MIMESIS
INTERNATIONAL

PHILOSOPHY
n. 39

Giacomo Maria Arrigo

GNOSTIC JIHADISM

A Philosophical Inquiry into Radical Politics

MIMESIS
INTERNATIONAL

www.mimesisinternational.com
e-mail: info@mimesisinternational.com

Isbn: 9788869773044
Book series: *Philosophy,* n. 39

P.I. C.F. 02419370305

CONTENTS

ACKNOWLEDGMENTS

This book is essentially my PhD thesis and I am deeply indebted to a number of people for their support while working on it. First, I would like to thank my two supervisors: I am extremely grateful to Alberto Ventura (University of Calabria), who had confidence in me during a crucial period of my life, and to John Nawas (KU Leuven), who accepted to supervise my doctoral thesis with dedication and care. They entrusted me to conduct my own research, helping me refining many ideas and concepts, but always leaving me great freedom in organizing the large amount of material presented here.

During my academic career, I have been lucky enough to meet many people who have encouraged and supported me despite the many difficulties of this job choice. I am indebted to Paolo Branca of the Catholic University of the Sacred Heart, in Milan, for his constant presence each time I sought him out. I must thank Giacomo Samek Lodovici of the same University, who has distinguished himself as an important and precious teacher and friend. The many conversations with Luciano Pellicani have been of great help in defining the notion of revolutionary Gnosticism, and I owe a lot to him.

Many thanks go to Dario Tomasello of the University of Messina, who has proved to be a great friend. Nicoletta Scotti had the patience to read the section on Eric Voegelin, giving me precious tips on his thinking. Marco Rainini gave me a solid background on the figure of Joachim of Flora. All of them heard parts of the dissertation in its nascent form and encouraged me to keep at it.

I must mention Francesco Botturi of the Catholic University of Milan, always present whenever I looked for him; Alessandro Orsini of LUISS University of Rome, who was so kind to give me detailed comments on the radical mindset of violent extremists; and Claudio Bonvecchio of the University of Insubria for his suggestions on the gnostic religion.

Spartaco Pupo of the University of Calabria and Bert Broeckaert of KU Leuven have provided me interesting and insightful tips on the use of the category of revolutionary Gnosticism in relation to other disruptive historical experiences.

I will never forget the night spent with Pietrangelo Buttafuoco in Rome, talking about my dissertation, Islam and Christianity, ranging up to the spiritual future of the European continent.

I am grateful to father Giuseppe Tanzella-Nitti of the Pontifical University of the Holy Cross and to the school he runs, the Advanced School for Interdisciplinary Research, for having let me open my research to new and unexpected horizons.

I have benefitted from numerous exchanges over the years with many friends, old and new. I would like to mention the colleagues of *Occhialì – Laboratorio sul Mediterraneo islamico*, a research center based at the University of Calabria and directed by Alberto Ventura. From the very beginning of my doctoral experience, Alberto included me in the center's pool of researchers, which has been an exciting experience for my study and for my own personal growth. *Occhialì* researchers encouraged me to do better and better, particularly Gianfranco Bria.

A mention to the team of *theSquare – Mediterranean Centre for Revolutionary Studies* and to Jacopo Franceschini, with whom I have had so many discussions on every single topic of this book.

For their friendship and support, I would also like to thank Aldo, Mario, Massimiliano and Federico.

My greatest debt is to my family: my parents, Dino and Rossella, and my brother, Massimiliano. Without their constant support, I could not have done it – and I am grateful to them for more than I could ever say.

Finally, this book is dedicated to Fernanda, my love.

NOTE ON CONVENTION

The transliteration system adopted in the book is the one used by International Journal of Middle East Studies (IJMES), which is considered a leader in the field of Middle East studies. Some place and people names are transliterated, but names familiar in English are given their usual English spelling (for example Mecca and Baghdad for place names, and Osama bin Laden for people names). For reasons of clarity and consistency, dating throughout this research is according to the Christian Era. The *aḥādīth* (sing. *ḥadīth*) cited in this study have been recovered from the website *sunnah.com*; therefore, for each *ḥadīth* quotation I have provided a direct link to the *sunnah.com* site, so as to compare the different forms of possible quotations.

PREFACE

Why do some people kill other people in the name of Islam? Newspapers and news agencies refer to these people simply as "terrorists". Others, who want to show some degree of being informed, call them Salafi-Jihadis. But names as such do not explain why adherents to Salafi-Jihadism do what they do. An outsider might say that Salafi-Jihadis just kill other people who happen not to be Muslims, but it remains a mystery to that outsider why they kill their co-religionists as well, sometimes by entering a mosque when people are praying in order to blow themselves up – in the name of the very same God to whom the people assembled were praying. Why do Salafi-Jihadis cut the throats of others or burn a Muslim pilot to death? Why? Why? Why?

Many wonder why and find no answer. An answer is to be found in the book you are now holding. This is the very first attempt to study Salafi-Jihadism as an ideology that is tied to revolutionary Gnosticism. In this study, you will find an interpretative framework that explains Salafi-Jihadism. After reading it, you will understand more of this ideology and why its followers commit crimes in the name of that ideology, which they call religion.

This study adopts an innovative viewpoint to study radical Islamist thought in general. Previously used by other notable scholars, the theoretical notion of revolutionary Gnosticism helps to frame and understand revolutionary phenomena such as Nazism, Bolshevism and Jacobinism, but never before has this notion been adopted in relation to Salafi-Jihadism to help explain it. Studying Salafi-Jihadism from this perspective reveals its intent of saving humankind from Evil (with a capital letter) in order to construct the perfect society.

The consistency of Salafi-Jihadism with revolutionary Gnosticism reveals that the ideological foundation of radical Islamist groups is basically at odds with Islam *tout court*.

By writing this book, Dr. Giacomo Maria Arrigo offers us a daring and cogent explanatory framework to understand Salafi-Jihadism as a revolutionary gnostic movement and at once he offers us a glimpse at what the future might bring. By reading this book, the reader will gain more insight into the motives of Salafi-Jihadism and will acquire a better understanding of this extremist ideology. After finishing this book, the reader will also have found answers to the questions posed at the outset of this preface. The publication of this book comes at a time in which humanity is confronted with Covid-19, economic recession, changes in world order, and racial conflict. Yes, it is a time to read such a book!

Prof. Dr. John Nawas
Professor of Arabic and Islamic Studies
University of Leuven, Belgium

[Matthew 19]
{19:25} And upon hearing this,
the disciples wondered greatly, saying:
"Then who will be able to be saved?"
{19:26} But Jesus, gazing at them, said to them:
"With men, this is impossible.
But with God, all things are possible."

INTRODUCTION

The study of revolutionary Gnosticism as a philosophical concept is rather new in the academic debate. The same could be said of Salafi-Jihadism, which is the ideological foundation of radical groups such as al-Qāʿida and the self-proclaimed Islamic State. The present research is therefore at the intersection of two underdeveloped areas of study, having to deal with issues that few have written about. However, it is not for a mere exercise in style that I put both notions in relation to each other. There is something more that guides the entire research, something I will explain in this brief introduction.

Revolutionary Gnosticism was introduced in the academic debate by the philosopher Eric Voegelin (1901-1985). He considers this notion as "the propulsive force of the Western revolution,"[1] a rather unusual and intriguing statement indeed. As a matter of fact, in all his intellectual work he delves into the very nature of revolutionary movements in European history, from the 17th-century Puritans to the 20th-century totalitarian experiences of Nazism and Bolshevism. Intrigued by the revolutionary mindset, he first uses the concept of political religion, but then he rejectes it for a more comprehensive theoretical model, that is, revolutionary Gnosticism. By adopting it extensively in his work, Voegelin has been able to understand the underlying purpose of every revolutionary movement, namely, to redeem humankind from Evil (with the capital letter) and to build the perfect society ever existed. This claim reveals the Promethean project of the gnostic revolution, which is to eliminate God from the revolutionary perspective and to pretend to take on His creative and redeeming power.

The efficacy of the concept of revolutionary Gnosticism has led several other philosophers and sociologists to adopt it as a useful explanatory notion to frame and define numerous modern and contemporary revolutionary phenomena. Scholars such as Augusto del Noce (1910-1989), Vittorio Mathieu (1923-2020), Emanuele Samek Lodovici (1942-1981) and Luciano

---

1 Eric Voegelin, *La nuova scienza politica* (Roma: Borla, 1999), p. 189.

Pellicani (1939-2020) used the Voegelian concept in their research to give reason to disruptive political and cultural phenomena in the modern era.

The historian and social critic Christopher Lasch writes:

> Recent commentary on Gnosticism tends to divide into two types: call them scholastic and prophetic. The *scholastic* enterprise is driven by questions internal to the various disciplines that have converged on Gnosticism, with a concentration of purpose bordering on the rapacious: ancient history, classical languages and literature, the history of religion, paleography, archaeology. [...] The second type of study [is] *prophetic* in the sense that it puts the study of Gnosticism at the service of social criticism. [...] Here the study of Gnosticism is shaped not by questions growing out of a tradition of specialized scholarship but by suspicion that an understanding of the gnostic sensibility will shed light on the spiritual condition of our own times.[2]

Hence, it is possible to say that the use of Gnosticism which all these authors adopt is the prophetic one, in that they place it at the service of a better understanding of modern political phenomena; this operation is also useful to recognize the spiritual condition of these same movements, which, in turn, says something about the spiritual condition of our age. It is not by chance that Eric Voegelin employs the notion of "pneumopathology" (disease of the spirit) to explain what revolutionary Gnosticism is.

The great revolutionary movements that academia has so far framed in gnostic terms are the radical Anabaptist seizure of Münster, Germany, during the 16th century; the Puritan revolution in England of the 17th century; the Jacobin takeover during the French Revolution in 1792; and the totalitarian projects of Nazism and Bolshevism.

However, the researches related to revolutionary Gnosticism do not address the chronologically last radical political experience. I am referring to Salafi-Jihadism, the latest existing revolutionary ideology and perhaps one of the most challenging ideologies of the moment. No one has yet studied radical Islamism in gnostic terms, despite the fact that the academic production has dealt with several similar revolutionary experiments, with particular reference to those attempting to create a completely new society

---

2 Christopher Lasch, 'Gnosticism, Ancient and Modern: The Religion of the Future?', *Salmagundi*, no. 96 (Fall 1992): pp. 28-29. Similarly, Jacob Taubes asserts: "The history of research into Gnosticism can be interpreted in two ways. First and foremost, and above all else, it concerns the study of Late-Antique Gnosticism. But, from the point of view of a more general approach, it is also possible to consider it as a way of defining the present" (*Messianismo e cultura* [Milan: Garzanti, 2001], p. 373).

with nothing in common with the previous world. In this respect, the attempt of establishing an Islamic state in the land of "Syraq" (Syria and Iraq), as well as the threatening claims of wiping out everything deemed un-Islamic from the face of the earth, are examples of an ideological force that has apparently something in common with the worldview shared by the other actors studied in terms of revolutionary Gnosticism. Could it be possible that Salafi-Jihadism, the mature ideological construction of the radical Islamist galaxy, is the last gnostic *avatāra* after the end of appeal of Western ideologies and in the so-called post-ideological era?

It is worth asking this question because of the very nature of Salafi-Jihadism. What is not yet fully understood, in fact, is whether such ideology is entirely Islamic or whether it shares a mentality that is alien to the traditional Islamic context. The consistence of Salafi-Jihadism with revolutionary Gnosticism would reveal that the ideological foundation of radical Islamist groups is basically at odds with Islam *tout court*. As a matter of fact, self-salvation is the foundational core of any revolution that shares a similar background: humankind does no longer need God's active power over earth, since it is now the militant group that knows *why* the world is evil and *how* to fix things. God is superfluous, He becomes unnecessary and even stands in the way of the revolutionary actor: it is better to get rid of Him, the gnostic believes.

If Salafi-Jihadism were a gnostic phenomenon, it would be very hard to call it religious; rather, it would reveal an atheist character, due to the fact that redemption would be in the hand of humankind only, leaving God without a clear possibility of intervening in human affairs, notwithstanding the apparently spiritual framework and religious justifications that jihadists provide.

It appears that studies carried out so far on Salafi-Jihadism tackle the problem from a strategic standpoint only, or from a doctrinal – and thus theological – perspective. The present research aims at analyzing Salafi-Jihadism from a philosophical point of view, adopting the category of revolutionary Gnosticism to recognize the very nature of Salafi-Jihadism. To that end, the literature on the topic of jihadism is fully taken into consideration, but the final goal is to move the debate to another level – the philosophical one, indeed.

Even though it is a purely philosophical study, this research fits the counter-narrative strategy to combat Islamist extremism; in fact, if it was successful at demonstrating that revolutionary Gnosticism and Salafi-Jihadism are consistent to one another, al-Qāʿida and the Islamic State would disclose their gnostic, Promethean, and thus atheist nature, losing their appeal on a genuine, sincere and well-informed Islamic community.

The structure of the book follows a clear-cut scheme. Chapter 1 is devoted to the literature review on the topic of revolutionary Gnosticism, analyzing the theoretical elaboration of the main thinkers such as Eric Voegelin, Augusto Del Noce, Hans Jonas, Vittorio Mathieu, Emanuele Samek Lodovici and Luciano Pellicani. The comparison with Late-Antique gnostic religion will be a constant in the investigation of all authors.

Once the thought of the main authors on the topic is reviewed, it is the turn of univocally defining the category of revolutionary Gnosticism. The first part of Chapter 2 attempts to draw a paradigm that isolates the essence of this category, i.e., a six-point *gnostic pattern* that provides a coherent theoretical architecture to such a philosophical notion. The six features are anti-cosmism, tripartition of history, immanentizing of the *eschaton*, Gnosis, political-revolutionary self-redemption, and sociological dualism – each of these elements is going to be examined in depth. The chapter intends to clarify what revolutionary Gnosticism is by finding a recurrent pattern that reflects its functioning.

The second part of Chapter 2 addresses the actual gnostic revolutions that, according to the literature on the topic, have occurred in history, hence the above-mentioned radical Anabaptists in Münster, the Puritans in England, the Jacobin totalitarian experience during the French Revolution, Nazism, and, finally, Bolshevism. The six features of the gnostic pattern will be found in each of these cases, proving their effectiveness and helpfulness in understating the common mechanism of the phenomena in question.

Chapter 3 is the introductory part to Salafi-Jihadism. What is Salafism taken by itself, and analogously, what is jihadism *per se*? These questions are addressed singularly, placing Salafi-Jihadism into a larger historical and conceptual context.

The first part of Chapter 4 concentrates on Salafi-Jihadism looking both at its historical evolution and at its doctrinal equipment, with particular reference to the two most lethal groups, al-Qāʿida and the self-proclaimed Islamic State. Relying on Shiraz Maher's conceptualization[3], the chapter directs its attention to the five essential characteristics of Salafi-Jihadism, namely, *tawḥīd*, *ḥākimiyya*, *al-walāʾ wa-l-barāʾ*, jihad, and *takfīr*. This set of conceptual aspects constitutes the essential doctrinal core of Salafi-Jihadism.

Finally, the second part of Chapter 4 applies the gnostic pattern to Salafi-Jihadism. If that attempt was successful, then al-Qāʿida and the

3 Shiraz Maher, *Salafi-Jihadism: The History of an Idea* (London: Hurst & Company, 2016).

self-proclaimed Islamic State would reveal an exogenous nature with respect to Islam. The issue is addressed focusing on each of the six points of the gnostic pattern, putting them in relation with the five features of Salafi-Jihadism. The attempt of transferring the category of revolutionary Gnosticism to an extra-Western ideology is unprecedented, and therefore the Islamic doctrinal context is taken into consideration so as not to risk a weak and inadequate application.

Lastly, the Appendix is dedicated to Luciano Pellicani, a prominent Italian sociologist who is well-known for his studies on the revolutionary mindset. In July 2019, I went to his house in Rome to have a conversation with him about Gnosticism and the relevance of this category for current world politics. The Appendix is a report of that meeting, full of thought-provoking accounts and noteworthy comments.

CHAPTER 1
GNOSTICISM AS A PHILOSOPHICAL CATEGORY: A LITERATURE REVIEW

1.1 *Introduction*

The category of revolutionary Gnosticism, which will be extensively used in the present research as the main explicative concept, needs to be first investigated from top to bottom in order to isolate its essence, laying the basis for further elaboration. Hence, before applying it to the Salafi-Jihadi ideology, we need to survey the vast literature on this concept.

Gnosticism is *per se* a problematic notion. There is no clear definition of what Gnosis is. Moreover, we do not even know for sure whether a distinct religion known as Gnosticism ever really existed somewhere in the past.[1] Nevertheless, philosophers and sociologists, as well as historians and political scientists, have recently adopted Gnosticism as an explanatory notion useful to frame and define several modern and contemporary political and cultural movements. In this chapter we will deal with the most relevant authors of the field, and namely, Eric Voegelin, Augusto Del Noce, Hans Jonas, Vittorio Mathieu, Emanuele Samek Lodovici, and Luciano Pellicani. According to them, there is an actual stream, an underground chain of gnostic movements stretching from the 2nd century A.D. until the present day, which follows a contorted and blurred path – a path that is theoretical, but more frequently practical, meaning that what I call the gnostic pattern (I will discuss this later) has spread out more on a phenomenological level than on an intellectual one.

"Revolutionary Gnosticism" is a combination of two words: "Gnosticism" and "revolutionary". The adjective "revolutionary" is central to our discourse because it enables us to discriminate between different types of Gnosticism (for instance, speculative Gnosticism, religious

1 "To the question 'Can we really talk of Gnosticism?' we should probably answer 'no', if by 'Gnosticism' we mean a unitary and cohesive phenomenon; 'yes', if we assume it exclusively as a working hypothesis" (Paolo Pizzimento, *L'apocrifo di Giovanni. Lo Gnosticismo, il mito e la metafisica* [Catania: Tipheret, 2018], p. 25).

Gnosticism, artistic Gnosticism…) Additionally, the word "revolutionary" highlights the disruptive element intrinsic to Gnosticism, evoking a proximity between such peculiar religious tendency and political violence as the means to reach and maintain power.

More precisely, in the current understanding the word "revolution" refers to a way to seize power in a violent manner and by pugnacious means, creating an absolutely innovative foundation for the society and, eventually, for all humankind. However, contrary to common sense, revolution is not inherently linked to the idea of a totally new beginning – such an appraisal is quite recent, as Hannah Arendt has demonstrated in her 1963 work *On Revolution.*[2] The etymological sense of the word "revolution" helps to trace its original and subtle meaning. "In its full meaning," writes Julius Evola, "the word 'revolution' consists of two ideas: in the first place, the idea of a revolt against a state of affairs; secondly, the *idea of a return*, of a conversion – which is why in the ancient astronomic language the revolution of a star meant its return to its starting point, its ordered movement around a center".[3] Hannah Arendt emphasizes the same point, saying that originally "revolution" had the same meaning of "restauration", a cyclical motion that follows a preordained order.[4] In this view, though today "restauration" and "revolution" are usually seen as two contradicting terms, at the beginning they went hand in hand. Even the French and the American Revolutions "where played in their initial stages by men who were firmly convinced that they would do no more than restore an old order of things that had been disturbed and violated by the despotism of absolute monarchy or the abuses of colonial government. They pleaded in all sincerity that they wanted to revolve back to old times when things had been as they ought to be."[5] The notion of novelty and newness as connected to revolution started to play a central role only in a second moment, but it is very alien

2 Cf. Hannah Arendt, *On Revolution* (1963; repr., London: Penguin Books, 1990).

3 Julius Evola, introduction to *La crisi del mondo moderno*, by René Guénon (Roma: Edizioni Mediterranee, 1972), p. 7. Emphasis added.

4 Arendt, *On Revolution*, p. 42: "The word 'revolution' was originally an astronomical term which gained increasing importance in the natural sciences through Copernicus's *De revolutionibus orbium coelestium*. In this scientific usage it retained its precise Latin meaning, designating the regular, lawfully revolving motion of the stars, which, since it was known to be beyond the influence of man and hence irresistible, was certainly characterized neither by newness nor by violence. On the contrary, the word clearly indicates a recurring, cyclical movement."

5 Arendt, *On Revolution*, p. 44.

to the true implication of the word "revolution", which is closer to a kind of oscillation between two poles rather than to a blind leap toward a mysterious and newfound end.

The above mentioned philosophers and sociologists have applied the paradigm of revolutionary Gnosticism to different revolutionary phenomena. Actually, for the peculiar nature of such category, being very specific, it can be applied only for limited cases – history witnesses only few gnostic revolts, and this acknowledgement is quite important since the present research aims at demonstrating that Salafi-Jihadism is one of those rare gnostic chapters.

According to the leading scholars on the topic I am about to review, the main gnostic revolutions are the following five: (1) the radical Anabaptist seizure of Münster (1534-1535); (2) the Puritan revolution in England (17th century); (3) the Jacobins' Terror (1793-1794); (4) Russian Bolshevism; and (5) Nazism. It is difficult, if not impossible, to identify other gnostic experiences (with the exception of some minor phenomena as the Italian Red Brigades).[6] Each of these revolutions was aimed at purifying the world and establishing the perfect society that, in the end, would have coincided with the lost golden age. Their action, in other terms, was a redeemer action, a benediction for humanity in its entirety, a behavior rooted in the faith in historical transfiguration. Woe to the person who tries to stop the pure party to fulfil its duty!

As is apparent, a regular political actor does not think to be saving humankind. This is why the revolutions mentioned above are the only political experiences that belong to revolutionary Gnosticism: they are part of a different mentality, of a way of thinking that does not operate within the rational means-ends relation, and that does not fit with any rational political philosophy or with any coherent strategical behavior.

The gnostic structure in its full political form emerged for the first time in the Late Middle Ages. Why in the Late Middle Ages? Because at that time the tension of the In-Between[7] began to vacillate, and the trust in

---

6 The Red Brigades (Brigate Rosse) was a violent radical left-wing organization that operated in Italy in the 1970s and the 1980s. The sociologist Alessandro Orsini, pupil of Luciano Pellicani, wrote a book to demonstrate that the Red Brigades was a gnostic group. See Alessandro Orsini, *Anatomy of the Red Brigades. The Religious Mindset of Modern Terrorists* (Ithaca and London: Cornell University Press, 2011).

7 The "In-Between" is a neologism coined by Eric Voegelin. It means the realization of the difference between two poles, the transcendent and the immanent, experienced as a condition of tension. As a consequence, the human nature lives in such a tension. See the first section of this chapter for a deeper analysis of the concept.

God was weakened daily. The hope in a top-down transfiguration was gradually and even unconsciously substituted by a bottom-up approach: it was no longer God the leading actor in the historical drama but humankind itself with its political and revolutionary initiative. Late medieval people acquired much more confidence in their own power: this is why the process of secularization is not a modern innovation but rather a long-lasting spiritual movement in Western thought. Moreover, the historian Norman Cohn has found in the socio-economic developments of the Late Middle Ages the sparkle for the eruptions of social upheavals and outbursts of apocalyptic fever.[8]

In a certain sense, *the story of revolutionary Gnosticism is contiguous to the larger issue of secularization*: when God ceases to be the only trusted authority, humankind does not hesitate to take His place, and politics, along with violent means, supplants the whispered prayers, the waits full of hope, the reflections on the Sacred Scriptures and the meaningful silences. As Luciano Pellicani clearly shows, revolutionary Gnosticism is also contiguous to the process of modernization; that is undeniably true, but modernization does not necessarily go along with secularization;[9] hence, secularization, i.e., the loss of credibility and the decreasing of public relevance of religion, is the leading factor in the emergence of gnostic revolutions. The intolerability of the tension[10] of the In-Between, which is the most visible symptom of Gnosticism, is a sign that the traditional faith in the trustworthy and supreme Beyond is inexorably cracked. Humankind has to rely on its own forces.

---

8 Norman Cohn, *The Pursuit of the Millennium: Revolutionary Millenarians and Mystical Anarchists of the Middle Ages* (1957; revised and expanded, New York: Oxford University Press, 1970).

9 See, for example, Shmuel N. Eisenstadt, 'Multiple Modernities', *Daedalus*, no. 1 (2000); Dipesh Chakrabarty, *Provincializing Europe. Postcolonial Thought and Historical Difference* (Princeton and Oxford: Princeton University Press, 2000).

10 In this respect, the French Catholic philosopher Jean Guitton hits the mark when he writes that "the pure is not the colorless, the odorless, the air conditioning, the mineral water, a uniform textile, the banality, the elementary. […] The true purity is not achieved through negation, or through resetting, or through indifference, but on the contrary, through a tension" (Jean Guitton, *Il puro e l'impuro* [Casale Monferrato: Piemme, 1993], p. 63). In fact, "we are median and mediator beings, and our role is to help the matter, the body, the flesh, to exist in a higher and noblest way" (ibid., p. 52). This last idea is quite unequivocally a Christian-Catholic conception, but it is useful in order to present Guitton's proposition how to cope with what he calls the "eternal Catharism" (ibid., p. 109) – and Catharism was a Christian heresy and a gnostic movement that was active between the 10th and 14th centuries.

It therefore appears as a consequence that talking of revolutionary Gnosticism as a reaction to the fact that the structural tension of human existence is no longer viable makes it irrelevant to find a genetic derivation, or a family tree, derived from ancient Gnosticism. Many authors have wondered how such a secular form of Gnosticism could have reached modernity. Well, the question has been put in the wrong way: it is true that doctrinal elements have reached the following generations and have inspired some specific conceptions of the world (the Joachim of Flora's Three Realms have deeply influenced Late Middle Ages, for instance), but such symbolic components were, and still are, *only occasions* for political and revolutionary re-actions to the same stirring, that is, that the world is radically evil and must be turned upside down.

The historian Jean Doresse writes that precisely because the Church persecuted the gnostics and the Manicheans between the 4th and the 6th centuries, Gnosticism was completely eradicated from the West. Hence,

> dualistic reminiscences during Medieval Europe in the cases of Bogomils, Cathars and Albigenses, as well as millenarian movements of the Late Middle Ages, have very tenuous links with ancient sects and with Manicheanism, so that it is hard to discern a true derivation. At most, one can speak of revivals determined by the transmissions of gnostic books disguised as Christian apocryphal texts and partially purged of more violent doctrines.[11]

In his essay, Doresse probably reveals more that he would have liked to: by talking of gnostic symbolisms employed by modern writers and poets (e.g., Edgar Allan Poe and Novalis), he first rules out the possibility of any clandestine survival and transmission of secret doctrines, and then he argues that "the powerful gnostic images used by poets can be explained by the *spontaneous* character of certain expression of the pessimism of ancient sects – they are symbols that human despair revives in front of the material weight of this low world and in front of the unintelligible silences of Providence."[12] A similar statement reveals something about human nature and claims Gnosticism to be a sort of constant of humankind.

Similar to Jean Doresse, the historian of religion Giovanni Filoramo draws an important distinction between the *awakening* (*risveglio*) of Gnosis and the *return* (*ritorno*) of Gnosis: in fact, he admits the existence

---

11 Jean Doresse, 'La Gnosi', in *Gnosticismo e manicheismo*, ed. by by Henry-Charles Puech (Roma-Bari: Laterza, 1988), p. 55.

12 Ibid., pp. 57-58. Emphasis added.

of "spontaneous gnostic outbreaks,"[13] a phenomenon that makes it possible to think of a phenomenological, and not historical, continuity with ancient Gnosticism. In his own words: "To talk, today, of *awakening* of Gnosis is licit from a comparative and phenomenological point of view, even though the price to pay is to understand too vaguely the term in question. Instead, to talk of *return* of Gnosis implies more than a phenomenological affinity among ancient Gnosis and recent forms of it."[14]

I tend to agree with Filoramo in saying that the *awakening* of Gnosis is more likely than the *return* of Gnosis, and that we should speak of phenomenological affinities rather than genetic derivations.[15] After all,

---

13 Giovanni Filoramo, *Il risveglio della gnosi, ovvero diventare dio* (Rome-Bari: Laterza, 1990), p. 6.

14 Ibid., pp. 6-7.

15 Many have been the attempts to trace the genealogy of Gnosticism in the Western thought. However, it is impossible to follow all the numerous evolutions of Gnosticism, and sooner or later any scholar would bump into a break, or missing link, in the transmission of the doctrine. It remains a dead-end effort. In this regard, Eric Voegelin has mostly followed Edward Gibbon's *Decline and Fall of the Roman Empire* (1776-1789), a voluminous study on Western civilization from the Roman Empire to the fall of Byzantium. "It is the merit of Gibbon – Voegelin writes – to have drawn attention for the first time (in chapter 54 of his treatise) to the origins and range of the movement that culminates in the outburst of the Reformation of the sixteenth century. He drew the line of direct continuity from the Paulician movement of the seventh century in Syria, through the transplantation of the Paulicians to the Balkans, through their ramification into the Bogomil sect, and through the migrations of Paulicians and Bogomils to upper Italy, to the appearance of the Cathars in southern France in the eleventh century. From the Cathars, the line is continued through the Waldenses and Franciscans into the later sectarian movements that spread over all Europe and reached their height in the Lollard movement in England and the Hussite movement in Bohemia in the fourteenth and fifteenth centuries. The Reformation of the sixteenth century is carried by a broad movement that manifested itself in the Peasant War as well as in the Anabaptist movement that spread from Holland to Switzerland and from Alsace to Moravia, with its continuation in the sect life of Holland, England, and America. In the seventeenth century, again, we see the Puritan movement proper carried by abroad movement with its fringes in the Diggers, Seekers, and Ranters. And in the eighteenth century, finally, we can observe the transition from the Deist and Unitarian groups into the clubs and movements of Enlightenment, Utilitarianism, and Socialism" (Eric Voegelin, 'The People of God', in *The Collected Works of Eric Voegelin.* Vol. 22, *Renaissance and Reformation*, ed. by David L. Morse and William M. Thompson [Columbia: University of Missouri Press, 1998], pp. 138-139). A similar genealogical line, which represents the stream of "sentiments and ideas that are in revolt against the institutional superstructure of our civilization" (ibid., p. 132), is nonetheless difficult to investigate, and Voegelin himself is aware of this. Since "these movements do not easily crystallize into a rational system of ideas that could be transmitted as a body of doctrine" (ibid., p.

revolutionary Gnosticism is a mentality – as Augusto Del Noce and Emanuele Samek Lodovici define it (see below) – and it could potentially rise where dissatisfaction with the current world takes root, where secularization erodes the traditional authority of the Sacred, and where the belief in a lost earthly paradise begins to assume a political form and is judged as a viable political program. Revolutionary Gnosticism is a structure of thought that does not belong to traditional societies, even in the specific cases of religious revolutions; instead, it is typical of secular societies, or societies in the process of secularization.

But what exactly is revolutionary Gnosticism? Eric Voegelin defines Gnosticism as "the propulsive force of the Western revolution."[16] This statement is equivocal, and the current chapter will elaborate on Voegelin's perspective as well as on all main scholars' works that are devoted to the peculiar phenomenon of revolutionary Gnosticism. In turn, this literature review will lead to a sketch of a gnostic pattern, a six-feature scheme that illustrates the structure of such a philosophical category.

1.2 *Eric Voegelin and the foundation of a theoretical paradigm*

Eric Voegelin (1901-1985) is one of the main political philosophers of the 20th century. His work covers many subjects, ranging from the status of political science to the problem of political representation, the idea of race, the authoritarian state, and the significance of ideology for a society as a whole. However, his main concern was to analyze the idea of order as the structuring force of history, on the one hand, and to develop a theory of consciousness, on the other. In studying these topics, Voegelin met Gnosticism. According to him, Gnosticism is the nature, or the essence, of

---

139), it is even harder to study them as a whole. Therefore, "they are clearly related to each other through the centuries by *the general structure of their sentiments and attitudes*; but whether this affinity is always due to an actual historical influence from one wave of the movement to the next, or whether the experiences that supply the drive of the movements spring up anew every time, without close determination by preceding similar movements, is largely an open question" (ibid.). So, to follow a historical genealogical line is one option, although it is the most difficult and, more likely, the most unsuccessful route to follow. Conversely, a phenomenological analysis based on a strong definition of the paradigm – and even grounded on what Voegelin calls "sentiments" and "attitudes" – is the other option; and I think it is a more useful approach in framing similar revolutionary phenomena. The present research is based on this second assumption.

16 Eric Voegelin, *La nuova scienza politica* (Roma: Borla, 1999), p. 189.

Modernity. Voegelin examined Gnosticism in many of his books, e.g., *The New Science of Politics* (1952), *Science, Politics and Gnosticism* (1968), *Order and History. Vol. IV* (1974), as well as in other minor volumes and articles. In order to properly understand the problem of Gnosticism as defined by Voegelin, one has to begin with the first work in which Voegelin studied modern ideologies as a link to ancient political and religious experiences, as he formulated these thoughts in his *Die politischen Religionen* (1938). In this book, the philosopher devotes his efforts to a "comparative analysis of symbolic phenomenon,"[17] with the intent of framing the then-spreading Nazi ideas within a larger tendency that had emerged throughout history, i.e., what Voegelin calls political religion.

As maintained by Voegelin, every political collectivism has something to do with religion: its *radix* (root) lies in religiosity. Therefore, to counter all political collectivisms that claim to represent a specific people, it is crucial to recognize how they are anchored in religious ideas and structures. And Eric Voegelin was fully aware of the threat posed by German Nazism, thus he was quick to try to come to grips with this movement from an intellectual point of view.

The first and main distinction that he draws is between spiritual religions and inner-worldly religions: "The spiritual religions, which find the *realissimum* in the Ground of the world (*Weltgrund*), should be called trans-worldly religions (*überweltliche Religionen*); and all others, i.e., those that find the divine in subcontents of the world,[18] should be called inner-worldly religions (*innerweltliche Religionen*)."[19] So far as inner-worldly religions come to terms with politics, they became political religions. In early Voegelian language, the *realissimum* is defined as the paramount reality, the most real, the Sacred. Hence, the relocation, or transfer, of the Sacred (the *realissimum*) to some subcontents of the creation, which is by nature finite, creates a sort of short circuit in political management and a recrystallization of social reality around an inner-worldly content, the political body, which "takes the place of the world-transcendent God as the ultimate condition and the origin of its own existence."[20] In particular, in

17 Sandro Chignola, introduction to *La politica: dai simboli alle esperienze*, ed. by Sandro Chignola (Milan: Giuffrè Editore, 1993), p. 10.

18 By that, Voegelin means any immanent *thing*, e.g., the blood, the social class, or everything pertaining this world and not the transcendent Beyond.

19 Eric Voegelin, 'The Political Religions', in *Modernity without Restrain*, ed. by Manfred Henningsen (Columbia: University of Missouri Press, 2000), pp. 32-33.

20 Ibid., pp. 28-29.

modern times the state became the true reality, a superhuman entity where each individual disappears, resembling "a mystical process."[21]

In the essay, Voegelin sketches the historical itinerary of political religions, tracing back its birth to pharaoh Akhenaton's epoch, then focusing on Hobbes and, finally, on the Third Reich. It is noteworthy that Voegelin's effort to identify four symbols used to link the political sphere with the divine now marks the distinctiveness of every political religion: (1) the *hierarchy*, that is the radiation of the divine power and legitimation through a chain of rulers; (2) the *Ecclesia*, "the order of domination [that] is sacral in character, but it is not the Most Holy Sacrament,"[22] an organized community that resembles the mystical Body (*corpus mysticum*) of Christ; (3) the *distinction between the spiritual and temporal*; and (4) the *apocalypse* as the revelation of the Reign. In explaining the last symbol, Voegelin introduces an element that attained much importance in the future elaboration of Gnosticism, that is the speculation of Joachim of Flora (ca. 1130-1202), a Calabrian monk known for his elaboration of Christian eschatology.[23] In Joachim's tripartite division of history, the last stage of time is characterized by the realization of the spiritual *in* the mundane, in the world, and not *outside* of it; hence, the belief in the *perfectibilitas* of humankind is immanentized, and historically it was going to become the belief in progress so common in the nineteenth century.

These four symbols (hierarchy, Ecclesia, spiritual/temporal distinction, apocalypse) are clearly borrowed from the Christian order and, as such, Voegelin says, they are secularized Christian symbols. Thomas Hobbes's thought serves as an example: the contract replaces the Covenant; the state is recognized as a collective person (near to an *unio mystica*) and becomes church; the "Mortal God", i.e., the state, takes the place of the traditional

---

21 Ibid., p. 30.

22 Ibid., p. 44.

23 Joachim of Flora has deeply influenced the Western thought in the centuries that followed his death. From the very beginning, his theoretical elaboration represented a challenge to the vision of history widely accepted by Christians in the Middle Ages, especially that proposed by Saint Augustine. "The *novitas* of this interpretation can be measured in particular by the vision of history conveyed by the Bishop of Hippo [Augustine], particularly in *De Civitate Dei*, and in fact assumed by subsequent centuries. [...] The characters of the third *status* of the Spirit, as Joachim da Fiore imagined it, collide with the vision of those who expect only the worst for the future, the world having entered into its *aetas decrepita*." (Marco Rainini, 'Apocalittica e/o progresso. Le molte reputazioni di Gioacchino da Fiore,' in *Filosofia ed escatologia*, ed. by Claudio Ciancio, Maurizio Pagano, and Ezio Gamba [Milan: Mimesis, 2017], p. 165).

Immortal God; the sovereign obtains the same position of Abraham (God speaks only to him). Finally, in recent history the Leviathan has been transformed in a new political-religious construction: the spirit of the people, or the national spirit (*Volksgeist*): "The Führer is the point where the spirit of the people breaks into historical reality; the inner-worldly god speaks to the Führer in the same way the transcendent God speaks to Abraham, and the Führer transforms god's words into commands for his immediate followers and for the people."[24]

As a final remark, Voegelin argues that every political religion entails the "abandonment of God,"[25] an observation that discloses the atheist character of similar experiences despite their religious appearances.

After the mid-1950s, however, Voegelin rejected his own analysis elaborated in *Die politischen Religionen*, saying that

> the interpretation is not all wrong, but I would no longer use the term "religions" because it is too vague and already deforms the real problem of experiences by mixing them with the further problem of dogma or doctrine. Moreover, in *Die politischen Religionen* I still pooled together such phenomena as the spiritual movement of Akhenaton, the medieval theories of spiritual and temporal power, apocalypses, the Leviathan of Hobbes, and certain National Socialist symbolisms. A more adequate treatment would have required far-reaching differentiations between these various phenomena.[26]

The loss of transcendence in political ideologies as well as the total immanence of their *Weltanschauung* remained the focal point for the philosopher. Yet, Voegelin shifted his interest from ideas to experiences, and in doing so he encountered the issue of Gnosticism. During the 1940s and 1950s, he discovered gnostic symbolizations and the question on whether or not there are parallelisms with modern political experiences. The reading of Hans Urs von Balthasar's *Prometheus* (1947) was significant. In his *Autobiographical Reflections* (1973), Eric Voegelin remembers that

> before publishing anything on the applicability of gnostic categories to modern ideologies, I consulted with our contemporary authorities on Gnosticism, especially with Henri Charles Puech in Paris and Gilles Quispel in Utrecht. Puech considered it a matter of course that modern ideologies are gnostic

24 Voegelin, 'The Political Religions', p. 65.

25 Ibid., p. 71.

26 Eric Voegelin, *Autobiographical Reflections* (Columbia and London: University of Missouri Press, 2011), chap. 14, Kindle.

> speculations; and Quispel brought the Gnosticism of Jung, in which he was especially interested, to my attention.[27]

His first applications of Gnosticism to modern phenomena occur in *The New Science of Politics* (1952) and then in *Wissenschaft, Politik und Gnosis* (1959). It is precisely in *The New Science of Politics* that Voegelin claims Gnosticism to be the essence of modernity. James L. Wiser suggests that such statement is "Voegelin's second attempt at specifying the character of the modern crisis,"[28] the first attempt already made in *Die politischen Religionen*. In fact, the question to be answered was: what is the peculiar soul of the modern and basically post-Christian era? By now dissatisfied with the concept of political religion, Voegelin moved his focus to Gnosticism. According to Voegelin, such a religious structure, which originated in the 2nd century A.D. in the Middle East and which at first sight does not have anything to do with modern Europe, is instead a constant feature of Western culture, albeit little-known to scholars because of its underground flowing and clandestine transmission. In the light of such an explanation, modern ideologies are understood as last manifestations of a major, ancient and mutant historical force in Western politics.

The very core of the gnostic experience is the understanding of the world as deeply evil and alien; yet, human beings could change such wicked condition by revolting against it, meaning that an appropriate human effort (theoretical or practical) could fix the painful and tragic situation in which the gnostic man lives. The Valentinians, a 2nd-century gnostic group, formulated the content of their doctrine as follow: "What liberates is the knowledge of who we are, what we became; what we were, whereinto we have been thrown, whereto we speed, wherefrom we are redeemed; what birth is and what rebirth."[29]

In *The New Science of Politics*, Voegelin explains Gnosticism as a reaction to the Christian de-divinized world.

> By de-divinization shall be meant the historical process in which the culture of polytheism died from experiential atrophy, and human existence in society

---

27 Voegelin, *Autobiographical Reflections*, chap. 17.

28 James L. Wiser, 'From Cultural Analysis to Philosophical Anthropology: An Examination of Voegelin's Concept of Gnosticism', *The Review of Politics*, vol. 42, no. 1 (January 1980): p. 94.

29 Quoted in Alexander S. Kohanski, *Greek Mode of Thought in Western Philosophy* (Madison, NJ: Fairleigh Dickinson University Press, 1984), p. 90.

> became reordered through the experience of man's destination, by the grace of the world-transcendent God, toward eternal life in beatific vision.[30]

In the Christian worldview, no longer gods or fairies inhabit the surrounding nature: now God is in the transcendent reality and human existence is directed to an eschatological end. Perfection would be reached in the Afterlife: it is trans-historical, eschatological, and not something that could be realized inner-worldly, in the immanent world. The Christian God becomes available to humankind only through faith. The experience of a world full of gods being lost, the connection with the only world-transcendent God "is reduced to the tenuous bond of faith."[31] But now – and this is the real problem – not everyone can endure it. On this very point, Voegelin's words are illuminating:

> The bond is tenuous, indeed, and it may snap easily. The life of the soul in openness toward God, the waiting, the periods of aridity and dullness, guilt and despondency, contrition and repentance, forsakenness and hope against hope, the silent stirrings of love and grace, trembling on the verge of a certainty that if gained is loss – the very lightness of this fabric may prove too heavy a burden for men who lust for massively possessive experience.[32]

The keyword here is "possessive experience": the majority of humankind wants to know rather than believe. "Knowing" is more gratifying and provides more security than "believing". Historically, the consequences of the de-divinization of the world and of the too heavy seriousness of Christianity led to what Voegelin calls a *fall from faith*, an alternative experience that has accompanied Christianity from its birth, or, in other words, Gnosis, a remedy to the uncertainty of faith.

Stated differently, the meaning of reality, assigned in the Christian worldview to the world-transcendent and eschatological reality, was too far from many people who were not ready to tolerate the uncertainty of faith. Hence, they tried to immanentize the meaning of existence, to bring it back to the empirical world. "The attempt at immanentizing the meaning of existence," – Voegelin writes – "is fundamentally an attempt at bringing our knowledge of transcendence into a firmer grip than the *cognitio fidei*,

30 Eric Voegelin, 'The New Science of Politics', in *Modernity Without Restrain*, ed. by Manfred Henningsen (Columbia and London: University of Missouri Press, 2000), p. 175.
31 Ibid., p. 187.
32 Ibid., pp. 187-188.

the cognition of faith, will afford."[33] Gnosis is precisely the penetration of the mystery of existence, a possessive experience that has the power to thin out existential angst and to escape the uncertainty of existence.

Yet there are many gnostic varieties. There is a *speculative* Gnosis, i.e., a theoretical possession of the truth; there is an *emotional* Gnosis, the "indwelling of divine substance in the human soul;"[34] and also a *volitional* Gnosis exists, which "assumes the form of activist redemption of man and society, as in the instance of revolutionary activists like Comte, Marx, or Hitler."[35] This third variety of Gnosis will be the focus of the discussion that follows.

The immanentization of the Christian *eschaton* (the final stage of history, the reign of perfection) was, and still is, the main consequence of the gnostic attitude in the political sphere. The possibility of reaching perfection *within* history – and not *beyond* history – is the hallmark of any gnostic political-revolutionary activity. Humanity is capable of self-redemption, is "absolutely powerful [...] and able to build a new world where iniquity is abolished and overcome."[36]

In *Science, Politics and Gnosticism*, Voegelin elaborates more on the identity of modern Gnosticism. In this essay, he lists six features. First of all, he states, "the gnostic is dissatisfied with his situation:"[37] this is the mood of every gnostic of all times, he says. The second element is the gnostic's self-explanation of such dissatisfaction, that is, "the world is poorly organized."[38] In the gnostic narrative, human beings are not inadequate; rather, the responsibility of the wicked condition lies on the same world and on its intrinsic disorder. The third feature is "the belief that salvation from the evil of the world is possible,"[39] and this is quite crucial since the bad and dreadful condition is not inescapable or unavoidable, as one may be inclined to think. Nonetheless, the proclivity for hope is common with the Christian worldview. And it is precisely the fourth characteristic that specifies the essential quality of modern Gnosticism: the gnostic believes that "the order of being will have to be changed in a historical process"[40], following a fully

33 Ibid., p. 189.
34 Ibid.
35 Ibid.
36 Mario Marcolla, introduction to *Il mito del mondo nuovo*, by Eric Voegelin (Milan: Rusconi, 1970), p. 11.
37 Eric Voegelin, 'Science, Politics and Gnosticism', in *Modernity Without Restrain*, ed. by Manfred Henningsen (Columbia and London: University of Missouri Press, 2000), p. 297.
38 Ibid.
39 Ibid.
40 Ibid.

earthly path. This feature clashes with the Christian narrative because, according to Christianity, man's salvational fulfilment takes place *beyond* the world and not *within* it. The fifth aspect of Gnosticism is quite peculiar: while in Christianity salvation is offered by God, in Gnosticism salvation is gained by humans themselves. Voegelin is clear: for the gnostic man, "the change in the order of being lies in the realm of human action, [...] this salvational act is possible through man's own effort."[41] Thus, the gnostic is similar to a man who steals his own redemption, illicitly appropriating something he should have earned by moral conduct and true devotion. The sixth and last element that circumscribes the identity of Gnosticism is Gnosis itself: Gnosis is "knowledge of the method of altering being [...] a formula for self and world salvation"[42] that should be employed and implemented in worldly life, both in organizing a political community and in fighting the enemies of truth.

The gnostic individual revolts against the structure of being. He does not humbly subordinate to the constitution of the world; rather, he wants to realize an immanent eschatology by actively overcoming every obstacle.

The psychic gains of every individual who follows such a system of thought are "a stronger certainty about the meaning of human existence, a new knowledge of the future that lies before us, and the creation of a more secure basis for action in the future."[43] The uncertainty of faith, and especially of Christian faith, is left behind: the gnostic knows the inner secrets of Being and does not wait for anything from the divine – the gnostic *is* the divine, now transfigured by the possession of the salvific knowledge that is Gnosis.

Voegelin's six features of Gnosticism have been questioned by the scholar Eugene Webb, who acknowledges the German-American philosopher Hans Jonas's influence on Voegelin's image of Gnosticism, and recognizes that

> the first three characteristics are in line with Jonas's idea of the essence of ancient Gnosticism. The fourth begins to introduce an idea from Voegelin's own system of thought, and the fifth and sixth depart from the standard use entirely in their emphasis on salvation within history through changes one is able to bring about in the world, whereas Jonas's gnostics despaired of the world and its history and looked for salvation elsewhere.[44]

41 Ibid., p. 298.
42 Ibid.
43 Ibid., p. 309.
44 Eugene Webb, 'Voegelin's "Gnosticism" Reconsidered', *Political Science Reviewer*, vol. 34, no. 1 (Fall 2005): p. 60.

This is undeniably true. However, Voegelin does not talk exclusively about ancient Gnosticism. The six-point scheme depicts the gnostic attitude as it can be found in revolutionary gnostic movements throughout history, e.g., Puritanism, Communism and Nazism. Giving birth to such different political experiences, ancient Gnosticism had to travel across two continents and over a long period of time before embodying in, for instance, the Puritans and Jacobinism, which means that it had inevitably acquired new features over time and many geographic location, gradually adapting to the understanding of each era. Hence, there are by necessity some relevant differences within Gnosticism itself: "While the ancient varieties sought escape from an irredeemably evil cosmos, their modern counterparts pin their hopes on its transformation."[45]

Nevertheless, yesterday and today, despite any differences, the gnostic individual reacts to the same basic assumption: the world is bad, humankind feels alien to reality, and something has to be done in order to mend the situation, either by escaping from the world or fixing the world. The possessive experience of Gnosis is a remedy to the uncertainty and insecurity not only of faith but also of the same human condition.

However, Voegelin "never managed to clarify the nature of the historical link suggested in *The New Science of Politics*"[46] between ancient and modern Gnosticism. Voegelin frequently asserted the continuity between the two, but he never analyzed the transmission of such a presumed tradition over the centuries. Yet, Voegelin's analysis "*is primarily an analysis of gnostic consciousness*. He is not an intellectual historian who is concerned with discovering the remnants of a premodern creed within modernity."[47] Voegelin's interest is not directed to, for instance, the archaeology of the concept; more exactly, his focus is human consciousness and openness toward reality.

To delve into this important point and explain better what Voegelin means with it, it must be stressed that Gnosticism – the quest for certitude – is not only a phenomenon that occurs in response to the uncertainty

45 David Walsh, 'Voegelin's Response to the Disorder of the Age', *The Review of Politics*, vol. 46, issue 2 (1984): p. 270.

46 Stefan Rossbach, 'Understanding in Quest of Faith. The Central Problem in Eric Voegelin's Philosophy', in *Politics & Apocalypse*, ed. by Robert Hamerton-Kelly (East Lansing: Michigan State University Press, 2007), p. 229.

47 Wiser, 'From Cultural Analysis to Philosophical Anthropology', p. 97. Emphasis added. See also Gian Franco Lami, *Introduzione a Eric Voegelin* (Milano: Giuffrè Editore, 1993), p. 256: "For Voegelin Gnosticism is more a philosophical category rather than a historical-sociological one."

of the Christian faith; on the contrary, the gnostic closure (the denial of transcendence, the levelling down of the consciousness to the inner-worldly reality only, an artificial truncation of reality) is "a universal human possibility."[48]

For example, in *Science, Politics and Gnosticism* Voegelin talks briefly, poetically and efficiently also about the Islamic case:

> The Islamic prayer exercises that have developed since the ninth century will serve as the final example of a high demand in spiritual tension. Structurally, this meditation, which preceded prayer, is most closely related to the meditative experiment on which the Platonic myth of the Last Judgment is based. When I want to pray, says the rule, I go to the place where I wish to say my prayer. I sit still until I am composed. Then I stand up: the Kaaba is in front of me, paradise to my right, hell to my left, and the angel of death stands behind me. Then I say my prayer as if it were my last. And thus I stand, between hope and fear, not knowing whether God has received my prayer favorably or not. Perhaps, for the masses, this high spiritual clarity is made bearable through a connection with the neither high nor especially spiritual extension of God's realm by force of arms over the ecumene.[49]

In this passage, Voegelin argues that the same uncertainty of Christian faith is also present in Islam. What he calls "not especially spiritual extension of God's realm by force of arms", by which he refers to jihad, is the gnostic response of Muslims to such insecurity and doubt. Unfortunately, the philosopher writes nothing more on Islam besides the passage just cited. The present research will fill in this gap by specifying which kind of jihad could be read as a gnostic reaction and in relation to what socio-political conditions is triggered. But for the moment let us go back to Voegelin.

Voegelin developed over time a useful and effective terminology to explain the state of mind of the gnostic: he spoke of *pneumopathology* as something distinct from psychopathology. Already in 1952, the philosopher says that "the essence of gnostic politics must be interpreted as a spiritual sickness […], a disturbance in the life of the spirit".[50] It consists in the *derailment* from the regular perception of reality and in the creation of a second reality, also called "dream reality". Gnostics "have to speak [about dream reality] as if they have had experience of it; and they have to act as if

48 Wiser, 'From Cultural Analysis to Philosophical Anthropology', p. 100.

49 Voegelin, 'Science, Politics and Gnosticism', p. 313.

50 Eric Voegelin, 'Gnostic Politics', in *The Collected Works of Eric Voegelin,* vol. 10, *Published Essays 1940-1952*, ed. by Ellis Sandoz (Columbia and London: University of Missouri Press, 2000), p. 226.

they were capable of bringing it about."[51] In the mind of gnostics, the dream reality is the perfect society, the finally immanentized *eschaton*, the final stage of history that gives meaning to the flow of events and that should be reached within history. But it is impossible to realize it anywhere and at any time: the friction with true reality is insurmountable and constant. Hence, the violence of the gnostic over reality, besides being extreme and tremendous, would be endless. Destruction (the negative phase of the pantoclastic program) is the only part of any gnostic construct that could be really implemented in the world.

To sum up, "there are then, if this pneumopathic condition has occurred, two realities: the first reality, where the normally ordered man lives, and the second reality, in which the pneumatically disturbed man now lives and which thus comes into constant conflict with the first reality."[52] In an essay written in 1970, Voegelin argues that such pneumopathic condition is a "disturbance within reality,"[53] which tends to eclipse reality, even though it cannot ever abolish it, eventually resulting in a permanent state of revolt, a *permanent revolution* aimed at eroding reality in a never-ending effort. Thus, it is evident that gnostic politics is a combination of lust for domination and resentment – a lethal cocktail ready to explode within the healthy body of any civilization.

In an important paper titled *Wisdom and the Magic of the Extreme: A Meditation* (1977), Voegelin discusses in more depth the problem of the pathological creation of a second reality. In creating a dreamworld, the pneumopath (the gnostic) lives a sort of suspension of consciousness, as Voegelin defines it, pretending to overcome the imperfection of man's existence: "Since our imperfection does not make sense to dreamers who know how to achieve perfection, it has acquired in the world of their phantasy the character of an Absurdity."[54] Here the ancient gnostic character of the revolt against every limit and against the creatural nature of human beings is easily discernable since imperfection is an element that impedes the achievement of an immanent *eschaton*. Therefore, although it is impossible to overcome the limitedness as such, it has to be denied or,

---

51 Ibid., p. 227.

52 Eric Voegelin, 'Hitler and the Germans', in *The Collected Works of Eric Voegelin*, vol. 31, eds. Detlev Clemens and Brendan Purcell (Columbia and London: University of Missouri Press, 1999), p. 108.

53 Eric Voegelin, 'The Eclipse of Reality', in *Phenomenology and Social Reality*, ed. by Maurice Natanson (The Hague: Martinus Nijhoff, 1970), p. 186.

54 Eric Voegelin, 'Wisdom and the Magic of the Extreme: A Meditation', in *The Collected Works of Eric Voegelin,* vol. 12, ed. by Ellis Sandoz (Columbia and London: University of Missouri Press, 2000), p. 317.

at least, omitted in sketching the dreamworld. "The burden of existence" – Voegelin says – "loses its sense, and becomes absurd, only when a dreamer believes himself to possess the power of transfiguring imperfect existence into a lasting state of perfection."[55] The foolish dreamer claims to hold a true Gnosis to be applied in order to transfigure reality and to bring history to its end, the final and perfect stage of human time. It goes without saying that such "unwillingness to distinguish between dream and reality"[56] is the herald of revolutions, wars and disorders.

Eric Voegelin goes further in developing the concept of Gnosticism, discussing it within the dynamics of consciousness and in relation with much larger historical evolutions. In his five-volume work *Order and History* (1956-1987), Voegelin treats Gnosticism in light of the problem of the balance of consciousness[57] as it has occurred over millennia. In the first volume, Voegelin examines the understanding of order in ancient Near Eastern imperial civilizations. Here the conception of order is the one that Voegelin calls "cosmic" or "cosmological": "The society is not conceived as secular, i.e., a simple organization of powers whose function is merely pragmatic and utilitarian. More accurately, the society is a *cosmion*, an essential part of the *cosmos* as a whole and a consubstantial community of man and god."[58] Human order and divine order are interconnected, constantly communicating with each other, forming one solid block. The gods are intra-cosmic, which is the reason why humankind can participate in the reality of the divine. There are no breaks in such structure. The firmness of the socio-religious construct testifies the oneness of being and order. But eventually, between 800 and 300 B.C. – more or less the same period that Karl Jaspers calls the "Axial Age"[59] – something happens: Voegelin speaks

---

55 Ibid., p. 318.

56 Ibid., p. 322.

57 Not all agree on seeing continuity in Voegelin's consideration of Gnosticism. Some (e.g., David Walsh, Bruce Douglass) think that the philosopher has set off along a new path after having acknowledged the dead end of tracing connections between ancient and modern Gnosticism. However, other scholars (e.g., James L. Wiser) disagree, and affirm homogeneity in Voegelin's researches across time.

58 Stephen A. McKnight, 'Il contributo di Eric Voegelin alla filosofia della storia', in *La scienza dell'ordine. Saggi su Eric Voegelin*, ed. by Gian Franco Lami and Giovanni Franchi (Rome: Antonio Pellicani Editore, 1997), p. 96.

59 The Axial Age, or Axis Age, is a period that goes from the 8th to the 3rd century BC. It is a term coined by the German philosopher Karl Jaspers, who went into the concept in his book *The Origin and Goal of History* (1949). He describes this period as following: "The most extraordinary events are concentrated in this period, Confucius and Lao-tse were living in China, all the schools of Chinese philosophy came into being, including those of Mo-ti, Chuang-tse, Lieh-tsu and a

of "spiritual outbursts" that break with the previous cosmological order; he also talks of "leaps in being", theophanic revealing experiences, qualitative leaps in the comprehension of reality. Examples of these spiritual outbursts are the prophets of Israel and the elaboration of philosophy in Greece. "While the cosmological order understands men as living in a natural and social cosmos that is 'full of gods', the 'spiritual outburst' consists in a human experience of participation in a transcendent divinity beyond both the natural and social tangible existence."[60]

This incredible experience produces what Voegelin calls "differentiation of consciousness", which is, briefly, the realization of a difference between two poles, the transcendent and the immanent, experienced as a condition of *tension*. The so-called "primary experience of the cosmos" is now totally broken: man is pushed out toward the Beyond, he lives in the "In-Between" (which Voegelin calls also *Metaxy*).[61] The spiritual outbursts

> are experienced as meaningful inasmuch as they constitute a Before and After within time that points toward a fulfillment, toward an *eschaton*, out of time. History is not a stream of human beings and their actions in time,

---

host of others; India produced the Upanishads and Buddha and, like China, ran the whole gamut of philosophical possibilities down to scepticism, to materialism, sophism and nihilism; in Iran Zarathustra taught a challenging view of the world as a struggle between good and evil; in Palestine the prophets made their appearance, from Elijah, by way of Isaiah and Jeremiah to Deutero-Isaiah; Greece witnessed the appearance of Homer, of the philosophers Parmenides, Heraclitus and Plato of the tragedians, Thucydides and Archimedes. Everything implied by these names developed during these few centuries almost simultaneously in China, India, and the West, without any one of these regions knowing of the others. What is new about this age, in all three areas of the world, is that man becomes conscious of Being as a whole, of himself and his limitations. He experiences the terror of the world and his own powerlessness. He asks radical questions. […] All this took place in reflection. Consciousness became once more conscious of itself, thinking became its own object. Spiritual conflicts arose, accompanied by attempts to convince others through the communication of thoughts, reasons and experiences. […] In this age were born the fundamental categories within which we still think today, and the beginnings of the world religions, by which human beings still live, were created" (Karl Jaspers, *The Origin and Goal of History* [New Haven: Yale University Press, 1953], p. 2).

60 Gerhart Niemeyer, 'Eric Voegelin's Philosophy and the Drama of Mankind', *Modern Ages*, no. 20 (Winter 1976): p. 29.

61 He first uses the term "Metaxy" in the essay *The Ecumenic Age*. See Eric Voegelin, 'Order and History, vol. IV, The Ecumenic Age', in *The Collected Works of Eric Voegelin,* vol. 17, ed. by Michael Franz (Columbia and London: University of Missouri Press, 2000), p. 50.

> but the process of man's participation in a flux of divine presence that has eschatological direction.[62]

The natural cyclical rhythm, until now understood as the law of human time, is promptly set aside. From this moment on, human time becomes a movement towards a direction – a direction that is discovered to be eschatological, pointing to an order, the perfect and everlasting order, that is beyond the cosmos. According to Voegelin, "the Beyond of all mundane existence is the source of order within the soul of man and the man who has experienced and realized the reality of the Beyond is the measure of political order and human existence."[63]

But inevitably a problem arises. In fact, despite the spiritual outbursts and the awareness of a Beyond, of a transcendent pole, human beings "continued to be subject to the biological rhythms of nature, and even those who had experienced the immortalizing movement of the soul were not immune to biological death. […] The structure of reality revealed itself, therefore, to be paradoxical."[64] Reality is moving beyond itself while remaining constant. And this, Voegelin maintains, is the same structure of reality, the very condition of the existing.

The historical process is a *mystery*, it is beyond human control, and it is "unpredictable and mysterious."[65] To have a healthy consciousness means to live in the In-Between without forcing the process, accepting the mystery of history and existence, participating in the tension and avoiding distortions, constantly confronting the two nodes of existential reality. "Whether Voegelin calls these nodes time and eternity, limitedness and un-limitedness, being and non-being, death and transfiguration, Aperion and thinghood, History I and History II, Beginning and Beyond, or immanence and transcendence, the challenge is to avoid distorting or rejecting either node."[66] Otherwise, the consciousness would not be longer healthy but sick. Therefore, altering the perception of such tension is a form of pneumopathology. And pneumopathology is "the perennial danger

62 Voegelin, 'Order and History, vol. IV, The Ecumenic Age', p. 50.

63 E.H. Wainwright, 'Eric Voegelin: An Inquiry into the Philosophy of Order', *Politikon: South African Journal of Political Studies*, vol. 5, no. 1 (June 1978): p. 75.

64 Bruce Douglass, 'The Break in Voegelin's Program', *The Political Science Reviewer*, vol. 7, no. 1 (Fall 1977): p. 11.

65 Ibid., p. 12.

66 Richard Avramenko, 'The Gnostic and the *Spoudaios*', *The Political Science Reviewer*, vol. 41, no. 1 (June 2017): p. 83.

of losing out of sight the world of things over its vision of the Beyond,"[67] or, in other terms, Gnosticism.

The reality is mysterious, unsteady and uncertain – only a pneumopathic mind can replace the intrinsic insecurity of existence with a made-up dream reality. The gnostic declares to possess the key for interpreting the whole, to possess the answer to the Question, even though, as Voegelin writes, "there is no answer to the Question other than the Mystery as it becomes luminous in the acts of questioning."[68] This is the reason why Gnosticism is a universal experience not limited to the West: the reaction to the mystery of reality is common to human beings and belongs to all humankind, meaning also that the rejection of the mystery of reality is a human constant.[69] "One does not *know* divine reality, one can only experience it"[70] – on the contrary, the gnostic claims to know, to have the Gnosis. To immanentize the *eschaton*, for example, is a form of impatience regarding the (unknown) destination of reality: "The mystery of the stream [of history] is solved through the speculative knowledge of its goal."[71] In other words, it appears that truth is essentially mysterious, hence *truth* is something different from *certainty*.

Voegelin uses this explanation in *Order and History* to clarify also the differences between ancient Gnosticism and modern Gnosticism: "While these early movements attempt to escape from the Metaxy by splitting its poles into the hypostases of this world and the Beyond, the modern apocalyptic-gnostic movements attempt to abolish the Metaxy by

67 Niemeyer, 'Eric Voegelin's Philosophy and the Drama of Mankind', p. 34.

68 Voegelin, 'Order and History, vol. IV', p. 404.

69 It is important to stress that in *Order and History*, vol. IV, *The Ecumenic Age*, Voegelin places more emphasis on consciousness rather than on the history of political systems, as opposed to how he did in the previous three volumes. In *The Ecumenic Age* he examines deeper what we can call *constants* of human consciousness. For example, he writes: "An observation on historical influences does not resolve the problem [of Gnosticism]. The question is rather what causes Gnosticism to appear" (Voegelin, 'Order and History, vol. IV', P. 64). In this brief passage, it is openly stated that a historical study is insufficient; something deeper must be analyzed, i.e., human consciousness and its constant reaction to the existential tension. Michael Franz also highlights this point: "Voegelin's emphasis on the phenomenal realm of worldly action in time is lightened in favor of a heavier emphasis on the realm of consciousness in the divine-human In-Between" (Michael Franz, introduction to *The Collected Works of Eric Voegelin,* vol. 17, ed. by Michael Franz [Columbia and London: University of Missouri Press, 2000], p. 14).

70 Wainwright, 'Eric Voegelin: An Inquiry', p. 77. Italics in the text.

71 Voegelin, 'The New Science of Politics', p. 224.

transforming the Beyond into this world."[72] Gnosticism is a way out from the uncertainty of the In-Between: the quest for certitude is its core. Its aim is always the same, notwithstanding the differences of the responses over centuries.

Questions present themselves. Why did Gnosticism become a threat only when the "leaps in being" had already occurred in history? Could Gnosticism also have appeared in the so-called cosmological empires, before the Axial Age? According to Voegelin, the answer is no. In fact, for the first time in history, after the spiritual outbursts, the quest for meaning "contracted from the society that had delineated the order of existence for the individual into the realm of personal existence."[73] Cosmological societies never experienced the In-Between, the Metaxy, the tension of existence, for reality was a compact whole. Consequently, the elements needed to trigger a gnostic reaction are three: alienation and revolt are the first two, but they are not enough; the third element is "a consciousness of the movement toward the Beyond of such strength and clarity that it becomes an obsessive illumination, blinding a man for the contextual structure of reality"[74] – such are Voegelin's own words.

Historically, humankind tends to create political systems that reflect the order experienced in the structural tension toward the Beyond. But since there is no clear and once-for-all-given order, the political effort is a never-ending search for order, a precarious explanation of the reality of society's existence, and the order gradually implemented is the self-interpretation of each society. In the light of this understanding, "the symbols that extend meaning into the factuality of existence are gnostic for they create the static society such as the Reich that would last for the proverbial Millennium."[75] To freeze human effort and to (fictitiously) reach the presumed last stage of history (immanentization of the *eschaton*): this is the last goal of Gnosticism. In other words, it is a consequence of the loss of the soul's balance – a real pneumopathology, an undeniable illness.

Voegelin's analysis emerges, overall, as a complex inquiry into the human soul. He structured his study in the form of "a philosophical anthropology informed by a theory of consciousness and a philosophy of history,"[76] a

---

72 Voegelin, 'Order and History, vol. IV', p. 302.
73 E.H. Wainwright, 'Political Gnosticism and the Search for Order in Existence', *Politikon: South African Journal of Political Studies*, vol. 6, no. 1 (June 1979): p. 57.
74 Voegelin, 'Order and History, vol. IV', p. 65.
75 Wainwright, 'Political Gnosticism', p. 55.
76 Michael Franz, *Eric Voegelin and the Politics of Spiritual Revolt* (Baton Rouge and London: Louisiana State University Press, 1992), p. 4.

multifaceted theoretical structure aimed at identifying two patterns of consciousness, the closed, or (pneumo)pathological, consciousness, on the one hand, and the open, or healthy, consciousness, on the other. The concept of Gnosticism as employed by Voegelin is not (just) historical Gnosticism or its literary transmission from person to person, from group to group, but it is something more profound, a kind of medical notion that classifies a spiritual disease, a diagnostic concept, the description of an attitude.

Modern ideologies are perfect examples of the gnostic disposition of consciousness – they are the last manifestations of political Gnosticism in the West. Their destructiveness derives directly from Gnosticism, as Dante Germino has explained in an important paper:[77] the consideration of reality as something deserving to be destroyed because of its wickedness originates in Gnosticism and it was very strong from its very outset, already in 2nd and 3rd centuries A.D. In all gnostic forms, the exaltation of violence is implicit, but not immediately manifest. "Although Gnosticism does not inevitably lead to the cult of violence," Germino clarifies, "Gnosticism does provide the essential ingredient, the *conditio sine qua non*, of such a cult: the rejection of the order of Being as a prison from which one must escape."[78]

The transformation of the world through violence – the rejection of the order of Being – is the hallmark of all modern ideologies. Indeed, ideologies are grounded on the idea of "*system*",[79] which is composed of beliefs that are mutually consistent *only* if put inside a closed intellectual circuit. As Voegelin writes in a letter to Leo Strauss, "the idea of 'system', of the possible exhaustive penetration of the mystery of the cosmos and its existence by the intellect, is itself a gnostic phenomenon."[80] System as a closed theoretical unity for the explanation of reality (Marx is the best example[81]) is surely violence against reality, and it also represents the opposite of an open mind, i.e., the philosophical mind. In this

---

77 Dante Germino, 'Eric Voegelin on the Gnostic Roots of Violence', *Occasional Papers*, VII (February 1998).

78 Ibid., p. 48.

79 "The system is a distinctly modern phenomenon though its modernity has been obscured by a climate of opinion in which the system as the mode of philosophical thinking is taken so thoroughly for granted that the reality of non-systematic philosophizing has been eclipsed" (Voegelin, *Autobiographical Reflections*, chap. 19).

80 Eric Voegelin to Leo Strauss, December 4, 1950, in *Faith and Political Philosophy. The Correspondence Between Leo Strauss and Eric Voegelin*, 1934 – 1964, eds. by Peter Emberley and Barry Cooper (Columbia and London: University of Missouri Press, 2004), p. 73.

81 Well-known is Voegelin's definition of Marx as a "speculative Gnostic" (Voegelin, 'Science, Politics and Gnosticism', p. 262).

sense, Voegelin's definition of systems as "systematizations of state of alienation"[82] is quite accurate: the state of existence in tension toward the divine ground is totally ignored and often even denied. Living in the In-Between is distorted, and the Beyond no longer exists for the ideologues. "Falsification of reality"[83] is the intrinsic and most real essence of systems. Here, the balance of consciousness is lost.

For a more detailed clarification on ideologies, we shall look at Voegelin's 1953 review of Hannah Arendt's *The Origins of Totalitarianism*. Arendt is more interested in the institutional aspects of the problem. From this perspective, "totalitarianism is the disintegration of national societies and their transformation into aggregates of superfluous human beings."[84] By contrast, Voegelin is fascinated by another and deeper aspect of the issue, namely, spiritual and intellectual affinities.[85] What associates different revolutionary movements is, indeed, a recurrent spiritual structure. It is worth quoting a crucial Voegelin's passage rather than paraphrasing it:

> The origins of totalitarianism would not have to be sought primarily in the fate of the national state and attendant social and economic changes since the eighteenth century, but rather in the rise of immanentist sectarianism since the high Middle Ages; and the totalitarian movements would not be simply revolutionary movements of functionally dislocated people, but immanentist creed movements in which mediaeval heresies have come to their fruition. […] Totalitarian movements do not intend to remedy social evils by industrial changes, but want to create a millennium in the eschatological sense through transformation of human nature. The Christian faith in transcendental perfection through the grace of God has been converted – and perverted – into the idea of immanent perfection through an act of man.[86]

Immanentist sectarianism is a gnostic manifestation, as is apparent from what has already been said above. The intolerability of finitude, coupled

---

82 Voegelin, *Autobiographical Reflections*, chap. 19.

83 Ibid.

84 Eric Voegelin, review of *The Origins of Totalitarianism*, by Hannah Arendt, *The Review of Politics*, vol. 15, no. 1 (January 1953): p. 71.

85 As Arendt writes in reply to Voegelin's review: "I think that what separates my approach from Professor Voegelin's is that I proceed from facts and events instead of intellectual affinities and influences" (Hannah Arendt, 'The Origin of Totalitarianism. A Reply', *The Review of Politics*, vol. 15, no. 1 [January 1953]: p. 80). See also Eric Voegelin, 'Apocalisse e rivoluzione', in *1867/1967. Un secolo di marxismo*, eds. Vittorio Frosini et al. (Firenze: Vallecchi Editore, 1967), pp. 116-121.

86 Voegelin, review of *The Origins of Totalitarianism*, p. 74.

with the perversion of the Christian idea of perfection, is the fuel for any revolution.

Stephen McKnight identifies a significant change in Voegelin's philosophical register. He underscores the fact that from the mid-1970s, the philosopher gradually avoided to use the concept of Gnosticism as the main explicative category: starting from an important conference held at Notre Dame University in 1971, Voegelin began to relativize such notion: "Gnosis is one element in the modern compound, but there are other elements of which we can talk later, for instance, the apocalyptic traditions and Neoplatonic experiences and symbolizations."[87] Likewise, in 1973 he declares that "Gnosticism is one factor in a very complex set of factors to which it also belongs: apocalypse, Neoplatonic immanentist speculation, magic, Hermeticism and so on."[88] Furthermore, in 1975 Voegelin states that the problems of modernity are caused "by the predominance of gnostic, Hermetic, and Alchemistic conceits, as well as by the Magic of violence as the means for transforming reality."[89] In light of these declarations, the question has to be answered whether this is a fundamental change in Voegelin's philosophical worldview or not. Does it represent a total shift towards other forms of understanding conscience, revolution and modernity? Stephen McKnight explains such comments as indicative that Voegelin was afraid that the explosion of interest in Gnosticism in the 1970s[90] would have obscured his real intent, making the term "less viable as a theoretical or an analytical category."[91] Becoming a mainstream concept, Gnosticism would have been eroded and compromised – as, in part, actually occurred. Thus, such comments should not be understood literary as a change of direction in Voegelin's philosophy; instead, they are

---

87 Eric Voegelin, quoted in Stephen McKnight, 'Gnosticism and Modernity: Voegelin's Reconsiderations Twenty Years After *The New Science of Politics*', *Political Science Reviewer*, no. 34 (2005): p. 127.

88 Eric Voegelin, 'Recovering Reality: An Interview with Eric Voegelin', by Peter Cangelosi and John William Corrington, *Voegelinview.com*, August 2013, https://www.voegelinview.com/recovering-reality-pt-1/ (accessed June 20, 2018).

89 Eric Voegelin, 'Response to Professor Altizer's "A New History and a New but Ancient God?"', *Journal of the American Academy of Religion*, vol. 43, no. 4 (December 1975): p. 769.

90 Especially because of the use made by Carl Jung in the psychoanalytic field, Voegelin says.

91 McKnight, 'Gnosticism and Modernity', p. 140. See also Stephen McKnight, 'Understanding Modernity: A Reappraisal of the Gnostic Element', *Intercollegiate Review*, no. 14 (1979).

a problematization of the whole theory of consciousness and are intended as a deepening of the matter at hand.

Yes, this most recent strategy is full of problems, above all the fact that "Voegelin's use of a single term to designate both historical Gnosticism and psychic 'Gnosticism' [which is an increasing tendency in his later writings] has the unfortunate consequence of blurring the important points of distinction that mark these patterns."[92] Nonetheless, this strategy doesn't completely miss the target, for at least one needs to stop and think Gnosticism as a real state of consciousness rather than simply a religious conglomerate of underground sects born in the 2nd and 3rd centuries A.D. – and thus a more complex phenomenon than it seems to be at first glance. To give an example, when Voegelin talks of magic, he refers to a feature already found in his previous studies: "When [the gnostic] acts, he expects such action to form the first reality into conformity with the Second Reality of his dream. The activist dreamer must know the trick action, as distinguished from ordinary action, that will have the extraordinary result of transfiguring the nature of things. He must imagine himself to be a magician."[93] Voegelin's use of the expression "magical politics" and "magical activism" is not at odds with "gnostic politics"; rather, it is a deepening and a development of its essence (for instance, the magical power to transfigure reality is a notion already included in the concept of self-redemption, though it emphasizes a specific aspect of it).[94] And in fact, the magic, or gnostic, act is the possibility of altering the order of being, gaining salvation here and now: the knowledge of therapeutic means directed to correct and renew the world is within human reach.

To end with the presentation of Eric Voegelin's definition of Gnosticism, an apparently marginal but very important intuition for the further analysis of Salafi-Jihadism must be mentioned here. The philosopher is quite worried by what he calls the "earthwide expansion of Western foulness."[95] Gnosticism is a disease of consciousness that has the potentiality of growing and expanding worldwide:

---

92 Michael Franz, 'Gnosticism and Spiritual Disorder in *The Ecumenic Age*', *Political Science Reviewer*, vol. 27, no. 1 (Fall 1998): p. 31.

93 Voegelin, 'Wisdom and the Magic', p. 324.

94 Actually, Voegelin had already adopted the notion of magic to explain gnostic politics. In *The New Science of Politics* he states that threats to gnostic activists are "met by magic operation in the dreamworld" ('The New Science of Politics', p. 227).

95 Voegelin, review of *The Origins of Totalitarianism*, p. 68.

> Modern Gnosticism has by far not spent its drive. On the contrary, in the variant of Marxism it is expanding its area of influence prodigiously in Asia, while other variants of Gnosticism, such as progressivism, positivism, and scientism, are penetrating into other areas under the title of "Westernization" and development of backward countries. […] Sill less can be said, for obvious reasons, about the probable reaction of a living Christian tradition against Gnosticism in the Soviet empire, and nothing at all about the manner in which Chinese, Hindu, Islamic, and primitive civilizations will react to a prolonged exposure to gnostic devastation and repression.[96]

Voegelin couldn't say anything about the prolonged exposure of Islamic civilization to Gnosticism. The present research posits that the ideology of Salafi-Jihadism is the Islamic reaction to gnostic ideas and behaviors – actually, a *mimetic* reaction that mirrors the same pneumopathological attitude by adopting an Islamic form. As such, Salafi-Jihadism is not a traditional Islamic form but a sick derivative within the classic Islamic tradition.

For any research dealing with Gnosticism, Eric Voegelin's philosophy is the starting point. His point of view will guide us through the whole book and it will be of the utmost importance in outlining the six-points gnostic pattern, which I will propose later.

1.3 *Augusto Del Noce, or grace replaced by revolution*

Augusto Del Noce (1910-1989) was a leading Italian political philosopher. He was well-versed in studies on the crisis of modernity, atheism, secularization, Marxism and contemporary nihilism. Del Noce was a Catholic and he took an active part in the Italian political life (he was elected Senator of the Italian Republic).

His encounter with Gnosticism is intimately linked to Eric Voegelin's thought. Starting from the publication in Italy of *The New Science of Politics*, Del Noce explicitly tackled the problem of Gnosticism as associated with the crisis of modernity. For the occasion, he wrote an introductive essay to Voegelin's Italian edition titled *Eric Voegelin e la critica dell'idea di modernità (Eric Voegelin and the Critique of the Idea of Modernity*) (1968). This paper is quite central for the development of his personal and innovative view on the topic.

96 Voegelin, 'The New Science of Politics', p. 222.

Talking about Voegelin's perspective, Del Noce himself acknowledges that the immanentization of the *eschaton* is the true spirit of modernity and that such tendency originates in what Voegelin calls Gnosticism. However, Del Noce feels the need to analytically define the concept: are we referring to a branch of ancient Gnosis that has reached modernity throughout centuries? Or is it something different, a sort of new creation recently set up following main historical changes and intellectual experiments? Del Noce seems to have little doubt: "We should carefully distinguish an ancient Gnosis from a post-Christian Gnosis."[97] According to the Italian philosopher, there are two types of Gnosticism; this approach is different from Voegelin's. In all likelihood, Del Noce doesn't recognize any development in Voegelin's thought, among others the theory of the balance of consciousness and the pneumopathological diagnosis of revolutionary dreams. Nothing suggests that he knows about Voegelin's other writings. To be sure, *Order and History. Vol. IV* was published only in 1974, while Del Noce's introductive essay dates back to 1968. Still, at the time Del Noce wrote this essay, Voegelin had already developed the concept of pneumopathology. But in order to avoid suggesting that Del Noce was ignorant about some elements of Voegelin's thought – in fact, I personally do not think this is true –, we are prone to suggest that his scientific approach to the issue is so different from Voegelin's that some elements are not useful for Del Noce's understanding of Gnosticism, as will emerge from the following pages.

Del Noce's answer to the problem regarding the difference between the two types of Gnosticism is the following: "Ancient Gnosis atheizes[98] the world (by denying its creation by God) in the name of the [absolute] divine transcendence; post-Christian Gnosis atheizes the world in the name of a radical immanentism."[99] He also adds: "It is possible to track down a common character, that is, the attempt to run from the sufferings of existence."[100] These remarks are useful to explain the feature of *anti-cosmism* as the inner soul of every form of Gnosticism: the world is evil and all laws governing and ordering the whole are but chains that compel human beings. The goal of the gnostic is to escape from the cosmos (ancient Gnosis) or to build another world order (post-Christian Gnosis).

97 Augusto Del Noce, 'Eric Voegelin e la critica dell'idea di modernità', in *La nuova scienza politica*, by Eric Voegelin (Roma: Edizioni Borla, 1999), p. 15.

98 The Italian word "ateizzare" has been translated as "atheize", even though it is not commonly used in English language. It means "to make or cause (someone or, in this case, something) to be atheist or to have no belief in God".

99 Del Noce, 'Eric Voegelin', pp. 15-16.

100 Ibid., p. 16.

Elaborating on this point, Del Noce writes that the main difference between the two forms of Gnosticism concerns pessimism and optimism: "[Ancient] Gnosticism deals with the rules that will permit to free the soul from the world; post-Christian immanentism, on the contrary, searches for rules to build a new world. The first possesses an aristocratic character. On the contrary, for the second it is essential the address to the masses."[101]

In light of similar comments, Augusto Del Noce does not hesitate to call post-Christian Gnosis by the name of "fallen" (*decaduto*) and "perverted" (*degenerato*) Gnosticism. In perverted Gnosticism, "the activist and revolutionary form prevails over the contemplative one,"[102] he says. The post-Christian gnostic is capable of self-redemption, meaning that salvation could be fulfilled through action. With an incisive expression, Del Noce talks of "grace replaced by revolution"[103] – humankind takes the place of God and gets rid of every transcendent reality, to the point that it becomes possible to talk of a real "fear of the supernatural."[104] The radical immanentism of the perverted Gnosis breaks up with any additional level of reality. To use Voegelian terminology, Gnosticism is the denial of the In-Between.

But it would be incorrect to argue that ancient Gnosticism is dead. Augusto Del Noce finds traces of it, for instance, in the thought of Simone Weil, where "a rationalistically-configured pessimism fights dramatically with Christianity."[105] In the introductive essay to the Italian edition of Weil's *Pensées sans ordre concernant l'amour de Dieu* (1962) translated as *L'amore di Dio* (1968), Del Noce finds the French mystical philosopher to be at a crossroad between Christianity and ancient Gnosticism. According to Del Noce, she seems to have "moved the Christian event [from the historical horizon] to the eternal level of essences, disavowing its unique and irreversible character."[106] Moreover, she seems to have adopted an anti-cosmic attitude toward creation, even agreeing on a quasi-Anaximander

101 Ibid.

102 Ibid., p. 17. On page 26 Del Noce writes: "The proper research of the perverted Gnosis is not the pursuit of truth but the pursuit of power."

103 Ibid., p. 7.

104 Ibid., p. 18.

105 Massimo Borghesi, 'Augusto Del Noce. Un pensiero non manicheo', *30Giorni*, no. 10/11 (2009), http://www.30giorni.it/articoli_id_21817_l1.htm (accessed August 17, 2018).

106 Augusto Del Noce, 'Simone Weil, interprete del mondo di oggi', in *L'amore di Dio*, by Simone Weil (Roma: Edizioni Borla, 1979), p. 22.

conception of birth.[107] Nevertheless, Simone Weil's Gnosticism is not so rigorous and all-embracing as it may appear: as Del Noce remembers, during her life she experienced a mystical encounter with Jesus Christ, and this experience, which is reported in the book *Connaissance surnaturelle*, "contradicts […] the thesis of the divine impersonalism, according to which talking of Christ as a 'person' would be diminishing him."[108] In this sense, Simone Weil's philosophy is characterized by the co-presence of two motifs, the Christian's and the ancient Gnostic's.

Returning to Del Noce's main exposition, it should be noted that he recognizes a clear break between the two forms of Gnosticism. The confusion between the two "could lead to an extremely serious misunderstanding […], that is to say, the idea of *unity* between pre-Christian and post-Christian Gnosis."[109] As a matter of fact, "ancient Gnosis existed as position of truth, while the new Gnosis emerges from the demand to satisfy a practical need; hence, it is impossible to talk of an evolution from the first to the second."[110] Nevertheless, like Eric Voegelin, Del Noce recognizes a common feature among the two, namely, the idea of a firmer grip than the *cognitio fidei* – which is the true element that makes it possible to call such experience by the name of "Gnosticism".

What is really interesting and original in Augusto Del Noce's discourse is that he admits a process of elaboration of Gnosticism, a kind of historical incubation of such theoretical and behavioral model: "The process of development of post-Christian Gnosis has been very slow: only in the past hundred years its theoretical definition has been manifested, and only in the last fifty years its practical nature came to light."[111] This recognition is not self-evident: Voegelin has talked of Gnosticism as a state of consciousness or, better, as a sick consciousness, a sort of permanent feature of the human soul, although it had become possible only after the destruction of ancient cosmological empires, after the main spiritual outbursts, and after the acknowledgement of living in the In-Between. In the case of Del Noce, instead, post-Christian Gnosis is something new and different from everything there was before; it is intimately linked to modernity and to the process of secularization. And if we take seriously Del Noce's assertion

107 With this, Del Noce means that birth is understood like a sort of a leak from an indistinct cauldron which must necessarily be returned to. It goes without saying that the individual is not exceptional in the eyes of this sort of impersonal divinity.

108 Del Noce, 'Simone Weil', p. 29.

109 Del Noce, 'Eric Voegelin', p. 18. Emphasis in the original text.

110 Ibid.

111 Ibid., p. 22.

that "it is impossible to talk of an evolution from the first to the second" type of Gnosticism, then post-Christian Gnosis, though picking from ancient Gnosis, has followed a completely new path, being in debt to other speculative traditions and innovative evolutions, first of all secularization. Indeed, one of the distinctive characteristics of post-Christian Gnosticism is "the absolutization of the political [...] for the followers of the perverted Gnosis replace religion with politics as *the* means to free and save man."[112] As such, Gnosticism is a product of the secularization, since the superiority of politics over religion as a way to save humankind is already a form of weakening of the Sacred in favor of the secular.

The final stage of history as it will be achieved by post-Christian gnostic politics is a transfigured humanity. Del Noce describes the immanentized *eschaton* of the gnostics as an "absorption [or incorporation] of individual consciousnesses in the universal consciousness."[113] This is why Marx and Engels were able to talk of the abolition of the state: individuality will disappear in the "immanent *Pleroma*,"[114] and all individual wills will be joined together in a superior, universal, common and finally peaceful will.

The gnostic revolution will be an "inimitable and painful event which will mediate the passage from the Reign of Necessity to the Reign of Freedom."[115] And, most importantly, the intuition of Del Noce is that a gnostic revolutionary attitude implies "the replacement of the research of the *meta-physics* (namely, the rationality that is inside reality, with the resulting primacy of contemplation of the order to whom one should conform) with the establishing of a *meta-humanity*, characterized by the recovery of those powers from which humankind had alienated himself in the past."[116] In this way, "the future takes the place of the afterworld"[117] or, in Voegelin's language, of the Beyond. The horizon is completely immanent. And humanity is deified.

The peculiarity of Christianity as compared to Gnosticism is very interesting:

112 Ibid., pp. 22, 24.

113 Ibid., p. 26.

114 Michael Henry, 'Civil Theology in the Gnostic Age: Progress and Regress', *Modern Age*, vol. 47, no. 1 (Winter 2005): p. 38. "Pleroma" means "fullness" and is a concept used by many ancient Gnostic sects.

115 Augusto Del Noce, 'Tradizione e rivoluzione', in *Tradizione e rivoluzione. Proceedings of the 27th Conference at Centro di Studi Filosofici, Gallarate, 1972* (Brescia: Morcelliana, 1973), p. 24.

116 Ibid., p. 25. Here Del Noce refers to the philosophical concept of the Superman as developed by Nietzsche and Marx.

117 Ibid.

> It is but one of the two: either the origin of evil is placed in the human will, or it is placed in an unjust […] social structure, whose end will bring the end of all iniquities. The first thesis stands for the distinction of religion and politics; according to the second thesis, politics replaces religion in the struggle against evil. It is legitimate to opt either for the first or the second thesis; however, it is not fair to contaminate them. There are no doubts that the saints have changed the world, but they have done it without intending it; the transformation is a surplus given to whom seeks primarily the non-temporal Reign of God: it follows to the irradiation of an authentic religious experience.[118]

The differences between Christianity and Gnosticism emerge quite evidently from this short quotation.

Let us move forward in the study of Augusto Del Noce's idea of Gnosticism. The Italian philosopher further developes his understanding of the topic in an important essay on violence. During a conference held in April 1979, Del Noce marks a difference between war and revolution: the first intends to reestablish peace, a conciliation between winners and losers, while the second aims to annihilate the enemy and all that pertains to the ancient "aeon". Hence, revolutionary violence points at creating a new human being by demolishing the past era. In this sense, violence becomes benign and benevolent, even creative and productive. And Del Noce has no doubts: "The idea of a creative violence has its source in the reaffirmation of the structure of a gnostic mentality."[119] In this essay, the philosopher gives a new and noteworthy definition of Gnosticism. In his own words:

> It is evident that with the term "Gnosticism" I am not referring to ancient Gnosis (indeed the latter is not an exhausting form of the whole gnostic phenomenon), but to a *spiritual essence* that is likely to arise in different forms and in several places; or to a *mentality* that, after having been an alternative to Christianity in the first centuries […], and after an underground transmission, has resurfaced in the last two centuries, reaching *after Christianity* its clearest form.[120]

---

118 Augusto Del Noce, 'Pensiero cristiano e comunismo: "inveramento" o "risposta a sfida"?', in *Opere 1945-1964*, by Felice Balbo (Torino: Boringhieri, 1966), pp. 980-981.

119 Augusto Del Noce, 'Il problema filosofico della violenza', in *Violenza. Una ricerca per comprendere. Proceedings of the 34th Conference at Centro di Studi Filosofici, Gallarate, 1979* (Brescia: Morcelliana, 1980), p. 10.

120 Augusto Del Noce, 'Violenza e secolarizzazione della gnosi', in *Violenza. Una ricerca per comprendere. Proceedings of the 34th Conference*, p. 202. Italics added.

Such a mentality, or spiritual essence, implies the already-mentioned anti-cosmic attitude, and thus a revolt against being. "From a kind of ethic that is autonomous from metaphysics and from theology it is not possible to draw a critic to violence."[121] The order of being is to be distorted, changed, and altered. In post-Christian Gnosis, violence appears as the means thanks to which humankind can free itself from the order that has ruled all over history, an order now judged oppressive and tyrannical.

But this kind of violence – *the* revolutionary violence – should not create a society that mimics the previous order; rather, the passage to the Reign of Freedom will be marked by the end of any kind of juridical infrastructure. Stated differently, "the production of legality is the sign of the failure of the passage from the Reign of Necessity to the Reign of Freedom."[122] Ancient Gnosticism and post-Christian Gnosticism differ on this very point, for second-century gnostics' goal was not to establish a new world but to run away from cosmic order in the direction of a totally Other. Nevertheless, "we cannot deny a degree of kinship represented by the negation of the order of being, of creation, of God's image."[123]

Remarkably, the end of legality and the beginning of true freedom in the Reign of Perfection stems from what we can call the "anarchic disposition" of ancient Gnosticism. The two opposite behavioral dispositions that distinguished many ancient groups are asceticism and libertinism, both directed to discredit and reject the order of creation. Del Noce formulates the following rhetorical question: "Isn't the revolutionary spirit a secularized version of gnostic asceticism, of moral nihilism, of gnostic libertinism?"[124]

Nihilism is the premise for any revolutionary action. In *The Suicide of Revolution* (*Il suicidio della rivoluzione*, 1978), Del Noce says that "the fulfillment of a revolution coincides with its own suicide."[125] What does it mean? The philosopher identifies two moments of a revolution that he refers to as *the* Revolution: the negative moment (the dissolution of the ancient order, the devaluation of any traditional values) and the positive moment (the instauration of a new order). To his mind, the suicide occurs if the two moments take place separately. But eventually the two moments *do* take place separately. Thus, "instead of the passage to a new order, there will be

121 Ibid.
122 Ibid., p. 204.
123 Ibid.
124 Ibid., p. 207.
125 Augusto Del Noce, *Il suicidio della rivoluzione* (Torino: Nino Aragno Editore, 2004), p. 8.

the return to the old order, but totally deconsecrated."[126] The revolutionary process starts from and ends up in nihilism. And such nihilism is highly totalitarian, for there will not be any ideal unity to bring people together but only brutal coercion. The natural end of gnostic politics is totalitarianism.

1.4 *Hans Jonas: an existential Gnosticism*

Among contemporary philosophers, the one who has studied the topic of ancient Gnosticism extensively is the German-American philosopher Hans Jonas (1903-1993). Since his doctoral dissertation on *Der Begreiff der Gnosis* (*The Concept of Gnosis*), Jonas dedicated most of his intellectual work to this ambiguous religious phenomenon. Even his most important and original theoretical elaboration, the well-known "imperative of responsibility,"[127] could be wholly interpreted as a response to the gnostic attitude in contemporary society.

At any rate, his interpretation of Late-Antique Gnosticism is still the point of departure for any further accounts of the phenomenon.

Hans Jonas's is one of the most influential analysis on Gnosticism in the field of Religious Studies. His work has followed new and innovative lines of interpretation, even adopting brave intellectual solutions in order to find the supposed unity behind different and often apparently incompatible gnostic variations and narratives. The gnostic principle, he maintains, is a complete novelty in the ancient world – in this sense, it is not a Christian heresy but a truly original development.

Jonas went beyond a rigorous historiographical reconstruction; he "has the merit of having launched the investigation of the *invariants*, trying to define Gnosticism through them."[128] What's more, he adopted a philosophical orientation that is close to existentialism; in fact, in Hans Jonas's work the philosophical dimension intertwines with the objective historical investigation. As Claudio Bonaldi writes,

> Jonas's prime objective is not philological-literary or merely historiographic, but [...] it consists in making visible the essential traits of the gnostic phenomenon by implementing a phenomenological-existential reinterpretation

---

126 Ibid.

127 See *The Imperative of Responsibility. In Search of an Ethics for the Technological Age* (Chicago: Chicago University Press, 1985).

128 Ioan Petru Couliano, *I miti dei dualismi occidentali* (1989; repr., Milan: Jaca Book, 2018), p. 82.

> of its testimonial basis. [...] It is properly this very wide perspective that allows Jonas [...] to prove Gnosticism as an ideal type that exemplifies a recurrent existential dynamic throughout history.[129]

What is important for the purpose of the present research is that Jonas's (re)interpretation of Gnosticism provides us with a key to see it as a recurrent phenomenon in history, a phenomenon that is not (only) linked to a distinguishable literary influence but a human constant that periodically emerges under similar socio-historical conditions. In other words, Jonas has demythologized the gnostic sources and brought to light its existential nucleus. "Jonas's hermeneutical paradigm"[130] is an important theoretical tool that permits us, on the one hand, to clarify the major themes of such a complex doctrine and, on the other, to synchronically study thoughts that have risen in different times.

A useful report on Jonas's account on ancient Gnosticism is the speech he gave at the Colloquium of Messina (April 13-18, 1966), a week-long conference on the origins of Gnosticism. Here, Jonas discussed the topic of *Delimitation of the Gnostic Phenomenon – Typological and Historical*. First of all, he circumscribes the content of Gnosis, which includes a theology (the transcendental genesis of the creation), a cosmology (the structure of the existing universe), an anthropology (the nature of man), and an eschatology (the doctrine of salvation). Then, he comes to define Gnosticism as a *movement of knowledge*: "*A lack of knowledge* is at work in the arrogance and delusion of demiurgical creation and is permanently embodied in the resulting world. *A want of knowledge*, inflicted by the world and actively maintained by its powers, characterizes man's inner-worldly existence. And *a restoration of knowledge* is the vehicle of salvation."[131] Jonas defines Gnosticism as a "metaphysic of pure movement and event, the most determinedly 'historical' conception of universal being prior to Hegel."[132] Finally, he summarizes the structure of gnostic myth:

---

129 Claudio Bonaldi, introduction to *Gnosi e spirito tardoantico*, by Hans Jonas (Milano: Bompiani, 2010), p. XI.

130 This expression has been coined by the historian Giuliano Chiapparini. See Giuliano Chiapparini, 'Gnosticismo: fine di una categoria storico-religiosa?', *Annali di Scienze Religiose*, no. 11 (2006): p. 190.

131 Hans Jonas, 'Delimitation of the Gnostic Phenomenon – Typological and Historical', in *The Origins of Gnosticism. Colloquium of Messina*, ed. by Ugo Bianchi (Leiden: Brill, 1967), p. 92. Emphasis added.

132 Ibid.

> The typical Gnostic myth [...] starts with a doctrine of divine transcendence in its original purity; it then traces the genesis of the world from some primordial disruption of this blessed state, a loss of divine integrity which leads to the emergence of lower powers who become the makers and rulers of this world; then, as a crucial episode in the drama, the myth recounts the creation and early fate of man, in whom the further conflict becomes centered; the final theme, in fact the implied theme throughout, is man's salvation, which is more than man's as it involves the overcoming and eventual dissolving of the cosmic system and is thus the instrument of reintegration for the impaired godhead itself, or, the selfsaving of God.[133]

Of course, according to such a creed, the world is evil: the cosmos, though ordered and governed by laws, is evil, and has an imprisoning and compelling structure. The foundational basis of any gnostic variation is, thus, anti-cosmism: "The generative existential principle, the true content of Gnosticism, Jonas recapitulates, is escape from, or negation of, the world (*Entweltlichung*)."[134] The behavioral pattern encouraged by Gnosticism is rebellion and protest, which can assume the double form of asceticism and libertinism – "the former refuses obedience to nature through abstinence, the latter through excess."[135] Therefore, the revolutionary and angry element in Gnosticism is intended to destroy any well-established traditions (from which anti-Judaism and opposition to Greek pro-cosmism are derived). Antinomianism and radical nihilism are two sides of the same coin.

What is particularly noteworthy in Jonas's hermeneutical reconstruction is that, by adopting the existential framework to explain ancient Gnosticism, he finds a path to a reciprocal interpretation of Gnosticism and existentialism. He "brings to light the structural connections between ancient Gnosis and contemporary existentialism and nihilism,"[136] enlightening in an innovative way the existential crisis of today's world. Such theoretical evolution occurs in his later writings, when a mature Jonas starts to investigate the unexpected parallels between the two currents of thought. Intrigued by such connections, he writes a central essay on the

---

133 Ibid., p. 94-95.

134 Michael Waldstein, 'Hans Jonas' Construct "Gnosticism": Analysis and Critique', *Journal of Early Christian Studies*, vol. 8, no. 3 (Fall 2000): p. 362.

135 Hans Jonas, "Gnosticism", in *Encyclopedia of Philosophy*, vol. 3 (New York: Macmillan and Free Press, 1967), p. 342.

136 Franco Volpi, *Il nichilismo* (Roma-Bari: Laterza, 2009), p. 123.

subject,[137] stating that "in retrospect, I am inclined to believe that it was the thrill of this dimly felt affinity which had lured me into the gnostic labyrinth in the first place."[138] Michael Waldstein is clear and acute:

> By the early fifties the former lock had turned into a key and the former key into a lock to be opened. When unlocked by the later Jonas with the ancient gnostic key, modern existentialism showed its true face: acosmic nihilism. [...] For the early Jonas, gnostic texts were a dim but forceful anticipation of existentialist philosophy, to be positively embraced as examples, even if ultimately unsuccessful examples, of the philosophical breakthrough achieved by existentialism, particularly Heidegger. For the later Jonas, modern existentialism was to be rejected as a symptom of nihilism, as a modern parallel of the ancient nihilism found in the gnostics.[139]

In this sense, the true heir of Late-Antique gnostic anti-cosmism turns out to be existentialist philosophy. Even the younger Heidegger, Jonas's former master, in a certain sense was gnostic.

In the essay titled "Gnosticism, Existentialism and Nihilism," Hans Jonas follows the evolution of the spiritual crisis of modern humankind, which he situates in the 17th century. At that time, Blaise Pascal was the first philosopher to realize the frightening implication of the modern mentality, namely, "man's loneliness in the physical universe of modern cosmology."[140] Humankind is estranged from the order of the whole and is now a foreigner in the world. Gone is the perception of the cosmos as an organic whole where man has its place. In Pascal's philosophy, God is still the transmundane creator but also an unknown God (*agnostos theos*), and the universe

> does not reveal the creator's purpose [...] nor his goodness [...] nor his wisdom [...] nor his perfection – but reveals solely his power by its magnitude, its spatial and temporal immensity. [...] A world reduced to a mere manifestation of power also admits toward itself – once the transcendent reference has fallen away and man is left with it and himself alone – nothing but the relation of power, that is, of mastery.[141]

137 Hans Jonas, 'Gnosticism and Modern Nihilism', *Social Research*, vol. 19, no. 4 (December 1952): pp. 430-52; reprinted as 'Gnosticism, Existentialism and Nihilism', in *Gnostic Religion: The Message of the Alien God and the Beginnings of Christianity*, by Hans Jonas (Boston: Beacon, 1963), pp. 320-40.

138 Jonas, 'Gnosticism, Existentialism and Nihilism', p. 320.

139 Waldstein, 'Hans Jonas' Construct "Gnosticism"', p. 344.

140 Jonas, 'Gnosticism, Existentialism and Nihilism', p. 322.

141 Ibid., p. 324.

Gradually, transcendence went lost, and the estrangement between humankind and the world reached a higher peak.

Jonas is adamant that a similar perception of the world was also present in ancient gnostic movements. The main characteristic of ancient Gnosticism is a radically dualistic mood: "The dualism is between man and the world, and concurrently between the world and God. It is a duality not of supplementary but of contrary terms; and it is one: for that between man and world mirrors on the plane of experience that between world and God, and derives from it as from its logical ground."[142] The Divine is alien to the world, the world is created by inferior principles, and humankind has the *pneuma* (spirit) that is not part of the world but belongs to the Divine principle, the unknowable totally Other. According to this view, the world is a prison which epitomizes the will to coerce, also representing ignorance, the lack of knowledge, having been created by the malignant and passionate demiurge. There is no a positive appraisal of the physical world nor of the physical body, so that it becomes possible to assert that "Gnosticism may well have been the most radical rebellion in Western history against the Greek notion of *physis*."[143] Anti-cosmism and antinomianism are inseparable.

Both ancient Gnosticism and modern nihilism share the same "devaluation or spiritual denudation of the universe."[144] The consequences are catastrophic in both cases:

> Nietzsche indicated the root of the nihilistic situation in the phrase "God is dead", meaning primarily the Christian God. The gnostics, if asked to summarize similarly the metaphysical basis of their own nihilism, could have said only "the God of the cosmos is dead" – is dead, that is, as a god, has ceased to be divine for us and therefore to afford the lodestar for our lives. Admittedly the catastrophe in this case is less comprehensive and thus less irremediable, but the vacuum that was left, even if not so bottomless, was felt no less keenly.[145]

For modern nihilism, God is dead and thus is irrelevant for human conduct; rather, according to ancient Gnosticism, God is the totally Other, a God that is not active in the cosmos. And "a transcendence withdrawn

---

142 Ibid., p. 326.

143 Benjamin Lazier, 'Overcoming Gnosticism: Hans Jonas, Hans Blumenberg, and the Legitimacy of the Natural World', *Journal of the History of Ideas*, vol. 64, no. 4 (October 2003): p. 620.

144 Jonas, 'Gnosticism, Existentialism and Nihilism', p. 330.

145 Ibid., p. 331.

from any normative relation to the world is equal to a transcendence which has lost its effective force."[146] Speaking of existentialism:

> his [of Heidegger] existentialist depreciation of the concept of nature obviously reflects its spiritual denudation at the hands of physical science, and it has something in common with the gnostic contempt for nature. No philosophy has ever been less concerned about nature than existentialism, for which it has no dignity left.[147]

As a final remark, Jonas acknowledges the difference in intensity between gnostic nihilism and modern nihilism. There is

> one cardinal difference between the gnostic and the existentialist dualism: gnostic man is thrown into an antagonistic, anti-divine, and therefore anti-human nature, modern man into an indifferent one. Only the latter case represents the absolute vacuum, the really bottomless pit. [...] From that nature [of modern science] no direction at all can be elicited. This makes modern nihilism infinitely more radical and more desperate than gnostic nihilism ever could be for all its panic terror of the world and its defiant contempt of its laws.[148]

This brief mention of Jonas's innovative and experimental study[149] is quite beneficial for the purposes of the present research due to two reasons: firstly, Eric Voegelin has been deeply inspired by Jonas in his definition of Gnosticism; and secondly, Jonas's attempt demonstrates the secret pervasiveness of Late-Antique Gnosticism in modern issues. Gnosticism continues to be a clandestine stimulus in the West, and by way of the so-called Westernization it is spreading throughout the world, causing unforeseen and unexpected mutations.

1.5 *Vittorio Mathieu and Emanuele Samek Lodovici: from revolution to protest*

In Italy many academics have recently dedicated their researches to the topic of Gnosticism. There are several reasons for this, but probably the main motivation can be found in the religion professed by the majority of

---

146 Ibid., p. 332.
147 Ibid., p. 337.
148 Ibid., pp. 338-339.
149 The same Jonas talks of his study as driven by "an experimental vein" (ibid., p. 320).

Italians. In fact, Catholicism has a long history of struggles, conflicts and disputes with gnostics – at the dawn of Christianity, almost all the heretics were labeled as gnostics, in spite of the differences between numerous non-orthodox doctrines and behaviors.

Two Italian philosophers who have produced valuable contributions for the advancement in knowledge of the relation between Gnosticism and contemporary world are Vittorio Mathieu and Emanuele Samek Lodovici.[150]

On this topic, Vittorio Mathieu (1923-2020) wrote an important book entitled *Hope in the Revolution* (*La speranza nella rivoluzione*, first edition 1972), where he analyzes the case of revolution from a phenomenological point of view. His investigation is quite innovative, for he distinguishes revolution from all other kinds of reform, also linking it with our topic, Gnosticism. It would be worthwhile to follow Mathieu's argumentation to understand the peculiarity of revolution as a gnostic resolution.

His starting point, which is also the leitmotiv throughout his entire reasoning, is that revolutionary actions have a distinctive *propitiatory function* in the same manner as prayer. To bring about revolution is the goal of any revolutionary actions – actions that are unescapably *liturgical*. To understand such an unusual statement, it should be clear how Mathieu uses the category of Gnosticism. The contact points between revolutionary thought and gnostic *Weltanschauung* are many, he maintains. According to several gnostic myths, as already seen thanks to Jonas's hermeneutical paradigm, the "fall" of God gives origin to the creation – the creation being something evil, something to be overcame. Hence, the drama of the Fall does not concern man but God himself. "Since there is no other reality outside of God, the illusory transition to another order of things is, ultimately, the exhibition of the same divine order but upside down. In fact, in any other conception there is a hiatus between God and the finite, but in

150 Vittorio Mathieu was a prominent philosopher and politicians. He wrote many essays on Philosophy of Science, Moral Philosophy, History of Philosophy and Aesthetics. He was professor first at University of Trieste and then at University of Turin. Emanuele Samek Lodovici was a young researcher who tragically died at 38 years old. Just before his death, Augusto Del Noce wrote him a letter saying: "Dear Samek, [...] you now have the opportunity to become a true master. Nor do I exaggerate at all in telling you that I don't see any others among those who are less than forty years old today." Samek Lodovici was an expert of Saint Augustine, Plotinus, Marx, and Gnosticism. He graduated at the Catholic University of the Sacred Heart, in Milan. Starting from 1974, he worked with Vittorio Mathieu for a small period of his academic career.

the gnostic view there is the overturning of the same and only reality."[151] The world, continues Mathieu, is the "transit area"[152] of the divine story. The finite reality where we live is the same infinite reality, but upside down, and so unrecognizable to humans (from which it comes "Gnosis" as "knowledge" in the sense of "acknowledgment"). "To recover the positive one should not move to another order of things; on the contrary, one should reverse the same:"[153] this declaration is quite common among contemporary revolutionaries, which are often atheist and anti-metaphysical. The whole (immanent) reality will be saved *through* humankind, through the act of recognition that humankind is God himself, and through the factual (and violent) overturning of nature: "Since the supernatural does not exist, nature will be saved all together [...] Revolution concerns the whole."[154] The transfiguration of reality is the end goal.

However, it is not humankind that saves reality; it is the same revolution that, *by means of* humankind, changes the Whole. Stated differently, it is the whole that will overturn itself *via* humankind. Mathieu explains this concept quite specifically: "One should only hope that the Whole changes from itself. At that point, technical operations, which still must be carried out, will be conceived not as 'causes' of the revolution understood as the 'effect', but just as many preparations for the Whole to change itself."[155] The definition of revolutionary actions becomes intelligible as liturgical and propitiatory for the Revolution to occur. Revolutionary actions are *the occasion* for the Revolution, just like the farmer who plants a seed: the technical action is required, but the seed will grow and develop from itself – or just like the priest in the Catholic mass, where the transubstantiation takes place through the priest, but the priest is not the author of it.

A consequence is that the subversion of the ancient order is aimed at a new, perfect and everlasting order "only indirectly, like a prayer."[156] The disorder has its own function, to bring chaos, to bring about a new order, an order that would no longer be extrinsic, external, purely mechanical, but finally vital, internal, not something different from things, but which will identify itself with things.

---

151 Vittorio Mathieu, *La speranza nella rivoluzione* (1972; repr., Rome: Armando Editore, 1992), p. 61.
152 Ibid., p. 62.
153 Ibid.
154 Ibid., p. 64.
155 Ibid., p. 67.
156 Ibid., p. 81.

Mathieu refers to some heretical sects from the Middle Ages, then draws a parallel between the ancient "sect" and the modern "party", both suggesting a split from the rest of the community – it is, in both cases, a portion of the society that claims to represent the Whole, bringing the banner of the "election". The sect, or the party, speaks for everyone because it speaks for the Whole. The revolutionary acts from the point of view of the totality, and "if he did not do so, he would not be a revolutionary but a reformist. In fact, it is the hallmark of any reform to be partial."[157] Any reform aims at transforming society through a specific technic; on the contrary, the Revolution (with a capital "R", the once-and-for-all event) is not tied to any technic in any sense of the word. Revolution is not something that one can do: "Revolution is always beyond everything that could be done in the *hope* that it happens."[158] Here the gnostic idea is all-pervading.

Besides, the revolutionary is against any kind of law. Jurisprudence is evil, the revolutionary says. The new order will rest on some kind of "non-juridical laws"[159] or, let us say, non-extrinsic norms. At that time, in the restored golden age, "only the morally right will be chosen [by the transfigured people]."[160] The restauration of the supposed lost golden age entitles all revolutionaries with a significant aura, for "actions are no longer motives of salvation, but only their clues. Salvation derives from the attitude with which the single actor acts."[161] In other words, salvation is already given, and *the revolutionaries are certain of their own salvation*. They are saints and they are on the right side of history. Such a revolutionary notion of redemption donates salvation to whom decides to be a revolutionary – it is an unescapable reasoning that has its roots in the gnostic worldview.

A corollary of the revolutionary thinking is the disposition to martyrdom: abnegation, self-denial and total devotion to the cause lead straight to self-sacrifice. And violence against the supposed enemy is justified as necessary – "the religious minister does not apologize to the victim offered as a sacrifice."[162] The dualism between the revolutionaries and the enemies of the revolution is total and absolute.

Interestingly, Vittorio Mathieu also speaks of Islam though he only devotes one single page to the topic; but still, a quite remarkable concept is expressed there. As a matter of fact, in a regular religious struggle Muslims

---

157 Ibid., p. 66.
158 Ibid., p. 77.
159 Ibid., p. 113.
160 Ibid., p. 116.
161 Ibid., p. 155.
162 Ibid., p. 117.

keep the transcendence, since God and the Afterlife are the compasses of the Islamic army and the mind of the warriors are turned to God. However,

> when transcendence disappears and the covenant [with God] remains exclusive, there is no more a pact with God, but [real] association, fusion, identification. […] The chosen people […] becomes an *élite*, thanks to whom everything will be saved. The holy war is still holy but only as an ideological war and no longer as a religious war, even keeping the same complete dissymmetry – dissymmetry that will be overcame at the end of the struggle. Thenceforward the everyone God will be found again in the finally united humanity.[163]

In a sense, the former religious revolutionary actor is liberated from the "weakness" of waiting salvation from the beyond. The "fusion" or "identification" to which Mathieu refers is the same "absorption [or incorporation] of individual consciousness in the universal consciousness"[164] that Del Noce analyzes in the small essay dedicated to Eric Voegelin: the individual loses or renounces to his individuality to reach the immanent Pleroma, the earthly communion of saints, the immanent (and only) Absolute, the situation when is not the individual to speak but the Whole, the Totality, the gnostic hidden God.

At the end of *Hope in the Revolution*, Mathieu proposes a curious explanation for the emergence of Gnosticism in the modern era. Romanticism, he explains, was the moment when certain counterforces disappeared, making way for a new force. Such counterforces can be ultimately recognized as "the push to the form [*l'impulso alla forma*]. And the push to the form is the sense of limit [*il senso del limite*]."[165] The new force that bursted into history was "the infinite transformability. […] Such is the origin of any revolutionary materialisms. […] This desire of infinite, which is grounded in the formless [*informe*], goes along the decline and the disappearance of the sense of the transcendence."[166]

To better understand this very point, I will now move to Emanuele Samek Lodovici (1942-1981), a philosopher who worked with Vittorio Mathieu for a small period of his academic career, as I said earlier. Samek Lodovici's main work is *Metamorphosis of Gnosis. Paintings of Contemporary Dissolution* (*Metamorfosi della gnosi. Quadri della dissoluzione contemporanea*, first edition 1979), an important contribution

---

163 Ibid., p. 203.
164 Del Noce, 'Eric Voegelin', p. 26.
165 Mathieu, *La speranza nella rivoluzione*, p. 271.
166 Ibid.

for the identification of Gnosticism in everyday life[167]. The book opens with a reference to Mathieu's understanding of Romanticism, adding that in the artistic field the Romantic attitude tends to do without any "mediations," e.g., forms and fixed techniques. In this way, the Romantic artist aspires to express everything immediately and straight away, failing to achieve a real balance as it is, for example, in classic masterpieces. Repercussions of such a Romantic mentality were not long in coming: "If the necessity of mediation falls because the Absolute is now instantly achievable, then the first result is the disregard for any institutional aspects of the Church, for any authority."[168] Faith becomes emotional, the conceptual mediation (philosophy and theology) is put aside. Hierarchy is smashed away.

The hate for the form is closely linked to *Prometheanism*: if a stable nature is not anymore, humankind becomes endowed with the task to shape the shapeless, to give order to the disorder. In fact, what has been really demolished by the eruption of the desire of a formless infinite is the very *sense of limit*. Samek Lodovici has no doubts in tracing this attitude back to Late-Antique Gnosticism: "2nd-century gnostics suddenly overturned the way of thinking one of the most important classic concepts, namely the idea of limit. Such a concept turns from a positive sense (limit is what actualizes me, what perfects me in a closed wholeness) to a negative one (limit is what incarcerates me, what restricts me, what suffocates me)."[169] The world is evil, as all gnostic narratives claim, and nature should be surmounted. Even my finite being, human finitude, should be fixed in some ways – and modern technics allow us to do so.[170]

Emanuele Samek Lodovici is rigorously concerned with contemporaneity. His study focuses on some modern trajectories such as feminism, media propaganda, egalitarianism, demythologization of Christianity, Marxism,

167 Unlike Augusto Del Noce, Samek Lodovici "considers the differences between ancient and modern Gnosticism to be less pronounced" (Sergio Fumagalli, 'Gnosi moderna e secolarizzazione nell'analisi di Emanuele Samek Lodovici e Augusto Del Noce' [PhD diss., Pontifical University of the Holy Cross, 2005], p. 39).

168 Emanuele Samek Lodovici, *Metamorfosi della gnosi. Quadri della dissoluzione contemporanea* (Milano: Ares Edizioni, 1979), p. 17.

169 Ibid., p. 106.

170 The gnostic total malleability of reality does not allow for a theoretical and contemplative approach to nature, but only for a practical-activist, or even a voluntarist, approach: all aspects of reality could, and should, be reshaped. See ibid., pp. 206-207. For a more detailed study, see Antonio Allegra, 'Trasformazione & perfezione. Temi gnostici nel postumanesimo', in *L'origine & la meta. Studi in memoria di Emanuele Samek Lodovici*, ed. by Gabriele De Anna (Milano: Edizioni Ares, 2015), pp. 151-168.

and the protest of 1968 – all of them are paintings, or aspects, of contemporary world, and parts of a massive gnostic renaissance.

In Samek Lodovici's analysis, Gnosticism is "a mentality"[171] that is dangerously resurging, causing the dissolution of every tradition, cutting any link with the past, twisting the understanding of limit, and opening the path for the total malleability of reality, in light of the oblivion of whichever norm and limit. Following the reasoning of the author of *Metamorphosis of Gnosis*, it is possible to list four points that circumscribe Gnosticism as a mentality: (1) the world is evil due to various reasons; (2) someone capable of fixing reality exists because he *knows* why the world is as it is; (3) a technique exists that allows humankind to achieve terrestrial paradise, and so fix the wicked existing condition; (4) it follows that the gnostic is deeply hostile to any kind of law, both positive and natural norms, because a law limits one's freedom (or, at least, such is the gnostic understanding of it), and because reality should be done all over again from scratch.[172]

The final stage of history (a communist society, a 1968 commune, the feminist utopia)[173] will be marked by perfect and complete equality among human beings. But – Samek Lodovici's intuition is precious – "it would be interesting to see whether behind such desire of equality there is a stronger refusal of whatsoever differences (and thus a deeper desire of unity) rather than the refusal of the mere visible social differences."[174] A similar idea mirrors the gnostic belief of the "fall" or "error" of the One, the creation of the world, the dispersion of divine fragments, and the final rejoining of the divine pieces in the Pleroma. The differences among individuals are obstacles for the final and eschatological reunion of the fragments.[175] It is

---

171 Samek Lodovici, *Metamorfosi della gnosi*, p. 7.

172 See ibid., pp. 8-10.

173 On Samek Lodovici's view regarding feminism, see Lucetta Scaraffia, 'Gnosticismo & femminismo', in *L'origine & la meta. Studi in memoria di Emanuele Samek Lodovici*, ed. by Gabriele De Anna (Milano: Edizioni Ares, 2015), pp. 169-182. According to Scaraffia, Samek Lodovici predicted the wave of gender studies and the deconstruction of sexual identity, which are all elements that mirror the gnostic wish of total equality and perfect fungibility, or substitutability, among individuals, "to the point that woman is no longer a clear biological fact" (ibid., p. 172).

174 Samek Lodovici, *Metamorfosi della gnosi*, p. 138.

175 Of course, a similar (immanent) gnostic unity wouldn't be real unity; rather, it would result in a condition of widespread uniformity. The degeneration of unity into uniformity – the latter being a mock of the former – has been analyzed by René Guénon in *The Reign of Quantity and the Signs of the Times* (1945; repr., Hillsdale NY: Sophia Perennis, 2001), pp. 49-54.

"the ancient Promethean desire of an impenetrable monism, a monism that is present in the myth of the divine androgynous. I'm finally God again."[176]

The belief in a new beginning derives from what Samek Lodovici calls "chronolatric theology,"[177] which can be explained as the veneration of a rosy and joyful future. In moving towards a perfect future, the gnostic destroys what belongs to the past – the cancellation of the past is necessary to the project of building a new world. "Il futuro è *nulla* delle cose presenti,"[178] states Samek Lodovici.[179] The gnostic transition is "the passage from a secular history to a holy history; and, by definition, in the holy history, in the Earthly Jerusalem, every norm is finally broken."[180] Total freedom, complete equality and everlasting peace are features of the rosy future. The gnostic timeline, continues Samek Lodovici, is like a *broken line*: according to ancient Gnosticism, through the acquisition of the salvific Gnosis humankind instantly escapes from time, now living in a non-flowing present; the same happens in modern Gnosticism through the success of the Revolution[181].

Samek Lodovici's study is of great help to frame contemporary society as an inherently gnostic civilization. The existence of gnostic elements in modern trends (gender studies, posthuman…) is significant, since it points out that revolutionary Gnosticism is still continuing its plan along (apparently) non-revolutionary developments, acting as an infection and obeying the belief in the infinite malleability of reality.

1.6 *Luciano Pellicani's sociological analysis*

Another important scholar who devoted many studies to the topic of revolutionary Gnosticism is the sociologist Luciano Pellicani (1939 -2020). His academic interests cover Marxism, the genesis of capitalism, radical politics and modernity. However, despite being perhaps an unusual field of study, Gnosticism is not unrelated to sociology. Pellicani "totally

176 Samek Lodovici, *Metamorfosi della gnosi*, p. 157.
177 Ibid., p. 18.
178 Ibid., p. 132.
179 As we will see in the further analysis of Salafi-Jihadism, the hate for the recent past, and therefore for the present as something deriving from the past, is a common feature of gnostic revolutionaries, bringing about the destruction of archaeological findings.
180 Samek Lodovici, *Metamorfosi della gnosi*, p. 209.
181 Emanuele Samek Lodovici has delved into such topic in 'Dominio dell'istante, dominio della morte', *Archivio di Filosofia* (1981): pp. 469-480.

agrees with Voegelin's considerations on gnostic history, from the English Puritans to Karl Marx."[182] Yet, unlike Voegelin, he adopts a sociological approach, trying to explain the gnostic outbursts as endemic reactions to the capitalist market.

His starting point is quite uncommon for the literature on the topic: he begins by taking into consideration the role of the intellectual. The main reference is Karl Mannheim, whose theoretical elaboration recognizes intellectuals as a class, or, better, as an "unanchored, *relatively* classless stratum."[183] Intellectuals, in fact, do not come from one single class.

> It is, of course, true that a large body of our intellectuals come from rentier strata, whose income is derived directly or indirectly from rents and interest on investments. But for that matter certain groups of the officials and the so-called liberal professions are also members of the intelligentsia. A closer examination, however, of the social basis of these strata will show them to be less clearly identified with one class than those who participate more directly in the economic process.[184]

At any rate, they have something in common which makes it possible to recognize them as a single group. In Mannheim's words:

> Although they are too differentiated to be regarded as a single class, there is, however, one unifying sociological bond between all groups of intellectuals, namely, education, which binds them together in a striking way. Participation in a common educational heritage progressively tends to suppress differences of birth, status, profession, and wealth, and to unite the individual educated people on the basis of the education they have received.[185]

Education as the unifying bond is a significant and useful sociological marker, for it allows Pellicani to identify the so-called "cultural capital"

---

182 Couliano, *I miti dei dualismi occidentali*, p. 312.

183 Karl Mannheim, *Ideology and Utopia* (1936; repr., London and Henley: Routledge & Kegan Paul, 1979), p. 137.

184 Ibid., p. 138. In particular, says Mannheim, such plural derivations of the figure of the intellectual are quite pronounced in the modern era: "One of the most impressive facts about modern life is that in it, unlike preceding cultures, intellectual activity is not carried on exclusively by a socially rigidly defined class, such as a priesthood, but rather by a social stratum which is to a large degree unattached to any social class and which is recruited from an increasingly inclusive area of social life. […] Not until we come to the period of bourgeois ascendency does the level of cultural life become increasingly detached from a given class" (ibid., p. 139).

185 Ibid., p. 138.

as the power and resource of the intelligentsia.[186] His conclusion is clear: "The intellectuals are a class characterized by specific social functions, namely the processing and transmission of knowledge; the spiritual guidance of the masses, and so on; and by specific interests, despite their claim that they have always been the one and only group representing the general interest."[187] Therefore, it is wrong to think of intellectuals as a non-class: intellectuals originate from what Mannheim calls a "relatively classless stratum", but they end up forming a specific class due to their common education.

Luciano Pellicani goes on in his reasoning by introducing in the analysis the modern, capitalist society and the transformations which have taken place in Europe between the 14th and the 16th centuries. Alluding to Alfred von Martin's sociological analysis, he maintains that two new classes have emerged from the traditional societal structure: men of letters and merchants. These new classes challenged the authority of the two groups that held power at the time, namely, the aristocracy and high clergy. But – and here is the point being made – "although the two new classes shared the same aversions, they were hardly allies, because they had completely different values and capital:"[188] on one side, knowledge and education, and on the other side, wealth and riches. Cultural capital versus material capital: such was the configuration of the new battle that was about to dominate the centuries to come.

The dissimilarities between the two new classes were so big and unbridgeable, and the attractiveness of material capital so powerful, that the outcome was the rise of a deep *resentment* against the merchants and traders. "People whose only capital was mental and whose aspiration was to live on that capital could only exist within a bourgeoisie, yet they felt confined to a position of inferiority and resented the attitude of a class that had accumulated wealth and, in so doing, had become

---

186 Pellicani talks of cultural capital in relation to Alvin Gouldner's essay *The Future of Intellectuals and the Rise of the New Class* (New York: Oxford University Press, 1979), where the author significantly writes (p. 19): "By gradually extending the sphere of those enjoying knowledge, the Industrial Revolution had allowed the formation of a huge cultural bourgeoisie that quietly took over the advantages of a cultural capital produced historically and collectively." Mannheim himself is aware that "a sociology which is oriented only with reference to social-economic classes will never adequately understand this phenomenon" (Mannheim, *Ideology and Utopia*, p. 138).

187 Luciano Pellicani, 'Produzione simbolica e potere: gli intellettuali come classe', *Orbis Idearum*, vol. 3, issue 2 (2015): p. 56.

188 Ibid.

powerful, in both economic and political terms."[189] Hence, intellectuals began to criticize and condemn modern capitalistic society, a place where cultural capital is not appreciated as it should be. Even today intellectuals are more prone to support anti-capitalist stances in the name of non-material values and non-economic standards. The profound sense of alienation and impotence experienced by intellectuals causes a deep frustration and dissatisfaction.

In fact, Pellicani writes, intellectuals often underestimate their influence over society: "People pursue their material and spiritual interests on the basis of what they believe to be reality; that is to say, on the basis of the images of the world [elaborated by intellectuals] that they have absorbed during the process of socialization and that have become common sense."[190] Nevertheless, the effect of ideas on society takes too long to provide gratification to intellectuals. The process takes too much time. And postponement of visible outcomes "leaves them with the sensation of living in a desert of indifference and even hostility."[191] Resentment, bitterness, anger, hatred and even neurosis become the regular conditions of the intellectual, who eventually happens to be the true actor behind any conflict between the haves and the have-nots.

Elaborating on this point, Pellicani believes Marx's theory to be ideological "in that it permits certain forms of protest against plutocratic bureaucracy to be presented as a fight of, and for, the proletariat, whereas the real actors, and those involved in a direct conflict with capitalism, are usually the more marginal elements of the modern intellectual class."[192] Such marginal elements of the modern intellectual class are what Pellicani calls a subclass of intellectuals, or *declassed intelligentsia*, that is to say, a more radical wing of the intellectual class that has been radicalized by the phenomenon of relative deprivation[193] (i.e., the discrepancy between status and legitimate expectations). Revolution originates from this very radical intelligentsia: "While *reformism* was the spontaneous

189 Alfred von Martin, *Sociologia del Renacimiento* (Mexico City: Fondo de Cultura Economica, 1946), p. 67. Quoted in Pellicani, "Produzione simbolica e potere", p. 57.

190 Pellicani, "Produzione simbolica e potere", p. 58.

191 Ibid.

192 Ibid., p. 60.

193 Interestingly, Diego Gambetta and Steffen Hertog extensively use this useful theoretical tool to explain why many Islamist terrorists have at least one academic degree; see Diego Diego Gambetta and Steffen Hertog, *Engineers of Jihad. The Curious Connection Between Violent Extremism and Education* (Princeton and Oxford: Princeton University Press, 2016).

reaction of the working class to the trauma generated by the uncontrolled accumulation of capital, *revolutionarism* was a solution proposed by alienated intellectuals."[194]

What about revolutionary Gnosticism? Luciano Pellicani is certain that the history of revolutionary Gnosticism and of the proletarianized intelligentsia is the same. "It is no coincidence that the first signs of the extraordinary events accompanying revolutionary movements should have emerged with the introduction of capitalism in European society."[195] As soon as the self-regulated market started to break its way into society, it eradicated many people from their traditional social ground. Social bonds were weakened in favor of utilitarian links and superficial ties. Solidarity was excluded from the world of market relationships. Society changed: the protection traditionally offered by the belonging community was no more.[196] The diffusion of self-regulated markets in traditional societies caused the angry outburst of the raising proletariat:

> Being marginalized from community life, they felt they were no longer an integral part of their macrocosm or bound by those moral and affective ties that once gave meaning and direction to their existence. Hence their receptivity to new messages, especially those favoring a radical overturning of the existing order that they hated and resented. Hence their search for a new group in the hope of recovering lost solidarity.[197]

And here lies the role of the radicalized intellectual, now actively involved in recovering ancient ways of life and lost harmonies, longing for the unity of the past and rejecting the existing order.

Luciano Pellicani's main literary reference in the reconstruction of the responsibility of the intellectual in shaping revolutionary movements is Norman Cohn (1915-2007), a British historian who dedicated many studies to Medieval fanaticism (and to its alleged resurrections in modern Europe). According to Cohn, in the late Middle Ages

---

194 Pellicani, 'Produzione simbolica e potere', p. 61.

195 Luciano Pellicani, *Revolutionary Apocalypse. Ideological Roots of Terrorism* (Westport and London: Praeger, 2003), p. 11.

196 Pellicani writes that "the man uprooted from his ancestral community of belonging, thrown on the capitalist market and subjected to his rigid economic laws, becomes a being who feels alien to himself, to others and to the 'new world' in which he lives" ('Capitalismo, modernizzazione, rivoluzione', in *Sociologia delle rivoluzioni*, ed. by Luciano Pellicani [Naples: Guida Editori 1976], p. 22).

197 Pellicani, *Revolutionary Apocalypse*, p. 12.

> there were always men [...] who in fact passionately desired to be seen as infallible, wonder-working saviours. In the main such men came *from the lower strata of the intelligentsia*. They included many members of the lower clergy, priests who had left their parishes, monks who had fled from their monasteries, clerks in minor orders. They included also some laymen who, unlike the laity in general, had acquired a certain literacy – artisans chiefly, but also some administrative officials and even occasionally a nobleman whose ambitions were loftier than his status.[198]

Such men took advantage of the dissatisfaction of the eradicated masses. From the 11th century onwards, indeed, Europe changed its socio-economic face: the population increased and commerce developed, causing the creation of new industrial centers, the rise of the surplus population, the movement of peasants from the countryside to new urban centers and the impossibility for the industry to absorb the surplus population... All these elements, grounded in "a rather primitive form of uncontrolled capitalism,"[199] created explosive conditions for revolutionary eruptions.[200] Traditional peasant families and strong kinship-groups, which used to contain any disorder, did not have the chance to take root in big industrial centers.

To sum up,

> journeymen and unskilled workers, peasants without land or with too little land to support them, beggars and vagabonds, the unemployed and those threatened with unemployment, the many who for one reason or another could find no assured and recognized place – such people, living in a state of chronic frustration and anxiety, formed the most impulsive and unstable elements in medieval society.[201]

And amongst these unstable elements, there was always a charismatic leader who belonged to the lower strata of the intelligentsia and who promoted a form of salvationist ideology. Very often such a leader imposed himself as the messiah, a prophet, the savior, who has the mission of

198 Norman Cohn, *The Pursuit of the Millennium: Revolutionary Millenarians and Mystical Anarchists of the Middle Ages* (1957; revised and expanded, New York: Oxford University Press, 1970), chap. 4, Kindle. Emphasis added.

199 Ibid., chap. 3.

200 To use Cohn's own words, revolutionary outbreaks became more likely "when population was increasing, industrialization was getting under way, traditional social bonds were being weakened or shattered and the gap between rich and poor was becoming a chasm" (ibid.).

201 Ibid.

bringing the world back to the golden age through a total transfiguration of society.[202] Sense of impotence and anxiety of the growing poor population was the fuel for this kind of designs fabricated by frustrated radical intellectuals. The revolutionary plan

> did not of course enable the helpless masses to overcome their dilemmas [namely, the chronic insecurity], and it often prompted them to courses of action that proved downright suicidal. But it did hold their anxieties at bay, and it did make them feel both immensely important and immensely powerful. […] Such shared fantasy […], though delusional, yet brought them such intense emotional relief that they could live only through it, and were perfectly willing both to kill and to die for it.[203]

Revolutionary plans always took the shape of eschatological turnings: the revolutionary effort aims at bringing about the Millennium, that is, a period of prosperity, wealth, peace and harmony before the Last Judgement and the End Time.

Luciano Pellicani follows Cohn's line of reasoning, but he adds a new important element already present in Cohn but not fully developed, i.e., the "hidden continuity"[204] between Medieval chiliastic movements and modern revolutionary-totalitarian experiences. "The *prophetae* of the millenarian movements of the Low Middle Ages and the professional revolutionaries of the twentieth century"[205] follow the same behavioral pattern, invoking an overturning that would have started from the subaltern classes. The "pantoclastic program"[206] has remained constantly the same, although "the demythologization of religious traditions conducted by the Enlightenment gave rational and scientific clothing to the wait of apocalypse"[207] (Rousseau's philosophy to the Jacobins, dialectical materialism to the Communists…)

From a sociological point of view, modern societies are experiencing the same social changes of the late Middle Ages but worsened, causing the most treacherous of the effects: the *crisis of meaning*. Peter L. Berger and

---

202 "This was the process," Cohn says, "which, after its first occurrence in the area between the Somme and the Rhine, was to recur in later centuries in southern and central Germany and, still later, in Holland and Westphalia" (ibid.)

203 Ibid., chap. 4.

204 Norman Cohn, preface to *I fanatici dell'Apocalisse*, by Norman Cohn (Torino: Edizioni di Comunità, 2000), p. 12.

205 Pellicani, *Revolutionary Apocalypse*, p. 11.

206 Luciano Pellicani, *L'Occidente e i suoi nemici* (Soveria Mannelli: Rubbettino, 2015), p. 219.

207 Ibid., p. 210.

Thomas Luckmann have excellently depicted the current condition in the book *Modernity, Pluralism and the Crisis of Meaning. The Orientation of Modern Man* (1995). The central idea of the monograph is the following:

> Population growth and migration and, associated with this, urbanization; pluralization in the physical, demographic sense; the market economy and industrialization which throw together people of the most different kinds and force them to deal with each other reasonably peacefully; the rule of law and democracy which provide institutional guarantees for this peaceful coexistence. The media of mass communication constantly and emphatically parade a plurality of ways of life and thinking: both printed material riding on mass literacy spread across the entire population by compulsory schooling and the newest electronic media. If the interactions enabled by this pluralization are not restricted by "fences" of one kind or another, this pluralism takes full effect, bringing with it one of its consequences: the "structural" crisis of meaning.[208]

Next to the crisis of meaning,[209] there is also another dangerous awareness rising, "a clamorous nostalgia for the good old days."[210] The eclipse of ends and the penetration of instrumental reason in all spheres of society are causing serious existential tumultuousness whose effects are revolutionary-totalitarian movements and other alterations in the individual as well as in the collective consciousness.

Pellicani sees in the coalition of two actors, "the 'plebeian proletariat' (the mobilized workers) and the 'aristocratic proletariat' (the declassed intellectuals),"[211] the nucleus of any revolutionary secession within a given society; the resentment against society and the will to overthrow it are the two attitudes that bring them together. And when the two kinds of proletariat come together, they form the party that is endowed to save the world, a self-proclaimed superior spiritual élite that *should* wage war on the existing situation in order to destroy it and to regenerate the whole reality. The declassed intellectuals become "*gnostic activists* who are convinced they know the method to uproot evil and live in and for action"[212] – this is the true meaning of "gnostic", that is to say, the denomination of who

208 Peter L. Berger and Thomas Luckmann, *Modernity, Pluralism and the Crisis of Meaning. The Orientation of Modern Man* (Gütersloh: Bertelsmann Foundation Publishers, 1995), pp. 37-38.

209 If modernity promotes changes and innovations, and "if novelty is perpetually awaited, this means that every moment is a moment of crisis" (Paolo Jedlowski, *In un passaggio d'epoca. Esercizi di teoria sociale* [Naples: Orthotes, 2012], p. 34).

210 Berger and Luckmann, *Modernity, Pluralism and the Crisis of Meaning*, p. 43.

211 Pellicani, *Revolutionary Apocalypse*, p. 13.

212 Ibid., p. 107.

knows the way to save the world. Gnosis is "science of self-redemption of humanity,"[213] being both a diagnosis and a therapy. But this kind of definition discloses the *atheist character* of any gnostic activists even when they claim to act in name of religious purposes; in fact, auto-salvation is incompatible with a divine redeemer – and the claim of fulfilling God's plan is equally atheist, since it tends to hasten the times fixed by God.

The final goal of any gnostic revolution is not the creation of a more just society, but rather of *the* perfect society, which requires some kind of regeneration of human nature. To this purpose, the gnostic prophet, the self-proclaimed Paraclete, must enjoy "*unlimited* dominion over reality, because the task set for the revolution is *unlimited*."[214]

Luciano Pellicani bases his analysis on a strong sociological structure. Pellicani's pupil Alessandro Orsini writes that "revolutionary Gnosticism is the response to the *rites of passage* that capitalism continually undergoes."[215] And he goes on by saying that

> when society is shaken by unexpected changes, whether favorable or not, individuals have to carry out a "cultural conversion" to enable them to respond suitably to the new challenges. But changes involving the cultural sphere are much slower and more difficult than economic ones. Culture and economy do not advance at the same pace. For some individuals, changing their values and models of behavior can require an intolerable effort. So the "conversion" fails, creating a feeling of rejection. Love for "tradition" becomes an obsession, increasing the mistrust, or even rejection, of the surrounding world.[216]

The gnostic cycle (original unity, break of unity, return to unity) is transferred to a temporal, historical dimension and it becomes nostalgia of the past, grievance for the present, desire to restore the golden age – restoration to be accomplished by a total revolutionary action. And such action should follow the instructions of *who knows*, the gnostic Paraclete, the alienated intellectual.

But what is revolutionary Gnosticism according to Luciano Pellicani? The definition given by the author is quite common among academics who have studied the topic. According to Pellicani, "Gnosticism is the tradition of soteriological thought that first developed in early Christianity

213 Luciano Pellicani, *La società dei giusti. Parabola storica dello Gnosticismo rivoluzionario* (Soveria Mannelli: Rubbettino, 2012), p. 281.

214 Ibid., p. 288.

215 Alessandro Orsini, *Anatomy of the Red Brigades. The Religious Mindset of Modern Terrorists* (Ithaca and London: Cornell University Press, 2011), p. 262.

216 Ibid., p. 112.

and periodically reemerged in the subsoil of Western civilization like an underground stream."[217] Pellicani also explains Gnosticism in terms of "a permanent temptation of the human spirit that derives from the ardent desire to possess a knowledge capable of solving every enigma and providing a method for ending the scandal of evil."[218] He then lists ten points that try to distinguish Gnosticism from any other revolutionary ideology: (1) "Before being a doctrine, Gnosticism is an existential disposition of the soul"[219] that makes the gnostic experience horror of the existing, seeing the world as an absurd and himself/herself as an alien; (2) the gnostic is oppressed by the fundamental question over evil, insistently asking himself/herself the origin of horrors in the world; (3) the gnostic believes in a cosmic-historic catastrophe that perverted all things, and he/she starts to feel a strong nostalgia for a putative golden age; (4) there is the possibility of going back to the state of perfection destroyed by whatsoever "fall", towards a "radical renewal, which is both *resurrection* and *restoration*;"[220] (5) history is divided into three periods or aeons: "a) the aeon of perfection (the remote past), b) the aeon of the fall and of alienation (the present), and c) the aeon of the restoration of great universal harmony (the future);"[221] (6) the means by which renewal of the totality becomes possible is the Gnosis, "which is a total complete knowledge (descriptive and normative) and contains a diagnosis-therapy of human alienation,"[222] being thus a liberating science that concerns the totality of being; (7) Late-Antique Gnosticism used to divide humanity in three classes – the pneumatics, the psychics, the hylics – and only the pneumatics are in possession of the divine soul; hence, "gnostic soteriology is elitist: it assumes that salvation is at hand only for a privileged segment of humanity;"[223] (8) the gnostic Paraclete (the radical alienated intellectual) is the indisputable leader, and he/she is endowed with the duty-right to guide the masses in accordance with the gnostic prescriptions; (9) gnostic movements organize themselves similarly to a church, where centralization is strong and the charismatic head totally dominates the whole structure; (10) there are only two parties

217 Pellicani, *Revolutionary Apocalypse*, p. 151. Similarly, Giovanni Filoramo wrote: "Gnostic imagination [is] an underground stream of our historical-religious tradition, which characteristically resurfaces with its myths, symbols and images" (*Il risveglio della gnosi, ovvero diventare Dio* [Roma-Bari: Laterza, 1990], p. VII).

218 Pellicani, *Revolutionary Apocalypse*, p.153.

219 Ibid., p. 151.

220 Ibid., pp. 151-152.

221 Ibid., p. 152.

222 Ibid.

223 Ibid.

facing each other, the party of Light and the party of Darkness, and the world is perceived as the battlefield of such cosmic-historic struggle.

Through all these passages, the gnostic activist, guided by the self-proclaimed Paraclete or prophet, seeks to restore the ancient Holy City against the Secular City, the latter being shaped by and rooted in commerce and trade,[224] whose values are antithetical to the true ancestral spiritual principles.

Luciano Pellicani reads the history of revolutionary Gnosticism through sociological lenses and in relation to the changes capitalism generates in any society. The erosion of traditional values and the increasing poverty, as well as other factors like unemployment and overpopulation, stimulate resentment and anger in the eradicated masses, and then declassed intellectuals take the reins of the explosive social situation by introducing a gnostic-like narrative and presenting themselves as (holy or secular) prophets who know how to save the world and the formula to transfigure humanity, going back to the golden age and overcoming the current situation.

Pellicani believes in the direct continuity of the gnostic narrative within Western thought – from late Medieval heresies to Puritanism, from the Jacobin experiment during the French Revolution to Marxism, Bolshevism and even Nazism. As such, Pellicani "explains [the doctrine of permanent revolution] as the effect of secularized gnostic religious concepts: the revolutionary Party is a gnostic church, the gnostic morality is now an intramundane ascesis, strategy and tactics of Revolution symbolize gnostic crusade against the enemy of Gnosticism."[225] The current situation outlined above using Berger and Luckmann's study is also quite tense – even today Gnosticism persists as a temptation for contemporary eradicated masses, with the difference that now other peoples too are participating to the process of modernization and to the dynamics of capitalist market.

Pellicani has also specifically contributed to the topic of jihad with a small but profound essay titled *Jihad: le radici*[226] (*Jihad: The Roots*), which will be studied subsequently in this research.

At any rate, Luciano Pellicani's study on revolutionary Gnosticism is of great importance for whoever intends to contribute to such topic. We will therefore refer to him more than once in the present study.

---

224 See Luciano Pellicani, 'La città sacra e la città secolare', *Filosofia e Questioni Pubbliche*, vol. 14 (2010): pp. 187-200.

225 Couliano, *I miti dei dualismi occidentali*, p. 314.

226 Luciano Pellicani, *Jihad: le radici* (Roma: Luiss University Press, 2004).

CHAPTER 2
WHAT IS REVOLUTIONARY GNOSTICISM?

2.1 *The gnostic pattern: six features of revolutionary Gnosticism*

Now that the main features of Gnosticism and the primary modern authors who have dealt with it have been reviewed, it is time to clearly and univocally define what revolutionary Gnosticism is. A post-Christian, or political form, of Gnosticism is naturally revolutionary (Mathieu), profoundly nihilistic (Jonas), perverted and activist (Del Noce), an enduring mentality (Samek Lodovici), a mutant soteriological thought (Pellicani), a pneumopathology (Voegelin). Moreover it is volitional, meaning that it "assumes the form of activist redemption of man and society."[1] The emphasis falls on self-redemption and the possibility given to humankind to shape a perfect everlasting society.

Nevertheless, a definition of revolutionary Gnosticism still eludes us. It is not a simple task. At this point it should be clear that this Gnosticism *it is not a faith nor a philosophy*.

First of all, revolutionary Gnosticism is not a faith, a belief, a religion. It should not be confused with ancient Gnosticism, namely, a cluster of religious myths grouped together by a common narrative structure. No gnostic revolutionary would ever recognize himself or herself to be gnostic, and probably that person would even ignore what Gnosticism is. It is unwise to think of this kind of Gnosticism as a real belief which someone literary believes in. Hence, it is not a faith, nor it should be conceived as the genetic derivation from Late-Antique Gnosticism.

Likewise, revolutionary Gnosticism is not even a philosophy. Angelo Campodonico, while labeling political Gnosticism in terms of an attitude, also defines it as a "rejection of any distinction between philosophy (an inquiry guided by reason) and religion (the revealed answer to the demand for salvation); also, within the same philosophy, it represents the denial of the diversity between the theoretical-contemplative dimension and the

---

1 Voegelin, 'The New Science of Politics', p. 189.

practical dimension of reason."[2] Analogously, Danilo Castellano suggests that "Gnosis could never be a philosophy because its starting point is an *assumption* on, and not the *apprehension* of, (ontic) reality, the latter being the foundation of any thought."[3] Thus, revolutionary Gnosticism is not a philosophy just like it is not a religion.

Rather, revolutionary Gnosticism can be considered as a *Weltanschauung*, a worldview that has inevitable repercussions in the behavior of a given individual or group. Revolutionary Gnosticism is thus a *mentality*, or a mental structure in the sense that it could adapt to any situation, wearing the clothes of every revolutionary actor – in this sense, it has no specific identity, as, for instance, being right wing or left wing, religious or atheist. To understand this point we can also speak of a *skeleton*, that is to say, the inner part of a body that is covered by skin and muscles – and it makes no difference if the skin is black or white, or if muscles are developed or not: the skeleton will remain the same under any circumstances, giving order and organizing the external material.

Accordingly, revolutionary Gnosticism is an existential attitude that has gradually dressed various clothes. In this sense, the Voegelian intuition about the difficulty of withstanding the tension of the In-Between is appropriate: the gnostic cannot stand the In-Between and impatiently wants to get rid of all sufferings. A revolutionary politics is the perfect means to achieve salvation as soon as possible. A similar vision of the world avoids seeing the finitude of human beings and of all creation; it rather escapes from reality and outlines a "dream-world" to be built by means of "sacral" violence. Surely the dream of overcoming all pains, ending poverty and even defeating death is as ancient as humanity itself – the discriminating factor, however, is whether one believes it is an achievable goal, a doable target (the revolutionary gnostic), or rather a regulative idea in the Kantian meaning.

There are six points that represent the content of revolutionary Gnosticism, a set of features that form what can be called the *gnostic pattern*. The identification of a recurrent pattern is useful for employing the category in various cases, in view of the fact that it allows us to isolate core components and to detect critical qualifications of a similar *Weltanschauung*.

---

2 Angelo Campodonico, 'Rifiuto del finito, dell'articolazione dei saperi e della diversità', in *L'origine & la meta. Studi in memoria di Emanuele Samek Lodovici*, ed. by Gabriele De Anna (Milano: Edizioni Ares, 2015), p. 139.

3 Danilo Castellano, 'La gnosi come "anima" dell'utopia rivoluzionaria contemporanea', in *L'origine & la meta. Studi in memoria di Emanuele Samek Lodovici*, ed. by Gabriele De Anna (Milano: Edizioni Ares, 2015), p. 269.

The six features that we think compose the distinctiveness of revolutionary Gnosticism are: (1) anti-cosmism; (2) tripartition of history; (3) immanentization of the *eschaton*; (4) Gnosis; (5) political-revolutionary self-redemption; (6) sociological dualism. The next sections will deal with the definition of each of these points. The acquisition of a solid theoretical basis will allow us to apply the gnostic paradigm to the case study of the present research, i.e., Salafi-Jihadism.

2.1.1 *Anti-cosmism*

The first aspect of revolutionary Gnosticism is anti-cosmism. The literature review made clear that aversion to the world is the peculiar feature that characterizes the gnostic attitude. "The world is evil" is the battle cry of any revolutionary – if this were not so, there would not be any need for a revolution. Anti-cosmism is an incitement and as such constitutes the first motivation for the gnostic. Ancient gnostics as well as modern activists seek to escape from, or radically change, the world because it is deemed wicked and sinful. "While the ancient varieties sought escape from an irredeemably evil cosmos, their modern counterparts pin their hopes on its transformation."[4] We can label both of them as forms of escapism. As such, "gnostic pessimism disavows the sentence *vidit quod erant bona* of Genesis."[5]

Anti-cosmism implies three elements: (1) the world is evil and therefore it must be turned upside-down; (2) the obsession with purity, from which opposition to the surrounding world emerges (eventually, "the 'obsession with purity' becomes the 'obsession with purification' or the implacable fight against the forces of evil,"[6] but this evolution concerns the fifth point of the gnostic pattern, see below); the last element closely tied to anti-cosmism is (3) antinomianism, the refusal and rejection of any norm – if the world is evil, then everything that concerns it is evil, even more so the laws on which it rests.[7] According to ancient Gnosticism, any kind of law

4 David Walsh, 'Voegelin's Response to the Disorder of the Age', *The Review of Politics*, vol. 46, no. 2 (1984): p. 270.

5 Giuseppe Faggin, 'Gnosi – Gnosticismo', in *Enciclopedia Filosofica*, vol. 7 (Milano: Bompiani, 2010), p. 4926.

6 Alessandro Orsini, *Anatomy of the Red Brigades. The Religious Mindset of Modern Terrorists* (Ithaca: Cornell University Press, 2011), p. 5.

7 For instance, let's read Michail Bakunin's words: "I do not believe in constitutions or in laws. The best constitution would leave me dissatisfied. We need something different. Storm and vitality and a new lawless and consequently free world" (Bakunin, quoted in Mannheim, *Ideology and Utopia*, p. 196). Eric Voegelin

was immoral because it was imposed by the will of the malevolent archons; in relation to modern Gnosticism, laws are linked to the in-between aeon, that is to say, the present time that represents a guilty departure from a hypothetical golden age.

The protest against the world is the door for *nihilism*. In fact, "there is [...] a blatant Gnosticism in the embittered nihilism who sees horror and shit as the kernel of reality."[8] In a conference held in 1974, Gershom Scholem denounces the refusal of valuing the world to be the root of gnostic nihilism, which has developed in opposition to the Greek cosmos and the Jewish doctrine of creation. Scholem defines the gnostic man in terms of a "mystic revolutionary"[9] who seeks to reject all norms, be they natural, moral and positive norms – only in this way can the gnostic achieve true freedom.

Scholem presents the example of Carpocrates, a gnostic thinker who lived in the first half of the 2nd century. Carpocrates's doctrine judges the world as made by inferior angels, and Jesus is the head of a revolt against the creators of the world.[10] According to Saint Irenaeus's account of heresies, Carpocrates and his disciples believe that "the body is a prison."[11] Saint Irenaeus describes their practices, which are full of "every kind of impious and godless deeds,"[12] for they say that humankind can achieve liberation only "until he has had experience in

writes that "the Marxian anthropology, just like the radical Puritan, is based on the belief that through a revolutionary transforming act the nature of man will change from its present imperfect state to a state of perfection that will make social compulsion unnecessary" (Voegelin, 'The People of God', p. 174).

8 Conor Cunningham, *Genealogy of Nihilism* (London and New York: Routledge, 2002), p. 257.

9 Gershom Scholem, *Il nichilismo come fenomeno religioso* (Firenze: Giuntina, 2016), p. 18.

10 Saint Irenaeus explains Carpocrates's doctrine as following: "Carpocrates and his disciples assert that the world and the things in it were made by Angels who are far inferior to the ingenerate Father, and that Jesus was begotten by Joseph and, though he was made like men, he was superior to the rest of men. Moreover, since his soul was vigorous and innocent, he remembered what he had seen within the sphere which belongs to the ingenerate God. For this reason, a power was sent down upon him by God, that by means of it he could escape from the makers of the world and that this [soul], having passed through all their domains and so remained free in all, might ascend to him [Father]. The souls that embrace things similar to it [Jesus' soul] will in like manner [ascend to him]" (St. Irenaeus of Lyons, *Against the Heresies* [New York and Mahwah: The Newman Press, 1992], p. 87).

11 St. Irenaeus of Lyons, *Against the Heresies*, p. 89.

12 Ibid., p. 88.

absolutely every kind of action that exists in the world."[13] Scholem is persuaded that "where the creator of the world was deemed as a lower, ignorant, blind and malicious power, or, in other terms, where it was considered in opposition to a true good god, the way to nihilism was opened."[14]

Anti-cosmism is the belief that current reality is degraded and corrupted. As reported by ancient gnostic cosmogonies, the world arose by an egoistic act of some inferior divine principle, and the task of humankind is to escape from it; to modern Gnosticism, similarly, the world fell from an original *but immanent* condition of beatitude, thus now humankind has to change the present condition and restore the pristine state. In both cases, the world as it is today is wicked and needs to be overcome, with the difference that in the first case humankind achieves salvation in a radical Beyond, while in the second case humankind finds liberation within the world and along an immanent timeline – in both cases, as Voegelin points out, the In-Between is broken: "While these early movements attempt to escape from the Metaxy by splitting its poles into the hypostases of this world and the Beyond, the modern apocalyptic-gnostic movements attempt to abolish the Metaxy by transforming the Beyond into this world."[15] The "pessimistic understanding of the world"[16] is at the heart of any gnostic thought.

An experiential outcome of anti-cosmism is "the human condition of *unrelatedness* [or extraneousness] to the world. Indeed, the world is no longer the order of cosmos, as it was for ancient Near Eastern empires and for the Greeks, nor the loving creation of God, as it is in the Judeo-Christian world, but instead it corresponds to a prison of darkness and sufferings that humankind finds itself compelled to live in."[17]

In summary:

> The gnostic has a negative opinion of the world: Its creation was not from God but from a demiurge, either by an act of disobedience or by ignorance, and it is the result of an error, or of a disordered desire, or of an unlucky incident.

---

13 Ibid., p. 89.

14 Scholem, *Il nichilismo come fenomeno religioso*, p. 26. Hans Jonas is clear on this point: "This antinomian libertinism exhibits more forcefully than the ascetic version the nihilistic element contained in gnostic acosmism" (Hans Jonas, *The Gnostic Religion* [Boston: Beacon Press, 2001], p. 46).

15 Voegelin, 'Order and History, vol. IV', p. 302.

16 Couliano, *I miti dei dualismi occidentali*, p. 135.

17 Stella Marega, 'L'attesa dell'Apocalisse: dall'antico Gnosticismo alla moderna rivoluzione', *Metábasis*, no. 1 (March 2006): p. 9.

> The gnostic does not see the world as a *cosmos* (order and beauty), but a place of exile that intensifies his angst and desire for the faraway homeland. The laws of the world and of society are not shared by the gnostic: only the Supreme Being can govern his inner self, while the decrees down here are exile laws, demiurge's laws.[18]

Humankind feels *alien* to the surrounding world and compelled by its laws, a foreigner in a hostile land. Something has to be done, but what exactly is not known. Where does the evil come from? Why is there so much pain and suffering? Something must have happened: it is impossible that humankind has always lived in such a dreadful conditions. Something must be done…

2.1.2 *Tripartition of history*

From the very outset Eric Voegelin firmly asserts that one of the main symbols used by revolutionary and totalitarian movements in the West is the third stage of time as the ultimate moment of human history. According to him, the Trinitarian division of history operated by Joachim of Flora has been deeply influential in the Western political thought. Briefly, based on the Holy Trinity, Joachim elaborated a

> conception of history as a sequence of three ages, of which the third age is intelligibly the final Third Real. As variations of this symbol are recognizable the humanistic and encyclopedist periodization of history into ancient, medieval, and modern history; Turgot's and Comte's theory of a sequence of theological, metaphysical, and scientific phases; Hegel's dialectic of the three stages of freedom and self-reflective spiritual fulfillment; the Marxian dialectic of the three stages of primitive communism, class society, and final communism; and, finally, the national-socialist symbol of the Third Realm.[19]

18 Luigi Moraldi, 'La nascita dello Gnosticismo', in *Gli arconti di questo mondo. Gnosi: politica e diritto*, eds. Claudio Bonvecchio and Teresa Tonchia (Trieste: EUT, 2000), p. 30.

19 Voegelin, 'The New Science of Politics', p. 179. In another work, Voegelin writes that according to Joachim's system, the present is a meaningful step toward a specific end. A similar conception was very fertile: "In order to arrive at a meaningful interpretation of the present […] we can use the pattern of the realms in combination with the line of progress and arrive at the conclusion that the present age is the Third Realm or that it is the period immediately preceding it. The system of Comte and Hegel are examples of Third Realm speculation of the first subtype; the system of Fichte and Schelling are examples of the second subtype" (Eric Voegelin, 'Joachim of Fiore (Flora)', in *The Collected Works of*

However, arguing that Joachim is a crypto-gnostic is of no help. It is quite undeniable that Joachim's tripartite division of history was significant and effective in shaping Western mentality to some degree, but it does not help to configure this triple classification of time as gnostic, notwithstanding Voegelin considered it as part of a greater gnostic emersion in the West.[20]

It cannot be denied that "the Joachitic speculation was an attempt to endow the immanent course of history with a meaning that was not provided in the Augustinian conception [... It was] the first Western attempt at an immanentization of meaning [of history]."[21] Joachim's speculation is a "theological historism"[22] that poses a great emphasis on the immanent world and on its temporal fulfillment.

But the three-phases periodization of history is not a Joachitic invention – rather, it derives eminently from actual gnostic narratives. In this respect, let us return to the feeling of the gnostic abandoned in a hostile world: the questions whence evil comes from and why humankind suffers so much deeply torment him/her. The impression of being a foreigner is stronger day by day. And, eventually, he/she develops the belief that something disastrous must have occurred: surely the past was full of justice and peace, but that is not how it now is.

As reported by Massimo Introvigne, gnostic myths tend to converge on the fact that history goes through three phases:

> (1) a vague original unity (Pleroma) where an original but unknowable God emanates couples of divine beings (aeons); (2) the "fall" from such unity of

---

Eric Voegelin, vol. 20, ed. by Peter Von Sivers [Columbia and London: University of Missouri Press, 1997], p. 130). Even Karl Löwith writes of modern transfigurations of Joachimism, including Friedrich Nietzsche among others because of his writings "On the Three Metamorphoses" on three figures that are "represented by the allegorical figures of a camel, a lion, and a child. But what else is the 'Thou shalt' of the camel than the law of the Old Testament; the 'I will' of the lion than the partial freedom of the second dispensation; and the 'I am' of the cosmic child than the perfect freedom of being reconciled with God or the world, respectively?" (Karl Löwith, *Meaning in History* [Chicago and London: University of Chicago Press, 1949], pp. 211-212).

20 Andrea Tagliapietra is sure that Joachim was by no means a gnostic, denouncing modern interpreters to have confused Joachim's apocalyptic thought with Gnosticism. See Andrea Tagliapietra, 'Gioacchino da Fiore e l'Apocalisse nella storia', in *Prospettive di filosofia della storia*, ed. by Roberto Mordacci (Milano: Bruno Mondadori, 2009), pp. 29-51.

21 Voegelin, 'The New Science of Politics', pp. 184-185.

22 Löwith, *Meaning in History*, p. 156.

> one or more divine beings, and the following birth of a malevolent god (the demiurge), who creates the material world on his own or with the help of some collaborators (the archons); (3) the presence in humankind of a divine sparkle that could be revitalized, allowing some to escape from the material world and from the finitude and to reach the prime divine reality.[23]

While discussing ancient Gnosticism, Hans Jonas describes the same periodization: an original pure divine unity; a primordial disruption of such a unity and the creation of the world; the dissolution of the cosmic system and the reintegration in the blessed prime divine state.

But still, one must discriminate between Late-Antique Gnosticism and what Del Noce calls post-Christian, or "fallen", Gnosticism. Here the most remarkable dissimilarity is the stress placed on temporality: for ancient Gnosticism, the drama of evil is half transcendent and half immanent, in the sense that the break of divine unity takes place before the creation of the world and thus beyond the time-space framework, while salvation is reached *in* time and *within* the material world; with regard to fallen Gnosticism, on the contrary, such structure is totally secularized, temporalized, immanentized: the original divine unity becomes a primordial golden age, the "fall" is now a degeneration that happened in time and that has led to the present state, and the reintegration in the Pleroma converts into the future restoration of the lost paradise, the terrestrial Jerusalem.[24]

To put it another way, post-Christian Gnosis, which ultimately is revolutionary Gnosticism, follows a tripartite scheme: *unity*, or the state of perfection (the past); *corruption*, an alteration of the original blessed condition (the present); *reintegration*, or restauration of the golden age (the future). The past, the present and the future acquire a specific meaning, and the gnostic system is irrevocably immanentized.

Two are the consequences of the gnostic tripartition of history: (1) iconoclasm and (2) apocalypticism.

Iconoclasm is the tendency to destroy religious images, icons and sculptures. In the context of revolutionary Gnosticism, iconoclasm is, more generally, the fury against the recent past pertaining the state of corruption – and in fact, what the gnostic wants to restore "is certainly

---

23 Massimo Introvigne, *Il ritorno dello Gnosticismo* (Varese: SugarCo Edizioni, 1993), p. 13.

24 A similar system of thought resembles what Zygumnt Bauman calls "retrotopia", namely, "visions located in the lost/stolen/abandoned but undead past, instead of being tied to the not-yet-unborn and so inexistent future" (Zygmunt Bauman, *Retrotopia* [Cambridge: Polity Press, 2017], Introduction, Kindle).

not the near past […] but a very distant past. […] In order to keep the traditional aspect, it was necessary to point to a very far distant past."[25] Indeed, the past is a limit to the effort of bringing back the perfect state. In the words of Samek Lodovici: "History, our past, is rejected because it is a limit, namely, the record of errors and unsuccessful attempts of humankind to break the limit and to build the perfect society and the New Man."[26] The past constantly reminds the gnostic of his or her wicked condition. So, the past should be destroyed in order to finally shape a new society and restore the earthly paradise. Nothing should lie outside the gnostic iconoclastic fury. The gnostic adopts a "*tabula rasa* policy"[27] to make room for the pristine condition, even provoking the destruction of cultural heritage[28] – as it was, for instance, among the Taliban and the self-proclaimed Islamic State.[29]

Speaking of book burning, Leo Löwenthal identifies "the erasure of history"[30] as the final goal of this barbaric practice. As a matter of fact, the burning of books is a "mad attempt to found anew the history of the world, to devise a new creation myth, the genealogy of a new history of salvation, which disowns, destroys, and erases all that precedes a new arbitrary calendar."[31] Every totalitarian movement has passed through it. It is a powerful rite that founds a new (renewed) beginning.

25 Maria Isaura Pereira De Queiroz, *Riforma e rivoluzione nelle società tradizionali* (Milano: Jaca Book, 1970), p. 129.

26 Samek Lodovici, *Metamorfosi della gnosi*, p. 107.

27 Pellicani, *Revolutionary Apocalypse*, p. 268.

28 "The history and memory of a community becomes the main obstacle to this pseudo-metaphysical 'new beginning', to this secular genesis that is the revolutionary pretension to the refoundation of reality" (Aldo Morganti, 'L'immagine e il nulla. Alcune metamorfosi contemporanee dello Gnosticismo di massa', *I Quaderni di Avallon*, no. 30 [1992]: p. 83).

29 It is worth recalling to mind the destruction of the Buddhas of Bamyan, in Afghanistan, dynamited by the hands of the Taliban in March 2001, and whose video was broadcasted by al-Qāʿida for propaganda purposes; and the Mosul museum in Iraq, looted and brutally destroyed by the Islamic State, whose images were released in a terrible propaganda video on February 2015. As I will write later, these actions, which were nominally justified in accordance with a presumed Islamic precept, are actually based on a gnostic mindset that aims at restoring the lost golden age, breaking with the surrounding cultural environment.

30 Leo Löwenthal, 'Caliban's Legacy', *Cultural Critique*, no. 8 (Winter 1987-1988): p. 9.

31 Ibid. The book burnings ordered by the Nazis followed the same reasoning. They were "Nazi ritual of annihilation that embody the perverse new creation myths of the thousand-year Reich; erasure of the past is the predominant theme of Goebbels's speech at the auto-da-fé in Berlin on May 10, 1933: 'Thus you do well, at this

Even Late-Antique Gnosticism developed distrustful stances toward tradition. Skepticism and mistrust towards Christian as well as Greek tradition were commonplace. "These gnostics, then, at least according to their enemies, rejected both Jewish-Christian and pagan heritage."[32] What's more, "they share a commitment to dismantle one of the most cherished cultural premises of their times, that of traditionalism – a commitment that one would be hard pressed to parallel in any other contemporary group or writing."[33]

The second consequence of tripartition of history is *apocalypticism*. The restauration of the first period of history, the golden age, is an ambiguous action indeed: it denotes a restauration. But a restauration is the action of going back by going further. In this sense, the extremes (the past and the future) coincide, and everything comes to full circle, history fulfills its meaning. It is time for the end of time, there is nothing else to be achieved. "The anticipation of the future allows history to embrace its totality."[34] It is not by chance that "apocalypse" derives from ancient Greek *apokalypsis* which means "uncovering", "revealing": history reveals its sense and achieves what it has to achieve. Time runs out all the possibilities, and nothing else is to be done. As a matter of fact, all revolutionary gnostic groups are obsessed by the end of the world – or, at least, they are persuaded that after the total victory of their side no significant enhancement could ever be achieved, freezing history in a tautological repetition of itself.

In conclusion, the tripartition of history is a decisive feature in defining revolutionary Gnosticism. It derives eminently from Late-Antique Gnosticism; however, it was shaped also by the Joachitic speculation of history, which was used ultimately as a political tool: "The political applications of Joachim's historical prophecies were neither foreseen nor intended by him. Nevertheless, they were plausible consequences of his general scheme."[35] And a little bit further: "The third dispensation of the

---

nocturnal hour, to commit the evil spirit of the past to the flames. That is a great, powerful, and symbolic act… that will show the world: here the spiritual basis of the November Republic sinks to earth, but from these ruins, the phoenix of a new spirit will rise victorious' – and so forth" (Löwenthal, 'Caliban's Legacy', p. 10).

32 Jonathan Cahana, 'None of Them Knew Me or My Brothers: Gnostic Antitraditionalism and Gnosticism as a Cultural Phenomenon', *The Journal of Religion*, vol. 94, no. 1 (January 2014): p. 56.

33 Ibid., p. 72. Jonathana Cahana says so after a brief analysis of some gnostic movements and texts (e.g., Marcion and Marcionism, the *Second Treatise of the Great Seth*, the *Apocryphon of John*, the *Gospel of Thomas*, Zostrianos' work).

34 Ignacio Rojas Gálvez, *I simboli dell'Apocalisse* (Bologna: EDB, 2016), p. 79.

35 Löwith, *Meaning in History*, p. 154.

Joachites reappeared as a third International and a third Reich, inaugurated by a *dux* or a *Führer* who was acclaimed as a savior and greeted by millions with *Heil!*"[36]

To sum up, the gnostic believes history to be composed of three stages and he/she to be living in the middle era, the present state of corruption; hence, the gnostic must overcome such a stage by destroying everything that is linked to it (iconoclasm), because the last era will be faultless and perfect; beyond this last epoch there will be nothing else to be achieved, and consequently history will come to an end (apocalypticism).

2.1.3 *Immanentization of the* eschaton

At this point, the third feature of the gnostic pattern is self-evident: the final, heaven-like stage of history, the reign of perfection, will be reached in history and not beyond history. The reintegration in the immanent Pleroma will take place on earth. The destination of humanity is no longer supernatural. As said above, the immanentization of the *eschaton* is an expression coined by Eric Voegelin. And so, "immanentist eschatology"[37] is the fulcrum of revolutionary Gnosticism.

Eschatology (from ancient Greek ἔσχατος, "last") is "a concept that is present in the whole Christian theology as the investigation on 'the last things', i.e., the final destiny of man and the world."[38] As such, it is not a prerogative of Christianity; instead, it is a constant in every religion and philosophy.

From a historical and doctrinal point of view, St. Augustine transferred the *eschaton* in the afterlife, freeing humankind from the obsession of reaching here and now the condition of perfection. However, the re-emersion of Gnosticism as a post-Christian, secularized attitude was to break the Augustinian effort: according to it, the City of God is no longer transcendent but an earthly state that humanity will reach in one way or another.

In a secular perspective, the *eschaton* overlaps with the idea of the Millennium. The sociologist Maria Isaura Pereira de Queiroz has profoundly studied the issue of millenarianism, or chiliasm.[39] Her definition

---

36 Ibid., p. 159.

37 Voegelin, *The New Science of Politics*, p. 189.

38 Gerardo Cunico, 'Escatologia', in *Enciclopedia Filosofica*, vol. 5 (Milano: Bompiani, 2010), p. 3579.

39 Traditionally, "millenarianism", "or millennialism, the Latin equivalent of the Greek term 'chiliasm', is that view of the future which looks for the coming of Jesus Christ

of millenarianism is quite useful for describing the immanentization of the *eschaton*: "Strictly speaking, millenarianism is the belief on the return of Christ in a specific time. In a broader sense, millenarianism is the faith in a future era that will be secular but sacred, terrestrial but heavenly; all discriminations will be mended, all injustices will be absolved. It is typical of millenarianism being religious and socio-political."[40] So, from a Christian point of view, the Millennium will last one thousand years and will be followed by the Last Judgement and the End of Time, whereas from a secular point of view, the Millennium is the time of the regeneration of the world and the instauration of a peaceful and harmonious time. Millenarian groups impatiently wait such coming major transformation of society – and gnostic groups are those who actively strive to hasten its coming (however, this last point is related to the fifth feature of the gnostic pattern).

The joyful last reign is a potent myth that functions as a model for many political narratives. It is "the New Jerusalem announced in the book of *Apocalypse*, it is the Age of the Spirit foretold by Joachim of Flora, it is the Land of Bengodi recounted in the *Decameron*, it is the alchemical *Unus Mundus*, it is the social utopia sometimes historically shaped in dystopic political forms."[41] Each of these examples suggests a transfiguration of humanity, a radical change in the spiritual structure of humankind that would allow for a break with current history, opening the possibility for the establishment of the last era.

The immanentization of the *eschaton* is intertwined with the ancient myth of the golden age, a time of primordial peace and prosperity. Norman Cohn has elaborately studied the issue of the egalitarian state of nature as interconnected with apocalypticism. In his *The Pursuit of the Millennium*, he dedicates four chapters to the symbol of the egalitarian millennium.

> Egalitarian and communistic phantasies can be traced back to the ancient world. It was from the Greeks and Romans that medieval Europe inherited the notion of the "State of Nature" as a state of affairs in which all men were equal in status and wealth and in which nobody was oppressed or exploited by anyone else; a state of affairs characterized by universal good faith and brotherly love and also, sometimes, by total community of property and even of spouses. In

---

to the earth a second time in bodily form to reign personally over a visible kingdom of the whole world for a thousand years" (Geroge Cross, 'Millenarianism in Christian History', *The Biblical World*, vol. 46, no. 1 [July 1915]: p. 3). The scriptural source of the Millennium is John's Book of Apocalypse (20, 1-7).

40 Pereira de Queiroz, *Riforma e rivoluzione*, pp. 21-22.

41 Stella Marega, 'Il regno della fine dei tempi: una premessa mitico-simbolica all'analisi delle politiche apocalittiche', *Heliopolis*, no. 2 (2016): p. 148.

> both Greek and Latin literature the State of Nature is represented as having existed on earth in some long-lost Golden Age or "Reign of Saturn".[42]

Ovid's *Metamorphoses* and Hesiod's *Works and Days* sketch the traits of the golden age; then, this myth has been recalled by Greek Stoics (e.g., Zeno), Diodorus Siculus's *Historical Library*, Roman Stoics (Seneca) and other authors up until the Middle Ages. "Although it was hardly possible to talk of social and economic organization of the Garden of Eden", Cohn writes, "orthodox theologians nevertheless managed to use the Graeco-Roman myth to illustrate the dogma of the Fall"[43]. Some elements of the myth, especially the primordial egalitarianism, became part of the catechesis.[44]

> Until almost the end of the fourteenth century it would seem to have been only a few obscure sectarians, such as some of the adepts of the Free Spirit, who tried to call the egalitarian State of Nature out of the depths of the past and to project it into the future. But however few might undertake it, this attempt to recreate the Golden Age was not without importance. It produced a doctrine which became a revolutionary myth as soon as it was presented to the turbulent poor and fused with the phantasies of popular eschatology.[45]

Therefore, the idea of a golden age that in some way could come back began to spread in the Late Middle Ages. Eventually, it fused with the gnostic Pleroma, the first and impeccable divine unity, because of their similarities, and together they gave birth to the disruptive attitude of revolutionary Gnosticism.[46]

---

42 Cohn, *The Pursuit of the Millennium*, chap. 10.

43 Ibid.

44 Norman Cohn's study on the transmission of the myth is rather noteworthy. He utters that "in the later Middle Ages it became a commonplace amongst canonists and scholastics that in the first state of society, which had also been the best state, there had been no such thing as private property because all things had belonged to all people" (ibid.)

45 Ibid.

46 Cohn's analysis is fascinating because it identifies the symbol of the golden age as a component that has played a strong influence over many Medieval apocalyptic movements. Moreover, Cohn suggests that three were the elements that merged into the revolutionary attitude: the ancestral egalitarian communism; the apocalyptic tension triggered by Joachim of Flora; and Gnosis as an antinomian tendency. Cohn shows how the gnostic attitude built its strength and appeal using different myths and elements: all these elements have given substance to the revolutionary gnostic *Weltanschauung*.

The immanent *eschaton* will be characterized by the same perfection that existed in the first age of history. There will no longer be a lust for wealth or private property, and humanity will live in peace and justice. The gnostic believes that he or she can reach this stage. But how? How would it be possible? There should be a way to escape from the present age of corruption…

2.1.4 *Gnosis*

One might ask why the category of revolutionary Gnosticism has such name. Well, the answer is simple: the gnostic who possesses an anticosmic feeling and believes in a lost golden age that will also be the next age of humanity claims to know *why* the world is as it is and *how* humankind can change its course: this kind of knowledge is the Gnosis. One of the best definitions of "Gnosis" has been given by Luciano Pellicani:

> … a total complete knowledge (*descriptive and normative*) [that] contains a *diagnosis-therapy* of human alienation. Thanks to the Gnosis, the gnostic knows the matrix of the (temporary) unhappiness of man – the catastrophe that overturned and degraded the world, filling it with horrors of all kinds – and the way to the Promised Land. In other words, those in possession of the gnosis know what humanity has been and has become because of the fall, as well as when and how redemption will take place. This knowledge is therefore a veritable soteriology, a liberating science, since, along with the awareness of degradation, it gives humanity the certainty of restoration of original being.[47]

Gnosis, then, is a descriptive knowledge ("the world is evil because of *these* factors") and a normative knowledge ("it is possible to change the world following *this* recipe"). Gnosis is a total liberating science (diagnosis-therapy) whose possession and application would save humanity from evil and from corruption and even from finitude, as it was in ancient Gnosticism. It is the key for escaping from the present situation and regaining the Garden of Eden.

In ancient Gnosticism, Gnosis is a superior and godly knowledge, the total understanding of the human, cosmic and divine realms, "a non-intellectual but mystical knowledge,"[48] a sort of mystical illumination superior to philosophy and faith, "an awareness of the true character of ourselves, which cannot be mediated through nature but can only come to

47 Pellicani, *Revolutionary Apocalypse*, p. 152. Emphasis added.

48 Pontifical Council for Culture, Pontifical Council for Interreligious Dialogue, *Gesù Cristo portatore dell'acqua viva. Una riflessione cristiana sul New Age* (Bologna: EDB, 2003), p. 69.

us as some sort of revelation. That revelation is of our transcendent nature and origin."[49] In post-Christian and revolutionary Gnosticism, Gnosis is the exhaustive comprehension of the mystery of evil, the acknowledgment of the means to overcome it, and, principally, the knowledge of the stream of history ("The mystery of the stream [of history] is solved through the speculative knowledge of its goal")[50] – once you know the end of history, the gnostic believes, you should act to hasten it, and only in this way will you be on the right side of history.

The 1966 Messina Colloquium on the origin of Gnosticism defined "Gnosis" more generally in terms of "a knowledge of the *divine* mysteries reserved for an élite."[51] In the perspective of a post-Christian and immanentized Gnosis, Gnosis is the knowledge of the *historical* mysteries reserved for an élite (what Pellicani and Cohn call the declassed intelligentsia) who eventually tends to include the masses.

Again in Pellicani's words: Gnosis is

> … a speculative knowledge […] that is capable of indicating the method for eradicating alienation and changing the ontological nature of reality. It presents itself as the last avatar of the savior-saved myth, in which the desire for self-redemption of the ancient gnosis combines with expectation of a rupture with the past, which is so radical that it is capable of putting an end to the prehistory of humanity and restoring the great universal harmony destroyed by the desire for profit.[52]

Unlike Late-Antique Gnosticism where anticosmism was a constant feature of creation, in revolutionary Gnosticism anticosmism only concerns the present age of general corruption. In this sense, Gnosis would be the knowledge on how to wipe out all sufferings, sins and iniquities from the current situation. Giovanni Filoramo writes that ancient Gnosticism "deals with the rules that would make possible the freeing of the soul of humankind from the prison of cosmos, [while modern Gnosticism] deals

49 Alastair Logan, 'Truth in a Heresy? Gnosticism', *The Expository Times*, vol. 112, issue 6 (March 2001): p. 191. Serge Hutin describes the Gnosis as "total, instant knowledge, which the individual possesses or doesn't possess at all; it's the absolute knowledge of everything, Man, Cosmos and Divinity. It's only through such knowledge – and not by virtue of faith or works – that the individual could save himself" (Serge Hutin, *Lo Gnosticismo. Culti, riti, misteri* [Roma: Edizioni Mediterranee, 2007], p. 18).

50 Voegelin, 'The New Science of Politics', p. 224.

51 Aa.Vv., 'Final document', in *The Origins of Gnosticism. Colloquium of Messina*, ed. by Ugo Bianchi (Leiden: Brill, 1967), p. XXVI. Italics added.

52 Pellicani, *Revolutionary Apocalypse*, p. XI.

with the rules for the liberation from the present world and, even more, with the rules for the construction of an absolutely perfect world."[53]

Again, the revolutionary Gnosis is a diagnosis-therapy of evil; it follows an inner-worldly framework; and it involves the *why* and the *how* – why the world is full of evil and how to free it from evil. Gnosis is "knowledge of being and thus, it symbolizes the power *of* being and power *over* being."[54]

Revolutionary Gnosticism being a mentality, its Gnosis can be filled with any content, whether religious or materialistic. As we will see later, several are the ways in which revolutionary movements throughout history have given substance to Gnosis.

2.1.5 *Political-revolutionary self-redemption*

The fifth feature of revolutionary Gnosticism is quite relevant. The gnostic who holds the Gnosis (diagnosis-therapy of human alienation) needs to implement it: the diagnosis affects the way in which the gnostic perceives himself/herself and the world around him/her, whereas the therapy involves the praxis – a praxis that eventually develops into orthopraxis.

By implementing the Gnosis, the gnostic has the certainty that the world will turn upside down ("the turning of the tables, in the sense of Israelitic eschatology, remains a fundamental feature of the movement down to the Marxian formula of the 'expropriation of the expropriators'")[55], that society will finally become just and right, and that all sufferings will disappear – it will represent not only a drastic transformation of social conditions but also a "revolutionary transfiguration of the nature of man."[56] Acting in this way, the gnostic is sure to be fulfilling the meaning of history, or the will of God, or the imperative of any supreme principle. The immanent eschatological society will be a value in itself – there will be nothing left to achieve. Humanity would accomplish its goal, and revolution would take the place of grace.

The distinctive trait of revolutionary Gnosticism is "the tendency [...] to solve any problem – both practical and theoretical – in terms of praxis."[57]

---

53 Filoramo, *Il risveglio della gnosi,* p. 14.

54 Claudio Bonvecchio, 'Potere della gnosi e gnosi del potere: un percorso sapienziale', in *Gli arconti di questo mondo. Gnosi: politica e diritto*, eds. Claudio Bonvecchio and Teresa Tonchia (Trieste: EUT, 2000), p. 345.

55 Eric Voegelin, 'The People of God', in *The Collected Works of Eric Voegelin,* vol. 22, ed. by David L. Morse and William M. Thompson (Columbia and London: University of Missouri Press, 1998), p. 173.

56 Voegelin, *The New Science of Politics*, p. 186.

57 Giacomo Marramao, *Potere e secolarizzazione* (Torino: Bollati Boringhieri, 2005), p. 42.

To be more precise, the aim of saving humanity is achieved not by praying or adhering to pious and devout acts, but instead by implementing disruptive, revolutionary and political actions. The salvation is not given by God to those who deserve it because of their devotion and faith, but it is guaranteed to those who practically seek to achieve it. Such revolutionary-political action is a "gnostic theopolitics."[58] Any revolutionary-gnostic ideology achieves its aim through a revolutionary politics. And despite its anti-cosmism, "gnostic sectarian does not withdraw from the world but seeks to use his special knowledge for his own advancement, of that of the movement, in the world."[59]

Similar revolutionary politics is a clear form of self-redemption. God is no more. Humankind saves itself by alone – politics is the gnostic's field, the gnostic's specific area. Gnostic revolutionary politics is directed to redeem humanity; hence, it is a "soteriological practice."[60] And if salvation is accessible in this life, the Beyond disappears from the scope of political action, and the tension of the In-Between is shattered. Even in the case of religiously rooted groups, God is equally dead because the revolutionary presumes to be fulfilling God's will… without God. Once again, Eric Voegelin's words are enlightening:

> The forces of the world-immanent human creatures blend with the transcendental forces of the divinity in an ineffable manner so that the action of man is no longer the action of man but the effectiveness of divine energy working through the human form. What in reality happens through political action and violence is understood as an operation of transcendental Spirit. Moral judgment that is valid in ordinary human existence obviously does not apply to the spiritual operation.[61]

The belief that "human salvation is worked out in history,"[62] the "faith in the liberating power of violence,"[63] and the blind reliance on "political action [as the means that] can bring about an alteration in

58 Massimo Borghesi, *Critica della teologia politica* (Genova-Milano: Marietti, 2013), p. 14.
59 Bryan R. Wilson, 'An Analysis of Sect Development', *American Sociological Review*, vol. 24, no. 1 (February 1959): p. 7.
60 Pellicani, *Revolutionary Apocalypse*, p. 20.
61 Voegelin, 'The People of God', p. 174.
62 John Gray, *Black Mass. Apocalyptic Religion and the Death of Utopia* (London: Penguin Books, 2008), p. 31.
63 Ibid., p. 37.

the human condition"[64] are the topics of one of the most significant books on apocalyptic politics, *Black Mass* (2007) by the English political philosopher John Gray. In his work, Gray detects in Christian millenarianism the core of all Western revolutionary experiences. Believing that "modern politics is a chapter in the history of religion"[65] and that "modern revolutionary movements are a continuation of religion by other means,"[66] Gray denounces the early Christian hope in an imminent apocalypse to have become much too militant over the centuries. Recalling St. Augustine's distinction between the City of Man and the City of God and the further philosophy of history elaborated by Joachim of Flora, Gray is sure that the movement of secularization has hit the same idea of end-time, so that "in secular version of the Apocalypse the new age comes about through human action."[67]

The Polish philosopher Leszek Kolakowski has deeply studied revolutionary mentality, which he defines as a "constant element of European

---

64 Ibid., p. 29.

65 Ibid., p. 1.

66 Ibid., p. 3.

67 Ibid., p. 13. Yet Gray does not believe Gnosticism to be the core of revolutionarism. Commenting on Voegelin's thought, Gray utters that "there can be no doubt that gnostic beliefs have had a far-reaching influence in shaping western thought, and there may well have been gnostic influences on medieval millenarian movements, but there are few points of affinity between Gnosticism and modern millenarianism. [...] While it undoubtedly has an influence, the impact of Gnosticism on modern political religion was not formative. The decisive influence was the faith in the End that shaped Christianity from its origins. In expecting a final struggle between good and evil forces, medieval millenarians harked back to this eschatological faith, as did modern totalitarian movements" (ibid., pp. 96-97). However, Gray also remarks that "modern politics has been driven by the belief that humanity can be delivered from immemorial evils *by the power of knowledge*" (ibid., p. 20, emphasis added), and this very point is quite central, for it reveals the gnostic nature of revolutionarism. Moreover, Gray finds Zoroaster, or Zarathustra, to be "the ultimate source of the faith-based violence that has broken out again and again throughout western history" (ibid., p. 14), eventually influencing early Christianity, and then, through Christianity, reaching the whole Western civilization. But the sole eschatological belief does not explain the nature of revolution, radical politics, terrorism and totalitarianism; rather, what triggers revolutionary politics is the high degree of certainty that knowledge (Gnosis) gives to humankind. Likewise, the ingredient that activates the movement towards the Beyond (ancient Gnosticism) or towards earthly reality (revolutionary Gnosticism) is the break of the In-Between. In other words, John Gray does not categorize Gnosticism, and omitting such a central element made Gray to think both Nazi totalitarianism (1933-1945) and the policies of American president George W. Bush (2000-2008) as both apocalyptic political religions.

culture."[68] He then isolates the features of revolutionary mentality, finding out that faith in a total liberation of mankind and the rejection of the present world are inescapably the two key-attributes of it. He then recognizes the issue at hand, namely, the "Promethean faith in auto-liberation of humanity:"[69] humankind will save itself by means of revolutionary politics. In the same way as Luciano Pellicani, Kolakowski believes that the vision of a universal revolution is due to the declassed intelligentsia and to individuals who have been eradicated from their social roots during crisis periods. He observes the tendency of revolutionary ideologies to emphasize the "radical cultural discontinuity"[70] (what we have called "iconoclasm"), which means that in order to give birth to a new world, the past should be destroyed, so that "the break of human cultural continuity"[71] does appear as a liberating operation. This justifies destruction of libraries and blind militantism.

Apocalypticism, which we have already framed as a consequence of the tripartition of history, is also an integral part of the idea of an active self-redemption. The extreme violence that the gnostic militant implements is deemed to be the *last* violence, the violence that will put an end to any other violence. It is considered to be the chronologically last coercion before a liberated and finally reconciled humanity. Revolution will transfigure, alter, change and convert humanity in order that humankind will no longer be able to hurt anyone. Envy, jealousy, lust, need and poverty will be no more. Revolution will be like surgery, "the great surgical operation that would finally heal the structure of society:"[72] it needs to use a degree of violence, but in the end everything will be fine. In this sense, the gnostic wants to force and compel times; he or she desires to hasten the "apocalypse", that is, the revelation of what humanity should be and will be. Once that a single human being *knows* the mystery of history, it is impossible to avoid

---

68 Leszek Kolakowski, *Lo spirito rivoluzionario. La radice apocalittico-religiosa del pensiero politico moderno* (Milano: PGreco Edizioni, 2013), p. 8.

69 Kolakowski, *Lo spirito rivoluzionario*, p. 13. As John Gray, Kolakowski does not rely on Gnosticism in explaining the revolutionary mentality. Instead, he believes that the idea of total liberation and of an imminent Apocalypse "is without doubt the cornerstone of Christianity" (ibid., p. 8). However, when he turns to study Marxism, he has to admit that even though the idea of a total liberation results from Christianity, "unlike Christianity, [Marxism] is built on the Promethean faith in auto-liberation of humanity" (ibid., p. 13). Auto-liberation is an element that makes sense only if studied through the concept of Gnosticism.

70 Ibid., p. 18.

71 Ibid., p. 21.

72 Pellicani, *Revolutionary Apocalypse*, p. 59.

acting in some way or another to reach the end of the historical process. Politics becomes the vehicle to implement the Gnosis, and revolution turns to be the favorite means of such great operation.

Furthermore, even in the case of a religiously dressed gnostic ideology (Puritanism, radical Anabaptism…), God is set aside, since humankind does not wait for salvation from Him but is focused on achieving redemption actively and politically. In other words, humanity takes the place of God, and *revolutionary politics takes the place of devotion and prayer*.

2.1.6 *Sociological dualism*

The last aspect of revolutionary Gnosticism is what Emanuele Samek Lodovici calls "sociological dualism:"[73] there are only two camps, the good and the bad, the one who possesses the Gnosis and the other who is ignorant. History will prove the victory of the first side and the annihilation of the second side. Alessandro Orsini has dedicated many pages to the concept of the "binary code" or black/white mentality, a dichotomous thought according to which "the world appears divided into two sides: on one side there are your friends, and on the other your enemies. Your enemies are not human beings but just symbols to be attacked. This way of perceiving the political conflict strips the enemy of their humanity."[74] In this sense, gnostic militants "can now look at the world through the eyes of a redeemer"[75] because they line up with the right side of history. Hence, those who do not possess the Gnosis are not only simple political adversaries but rather cosmic enemies who should not only be defeated but totally annihilated. It follows that the conflict between the two sides is "the final battle before the establishment of the free society,"[76] the ultimate war that will eventually lead to the immanent *eschaton*, or Millennium, and then to the apocalypse, or the end of time.

The intrinsic elitism of Late-Antique Gnosticism is of some help in framing this last feature of the gnostic pattern; as Filoramo writes,

> by destroying the basis of mundane power through a strong condemnation of the Demiurge, the sovereign of this world, and by self-portraying themselves as the progeny of *abasileutoi*, i.e., those who are devoid of any form of human and divine power, the gnostics outline a political theology that delegitimizes any

---

73 Samek Lodovici, *Metamorfosi della gnosi*, p. 10.
74 Orsini, *Anatomy of the Red Brigades*, p. 18.
75 Ibid., p. 19.
76 Marega, "L'attesa dell'Apocalisse", p. 19.

> cosmic power and that finds a new form of legitimation in their own separation from other groups.[77]

For this reason, Filoramo concludes that the gnostics are in search of a new principle of authority, which is ultimately found in the Gnosis, and thus, in those who possess it.

Quite interesting are the considerations of the philosopher Jean Guitton:

> I call a 'pure party' each group that originates within a society that is otherwise considered corrupt, unclean, and that seeks its lost purity. […] You may already understand that there are two species of parties of the pure. There is the party that acts to improve society by cooperating in it. […] And there is […] the party of the Pures, that instead of serving power, works to destroy it in order to replace it with its own.[78]

Guitton's focus is dedicated to those groups that have labeled themselves as pure and that have self-represented themselves as identical to some kind of redeemer or savior. "Since a pure society is the social image of inner purity", Guitton writes, "belonging to a pure party is sign of being loved by the gods."[79] Once again, here emerges that the only belonging to a group guarantees the salvation of the militants, forgives any sin and exonerates them from asking for forgiveness – that is, self-redemption: the salvation is granted to those who belong to the "pure party".

To fulfill their goal, the self-redeemers have to abolish evil and annihilate sufferings. But the existence of people who are not part of their group slows down, or even prevents, any transfiguration of the world. Hence, these enemies must be annihilated. "The immaculate character of the purpose transfers its innocence to the bloody means. This is why the 'pures' are violent and the violent people believe to be pure. The more intense the violence is, the more it seems benevolent, since it saves time of pain. […] Violence […] is compassionate."[80] Guitton provides the example of the Bolsheviks and Jacobins: "Rational societies under the Terror, in France and in Russia, have always considered themselves

77 Giovanni Filoramo, 'Riflessioni in margine alla teologia politica degli gnostici', in *Gli arconti di questo mondo. Gnosi: politica e diritto*, eds. Claudio Bonvecchio and Teresa Tonchia (Trieste: EUT, 2000), pp. 40-41.

78 Jean Guitton, *Il puro e l'impuro* (1991; repr., Casale Monferrato: Piemme, 1993), pp. 21-22. I would like to thank Luciano Pellicani for bringing the book to my attention.

79 Ibid., p. 24.

80 Ibid., p. 31.

as germs of a pure society that must be extended over the whole Earth."[81] The Terror is the means by which the Jacobins and the Bolsheviks have tried to carry out policies for establishing a virtuous order; moreover, the Terror was used to crash the enemies of the "pure party", enemies who were regarded same as pollutants, impurities, whose mere existence endangers the pantoclastic project.

The Manichaean friend-enemy configuration recalls Carl Schmitt's definition of the political. In *The Concept of the Political* (1932), Schmitt identifies the essence of the political in the friend-enemy distinction, where the "enemy is not the *inimicus*, the one who has unfriendly attitude on a personal level, nor the *rivalis*, who is the competitor, nor the *adversarius*, the generic adversary, but the *hostis*, the enemy of the fatherland, the public and political enemy,"[82] who remains the stranger who poses an existential threat to a specific community.

With the emersion of non-state actors, for whom Schmitt uses the category of "partisan", the European landscape changed completely – and even the same concept of the political did not resist its previous form. Schmitt lists four traits of the partisan: irregularity, increased mobility, intensity of political commitment, and tellurian character. Irregular warfare (1) is characterized by speed and agility (2) on a specific ground that is well known to the partisans (3) who is moved by an intense political enthusiasm (4). "The intense political character is crucial as it distinguishes the partisan from other fighters, from the thief and criminal, or the pirate, for whom violence is carried out only for private enrichment."[83] The intention of this kind of local partisan is merely defensive, since the partisan is linked to a specific territory and is concerned about freeing his or her own country. "His grounding in the tellurian character seems necessary to me in order to make spatially evident the defensive character, i.e., the limitation of enmity, and in order to preserve it from the absolutism of an abstract justice."[84] However, the partisan has drastically changed over time. The encounter with a revolutionary ideology such as Communism, Schmitt explains, has completely changed the nature and the structure of the partisan. The global approach of universalistic ideologies as well as the technical-industrial progress have made the partisan lose the tellurian character. The

81 Ibid., p. 29.
82 Volpi, *Il nichilismo*, p. 136.
83 Tarik Kochi, 'The Partisan: Carl Schmitt and Terrorism', *Law Critique*, no. 17 (2006): p. 278.
84 Carl Schmitt, *The Theory of the Partisan* (1963; repr., Michigan: Michigan State University, 2004), p. 13.

complete dislocation of the so-transformed partisan has converted him into a *revolutionary combatant*. This last figure is pernicious. In addition to the loss of tellurian character, William Hooker suggests that "the key distinction [between the partisan and the revolutionary] lies in the political potentiality of their relationship with the law. In other circumstances, the partisan could subscribe to a system of order in which he is, in essence, left alone. The global revolutionary cannot."[85] The revolutionary has global expansionist ambitions that are not limited to a particular territory.

Lenin is the key figure of the revolutionary, its real ideologue. He is guilty of having internationalized the partisan, who now does not fight a "real" enemy but an *"absolute" enemy*. Lenin has brought the partisan in the field of total and unlimited enmity, outside the conventional game of wars. And "the war of absolute enmity knows no containment."[86] Absolute war, absolute enmity and absolute enemy became the coordinates of a new lethal warfare.

But eventually, Lenin's theoretical structure was further developed by Stalin. Schmitt writes: "Stalin was successful in linking the strong potential for national and local resistance – the essentially defensive, telluric power of patriotic self-defense against a foreign conqueror – with the aggressive nature of the international communist world-revolution. The connection of these two heterogeneous forces dominates partisan struggle around the world today."[87]

Absolute enmity is a key feature of Guitton's "pure party": there are no rules in the battle against the enemies of the Revolution; they must be completely eradicated.

Therefore, the sixth feature of sociological dualism defines the position of the gnostic individual in society and of the gnostic group in history.

2.2 *Gnostic revolutions throughtout history*

The present section will briefly study the main gnostic revolutions throughout history, trying to find in each of them the six features of the gnostic pattern. According to the leading scholars on the topic we have reviewed earlier, the main gnostic revolutions are the following five: (1) the radical Anabaptist seizure of Münster (1534-1535); (2) the Puritan

85 William Hooker, *Carl Schmitt's International Thought* (Cambridge: Cambridge University Press, 2009), p. 181.
86 Schmitt, *The Theory of the Partisan*, p. 36.
87 Ibid., 38.

revolution in England (17th century); (3) the Jacobins' Terror (1793-1794); (4) Bolshevism; and (5) Nazism.

This exercise would prove the gnostic pattern as a useful theoretical tool, being also helpful for the further analysis of Salafi-Jihadism, since looking at the functioning of actual gnostic revolutions would help comparing their structure to our case study.

2.2.1 *John of Leiden, the Paraclete of Münster*

The first gnostic attempt to establish the city of God on Earth by means of a revolutionary-political action goes back to 1534 and to the city of Münster, in north-western Germany. Here a radical form of Anabaptism[88] took root and became difficult to eradicate. Anabaptism is a Christian movement whose central practice is rebaptism seen as the seal of its separation from the rest of the world and their departure from the teaching of the Church. "Their communities were modelled on what they supposed to have been the practice of the early Church and were intended to realize the ethical ideal propounded by Christ."[89] Such a doctrine, whose origin can be found the 16th century, was quite widespread in Germany, Switzerland and Low Countries.

The seizure of Münster by a community of radical Anabaptists lasted for a little more than a year (February 1534 – June 1535). If the historical chronicles are correct, it was a terrible communistic experiment. The self-proclaimed prophet Melchior Hoffman[90] contributed in propagating an apocalyptic form of Anabaptism based on the close advent of the Millennium. In 1533, many Anabaptists who had been influenced by Hoffman, arrived in Münster and spread the new faith. Soon the population was captured by this appealing belief on the imminent end of times. Bernhard Rothmann, the Lutheran minister of the city, soon converted to this radical form of Anabaptism. When Hoffman was arrested, the Dutch baker Jan Matthys (c. 1500-1534) became the one who now possessed the gift of prophecy. But

88 George Cross sketches a possible genealogy of ideas deriving from Joachim of Flora, through the Franciscan monks known as the Spirituales, to the Wycliffites and Hussites and, finally, to the millenarian Anabaptists. See Cross, 'Millenarianism in Christian History', p. 8.

89 Cohn, *The Pursuit of the Millennium*, chap. 13.

90 Melchior Hoffman (c. 1495-1543) was a visionary Anabaptist leader who preached in the norther lands of Germany and the Netherlands. He spread the belief that Apocalypse would have been in 1533, basing his words on presumed visions – and so giving boost to the Münster rebellion.

> this change of leadership changed the whole tone of the movement. Hoffmann was a man of peace who had taught his followers to await the coming of the Millennium in quiet confidence, avoiding all violence. Matthys, on the other hand, was a revolutionary leader who taught that the righteous must themselves take up the sword and actively prepare the way for the Millennium by wielding it against the unrighteous.[91]

With the arrival of two new Anabaptist apostles, the political landscape of Münster changed completely: in fact, one of the newcomers was Jan Bockelson, better known as John of Leyden.[92] When Matthys died (April 1534), Bockelson assumed the leadership of the movement and of the city of Münster. In the meantime, the Catholics and the Lutherans joined together to expel the Anabaptists from the city. The war between the Millenarian Anabaptist city and the forces of evil had begun.

One of the best reports on the happenings in Münster has been written by Friedrich Reck-Malleczewen[93] in his *A History of Münster Anabaptists*. Reck-Malleczewen depicts in detail all the horrors that Münster witnessed in those dark months. The apocalyptic belief was the cornerstone of the whole radical ideology. "The Judgment Day will come between Lent and Easter – horribly soon, gentlemen – and engulf the whole world. But here not one in ten people will escape, and only Münster, God's own city, will be spared:"[94] this is the apocalyptic faith that burst forth in Münster. People were talking of the Lord's trumpet that, at any moment, would sound thrice from the clouds to announce the forthcoming end. Therefore, "Münsterites sought to reshape the social and physical order so as to conform to the biblical apocalyptic pattern."[95]

As Reck-Malleczewen reports, another self-proclaimed prophet, the goldsmith Dusentschnuer from Warendorf, even started to

---

91 Cohn, *The Pursuit of the Millennium*, chap. 13.

92 John of Leyden (1509-1536) is the infamous hero of the seizure of Münster. Raised in poverty and soon converted to Anabaptism, he moved to Münster attracted by the fact that there were many Anabaptist preachers there.

93 Friedrich Reck-Malleczewen (1884-1945) was a German writer. He strongly opposed the Nazi regimes, and he tragically died at the Dachau concentration camp. The book *A History of Münster Anabaptists* (first published in 1937) depicts John of Leiden's bloody Anabaptist experiment as a forerunner of Nazism. For that reason it was banned by the Nazi authority.

94 Friedrich Reck-Malleczewen, *A History of the Münster Anabaptists* (1937; repr., New York: Palgrave Macmillan, 2008), p. 40.

95 Claus Bernet, 'The Concept of the New Jerusalem among Early Anabaptists in Münster 1534/35. An Interpretation of Political, Social and Religious Rule', *Archiv für Reformationsgeschichte*, vol. 102, issue 1 [2011]: p. 176.

> run out on the market square, crying that God's own holy man Johann Bockelson shall henceforth be King... not only of Münster but rather King of the entire world[96], over all the imperial princes and, of course, King over Emperor Carolus himself. Dusentschnuer proclaims this, he is handed a sword by one of the elders who have been summoned, and he presents it to Bockelson, "so that he may carry it until God himself shall take his dominion from him." Dusentschnuer also takes some chrysma oil and "on the orders of the Father" anoints the tailor and pronounces him as "successor to the throne of David" to be King of Zion.[97]

Eric Voegelin subsumes John of Leyden under the category of the *Paracletes*, i.e., strong personalities who appear as incarnations of the Spirit and lead a specific community thanks to their great charisma.[98] John of Leyden legitimized his takeover by claiming that he alone could have ruled until the actual Second Coming.

Soon in Münster the iconoclastic fury became savage: the destruction of the old cathedral was a traumatizing event. Here is how Reck-Malleczewen describes it:

> The inner sanctum is befouled in the time-tested old ways of all burglars, the glass windows are smashed, and with a blacksmith's hammer they beat on the clock whose artful construction was the life's work of an unknown master. They defile the cathedral library with human feces, and in the days that follow they burn the collection of incunabula and etchings imported from Italy by Herr Rudolf von Langen. The altar panels painted by Master Franke are sawed into boards for a latrine, the Roman baptismal font shatters under their hammers. With hammers and axes they hack away at wooden and stone sculptures, and the organ is carefully destroyed pipe by pipe.[99]

---

96 Norman Cohn adds that John od Leyden was welcomed as "a Messiah of the Last Days" (Cohn, *The Pursuit of the Millennium*, chap. 13).

97 Reck-Malleczewen, *A History of the Münster Anabaptists*, p. 89. Moreover, "the inscription on the King's seal not merely read 'King of Münster,' but ambitiously 'King of the New Temple', and van Leyden's title was 'John by the Mercy of God, King of the New Temple'. From other sources we read that he was simply 'King of Zion or of the New Jerusalem,' 'Johann von Leyden, King of the New Jerusalem', or 'King of Jerusalem and All the World'" (Bernet, 'The Concept of the New Jerusalem', p. 179).

98 Voegelin finds many doctrinal formative forces for the figures of the Paracletes: "Most obviously, the Johannine Paraclete exerted its influence, nut we have also to keep in mind the broad and deep reservoir of gnostic symbolism, as well as the Neoplatonic tradition. Fränger has drawn special attention to a Pythagorean fragment: 'There are three kinds of reason-endowed [*logikos*] being, that is God, man, and beings like Pythagoras'" (Voegelin, 'The People of God', p. 190).

99 Reck-Malleczewen, *A History of the Münster Anabaptists*, p. 29.

Many churches were destroyed, for "in the Heavenly Jerusalem [as described in the Book of Apocalypse] holy space would not only be unnecessary but also proscribed."[100] And even the clock of the Cathedral of St. Lambert was destroyed, given that "with the beginning of God's Kingdom, according to Revelations x, 6, earthly time would run out."[101] Musical instruments were banned. All books, with the exception of the Bible, were burned. All church spires were leveled. Streets and buildings were given different names, "an innovation that would be followed by the Jacobins."[102] Hence, "the social revolution in Münster was uncompromisingly anti-intellectual,"[103] which eventually led to "*a complete break with the past*."[104] A new calendar was issued: "since every day would be holy, there would no longer be need for Sundays, apostles' days, and saints' days. The Anabaptists annulled them all."[105] Newborns were given only biblical names.

An eyewitness of the events in Münster, Heinrich Gresbeck, recounts that "everything they [the Anabaptists] did, it just had to be good; it was after all God's will."[106] The technique adopted by the king of the new Sion was to claim to act by visions and voices revealed by God directly to him. Correspondingly, all the legislation had to be based to the letter on the Sacred Scriptures. The establishment of a new council that "will no longer be concerned with matters of the flesh but rather with matters of the spirit"[107] is the crucial passage toward the new repressive regime. "All of these ordinances, lacking only a regulation pertaining to your dog's fleas, are concluded with a Bible passage:"[108] the prophets in charge always had biblical quotations and mystical visions at hand to justify their actions and ordinances. Public executions were countless.

Believing that at the beginning of Christianity the Christian community lived in a communistic manner, all money and all precious metals were confiscated – whoever tried to keep some money or gold was beheaded. No one should have locked his/her door at night, "for the gates of the Heavenly

100 Bernet, 'The Concept of the New Jerusalem', p. 186.
101 Ibid., p. 187.
102 Gray, *Black Mass*, p. 19.
103 Cohn, *The Pursuit of the Millennium*, chap. 13.
104 Ibid. Emphasis added.
105 Bernet, 'The Concept of the New Jerusalem', p. 188.
106 Heinrich Greskeck, quoted from Reck-Malleczewen, *A History of the Münster Anabaptists*, p. 3.
107 Ibid., p. 27.
108 Ibid., p. 56.

Jerusalem never closed."[109] Polygamy was legalized and enforced (soon Bockelson's harem included up to sixteen women).

For these radical Anabaptists, the city of Münster was the "most Christian city"[110] and "God's most elevated city,"[111] which would have expanded over the whole world. In a letter distributed among the adversaries lined up outside the city, the Anabaptists wrote: "We know that we are the children of anger and that we can only be justified by our faith in Jesus Christ. But the belief that He died for us does not accomplish anything, and the Kingdom of God cannot be won that easily, and it is written: 'The Kingdom of Heaven suffereth violence, and the violent shall take it by force.'"[112] Unmistakably, such "children of anger" had the goal of actively establishing the Kingdom of God on Earth. "The door of mercy is closed,"[113] Jan Bockelson uttered. It's no longer time for God's action: it's the time of men.

Reck-Malleczewen diagnoses a "mass insanity, a mysterious psychosis overwhelming an entire community."[114] Furthermore, he writes: "The collective of Münster – cut from the cloth of the Old Testament, born of the rejection of German mysticism – shows early on all the symptoms which come from the secularization of life: not least of all the terroristic claims to power of mass-man."[115] The secularization, or immanentization of life was the primary cause of the gnostic experiment, which means that a truly religious life was no longer popular as one might think. This very element reinforces the assumption that revolutionary Gnosticism detonates where the predominance of the Sacred is no more. Like Luciano Pellicani, Friedrich Reck-Malleczewen is also convinced that the "collapse of the old ideas at first produces a deep sense of helplessness and severe shock, and consequently we always see the mass psychoses of a people in their years of transition."[116] Indeed, referring to the Münster inhabitants, he talks of "discontented masses, already rebelling against early capitalism."[117] Hence, "we would perhaps do well to hunt for the infectious germs of the entire movement not in religious but rather in anticapitalistic problems,

109 Bernet, "The Concept of the New Jerusalem", p. 181.

110 Reck-Malleczewen, *A History of the Münster Anabaptists*, p. 58.

111 Ibid., p. 59. In Norman Cohn's word: "The regime was a theocracy, in which the divinely inspired community had swallowed up the state" (Cohn, *The Pursuit of the Millennium*, chap. 13).

112 Quoted in Reck-Malleczewen, *A History of the Münster Anabaptists*, p. 60.

113 Quoted in ibid., p. 44.

114 Ibid., p. 1.

115 Ibid., p. 41.

116 Ibid., p. 72.

117 Ibid., p. 96.

not in the controversial theological questions but rather in the dreary social longings of the late-medieval masses, and finally in the fulfillment of those wishes through the communism that manifested itself in the Anabaptist rule of Münster."[118]

Accordingly, the Anabaptist revolution is defined by Karl Mannheim as the moment when "longings which up to that time had been either unattached to a specific goal or concentrated upon other-worldly objectives suddenly took on a mundane complexion. They were now felt to be realizable – here and now – and infused social conduct with a singular zeal."[119] In this respect, Mannheim talks of "spiritualization of politics."[120]

The millenarian experiment of Münster shows an extraordinary "blend of millenarianism and primitivism,"[121] a lethal cocktail that follows the scheme of the tripartition of history: there was a golden age that went lost, thus in order to restore it we should move toward the end of history, toward the moment when the enemies will be challenged and annihilated, following apocalyptic prophecies to be read as instructions to literary stick to and implement in history. It is because of this cosmic project that the saints need to "bear all the world's enmity,"[122] especially "the papists, the true Babylonians."[123]

The attempt to set up an earthly Jerusalem in Münster ended in a bloodshed: with the help of the Münsterite carpenter Heinrich Gresbeck, in June 1535 the Bishop's army penetrated the city. From the further interrogatories to the leaders of the movement, we know that "the affinity to the Heavenly Jerusalem was not a game, a drama or a liturgical performance, but that the Anabaptists genuinely believed in 'their' Heavenly Jerusalem. We are dealing with *literal biblical acting* rather than allegorical or symbolic play."[124] In other terms, they were using the Sacred

118 Ibid., p. 182.

119 Mannheim, *Ideology and Utopia*, pp. 190-191. And he adds: "Even though this stage is, as already indicated, still very far removed from the stage of 'proletarian self-consciousness', it is nevertheless the starting point of the process gradually leading to it" (ibid., p. 191).

120 Ibid., p. 191.

121 Cohn, *The Pursuit of the Millennium*, chap. 13.

122 Anabaptists' letter, dated January 10, 1535. Quoted in Reck-Malleczewen, *A History of the Münster Anabaptists*, p. 119.

123 Quoted in ibid. It is noteworthy the use of the term "Babylonian", a Biblical name for those who oppose the gnostic project of the Anabaptists. Likewise, the radical Islamist militants will use the term *jāhiliyya* for the same purpose.

124 Bernet, 'The Concept of the New Jerusalem', p.193. Emphasis added.

Scriptures with the certainty that their understanding was superior and did not need any compromises or any rational discussion whatsoever.

In any case, John of Leyden is a clear example of a gnostic Paraclete who anticipated many other similar, and even more violent, experiments. Friedrich Reck-Malleczewen defines him an "anticipation of Cromwell,"[125] and considers his rhetorical strategy ("Beware of whom tries to stop me, because I am on the path of God!") to be the same approach adopted "in 1792 in Paris and in Moscow of 1917."[126]

2.2.2 *Puritanism and the revolution of the saints*

Radical wings of the Puritan movement of the 17th century could be understood as "the development of an idea that already existed within the Anabaptist movement: the purpose of politics [as] the revolutionary transformation of the existing in the light of the Holy Scripture."[127] Even John Gray believes that 17th-century England was the theatre of a significant evolution, that is, "the millenarian currents of late medieval times started their mutation into modern revolutionary movements."[128] And Vittorio Mathieu considers that "the first true revolutionaries are the Puritans. They moved the revolution from heaven to earth [...] and transformed a religious attitude into a political force [...] following a basically political vision of renovation."[129]

At that time, England was a land where many religious personalities were spreading a recalcitrant form of Christianity. Indeed, the Puritans were "the 'hottest' members of the Calvinist Protestantism that constituted the mainstream of the Elizabethan Church."[130] Opposition to the established church[131] was the distinctive trait of such movement, and "the efforts of ascendant 'anti-Puritans' in the Stuart church – especially archbishop Laud – increasingly forced Puritans into non-conformity and open opposition to the Church of England"[132] – opposition that eventually turned into hostility toward the monarchy *tout court*. In fact, during the reign of Mary Tudor

125 Reck-Malleczewen, *A History of the Münster Anabaptists*, p. 56.

126 Ibid., p. 20.

127 Pellicani, *Revolutionary Apocalypse*, p. 27.

128 Gray, *Black Mass*, p. 31.

129 Mathieu, *La speranza nella rivoluzione*, p. 193.

130 Karl Gunther, 'The Origins of English Puritanism', *History Compass*, vol. 4, issue 2 (March 2006): p. 235.

131 This opposition was due to the original Puritan purpose of purifying the English church from any Catholic or "papist" remaining.

132 Gunther, 'The Origins of English Puritanism', p. 237.

(1553-1558), daughter of Henry VIII, many Calvinist preachers were forced to leave the country. Likewise, between 1629 and 1640, the Stuarts persecuted Calvinism, and about 20,000 Puritans went in exile. These two episodes summarize the resentment of Puritans against the monarchy. During the years of persecution the Puritans developed a deep sense of identification with the persecuted Jews: at the end of historical sufferings there will be the "promised land."[133]

Meanwhile, a strong dissatisfaction with the monarchy began to rise among members of Parliament. More exactly, "the political authorities had become power conscious,"[134] and this very element was highly problematic in the English political arena. The Petition of Right (1628) and the Triennial Act (1641) tried to restrict the royal power by balancing it with a stronger freedom of initiative of the Parliament. On 1 June, 1642, the Nineteen Propositions approved by the House of Lords and the House of Commons were rejected by King Charles I, and then the country came to civil war, witnessing Royalists versus Parliamentarians.[135] In 1645, the Parliamentarians established the New Model Army, an army mainly composed of fervent and radical Puritans and led by the military leader Oliver Cromwell. When the Royalist army was defeated, Charles I was executed (30 January, 1649). Cromwell proclaimed the Commonwealth which lasted up until 1660, when Charles II became king (the so-called Restoration).

Radical social changes accompanied the English revolution: a proto-industrial configuration of the economic production transformed society from within, provoking rapid enrichments and rapid impoverishments. During this period, the perception and the functioning of society inexorably changed: society was no longer considered "static and irreversibly stratified, but on the contrary, it was regarded as an alterable

133 It was especially John Brinsley (1600-1665) who stressed this similarity: "Our case being now the very same with Israel in the days of King Asah" ('The Saints Solemne Covenant With Their God' [1644], retrieved by http://downloads.it.ox.ac.uk/ota-public/tcp/Texts-HTML/free/A29/A29528.html [accessed May 9, 2017]).

134 Eric Voegelin, 'The English Revolution', *The Collected Works of Eric Voegelin,* vol. 25, *History of Political Ideas, vol. VII*, ed. by Jürgen Gebhardt and Thomas A. Hollweck (Columbia and London: University of Missouri Press, 1999), p. 76.

135 The Nineteen Proposition were a series of requests by which the Long Parliament called for a greater share of power in the governance of the kingdom. Among other things, there was the request of parliamentary supervision of foreign policy and the responsibility for the command of the militia, the non-professional body of the army.

fact such as to stimulate not a resigned quietism but the enthusiasm for new possibilities."[136] The same monarchy, until then deemed sacred, was perceived differently. The more Charles I and the archbishop of Canterbury, William Laud, acted fiercely against the Puritans, the more "the Puritan preachers found Antichristic characters in Charles, Laud, the bishops, the Anglican church."[137] The new perception of reality as something malleable merged with the rising sentiment of revenge against what we can call "the establishment". Hence, religious dissent and political dissent went hand in hand ("People's rage adopted Biblical expressions: but what was causing it was no longer only the [theological] sin, but an entirely earthly injustice.")[138] The victory of Cromwell over Charles I was the turning point of this story.

The rigid religious discipline that spread in English society and that was partially enforced during the period of the Commonwealth descends from the proliferation of many Puritan congregations and from the same mentality of the army: among the soldiers of the New Model Army there were members of many radical Puritan branches such as the Levellers and the Fifth Monarchy Men.[139] The latter was a group with a strong chiliastic belief that can be condensed as follow:

> The four monarchies of the past – the Assyrian, Persian, Greek, and Roman – were soon to disappear; the Rule of the Saints would soon begin; Christ would come again to earth and set up the Fifth and last Monarchy with Himself as King. The high duty of the Fifth Monarchy man was to work toward this goal, laying the earthly foundations of God's everlasting kingdom.[140]

---

136 Ugo Bonanate, introduction to *I puritani. I soldati della Bibbia*, ed. by Ugo Bonanate (Torino: Einaudi, 1975), p. 6.

137 Ibid., p. 13.

138 Ibid., p. 19.

139 The Levellers were a group of people organized in a form that resembles a modern and democratic political party. They "openly proclaimed that sovereignty resides wholly and solely in the people [...] and it was the first political party that dared to make religious tolerance a cornerstone of its program" (H. Noel Brailsford, *I livellatori e la rivoluzione inglese* [Milan: Il Saggiatore, 1962], pp. 43-44). Their radical egalitarianism, which comprised also common ownership, sure was a threat to the monarchy.

140 Eden Quainton, 'Cromwell and the Anabaptists during 1653', *Pacific Historical Review*, vol. 1, no. 2 (June 1932): p. 166. See also Piero Stefani, *L'Apocalisse* (Bologna: Il Mulino, 2008), p. 79: "The monarchy was qualified with the ordinal 'fifth' in that the four kingdoms described in the book of Daniel (cf. Dn 2, 14-45) would be succeeded by the final kingdom of the saints."

Oliver Cromwell himself remained close to the movement until 1653, when the establishment of the Protectorate turned the sect against him. Besides the Fifth Monarchy Men, there were many other groups (for instance, the Quakers, the Seekers, the Ranters, the Muggletonians) and individuals who believed in the imminent end of times. Richard W. Cogley defines 17th-century Puritanism as "an intensely biblical subculture, one that regarded the Scripture, including the Books of Daniel and Revelation, as an inerrant and all-sufficient guide for human affairs."[141]

Puritans stand as a historical force mainly preoccupied with history and its direction rather than with transcendent salvation: in this respect, millenarianism is a form of belief that has to do mainly with time and with the unfolding of proofs of the alleged essence of history. By identifying *in time* the "last things" (e.g., the Millennium, the Battle of Armageddon, the conversion of the Jews, the destruction of the Antichrist), the Puritans were able to declare that "they were aligned with the transcendent power that eventually would be victorious."[142] But what is extremely interesting here is that the "last things" were used as a tool "to make history intelligible"[143] – the importance of such principles should not be underestimated, for what we have identified a Gnosis is precisely the explanatory power of whatsoever narrative, for instance, of these apocalyptic elements.

The religious fervor that inflamed England in the 17th century has been deeply studied by the philosopher and political thinker Michael Walzer, who devoted many studies to the definition of the word "revolution" as linked to the Puritan case. He states that "the Puritan effort to transform English society and politics turned the civil wars into a revolution."[144] But what does "revolution" mean in this context? Walzer distinguishes two conceptions of warfare among the Englishmen fighting their king: the first conception is the old theory of just war, according to which one has the duty to wage war against whoever breaks the peace. In other terms, if a king invades another country, or if a tyrant violates the rights of his own subjects, a violent defense is legitimate and just. The second conception of warfare is the one that took place in England; according to this idea, there are two kinds of people, the wicked, or depraved, and the good, or

141 Richard W. Cogley, 'Seventeenth-Century English Millenarianism', *Religion*, vol. 17, issue 4 (October 1987): p. 392.

142 Ibid., p. 393.

143 Ibid.

144 Michael Walzer, 'War and Revolution in Puritan Thought', *Political Studies*, vol. 12, issue 2 (1964): p. 220.

saints, fighting each other in a perpetual conflict, whose end will witness the victory of the good over the evil.

> This was the war which the Puritans fought. It was not a just war, for its purpose was never the re-establishment of some shattered peace or violated legal order. The Puritans simply did not perceive a world at peace, or rather they believed, as the preacher Thomas Taylor declared, that "the world's peace is the keenest war against God". And among depraved men, the saints did not recognize a legal order. "Most nations in their civil constitution", argued the radical minister John Owen, "lie out of order for the bringing in of the interest of Christ; they must be shaken up and new disposed of, that all obstacles may be taken away". It was thus the creation of a new order – *total triumph over depravity* – which the self-designated saints sought in their wars.[145]

War against depravity is the gnostic attempt to change human nature once and for all by means of politics, violence and revolution.[146]

Now, just war requires an end (the termination of the conflict and the restoration of a period of peace); on the contrary, the war of the saints knows no limits. For this reason, Walzer acutely recognizes that the struggle against the wicked has its start in the self. In his own words: "Saints cannot war against worldlings until first there are saints, until, that is, some men have conquered the lusts of the fallen Adam. […] There was a continual tendency in Puritan thought and practice to turn the internal struggle against Satanic temptation into an external war against wicked men."[147] John Milton's famous eulogy of Cromwell is illustrative of this theory: "A commander first over himself, the conqueror of himself, it was over himself he had learnt most to triumph. Hence he went to encounter with an external enemy as a veteran accomplished in all military duties…"[148]

In view of that, in his famous *The Revolution of the Saints. A Study in the Origins of Radical Politics* (1965), Michael Walzer associates the struggle for self-control to the rapid social and economic changes mentioned above: "Whenever groups of men are suddenly set loose from old certainties"[149], Walzer writes, then the need for order and discipline becomes compelling.

145 Ibid., p. 225. Emphasis added.

146 "The revolutionary saints […] did not seek a remedy for a particular, narrowly defined evil, but for evil itself" (ibid., p. 228).

147 Ibid., p. 226.

148 John Milton, quoted in ibid., p. 226.

149 Michael Walzer, *The Revolution of the Saints. A Study in the Origins of Radical Politics* (Cambridge: Harvard University Press, 1965), p. 311.

When traditional society[150] begins to weaken and erode, as it was in Late Middle Ages, "individual men experienced at once a new and exhilarating sense of freedom and mobility and an acute anxiety and fearfulness."[151] The choice of sainthood (self-control, discipline, self-sacrifice, dedication to a cause) is a sort of remedy to the uncertainty of modernity, and Puritanism is accordingly defined as an "ideology of transition."[152] In a certain sense, Puritanism is "a response to the disorder of the transition period"[153] because "ideological zeal [...] makes it possible for men to feel secure outside the traditional system of connections;"[154] it would be unimaginable in a traditional society ("in traditional societies, this self-conquest is not necessary – except for relatively small numbers of men who for personal reasons choose monasticism as a way of life;"[155]) therefore, it is a strictly modern, or rather secular, attitude, which is a confirmation of the thesis that revolutionary Gnosticism is a secular and modern phenomenon.

Interestingly, Michael Walzer adopts such an explanation to clarify the emersion of other kinds of revolutionaries: "Englishmen became Puritans and then godly magistrates, elders and fathers in much the same way and for many of the same reasons as eighteenth-century Frenchmen became Jacobins and active citizens, and twentieth-century Russians Bolsheviks and professional revolutionaries."[156] The target of each of these revolutionaries was always the same: the impulse toward disorganization and spontaneity.[157] The creation of a new man through repression and collective discipline must precede the creation of a new social order – once the new man is settled, the war can take place. And in this war, the sides facing each other are only two, the saved versus the damned. In this

150 Walzer defines as traditional "a society in which hierarchy is the fundamental ordering principle; patriarchy, personal loyalty, patronage and corporatism are the key forms of human relations; and passivity is the normal political posture of common men" (Walzer, *The Revolution of the Saints*, p. 311).

151 Ibid., p. 311.

152 Ibid., p. 312. Walzer is sure that Puritans "had helped carry men through a time of change; they had no place in a time of stability" (ibid., 320).

153 Ibid.

154 Ibid., p. 319.

155 Ibid., p. 315.

156 Ibid., p. 310. The connection with Jacobins and Bolsheviks is noticed also by John Gray: "These [Puritans] groups began a modern revolutionary tradition of armed missionaries that was later embodied in the Jacobins and the Bolsheviks" (Gray, *Black Mass*, p. 32).

157 "All forms of radical politics make their appearance at moments of rapid and decisive change, moments when customary status is in doubt and character (or 'identity') is itself a problem" (Walzer, *The Revolution of the Saints*, p. 315).

scheme, the saved "discover in themselves a predestination, a firm and undeviating sense of purpose,"[158] which resembles the character of self-redemption of the gnostic pattern. And the Puritans' sense of enmity is indicative of what we have called sociological dualism: Puritans would have used the apocalyptic notion of "Satan's end-time 'wrath' to sustain themselves even under the worst of circumstances,"[159] and the mounting adversity of the world against them would have been a positive sign of the final victory.[160]

In light of Michael Walzer's thesis, it is possible to appreciate his definition of the English Revolution: "The English Revolution, as distinct from the resistance of Parliament to the 'tyranny' of Charles I, was precisely this self-disciplining, new modelling, fighting, purging and punishing in which the saints were eternally engaged."[161]

Eric Voegelin explores the issue by analyzing Richard Hooker's *Ecclesiastical Polity* (1594), a book that outlines the type of the Puritan:

> Hooker discerned that the Puritan position was not based on Scripture but was a "cause" of a vastly different origin. It would use Scripture when passages torn out of context would support the cause, and for the rest it would blandly ignore Scripture as well as the traditions and rules of interpretation that had been developed by fifteen centuries of Christianity.[162]

The selection of Biblical passages is quite significant, for it reveals the hatred against tradition and shows that the Bible was used as an instruction manual: "Radical scripturalism has become, in the field of social technique, the instrument through which the conscience of man can be kept within the limits of national jurisdiction."[163]

An example of this method is the interpretation of the evangelical statement "My Kingdom is not of this world", and the consequent distinction between the terms "world" and "earth": "Of course Christ said his Kingdom is not of this world; but did he say it shouldn't be established

---

158 Walzer, *The Revolution of the Saints*, p. 317.

159 Cogley, 'Seventeenth-Century English Millenarianism', p. 389.

160 "The saints expected the universal claim of their federation to call forth an equally universal alliance of the world against them. [...] The universal claim to dominion of the gnostic sectarian produces the universal alliance against him" (Voegelin, 'Gnostic Politics', p. 238-239).

161 Walzer, 'War and Revolution', p. 228.

162 Voegelin, 'The New Science of Politics', p. 200.

163 Voegelin, 'The English Revolution', p. 94. Catholicism was the first target of this strict attitude.

on earth? On the contrary, Rev. 5:10 explicitly assures us: 'And [thou] hast made us unto our God kings and priests: and we shall reign on the earth.' *World* and *earth* must therefore be distinguished from each other."[164] To give reason for this, Voegelin quotes a sermon preached in 1647 by Thomas Collier (1615-1691) in Cromwell's headquarters. The sermon shows also the affinity with the immanentization of the *eschaton*:

> We always had and we still have very lowly and carnal images of heaven, in so far as we take it to be a place of glory beyond the firmament, invisible, and we are to enjoy its joys only beyond this life. But God himself is the Kingdom of Saints, their pleasure, and their glory. Wherever God is manifest, there is his Kingdom and that of the Saints; and he manifests himself in the Saints. Here is the great and hidden mystery of the Gospel, this new creation in the Saints.[165]

What is extremely important is the radical break with Christianity that such a sermon represents. Only resorting to Voegelin's own words it is possible to get the idea of the great hiatus between the gnostic speculation of the Puritans and traditional Christianity:

> [According to Collier and the Puritans], the earth, as it exists, can be the world of darkness or the world of light, realm of the devil or Kingdom of God. This is the classical break with Christianity. The Christian world, as God's creation, is not a real of darkness; to be sure, it is darkened by the all-too-human factor of the Fall; but it is ennobled again by the Incarnation of God as the locus of fulfilled humanity within the limitations of creaturely being. This Christian tension between created and divine being, between the limits of being and transfiguration by grace in death, gets dissolved into an immanent historical process that embraces world and superworld as temporally unfolding eons. And this immanentization dissolves even the symbol of "heaven" inasmuch as it substitutes a materialist paradise for the mystery of the beatific vision of God in death and then against this "lowly image" calls for the temporal realization of the eternal Kingdom as its spiritual interpretation.[166]

Voegelin is especially interested in a peculiar treatise entitled *A Glimpse of Sion's Glory* (1641). Its author is still uncertain, but recently Mark R. Bell has argued[167] that it was Thomas Goodwin, a Puritan preacher who served as chaplain to Oliver Cromwell. A *Glimpse of Sion's Glory* is an

164 Voegelin, 'Gnostic Politics', p. 224.
165 Thomas Collier, quoted in Voegelin, 'Gnostic Politics', p. 225.
166 Ibid.
167 See Mark R. Bell, *Apocalypse How? Baptist Movements during the English Revolution* (Macon: Mercer University Press, 2000), pp. 69-70.

important pamphlet for our research, since it depicts a religious utopia akin to the immanentization of the *eschaton* – for this reason Voegelin highlights a crucial passage of the text, a sentence where the author writes that "not only heaven shall be your kingdom, but this world bodily."[168] Thomas Goodwin's concern is to disclose the future reality, a world where the presence of Christ will fill all creatures, "making legal sanctions superfluous"[169] (here again the theme of antinomianism). Such future condition would be an earthly paradise "free of poverty, sickness, death, oppression, and sexual need. The dreams of the *Glimpse* are concentrated on the political-economic needs – on poverty and coercive authority."[170] Hence, despite the semblance of religiosity, the *Glimpse* is a secular treatise.

The author of the pamphlet is also moved by the belief in an imminent eschatological event; he encourages the "saints" to "dasheth the brats of Babylon against the stones"[171] in order to hasten the coming of the new Jerusalem. He exalts the common people and demonizes the rich, the noble and the clergy. And he incites the common people to cooperate to the divine plan: "The people will start the glorious reign of Christ. [...] You all have begun this endeavor that consists in rebuilding the Church to which God will confer His grace. [...] This endeavor [...] will continue up until Christ's Coming."[172] It is an actual self-redemption, for the saints believe they are doing God's will and, in doing so, they are sure to be saved. Political-revolutionary action is the means by which they are going to inaugurate God's Kingdom – and God's Kingdom will last forever.[173]

The same program of "activist" salvation is also present in a 1646 sermon preached by Hugh Peters, a close collaborator of Cromwell, in front of Parliament: "What [our] means do, is actually God to realize it. It is the Lord who has given strength and success to our plans. [...] Now the sword should determine the dispute. [...] You are about to fulfill great and glorious prophecies."[174] Oliver Cromwell himself was fascinated by the inseparability of religion and politics. As Alessandro Orsini writes,

168 *A Glimpse of Sion's Glory*, quoted in Voegelin, 'Gnostic Politics', p. 230.
169 Ibid.
170 Ibid.
171 *A Glimpse of Sion's Glory*, quoted in Voegelin, 'The New Science of Politics', p. 183.
172 Thomas Goodwin, 'Un raggio della gloria di Sion', in *I puritani. I soldati della Bibbia*, ed. by Ugo Bonanate (Turin: Einaudi, 1975), pp. 75-76.
173 "The attempt at freezing history into an everlasting constitution is an instance of the general class of gnostic attempts at freezing history into an everlasting final realm on this earth" (Voegelin, 'The New Science of Politics', p. 218).
174 Hugh Peters, 'Le opera di Dio e il dovere degli uomini', in *I puritani. I soldati della Bibbia*, ed. by Ugo Bonanate (Turin: Einaudi, 1975), pp. 100-101 and 103.

driven by a "providentialistic" view of history – according to which God deals directly with earthly affairs – Cromwell regarded his victory as the direct result of the will of God. On 4 July 1653, he spoke to Parliament: "I confess I never looked to see such a day as this – it may be nor you neither – when Jesus Christ should be so owned as He is, at this day... And you manifest this, insofar as poor creatures can do, to be a day of the Power of Jesus Christ… Therefore hold steady your vocation: it is extraordinary and comes from God and has neither been designed nor thought by you or me".[175]

Beyond any ideological variances among different Puritan sects and groups, the idea of a lost pristine perfect condition on earth, pushed by a strong anticlericalism, was very common. John Brisley insisted on "reducing [episcopate] to the primitive semplicitie,"[176] Hugh Peters inveighed against the clergy because "Christ principally criticized scribes and Pharisee,"[177] and Edmund Calamy attacked "all Popery and Popish innovations:"[178] the primitive Christianity was the compass of any actions.

During the years of the revolution, symbolic acts were as crucial as actual facts. This is the reason why, on June, 1649, a group of people known as the Diggers and led by Gerrard Winstanley began to cultivate and plant vegetables in common land on St George's Hill, near London. In the manifesto of the group entitled *The True Levellers Standard Advanced* (1649) and written by the same Winstanley and other Diggers, one could recognize communistic motifs and dreams on an ancient golden age:

> In the beginning of Time, the great Creator Reason, made the Earth to be a Common Treasury, to preserve Beasts, Birds, Fishes, and Man. [… But] selfish imaginations taking possession of the Five Sences, and ruling as King in the room of Reason therein, and working with Covetousnesse, did set up one man to teach and rule over another. […] And hereupon, the Earth (which was made to be a Common Treasury of relief for all, both Beasts and Men) was hedged in to In-closures by the teachers and rulers, and the others were made Servants and Slaves. […] From the beginning it was not so. […] But when once the Earth becomes a Common Treasury again, as it must, for all the Prophesies of Scriptures and Reason are Circled here in the Community, and mankind must have the Law of Righteousnesse once more writ in his heart, and all must be made of one heart, and one mind. Then this Enmity in all Lands will cease, for

175 Orsini, *Anatomy of the Red Brigades*, p. 166.
176 Brinsley, 'The Saints Solemne Covenant'.
177 Peters, 'Le opera di Dio', p. 104.
178 Edmund Calamy, 'Gods Free Mercy to England' (1642), retrieved by http://tei.it.ox.ac.uk/tcp/Texts-HTML/free/A32/A32016.html. Calamy preached this sermon in front of the Parliament on February, 1642.

> none shall dare to seek a Dominion over others, neither shall any dare to kill another, nor desire more of the Earth then another; for he that will rule over, imprison, oppresse, and kill his fellow Creatures, under what pretence soever, is a destroyer of the Creation, and an actor of the Curse, and walks contrary to the rule of righteousnesse: Do, as you would have others do to you; and love your Enemies, not in Words, but in actions.[179]

This long quotation from the treatise exemplifies a great sensitivity to wickedness and iniquity of the present world (anti-cosmism) that was absent at the beginning of history (tripartition of history). Property should be abolished in order to establish justice on earth (immanent *eschaton*) as it was in the beginning (golden age). The Diggers represent a significant experience, for they are the paradigm of how much the Revolution stirred up new (and gnostic) sentiments among society.

The Puritan attempt "to reorder the political affairs of an entire nation, while simultaneously reforming the consciousness of its citizens"[180] miserably failed. The Restoration made people forget the experiment. Nevertheless, in the Puritan experience "there is already indicated the historical line along which gnostic politics will shift from Christian symbolic language to the anti-Christian symbolism of Marxism."[181]

2.2.3 *The French Revolution and the true Jacobin spirit*

At a certain moment in Western history, the paradigm of revolutionary Gnosticism shifted from a religious dress to a secular, even anti-religious, outlook. "With the French Revolution", Orsini writes, "the idea of rebellion broke away from its religious origin."[182] Modernity (with capital "M") violently broke the political life, shaking a nation and an entire continent.

The opening of the Estates-General at Versailles (May 5, 1789) represents the first chapter of a great transformation in Western civilization. The three estates (clergy, nobility and commoners) gathered to discuss the serious issue of the state deficit. On June 17, the deputies of the Third Estate declared the National Assembly, and on July 9, after the nobility and clergy joined the Third Estate, the National Assembly became the National Constituent Assembly: the legislative power moved from the king to the Assembly. When

179 Gerrard Winstanley and the Diggers, 'The True Levellers Standard Advanced', retrieved by https://scholarsbank.uoregon.edu/xmlui/handle/1794/863 (accessed May 19, 2017).
180 David Hawked, *Ideology* (London: Routledge, 1996), p. 33.
181 Voegelin, 'Gnostic Politics', p. 226.
182 Orsini, *Anatomy of the Red Brigades*, p. 170.

the famous Storming of the Bastille took place (July 14), the situation of the entire country was tense and now irreversible. The Constituent Assembly itself approved many laws that overthrew the ancient regime, especially the abolition of feudal rights and privileges of the nobility. During the month of August, freedom of speech and freedom of religion were enforced, and King Louis XVI lost his effective power. The most notable fact of the first stage of the Revolution was the drafting of the Declaration of the Rights of Man and of the Citizen (August 27), which announced the reign of reason, liberty, equality and fraternity. However, the new situation paralyzed the whole of France, and unemployment exasperated the citizens, especially the working class. The Revolution passed into a new radical phase when thousands of women marched on Versailles and invaded the royal palace (October 5). To quiet things down, the bishop of Autun, Charles-Maurice de Talleyrand-Périgord, proposed to place property of the Church at the disposition of the State: the proposal was incredibly intrepid, for at that time the Church was the largest economic power of the nation. The Assembly approved this motion on November 2 – it was the first strong symbolic act against religion. Religious vows were abolished and on February 13, 1790, all contemplative religious orders were dissolved. On July 12, the Assembly voted the Civil Constitution of the Clergy: it was a law that subordinated the Catholic Church in France to the French government, and that commanded the new bishops to be now elected by the people of France and no longer by the Pope. It was an attempt to weaken the still strong clergy and to create an episcopate that was devoted to the Revolution only. But this muscular initiative, which was patently and paradoxically in contrast with the principles of the Declaration, was the straw that broke the camel's back: the King refused to approve the Civil Constitution of the Clergy. The press fiercely criticized the king, and the latter was finally forced to promulgate the law. The Catholic community of the country abstained from participating in any further political initiative. The church in Paris dedicated to St. Genevieve – not yet consecrated – was then transformed into the Panthéon, a mausoleum for the most notable Frenchmen of history. The first to be buried inside the building was the Count of Mirabeau, a former president of the National Constituent Assembly – on July 11, 1791, the ashes of Voltaire were transferred into the building, too. On September 14, the king accepted the new Constitution, and the National Constituent Assembly became the new Legislative Assembly. The deputies of the Assembly counted 745 people. On January 1792, Prussia and Austria decided to invade France in order to defend the monarchy, while the economic crisis worsened: the situation was precarious, and the Assembly decided to suspend the authority of the king, eventually electing a new government, the Convention, which took the place of the king and created the Revolutionary Tribunal. In this period, many people were arrested, accused of being enemies of the Revolution. On September 21, the Convention voted for the abolition of the monarchy and the creation of the First French Republic, and on December 3, Robespierre, leader of the Jacobin club, publicly asked the king to be put to death – the accusation against the king was vague and ambiguous, for it blamed the king of having threatened the liberty of the nation. King Louis XVI was beheaded on January 21, 1793. Now at war with England, the Dutch Republic, Belgium and Spain, and experiencing a strong domestic rebellion in the Vendée, the Convention strengthened inner surveillance, and arrests of suspects increased in number. On April 6, the Convention voted for the creation of the Committee of Public Safety, which had the function of supervising the ministers and of deciding interior and exterior defense measures. Because of inner pressures, on June 2 the Convention arrested 29 Girondins deputies, the moderate wing of the Convention: now it was the turn of the radical side of the revolutionaries, namely, the Jacobins, to be fully in charge. Even though a new Constitution was quickly issued in those troubled days, the Jacobins asked for the postponement of the acceptance of it because of the war. The murder of Jean-Paul Marat (July 13) made Robespierre head of the Jacobins. On September 17, the Law of Suspects was voted and the Reign of Terror started. Capital executions were many. One month later, on October 16, Marie-Antoinette was guillotined and two weeks later 22 Girondins deputies were executed. Within a few weeks, the same leaders of the Revolution, Jacques-René Hébert and Georges Jacques Danton, were killed, and Maximilien Robespierre became the effective leader of France (April 5, 1794). In the beginning, he was very popular among all factions, but his success was not to last long. According to historical bulletins, the executions and unjustified arrests tripled. On June 8, Robespierre officially established the Cult of the Supreme Being, a secular deism aimed at replacing Catholicism. The extensive use of inner terrorism (the Terror) was too much for the French population and even for the deputies of the Convention. On 27 July, the Convention voted to arrest Robespierre, and the day after Robespierre was guillotined (Thermidorian Reaction) – a more moderate politics was enforced thereafter.

This short synopsis of the French Revolution is indispensable for a correct overview of the Jacobin phenomenon, or rather, the first secular version of revolutionary Gnosticism. The Jacobin coup inaugurated the idea of a transfiguration of human nature through a violent and total revolution. Such revolution was

> founded on an ethic premise, i.e., the *ab imis* transformation of humankind and society, following the utopian project of regeneration to be achieved with an incessant revolutionary, pedagogic and institutional action [...] until an abstractly egalitarian and palingenetic regime would take place, a regime where all oppositions and divergences are demonized and deemed as the absolute evil.[183]

The two gnostic elements of political-revolutionary self-redemption and of sociological dualism are both present in this very first description of the Jacobin mission.

The sociologist Guglielmo Ferrero is adamant that in reality two different French revolutions occurred, a constructive and a destructive revolution. The first revolution started in the year 1789 and ended in 1793: it was guided by the Enlightened ideals of reason, human rights, freedom and dignity. The second revolution was characterized by the Terror, and it was represented by the Jacobin despotism under Robespierre's leadership. This second revolution is "the total negation of the right to oppose and it led to the demolition of all political freedoms."[184]

Ferrero distinguishes two meanings of the word "revolution": the first is "a new orientation of the human spirit [... and the second is] the overturning of an old legality [set of rules]."[185] These two revolutionary forms could even occur separately. The Jacobin experiment embodies the revolution that aims at changing the human spirit by violently enforcing laws and norms in accordance with a meta-political and metaphysical "virtue". As Robespierre said,

> if the mainspring of popular government in peacetime is virtue, the mainspring of popular government in revolution is virtue and terror both: virtue, without which terror is disastrous; terror, without which virtue is powerless. Terror is nothing but prompt, severe, inflexible justice; it is therefore an emanation of virtue; it is not so much a specific principle as a consequence of the general principle of democracy applied to the homeland's most pressing needs.[186]

---

183 Emanuele Pagano, 'Giacobinismo', in *Enciclopedia Filosofica*, vol. 7 (Milano: Bompiani, 2010), pp. 4711-4712.

184 Guglielmo Ferrero, *Le due rivoluzioni francesi* (1986; repr., Soveria Mannelli: Rubbettino, 2013), p. 121.

185 Ibid., p. 9.

186 Maximilien Robespierre, 'On the Principles of Political Morality that Should Guide the National Convention in the Domestic Administration of the Republic. 5 February 1794', in *Virtue and Terror*, by Maximilien Robespierre (London: Verso, 2017), chap. 14, Apple Books.

The Slovenian thinker Slavoj Zizek speaks of "divine violence", an expression coined by Walter Benjamin and which Zizek explains in terms of "*fiat iustitia, pereat mundus*: it is justice, the point of non-distinction between justice and vengeance, in which the 'people' (the anonymous part of no-part) imposes its terror and makes other parts pay the price – the Judgement Day for the long history of oppression, exploitation, suffering."[187] A similar violence "is the highest form of clemency"[188] in the eyes of the executioners, for evil is finally being eradicated from the world, and therefore the succeeding social order, as well as the following human nature, will be purified and perfected – or, in another but more familiar word, virtuous. Robespierre had in mind a "metapolitical conception of revolution: this was *the* apocalyptic event, both terrible and sublime, that would put an end to an age of lies and corruption."[189] The radical change of reality was the underlying project of the Terror.

The idea of virtue is illustrative of the gnostic character of the Jacobin revolution. Such an idea "had a range of derivations, mingling classical republicanism, natural virtues, religious thought, and the theme of self-sacrifice for the public good."[190] Basically, being virtuous meant that "one was ready to put the public good before any other consideration"[191] – one's own self-interest should be silenced to make the public side of life total and totalizing. In Robespierre's own words:

> I said, virtue! It is a natural passion, no doubt about it; but how would they know it, those venal souls who only ever open themselves to cowardly and ferocious passions; those miserable schemers who never linked patriotism with any moral idea, who marched in the Revolution behind some important and ambitious character, behind I know not what despised prince, like our lackeys in times past in the footsteps of their masters? But there do exist, I can assure you, souls that are feeling and pure; it exists, that tender, imperious and irresistible passion, the torment and delight of magnanimous hearts; that deep horror of tyranny, that compassionate zeal for the oppressed, that sacred love for the homeland, that even more sublime and holy love for humanity, without which a great revolution is just a noisy crime that destroys another crime; it does exist, that generous ambition to establish here on earth the world's first republic. That selfishness of men who are not debased, which finds a celestial delight in the

187 Slavoj Zizek, 'Robespierre, or the "Divine Violence" of Terror', in *Virtue and Terror*, by Maximilien Robespierre, (London: Verso, 2007), p. XI.

188 Ibid., p. VIII.

189 Pellicani, *Revolutionary Apocalypse*, p. 33.

190 Marisa Linton, 'The Choices of Maximilien Robespierre', *H-France Salon*, vol. 7, Issue 14 (2015): p. 3.

191 Ibid.

> calm of a clear conscience and the ravishing spectacle of public happiness, you can feel it at this moment burning in your souls; I feel it in mine.[192]

The Jacobin virtue, Vittorio Mathieu writes, is precisely the "action of the universal,"[193] from which it derives the "guilt of the individual will."[194] A similar abstract universal is a secularized and depersonalized god whose will is embodied by the virtuous men. The universal is good, while the particular – the individual will – is bad. Therefore, "the Jacobins justify their extreme procedures due to their belief that they are acting in the true interest of the populace, but the people resist because they do not understand their own interests."[195] This attitude is typical of the gnostic savior who *knows* what is better for the whole humanity. History is approaching its end, thus the universal should finally appear in all its glory even with the use of violence. Robespierre utters: "The revolution's government is the despotism of liberty over tyranny."[196]

But before the apocalyptic time becomes reality, the Jacobins need "*to purge* all of the corrupt elements of society in order to begin anew."[197] Purification is the means by which gnostic militants redeem the world – *violent* purification, of course. The annihilation of the so-called "enemies of liberty" (or "enemies of the Revolution" or "the people's enemies" or "enemies of humanity")[198] is as urgent as the spreading of the new ideas and philosophies.

Speaking of philosophy, the fundamental theoretical reference of the Revolution is Jean-Jacques Rousseau, whose "ideal of the return of man to the state of nature"[199] could be intended as the guideline of the whole Jacobin action. Mathieu calls Rousseau "Robespierre's theoretical godfather:"[200] in fact, Rousseau's "general will" is the source of any virtue.

---

192 Maximilien Robespierre, 'Extracts from Speech of 8 Thermidor Year II. 26 July 1794', in *Virtue and Terror*, by Maximilien Robespierre (London: Verso, 2017), Apple Books.

193 Vittorio Mathieu, *Cancro in Occidente. Le rovine del giacobinismo* (Milano: Editoriale Nuova, 1980), p. 37.

194 Ibid., p. 38.

195 Allison M. Tanner, 'From Fraternity to Fratricide. Why the Jacobin Vision of Utopia Degenerated Into the Terror', *Athene Noctua*, no. 1 (Spring 2013): p. 4.

196 Robespierre, 'On the Principles of Political Morality', chap. 14.

197 Tanner, 'From Fraternity to Fratricide', 5. Emphasis added.

198 All these names have been used by Robespierre in several speeches.

199 Armando Plebe and Pietro Emanuele, *Storia del pensiero occidentale*, vol. 2 (Rome: Armando Editore, 1989), p. 220.

200 Mathieu, *Cancro in Occidente*, 44. Robert Nisbet says that "what we know for a fact is that such Jacobins as Robespierre and Saint-Just, at the height of the

The general will "isn't inferred from individual wills: on the contrary, it is primal, and it's not the product of some kind of conventional procedure. If similar procedures (e.g., parliamentary procedures) are needed, it's only *to reveal* [the general will] and not to shape it."[201] Mathieu uses a term that was already adopted by Voegelin in his study on political religions, that is, the mystical body (*corpus mysticum*): the general will is the spirit of the mystical body that is the Whole, and only few people understand what the Whole is saying – and when the Whole is listened to, it demands to be revealed to everyone. Consequently, the listeners (the gnostics) must convey the message to humankind and translate into facts the norms and precepts that they now *know*. Sometimes it could happen that the Whole "reveals itself to one prophet only, for example Robespierre,"[202] or, the Voegelian "Paraclete". But it should be clear that what the Paraclete does and says does not come from himself/herself but from the Whole, from the universal.

Interestingly, the Whole is no longer God as it was, for instance, among the Puritans. Now the (metaphysical) principle is entirely immanent – after all, self-redemption should have inevitably brought sooner or later to a break with the religious worldview.[203]

Rousseau was a proto-communist and insisted on the mutability (*perfectibilité*) of human nature, resembling Sartre's principle: "existence precedes essence."[204] The fading of the transcendent notion of human nature led Rousseau to theorize a historically determined human nature. "The notion of human nature is entirely dissolved within the notion of historicity,"[205] and contingent facts are the elements that shape humankind's identity and existential condition. In other terms, it is the external world that forms (and deformes) our consciousness, he believes. Hence, the beatific

---

Revolution, read Rousseau devotedly and regularly" (*Conservatism: Dream and Realty* [London: Routledge, 2002], p. 26).

201 Mathieu, *Cancro in Occidente*, p. 40.

202 Ibid., p. 41.

203 The meta-political Revolution, namely, the gnostic revolution, makes "a correlation between the elevation of politics to religion, on the one hand, and the negation of the supernatural, on the other hand" (Augusto Del Noce, 'Riflessioni sull'opzione ateistica', in *Il problema dell'ateismo*, by Augusto Del Noce [Bologna: Il Mulino, 2010], p. 362).

204 Jean-Paul Sartre, *Existentialism Is a Humanism* (1946; repr., New Haven: Yale University Press, 2007), p. 22.

205 Maria Moneti, 'Dalla storia provvidenziale alla filosofia della storia. Il Settecento francese', in *Prospettive di filosofia della storia*, ed. by Roberto Mordacci (Milano: Bruno Mondadori, 2009), p. 91.

condition of the state of nature, a state that precedes morality itself, went corrupted by the same course of history (first of all due to the introduction of private property and the division of labor).

History is a progressive barbarization, but it is also a process susceptible to change – indeed, the problem of theodicy is transferred to an immanent, empirical and historical level ("exteriority of evil,")[206] so that "the guilt of society [i.e., the origin of evil] is not a guilt within the essence of humankind [e.g., the original sin] but lies in its [social] relations."[207] To change such social structures and collective institutions would mean to alter human nature as well. And thus, humankind does have the power to operate for the transformation of its own essence.

Well, the possibility of altering the structure of social organization in order to start anew was one of the theoretical premises of the Jacobins, but their "error was to have assumed that Rousseau's 'state of nature' was an empirically attainable condition. [...] Rousseau says that people are by nature equal, and the revolutionaries are thereby led to assert something that is manifestly empirically not the case – that all men are equal *here and now*."[208]

The gnostic elements concerning the tripartition of history and the immanentization of the *eschaton* are both present in the Jacobin revolutionary ideology: the advent of a new era for all humanity and the emancipation from the alienating factors of the present aeon are on the Jacobin agenda. To bring about a time when humankind would be virtuous and freed from the inauspicious conditionings of history: this is the final goal of the Jacobin revolutionary attempt. "We want to fulfill Nature's desires, accomplish the destiny of humanity, keep the promises of philosophy, absolve Providence from the long reign of crime and tyranny:"[209] these are the words Robespierre proclaimed on February 5, 1794.

---

206 Roberto Gatti, *Filosofia politica* (Brescia: Editrice La Scuola, 2011), p. 129.

207 Roberto Gatti, '"*Nul N'Est Parfait Ici-Bas'*: Rousseau gnostico post-cristiano?', in *Gli arconti di questo mondo. Gnosi: politica e diritto*, eds. Claudio Bonvecchio and Teresa Tonchia (Trieste: EUT, 2000), p. 193. Augusto Del Noce comments Rousseau's political philosophy as following: "Religious liberation is replaced by political liberation: only the social contract can give virtue back to man. The problem of evil is transposed from the psychological and theological level to the political and sociological level: the dogmas of Fall and Redemption are transferred to the level of historical experience" ('Riflessioni sull'opzione ateistica', p. 364).

208 Hawkes, *Ideology*, p. 52.

209 Maximilien Robespierre, 'Sui principi di morale pubblica. 5 febbraio 1794', in *Il terrore e la rivoluzione giacobina*, by Maximilien Robespierre (Milano: PGreco Edizioni, 2012), Kindle.

Various authors have recognized the Jacobin legacy in several disruptive experiences of Western history, as if many revolutionaries have taken the cue from Robespierre. The sociologist Shmuel N. Eisenstadt defines the Jacobin tendency in terms of a "faith in the transformation of society by means of a totalitarian political action,"[210] and is certain that "none of the modern liberal democracies has been able to completely dismantle its Jacobin components nor its utopian dimension."[211] The Jacobin components are "totalizing orientations which deny the legitimacy of private interests and of different conceptions of the common good and which emphasize the totalistic reconstruction of society through political actions."[212] The Jacobin "salvationist vision"[213] is in common with Communism (the Jacobin legacy is "evident […] in the political structures established by the Bolshevik revolutionaries after 1917.")[214]

Likewise, the German historian Ernst Nolte is sure that Jacobinism is a cultural and political principle characterized by a radical sociological dualism ("an ideology that sees in the enemies not human beings but harmful insects")[215] and a vocation for internationalism, i.e., the conquest of the world, or, in other words, the totalitarian attempt to change humanity *tout court*. Nolte maintains that Jacobinism has been personified by the Bolsheviks and radical Islamism too: "Islamism is to be considered as the Jacobinism of the 21st century; outside of it there is no phenomenon today that is likely to have a similar historical-planetary significance."[216]

In conclusion, let us read Luciano Pellicani's words on the issue of Jacobinism:

---

210 Shmuel N. Eisenstadt, *Fondamentalismo e modernità. Eterodossie, utopismo, giacobinismo nella costruzione dei movimenti fondamentalisti* (Roma-Bari: Laterza, 1994), p. 33.

211 Ibid., p. 44.

212 Shmuel N. Eisenstadt, *Fundamentalism, Sectarianism, and Revolution. The Jacobin Dimension of Modernity* (Cambridge: Cambridge University Press, 1999), p. 69.

213 Ibid., p. 111.

214 Andrew Levine, 'Two Theories of Revolutionary Government', in *Jean-Jacques Rousseau and the Revolution. Proceedings of the Montreal Symposium, 1989*: 85. See also Michel Vovelle, *I giacobini e il giacobinismo* (1998; repr., Roma-Bari: Laterza, 2009), pp. 122-134.

215 Ernst Nolte, 'I nuovi giacobinismi: da Robespierre a Bin Laden', http://www.liberalfondazione.it/archivio/numeri-speciali/748-i-nuovi-giacobinismi-da-robespierre-a-bin-laden (accessed February 2, 2018).

216 Ibid.

> Strictly speaking, the history of the revolutions of the twentieth century is simply a repeat of Jacobinism, the development of the project to create an identity between civil society and State, to unify by means of a dictatorship the elements constituting the State in an organic and broader sense (State as such and civil society) in a desperate attempt to control the life of the nation and the people.[217]

2.2.4 *The twentieth century: Bolshevism and Nazism*

The two incarnations of revolutionary Gnosticism in the 20th century are Bolshevik and Nazi totalitarianisms. Though in many ways opposed, "Marxian blood-intoxication belongs to the same symbolic type as the National Socialist mystique that permitted the man of the millennium to be formed by the chemistry of blood and soil."[218] Both are manifestations of the gnostic attitude towards existence, and both share the same gnostic *Weltanschauung*.

The interpretation of Marxian philosophy as a gnostic speculation is the insightful intuition of Eric Voegelin, who devoted many studies to the issue at hand.[219] "Marx is a speculative gnostic"[220] and a "Paraclete in the best style of Medieval sects:"[221] such is Voegelin's final verdict. Indeed, Marx knows the course of history – *he claims to know it* – resembling the gnostic attitude of those who discern the inner secret of reality. Marx is not tormented by the intolerable uncertainty of the obscure future: he is no longer at the mercy of fate or of an impenetrable divine Providence. Communism is "the solution of the riddle of history and knows itself to be the solution,"[222] states Marx himself.

The rejection of religion is consistent with the gnostic attitude. He writes that "the criticism of religion is the prerequisite of all criticism,"[223] and from a certain point of view he is right. In fact,

---

217 Pellicani, *Revolutionary Apocalypse*, p. 49.

218 Voegelin, 'Gnostic Politics', p. 233. Similarly, Norman Cohn writes: "The Communist and Nazi ideologies, though extremely different, owe a lot to the doctrinal body of popular apocalyptic tradition" (Cohn, conclusion to *I fanatici dell'Apocalisse*, p. 343).

219 See Michael Franz, 'Voegelin's Analysis of Marx', *Occasional Papers*, XVIII (August 2000).

220 Voegelin, 'Science, Politics and Gnosticism', p. 262.

221 Eric Voegelin, 'Marx: la genesi del socialismo gnostico', in *Dall'illuminismo alla rivoluzione*, by Eric Voegelin (Roma: Gangemi Editore, 2004), p. 303.

222 Karl Marx, 'Economic and Philosophical Manuscripts', in *Marx/Engels Internet Archive*, https://www.marxists.org/archive/marx/works/download/pdf/Economic-Philosophic-Manuscripts-1844.pdf (accessed November 10, 2018).

223 Karl Marx, 'Introduction to a Contribution to the Critique of Hegel's Philosophy of Right', in *Marx/Engels Internet Archive*, https://www.marxists.org/archive/

> the aim of parousiastic Gnosticism is to destroy the order of being, which is experienced as defective and unjust, and through man's creative power to replace it with a perfect and just order [e.g., the Communist society]. Now, however the order of being may be understood […] it remains something that is given, that is not under man's control. In order, therefore, that the attempt to create a new world may seem to make sense, the givenness of the order of being must be obliterated; the order of being must be interpreted, rather, as essentially under man's control. And taking control of being further requires that the transcendent origin of being be obliterated: it requires the decapitation of being – the murder of God.[224]

That said, Marxian atheism is the final complete unfolding of the inner logic of the gnostic element of self-redemption: if humankind saves itself, then God is unnecessary and even an obstacle for the demiurgic and Promethean project of reshaping reality.

Talking about Marx's *Capital*, Karl Löwith writes that "all history is absorbed into an economic process moving toward a final world revolution and world renovation."[225] The Marxian division of history (a sinful capitalist prehistory and a joyful post-capitalist history) follows the gnostic tripartition of time: a golden age (*Urkommunismus*, or primitive communism), the fall (the present age) and a rising future (the final communist society). The passage from the realm of necessity to that of freedom suggests the end of alienation and the advent of emancipation from what is deemed to be the modern transposition of ancient fate, namely, the capitalistic mode of production. The *Communist Manifesto* (1848) is "scientifically relevant in its particular contents, eschatological in its framework, and prophetic in its attitude,"[226] writes Löwith – even Hans Kelsen is aware of this ambiguity, for he underlines the "tragic methodological syncretism"[227] in the Marxist discourse, i.e.,

---

marx/works/download/Marx_Critique_of_Hegels_Philosophy_of_Right.pdf (accessed November 16, 2018). It is not by chance that Marx's mythological reference figure is Prometheus. In his doctoral dissertation of 1840-41, Marx writes: "The proclamation of Prometheus – 'in a word, I detest all the Gods' – is his own profession, his own slogan against all the gods of heaven and earth who do not recognize man's self-consciousness as the highest divinity. There shall be none other beside it. […] Prometheus is the foremost saint and martyr in the philosophical calendar" (Karl Marx, 'Doctoral Thesis', in *Karl Marx: Selected Writings, ed. by David McLellan* [Oxford: Oxford University Press, 2000], p. 17).

224 Voegelin, 'Science, Politics and Gnosticism', p. 278.

225 Karl Löwith, *Meaning in History* (Chicago: University of Chicago Press, 1949), p. 33.

226 Ibid., p. 38.

227 Hans Kelsen, *Socialismo e Stato* (Bari: Donato, 1978), p. 10.

the compresence of "two different conceptions of science: the Galilean positive science and the Hegelian dialectical science."[228]

According to such great design, the long-lasting battle between oppressed and oppressors, the proletariat and the bourgeoisie, is the only true and essential conflict in history: two are the hostile camps (sociological dualism), the character of which is fundamentally Manichaean, as Löwith highlights: "What makes them antagonistic is that the one class is the children of darkness and the other the children of light."[229] The final victory of the proletariat will lead to the establishment of a communist society, which "is not an institutional reform; it is, indeed, a change in the nature of man,"[230] since it represents the "obsolescence of the state and politics"[231] and requires the "appearance of the 'total individual', or – in other contexts – of 'socialistic man',"[232] a perfectly free being.

Read through the lenses of revolutionary Gnosticism, the Marxian philosophical system appears thus as a secular socio-political eschatology – Voegelin talks of a "intramundane mystical derailment."[233]

> It not only conceives salvation as immanent – similar to certain medieval millenarian sects which sought to establish the "Heavenly Kingdom" on earth by mean of violence; it promises that the proletariat will soon "transcend" nature, faith, and the moral law itself by undergoing the convulsions of class warfare, by passing through the door of revolutionary social upheaval.[234]

Following the speculation of Emanuele Samek Lodovici, it is also possible to state that the Marxian project seeks to transcend the same finitude of reality: "Marx is that *typos* of human being who rejects any limits and thus thinks in terms of a new aeon, the future aeon when all antagonisms will be passed and where man will be released from his finitude, and humanity will be perfect."[235] Hence, the gnostic aspiration for

---

228 Luciano Pellicani, October 10, 2018, personal email.

229 Löwith, *Meaning in History*, p. 44.

230 Eric Voegelin, 'The Formation of the Marxian Revolutionary Idea', *The Review of Politics*, vol. 12, no. 3 (July 1950): p. 294.

231 Giuseppe Bedeschi, *Introduzione a Marx* (Laterza: Roma-Bari, 2012), p. 206.

232 Voegelin, 'The Formation', p. 293.

233 Voegelin, 'Marx: la genesi del socialismo gnostico', p. 328.

234 Ronald Osborn, 'On the Path of Perpetual Revolution: From Marx's Millenarianism to Sendero Luminoso', *Totalitarian Movements and Political Religions*, vol. 8, no. 1 (March 2007): p. 119.

235 Samek Lodovici, *Metamorfosi della gnosi*, p. 106. The quotation continues as follows: "2nd-century gnostics suddenly overturned the way of thinking one of the most important classic concept, namely the idea of limit. Such concept turns from

the "total emancipation from finitude"[236] is the underlying goal of Marxism, a consideration that follows R.T. Allen's reflection on the lack of a concrete content of the notion of "alienation":

> It is no accident that Marx and the Marxists have failed to give a determinate content to "alienation" which could be empirically tested. For alienation is ultimately the metaphysical malady of being finite, determinate and differentiated, of being *this* and not *that*. And there cannot be any cure for that in this world and so there cannot be any empirical tests for detecting freedom from "alienation".[237]

In light of this peculiar analysis of Marx's thought, many scholars have studied the Bolsheviks as gnostic revolutionaries enlightened by a specific Gnosis, namely, the Marxian salvific knowledge. Their final aim was to create a new type of human being, foreseeing a perfect future where no evils or iniquities will further exist. As mentioned above, Norman Cohn stresses the line of continuity between Bolshevism and Nazism, on one side, and Medieval eschatological experiences, on the other – he talks of a "hidden continuity",[238] making Bolshevism a lineal descendant of radical Anabaptism and other disruptive groups in Western history.

In this regard, Michael Barkun is extremely clear in showing the continuity between Russian indigenous millenarian ideas and Marxian eschatological thinking: Marxism, he writes, was "implanted in a situation where salvationist visions were known and accepted responses to crisis. Thus a convergence occurred between Marxism and traditional Russian messianic expectations. [...] The rise of the Soviet regime, far from appearing as an importation, struck roots among a people habituated to chiliastic thought."[239] It was the "replacement of the Third Rome messianism with the Third Communist International messianism"[240] – the third stage of history is always believed to be the last and perfect one, in accord with the tripartition of history and with the imperative of reestablishing the gone golden age.

---

a positive sense (limit is what actualizes me, what perfects me in a closed wholeness) to a negative one (limit is what incarcerates me, what restricts me, what suffocates me)."

236 Ibid., p. 169.

237 R.T. Allen, "Flew, Marx and Gnosticism", *Philosophy*, vol. 68, no. 263 (January 1993): p. 94.

238 Cohn, preface to *I fanatici dell'Apocalisse*, p. 12.

239 Michael Barkun, 'Millenarianism in the Modern World', *Theory and Society*, vol. 1, no. 2 (Summer 1974): pp. 137-138.

240 Luciano Pellicani, October 10, 2018, personal email.

Yet, the multiple disasters experienced by Russia in the period preceding the October Revolution (November 7, 1917) (for example, the humiliating defeat in 1905 against Japan, inflation, food rationing, the inefficiency of the army as well as the multiples mutinies during World War I) functioned as fuel for the spreading of communism.

The radical break with the past, as well as the destruction of society to create a new way of life, was the motivating duty of the Promethean project of Lenin and Stalin. "The Bolsheviks believed the new world could come into being only after the destruction of the old"[241] – which is, by the way, a form of gnostic iconoclasm, that in turn is a result of anti-cosmism and tripartition of history. Mass executions and deportations, concentration camps and developed techniques of repression were the means by which the Bolsheviks created the condition for a new world. "Purification" was the operative word. Luciano Pellicani's description of Lenin's mentality is quite fascinating: "Humanity emerged as divided into three spiritual families: a minority of pneumatics (the professional revolutionaries who believed themselves to be the conscious avant-garde of the proletariat); the mass of psychics (the workers who could be redeemed despite the bourgeois deceit); and all the hylics, corrupted and corruptors, to be exterminated"[242] – such a sociological division, which is the traditional trisection of humanity made by some Late-Antique gnostic sects, only apparently contradicts the fundamental dualism between the pures and the impures, for the pneumatics and psychics are those who are destined to save the world and to be saved, whereas the hylics are doomed to die.

As Lenin himself writes in *What is to be done?* (1902), "There could not have been Social-Democratic consciousness among the workers. It would have to be brought to them from without."[243] The role of a revolutionary intelligentsia is thus necessary, since "a revolutionary consciousness is not an automatic consequence of belonging to the working class,"[244] instead requiring the gnostic pneumatics, or the enlightened élite that possesses the Gnosis and "whose aspiration was to sweep away the plutocratic bourgeoisie and create a new social hierarchy, based not on the hegemony of the 'haves' over the 'have-nots,' but on that of the 'knows' over the 'know-nots'."[245]

241 Gray, *Black Mass*, p. 75.
242 Luciano Pellicani, October 10, 2018, personal email.
243 Vladimir Lenin, 'What is to be done?', in *Essential Works of Lenin*, ed. by Henry M. Christman (New York: Dover Publications, 1966), Kindle.
244 Pellicani, *Revolutionary Apocalypse*, p. 100.
245 Ibid., p. 101.

In conclusion, Bolshevism was a devastating gnostic attempt to create an earthly Heaven by way of violence and repression. All the gnostic features are present: anticosmism (the actual world is evil and needs to be overthrown), tripartition of history, immanentization of the *eschaton* (the atheist character of Marxism forces to this), Gnosis (Marx's dialectical materialism), political-revolutionary self-redemption, and sociological dualism. In the gnostic dream of Lenin and Stalin,

> heaven became the classless society, providence and the holy spirit became the inevitable course of history. Marx became God the father who handed down the new commandments to Lenin. Lenin began as the new Moses and ended as new Messiah, virtually equivalent in authority to the Father. The Vanguard Party was the Church, and Stalin became its pope, vested with infallibility and surrounded by the Politburo which served as his College of Cardinals.[246]

Despite being in many ways different, Nazism follows the same guidelines of Bolshevism. Yet, the same cannot be said of Italian Fascism, as Umberto Eco highlights about the different approaches that guided Hitler and Mussolini:

> Nazism had a theory of racism and of the Aryan chosen people, a precise notion of degenerate art, *entartete Kunst*, a philosophy of the will to power and of the *Übermensch*. Nazism was decidedly anti-Christian and neo-pagan. […] Italian fascism was certainly a dictatorship, but it was not totally totalitarian, not because of its mildness but rather because of the philosophical weakness of its ideology. […] Mussolini did not have any philosophy: he had only rhetoric.[247]

In other terms, Italian Fascism was focused on gaining power and giving renewed glory to the Italian nation, but in reality, it "did not aim to remodel humanity"[248] nor was it meant to bring about the *eschaton* and to free humankind from all evils.[249] Mussolini had, so to speak, a provincial

---

246 Leslie Armour, 'Gnosticism, the Dream Economy and the Prospects for Communism', *International Journal of Social Economics*, vol. 21, issue 2/3/4 (1994): p. 37.

247 Umberto Eco, 'Ur-Fascism', *The New York Review of Books*, vol. 42, no. 11 (June 1995), https://www.nybooks.com/articles/1995/06/22/ur-fascism/. Eco adds also that "Fascism was philosophically out of joint, but emotionally it was firmly fastened to some archetypal foundation" (ibid.)

248 Gray, *Black Mass*, p. 55.

249 See Pellicani, *La società dei giusti*, pp. 583-585: "Mussolini's program has not any palingenetic energy. He is not a gnostic Paraclete. The idea of regeneration of humanity through the eradication of evil is alien to him."

attitude, and its range reached only Italy and its needs. The same Nazis were aware of this not so slight difference: as Hannah Arendt writes in *The Origins of Totalitarianism*, quoting from Goebbels and Himmler:

> Goebbels: "[Fascism] is […] nothing like National Socialism. While the latter goes deep down to the roots, Fascism is only a superficial thing". […] "[The Duce] is not a revolutionary like the Führer or Stalin. He is so bound to his own Italian people that he lacks the broad qualities of a worldwide revolutionary and insurrectionist". Himmler expressed the same opinion in a speech delivered in 1943 at a Conference of Commanding Officers: "Fascism and National Socialism are two fundamentally different things. […] There is absolutely no comparison between Fascism and National Socialism as spiritual, ideological movements".[250]

Nazi ideology can be considered as a "racist Gnosis"[251] whose aim was to restore the ancient and lost purity of the Aryan race, opposing all forms of decaying that were destroying Germany (the soil) and the Germans (the blood). The cause of degeneration was located in a population, the Jewish one, ideologically transformed into a Satanic force, into a metaphysic principle, the origin of Evil. According to Adolf Hitler, a people can thrive exclusively by becoming aware of its own race, "for a racially pure people which is conscious of its blood can never be enslaved by the Jew. In this world he will forever be master over bastards and bastards alone,"[252] writes Hitler.

The reach of Nazism is universal and total, like any other gnostic attempt to re-create the world and reshape human nature. In Ernst Nolte's words: "For Hitler, the struggle for renovation is not only a German provincial question. Since this battle is fought against an illness that afflicts the whole world, by its very nature it is universal in scope and cannot end until the power of the disease has been broken everywhere."[253] The effort to modeling human nature could not be confined within narrow national borders.

As early as 1934, Emmanuel Lévinas was aware of such a paradoxical universal character of Nazism. He initially wonders how it was possible to conjugate racism with universality. Then, he replies:

---

250 Hannah Arendt, *The Origins of Totalitarianism* (1953; repr., San Diego, New York and London: Harcourt Brace & Company, 1976), p. 309.

251 René Alleau, *Le origini occulte del nazismo* (Roma: Edizioni Mediterranee, 1996), p. 137.

252 Adolf Hitler, *Mein Kampf*, http://childrenofyhwh.com/multimedia/library/Hitler/mein-kampf.pdf (accessed 16 September, 2017).

253 Ernst Nolte, *I tre volti del fascismo* (1963; repr., Milano: Mondadori, 1971), p. 582.

> The answer – to be found in the logic of what first inspires racism – involves a basic modification of the very idea of universality. *Universality must give way to the idea of expansion*, for the expansion of a force presents a structure that is completely different from the propagation of an idea. [...] The universal order is not established as a consequence of ideological expansion; it is that very expansion that constitutes the unity of a world of masters and slaves. [...] Its own form of universalization [is] war and conquest.[254]

Nazi symbolism closely reproduces gnostic idiom: the Third Reich is the actual third stage of history that will inaugurate the restored golden age; the Jews serve as the final enemy to be annihilated; the millenarian conception of the world is the belief in a near radical change of the same structure of reality; the awareness of one's own race is the awakening Gnosis; the blemished present generates the anti-cosmic feeling that triggers the revolutionary action ("The present time and the recent past were evil beyond redemption. The one hope lay in a catastrophe – only after an all-destroying event could the German *Volk* ascend to a condition of mystical harmony.")[255]

By saying that "today I believe that I am acting in accordance with the will of the Almighty Creator: by defending myself against the Jew, I am fighting for the work of the Lord,"[256] Adolf Hitler was sure to be doing what had to be done in order to save the world and accomplish the imperative of the Nordic race[257] ("according to Rosenberg, the Aryan blood was the same substance of the divinity.")[258]

Alfred Rosenberg (1893-1946), famous theorist and known as the most influential ideologue of the Nazi party, wrote a celebrated work, *The Myth of the Twentieth Century*, which by 1944 sold more than a million copies. Amit Varshizky has argued that Rosenberg's work should be seen as a modern version of Gnosticism. Talking of a racial soul, or race-soul (*Rassenseele*), as the inner principle from which the physiological manifestations of

---

254 Emmanuel Lévinas, 'Reflections on the Philosophy of Hitlerism', *Critical Inquiry*, vol. 17, no. 1 (Autumn 1990): pp. 70-71.

255 Gray, *Black Mass*, p. 94.

256 Hitler, *Mein Kampf*.

257 Eric Voegelin explicitly calls Hitler a pneumpathic: "There is no point, as is still so often done, in accusing Hitler of inhumanity; it was absolute humanity in human form, only a most remarkably disordered, diseased humanity, a pneumopathological humanity" (Voegelin, *Hitler and the Germans*, p. 108). His construction of a second, or dream, reality is the condition of every gnostic, as he or she loses any connection with the mysterious foundation of the world and put himself/herself in that very place.

258 Cohn, conclusion to *I fanatici dell'Apocalisse*, p. 343.

the race emanate, Rosenberg could say that "soul means race seen from within. And, conversely, race is the external side of a soul."[259] Theorizing a metaphysics of race, Rosenberg describes a cosmic battle between two opposing principles "whose clash dictates the course of human history. On the one hand is the racial element, creator of cultures and affirmer of life, whose most prominent representative is the Nordic race; on the other hand, an anti-racial element, manifested by Judaism and the Catholic Church"[260] – the gnostic sociological dualism becomes here a theoretical principle based on a rigorous, though fantastic, philosophy. The unveiling of such dynamic is *per se* an act of redemption, and "the racial-soul, similar to the gnostic 'spark', reflects 'real life', 'reality' as it is, and acknowledging it shall release the Nordic man from the shackles of an oppressive and false reality."[261] The awakening of the Nordic racial awareness is a great indicator of the counter-attack of the racial cosmic principle against the anti-racial element. Here the self-redemption passes through the re-appropriation of one's own race and the subjugation of the others.

Another frightening but curious Nazi experience is the Ahnenerbe (ancestral heritage), a research organization founded by Heinrich Himmler in 1935. The Ahnenerbe was a sort of prehistoric research institute that functioned as a modern think tank, with almost fifty sections each of them working on a distinct project (geography, anthropology, musicology, ethnography, botanic, popular tradition studies, astronomy, magic...) Several were the renown scientists united there by the same purpose, i.e., "to set the future dominant culture of the new world order, with its interdisciplinary relations between the different branches of knowledge, giving a prominent place to the Germanic ancestral heritage."[262] In other terms, the Ahnenerbe meant to know everything about the origin and diffusion of Germanic culture and the Aryan spirit, and to recover ancient popular and cultural traditions, with the ultimate aim of reintegrating them

259 Alfred Rosenberg, *The Myth of the Twentieth Century*, http://www.nommeraadio.ee/meedia/pdf/RRS/Alfred%20Rosenberg%20-%20The%20Myth%20of%20the%2020th%20Century.pdf (accessed September 26, 2017).

260 Amit Varshizky, 'Alfred Rosenberg: The Nazi Weltanschauung as Modern Gnosis', *Politics, Religion & Ideology*, vol. 13, no. 3 (September 2012): p. 320. A little further on: "On the one end stands an Aryan racial element that embodies life, vitality and cultural generation, while at the opposite end stands an anti-racial, universal element that is identified with the negation of life, static dogmatism, chaos and cultural degeneration" (p. 321).

261 Ibid., p. 322.

262 Gianfranco Drioli, *Ahnenerbe. Appunti su scienza e magia del nazionalsocialismo* (Milan: Ritter Edizioni, 2011), p. 25.

in the organic cultural environment of the Third Reich. The Ahnenerbe organized many archaeological explorations in several places such as Tibet, Antarctica and Mongolia, trying to discover legendary places like Agartha and Shamballa. Functioning also as an esoteric initiatory order in some of its deeper sections, the Ahnenerbe "presupposed the revival, on a practical and ideological level of daily National Socialist life, of the mythical world of the Germanic ancestors."[263]

Therefore, Nazis adopted science as a valid means for implementing racial ideas and for insisting on the belief that there has been in a distant past a pure Aryan race that now should have been recovered and restored. The Ahnenerbe is a prime example of the gnostic soul of Nazism: the tripartition of history is here re-elaborated as a scientific datum; Gnosis is the scientific outcome of the collective research work; self-redemption is attained through the recovery of the ancestral heritage; the *eschaton* is actively reached thanks to the reintegration in the current German life of the traditional materials that the institute founds around the world; and lastly, sociological dualism is in the eternal fight against Jews, guilty of having organized the plot of "racial pollution."[264]

Emmanuel Lévinas has developed a very interesting perspective about the philosophy of freedom underlying the entire Nazi *Weltanschauung*. If Judaism and Christianity have delivered the salvific message of the liberation from the past thanks to the redemption "from *what has been*"[265] ("Once the choice is made, it does not form a chain"[266] because Christ through the Eucharist emancipates every day), Nazism starts a new anthropology, a new conception of humankind that is no longer founded over the notion of freedom but over the original enchainment to the body: "To be truly oneself does not mean taking flight once more above contingent events that always remain foreign to the Self's freedom; on the contrary, it means becoming aware of the ineluctable original chain that is unique to our bodies, and above all accepting this chaining."[267] Only in this way, that is, by accepting the original chain to one's own personal body, can a person become more and more himself or herself. It is like the gnostic *pneuma* but upside down: humankind must discover its true nature to accept it and reach salvation, with the difference that for Late-Antique Gnosticism humankind is only

263 Marco Dolcetta, *Nazionalsocialismo esoterico. Studi iniziatici e misticismo messianico nel regime hitleriano* (Roma: Cooper & Castelvecchi, 2003), p. 138.
264 Hitler, *Mein Kampf.*
265 Levinas, "Reflections", p. 66.
266 Ibid., p. 65.
267 Ibid., p. 69.

its divine soul, while for the Nazi gnostic *Weltanschauung* humankind is exclusively its earthly and racially classified body.

Lévinas's discourse is quite similar to Ernst Nolte's caveat that the Nazis are afraid of the intrinsic transcendence of humankind, which he defines as the force that gives dynamics to human life, and that drives humankind to *go beyond* and shape its environment: Nazism was "the empirical and brutal resistance against transcendence."[268] Revolutionary Gnosticism reaches here its higher, or lower, peak, the total and complete disappearance of the transcendent reference and even the hatred of it ("The Christian doctrine will be convicted of absurdity,"[269] said Hitler).

Conclusively, Bolshevism and Nazism are two equal gnostic attempts to redeem humanity with sole human forces. Both have a Gnosis, a diagnosis-therapy of human alienation, and both are engaged in implementing a cultural-political project for the redemption of all humankind. "Marx rejected faith and instead found certainty through his scientific discovery of the process of history; the Nazis, by contrast, found it in the scientific explanation of Race:"[270] in other terms, to use a Voegelian theoretical framework, both tried to escape from the uncertainty of existence, and both sought certainty within the temporal sphere of existence. And both perceived political society in soteriological terms and gave no space for the autonomous initiative of the individual, for it is the community that offers salvation.

Activist redemption is the (false) optimism that lies behind all the totalitarian initiatives of the 20th century. "To the Marxist *Weltanschauung*, centered on the deadly war between the classes, Hitler opposed a *Weltanschauung* centered on the deadly war between the races. But the stakes remained the same: the destiny of humanity."[271]

---

268 Nolte, *I tre volti del fascismo*, p. 587.

269 Adolf Hitler, quoted in Voegelin, *Hitler and the Germans*, p. 125.

270 Clifford F. Porter, 'Eric Voegelin on Nazi Political Extremism', *Journal of the History of Ideas*, vol. 63, no. 1 (January 2002): p. 167.

271 Pellicani, *La società dei giusti*, p. 606.

CHAPTER 3
RADICAL ISLAM:
SALAFISM AND JIHADISM

3.1 *Pioneering studies*

The adoption of revolutionary Gnosticism to illuminate the very nature of Salafi-Jihadism raises some problems. Firstly, revolutionary Gnosticism is a Western concept, and, secondly, it is indeed a very modern notion. However, revolutionary Gnosticism, as seen above, does provide a potent description for revolutionary phenomena of different epochs, and it is not therefore confined to modern West only.

Contrary to other kinds of classification, revolutionary Gnosticism does not provide a too strict and excessively narrow categorization: in fact, both behavioral and doctrinal indicators are taken into consideration, they being matters the philosophical analysis is built upon. Thanks to the six-points pattern discussed earlier, revolutionary Gnosticism does not ignore any factor involved in the Salafi-Jihadi worldview, nor the strategic thinking of the militants nor their ideologization of the theological sphere nor the sociological ground in which Salafi-Jihadism happened to grew out of – actually, the latter point is quite relevant considering that the story of revolutionary Gnosticism is contiguous to the larger issue of secularization, as we have tried to clarify above.

Lastly, for the issue at hand the concept of revolutionary Gnosticism does not require a previous religious investigation into the early links between Islam and Late-Antique Gnosis, as many could mistakenly suppose. The definition of revolutionary Gnosticism as a mentality, a worldview, makes it a fully viable epistemological instrument through which one could scrutinize political experiences without bringing ancient times into the analysis. As such, revolutionary Gnosticism is independent from its original matrix insomuch as it does not need a constant reference to ancient gnostic sects. Rather, once the connection between revolutionary Gnosticism and the religiously-defined Gnosis is clear (in the way we have done in the previous chapter), it is no longer necessary to bring it into play. The lenses provided by revolutionary Gnosticism are thus rendered analytically objective and scientifically valid, making it a notion applicable to all kinds of experiences regardless if they are originally Western or belong to other geographical and cultural contexts.

Succeeding in understanding Salafi-Jihadi ideology in terms of a gnostic ideological construction would result in an unexpected achievement, namely, the assertion that such ideology, famous for being indisputable religious, is actually a profoundly secular and modern creation. Even though the jihadis claim to fight the secular Western world, they are essentially the worst part of it. In this sense, as I will argue in the following sections, "there is no clash of civilizations, but rather a conflict within the same form of civilization,"[1] as Alberto Ventura maintains. The "radical praxism"[2] of Salafi-Jihadis is inversely proportional to their spiritual commitment and true devotion.

The attempt of framing Islamism through philosophical categories borrowed from Eric Voegelin is not new. In his book *New Political Religions, or An Analysis of Modern Terrorism* (2004), Barry Cooper uses the Voegelian concept of pneumopathology to present violent Islamism, focusing on Islamists' disordered spiritual dimension. Cooper makes extensive and cautious use of Voegelian vocabulary (pneumopathology, derailment, metastasis), succeeding in understanding violent Islamists as apocalyptic warriors in wait for the metastatic transfiguration of the world. Accordingly, they see themselves as true saviors allowed to make violence over people and over nature in order to magically transform reality. Cooper states that "terrorism is a mode of fabrication,"[3] an assertion that reveals the purifying approach at the bottom of the terrorist's claim, that is, the "*altruistic omnicide*."[4] Needless to say, the aim is a final peaceful state, the "metastatic peace, inasmuch as it requires a transformation of reality in order to be achieved."[5] A similar purpose is a product of what Voegelin calls "derailment", the imaginary merging of the Beyond with the immanent world. Following this pathological track, the same religiously-defined faith mutates into "an instrument of pragmatic political action."[6]

1 Alberto Ventura, 'Alle radici del fondamentalismo islamico', in *Il fondamentalismo islamico*, eds. Angelo Iacovella and Alberto Ventura (Roma: ISIAO, 2006), p. 35.
2 I thank professor Francesco Botturi for this insightful definition.
3 Barry Cooper, *New Political Religions, or An Analysis of Modern Terrorism* (Columbia and London: University of Missouri Press, 2004), p. 39.
4 Ibid., p. 68. The emphasis is mine.
5 Ibid., p. 58.
6 Ibid., p. 90.

Cooper maintains that the fall from faith, which is another Voegelian concept, is a phenomenon that exists not only in Western history: "The history of Islam, from the Kharijites to the Ikhwan, recapitulates a structurally similar fall from faith in response to a series of historical crises."[7] The two main examples Cooper gives are Ibn Taymiyya and Muḥammad ibn ʿAbd al-Wahhāb, both leading figures in confronting situations of political and social crisis. Osama bin Laden's "pneumopathological expectation of an ecumenic transfiguration of human life"[8] is the final outcome of a very long-lasting historical incubation that seeks the "enactment of apocalyptic scenarios on the plane of history, in real time, in the real world"[9] – which is the same as saying the immanentization of the *eschaton*.

Barry Cooper's analysis is thought-provoking, stimulating and pioneering, but it does not cite Gnosticism nor Voegelin's assumption that any pneumopathological actor is a gnostic militant.[10]

Another scholar who has adopted Voegelin's philosophy as a conceptual tool for tackling Islamist thought is Michael Franz. Appearing on the online platform VoegelinView, the document entitled *Caution and Clarity in Thinking About ISIS and Apocalyptic Activism* (2018) focuses on the apocalyptic fervor of the so-called Islamic State (ISIS or Dāʿish). Franz acknowledges that Barry Cooper's work is and remains "the 'state of art' in terms of applying analysis of pneumopathology to the beliefs and actions of terrorist killers."[11] Franz, then, takes a step further: while deploring university social sciences departments for reducing all religious phenomena to factors that are not related to spirituality[12], he strongly affirms that religiously-

7 Ibid., p. 108.

8 Ibid., p. 147.

9 Ibid., p. 57. Today the apocalyptic imagination is more likely to spread among Muslim masses than in the past. On page 114 Cooper writes: "The doctrine of Muslim supersession toward Judaism, the sentiment that no country that has become Muslim can ever revert to being non-Muslim, and the fact that Israeli control over Muslim holy places are issues on which Muslims cannot easily compromise, enhances the attractiveness of apocalyptic 'solutions' to what is for common sense merely a pragmatic political impasse".

10 Actually, Cooper does cite a Voegelin's passage where the German philosopher connects pneumpathology with the condition of gnostic thinkers (see ibid., p. 41), but he does not elaborate on that at all.

11 Michael Franz, 'Caution and Clarity in Thinking About ISIS and Apocalyptic Activism', *VoegelinView*, January 21, 2018, https://voegelinview.com/caution-clarity-thinking-isis-apocalyptic-activism/ (accessed March 12, 2018).

12 "Many of us who work in university social science departments, steeped in secularist biases thereby, are accustomed to hearing people explain away religious phenomena by any available means. [… This approach] certainly does irritate me

marked violent extremism is a form of pneumopathology. "Pathological spirituality is spiritual nonetheless,"[13] he says, and it cannot "be neutralized by administration of a psychoactive medication,"[14] which makes it a true spiritual problem that should be tackled with appropriate instruments.

After that, Michael Franz defines what "pneumopathology" means according to Eric Voegelin's definition: "Individuals with particularities of character and consciousness that make them unusually sensitive to inherent aspects of the human condition (especially uncertainty, imperfection and mortality) engage in revolt against that condition,"[15] he writes. Such a revolt against finitude, which is a peculiar feature of the gnostic *Weltanschauung*, regularly arises in the recurrent phenomenon of apocalypticism today embodied by Dāʿish. As a conclusion, Dāʿish is labeled by Franz as an "apocalyptic and spiritually disordered based organization."[16]

While Michael Franz's analysis is remarkable, it does not adopt the concept of Gnosticism to clarify the "inner logic" of Islamist violence.

The 2008 essay entitled *The Mind of Jihad* by Laurent Murawiec is an attempt to implement the very category of Gnosticism to Islamic issues – however, it is no more than a limp attempt. It lacks analytical rigor, proceeds with vague similarities and makes loose historical comparisons. Murawiec does not quote the literature on revolutionary Gnosticism, barely citing Eric Voegelin and mentioning Hans Jonas only twice, omitting all other relevant scholars. The same concept of Gnosticism is confusingly defined: he speaks of it as an "ideology,"[17] unjustifiably jumping from Late-Antique Gnosticism to revolutionary Gnosticism without making any distinction between the two. In the course of the discussion on ancient Gnosticism (according to which "the this-worldly 'life' is depreciated"[18] and "the afterlife becomes the sole purpose of life on earth,"[19] he writes)

---

as an instance of ideological closure against evidence regarding an important phenomenon" (ibid.)

13 Ibid. And further on: "The problem posed by most ISIS members (and most religiously motivated terrorists more generally) is not that they are in-authentically spiritual, but rather that their spirituality is disordered in character."

14 Ibid.

15 Ibid.

16 Ibid.

17 Laurent Murawiec, *The Mind of Jihad* (Cambridge University Press: Cambridge, 2008), p. 82.

18 Ibid., p. 60.

19 Ibid., p. 62. The author also draws a parallel with Ayatollah Khomeini, whose statements "betray a fundamental devaluation of this life, and conversely, an overvaluation of the afterlife" (ibid.)

he suddenly discusses "the activist variant of Gnosticism"[20] as if it were a regular branch of ancient gnostic cults – whereas, as we have seen, in reality that is not the case.

Then Murawiec continues to review esotericism within Islam, surreptitiously drawing a parallel between ancient Gnosticism, revolutionary Gnosticism and esoteric tendencies. In his words:

> Islam truly is burdened by a heavy Gnostic content, inherited from the legacies of Persian-Zoroastrian and Manichean religions, from other ancient Middle Eastern mystery religions, from Jewish and Christian apocalyptic religions, and from heresies that preexisted or developed under Byzantine Christianity, itself often gnostically inclined. [...] A history of Islam cannot be told without examining the repeated blossoming of Gnostic sects within and around it.[21]

The author draws, or at least sketches, a genealogical derivation of gnostic tendencies within contemporary Islam to Late-Antique gnostic cults and sects, but he does not prove it with historical evidence other than declarations of principle.[22] Finally, in Murawiec's reconstruction, the contemporary Islamic groups that are "contaminated" by the gnostic spirit are so many that the reader soon get lost: Palestine Liberation Organization (PLO), the secular Arab socialist Ba'th Party, Wahhabism, the Muslim Brotherhood, Ayatollah Khomeini, the former President of Pakistan Muḥammad Zia ul-Haq (1924-1988), the Iranian revolutionary ideologue ʿAlī Sharīʿatī (1933-1977), the Algerian National Liberation Front, the Indian-Pakistani thinker Abū l-Aʿlāʾ al-Mawdūdī, as well as al-Qāʿida. Even the Islamic phenomenon of Mahdism (which will be dealt with subsequently in this book) is considered by Murawiec to be a gnostic manifestation, marked as a "Gnostic-eschatological expectation"[23].

In short, the problem with Laurent Murawiec's *The Mind of Jihad* is the vagueness of the terms involved. The impression one has after reading it is that the author ends up identifying not only (a very broad) radical Islam but Islam *tout court*[24] with a vague Gnosticism that inconsistently oscillates

---

20 Ibid., p. 85.

21 Ibid., pp. 90-91.

22 On the contrary, as I said earlier, I think we should speak of phenomenological affinities rather than genetic derivations, following Giovanni Filoramo's distinction between the awakening of Gnosis and the return of Gnosis, and Eric Voegelin's stress of sentiments and attitudes.

23 Ibid, p. 277.

24 Laurent Murawiec betrays an essentialist vision on Islam and Muslims. For example, he writes: "The very concept of *dar al-Islam*, the abode of Islam, is

between, on the one hand, the devaluation of this-world in favor of an other-world and, on the other hand, a profound activism completely immersed in this-world – as a matter of fact, lacking to differentiate between ancient Gnosticism and revolutionary Gnosticism is problematic and leads to great confusion.

Let's move to a 2013 article by Lazaros Miliopoulos. The author insists on the early Voegelian category of political religions to expound the ideological claims of Islamism. He undertakes an original explanation of Sayyid Quṭb's speculation on the basis of the four features Voegelin claims to be common to every political religion, namely, hierarchy, *ecclesia*, the spiritual and the temporal, and apocalypse. According to Voegelin, these traditionally religious symbols have been transformed by 20th century political religions in political tools, and the political collectivism was converted in the ultimate and only reality (the *realissimum*, the paramount reality). What Miliopoulos wonders about is whether the political religions theory is transferable to Islam. After all, the symbol of *ecclesia*, the Church, seems not to exist in Islam as it does in Christianity. To overcome this very problem, Miliopoulos takes the collective body of Islam, the *umma* (community of believers), as the equivalent of the Christian Church.

Starting from the symbol of the apocalypse, Miliopoulos recognizes it in the inner-worldly promise of salvation promoted by Islamist groups. Such fully empirical promise was for the first time openly affirmed by Sayyid Quṭb in his *Ma'ālim fī aṭ-Ṭarīq* ("Milestones"), a book that is universally judged as the handbook of all contemporary Islamist violent groups. The present state of *jāhiliyya*, or "age of ignorance", demands from humankind a strong and energetic action in defense of the Truth. Therefore, "by sacrificing their own lives, the conviction of the suicide bombers within al Qaeda is to 'participate' in both the Apocalypse as well as in the Islamic world order. There is no distinction anymore between world transcendence and world immanence."[25] In fact, Miliopoulos says, evil becomes wholly

perilously close to being in itself a Gnostic concept" (Murawiec, *The Mind of Jihad*, p. 92), just adding a page after that "the division between an *umma* – the 'Islamic nation' – and the rest of the world is of the same nature as the Gnostic division between the Elect (the Perfects) and the mass of mankind" (ibid., p. 93). This statement is nonsensical for the very fact that, if it made any sense, then even the Catholic Church could be considered gnostic because it establishes an in-group (the believers) and an out-group; and, for that matter, all religions could be deemed gnostic as well.

25 Lazaros Miliopoulos, 'The Revolutionary Global Islamism – Politicized or Political Religion? Applying Eric Voegelin's Theory to the Dynamics of Political Islam', *Religion Compass* 7, no. 4 (2013): p. 132.

reduced to the *jāhiliyya*, and the *jāhiliyya* is a historical phase – which leads to the inevitable conclusion that evil can be expelled from the earth relying solely on material means and along a temporal line.

With regard to the elements of hierarchy and *ecclesia*, Miliopoulos finds out that "by emphasizing the *umma* and its moral superiority in simultaneous discrimination of all those who are not Muslim, the highest form of reality (the *realissimum*) is practically moved into the earthly, inner-worldly existence."[26] The *umma* itself becomes the final goal of Islamist action. And even the distinction between the spiritual and the temporal – not to be confused with the evangelical "Render unto Caesar the things that are Caesar's, and unto God the things that are God's", indicating instead the constitutive tension between the two dimensions – is present in the Islamist narrative: "[Quṭb] degrades the spiritual struggle of every individual believer to a purely earthly battle between believers and nonbelievers. This focus on the earthly-immanent fight neglected the transcendent substance of the conventional religiosity beyond recognition."[27] The inevitable conclusion of Miliopoulos's research is that "revolutionary Islamists in theory only apparently situate God in the source of all power. Actually they are filling this source with natural contents of this world."[28]

Again, even Lazaros Miliopoulos omits Gnosticism from his curious and quite original analysis.

Another academic to have adopted Voegelin's perspective to deal with Islamism is Hendrik Hansen, in whose short essay (2009) he has tried to figure out whether Islamism is a political religion in Voegelin's sense or whether it is a politicized religion, the former being a pure immanent ideology and the latter an ideology formulated on the basis of religious design. His answer is that the concept of political religion is more useful provided that the gnostic perspective is acknowledged. In fact, two elements define political religions: "The political idea of a radicalization of the friend-foe distinction meets the religious idea of purging the earth of evilness by annihilating the enemy. This is the core of political religions, and in this respect revolutionary Islamism is a political religion."[29] Indeed, if on a truly religious level purgation is the purging of one one's sins, on a

26 Ibid.
27 Ibid., p. 133.
28 Ibid., p. 135.
29 Hendrik Hansen, 'Islamism and Western Political Religions', *Religion Compass* 3, no. 6 (2009): p. 1037.

political-religious level it becomes a collective task, ending up as being a synonym for the same politics.

Hansen closes his article with the following consideration:

> Whether one purges the earth of evil in the name of the socialist paradise (Lenin), of 'providence' (Hitler) or of Allah (Al-Banna and Qutb) certainly makes a difference in the analysis of the historical development of these ideologies, but it is not a key distinction. And one could question if a religion that is used to justify a purely earthly struggle between good and evil (as Islam is used by revolutionary Islamism) has not been turned into a secular religion, even if it still claims to be oriented towards a transcendent God.[30]

Quite interestingly, Hendrik Hansen introduces Gnosticism for the explanation of Islamism, and the notion of purgation stands out like a brave attempt to link gnostic features to the worldview of Islamist militants. However, the explicatory strength of Gnosticism has not fully come to light, and further researches are needed.

Another pioneering study that uses the notion of Gnosticism to describe a contemporary Arab political formation is an article written by Mordechai Nisan and entitled "PLO Messianism: Diagnosis of a Modern Gnostic Sect." (1984).[31] It is an ambiguous and equivocal study, indeed. It contains some thought-provoking ideas, but its analysis is limited and the case study is not in focus. The author refers to Hans Jonas only, quoting Eric Voegelin just once. His intent is quite polemical: apart from describing all Arabs as irrational, barbaric and deeply emotional[32], which is a clear sign of essentialism, Nisan's goal is to delegitimize the Palestine Liberation Organization's (PLO) objectives, and even presenting Israel's struggle against the PLO in Lebanon "the assertion of a natural force favoring equilibrium, as a principle of order arises to overcome disorder and reestablish balance in the political universe."[33]

---

30 Ibid., p. 1038.

31 Mordechai Nisan, 'PLO Messianism: Diagnosis of a Modern Gnostic Sect', *Terrorism: An International Journal*, vol. 7, no. 3 (1984).

32 "The Arabs continue to struggle with a deep cultural ailment that so-called 'progress' cannot cure" (ibid., p. 300); "The deeper, emotional, and surrealistic mental convolutions of the East are hardly understood, and often not even noticed" (ibid., p. 301); "The Arabs have 'a love of myths' in the way in which they abandon realism and rationality when involved in politics" (ibid., p. 310).

33 Ibid., p. 311.

Written before the establishment of Ḥamās in 1987, the article accuses the PLO of being a gnostic sect. It describes the PLO's view of history as a mythological narration about a pre-Israel Palestine, a sort of primordial Garden of Eden that was broken by the arrival of the Zionists, Satanic forces that embody Darkness itself. The Israeli-Palestinian conflict, thus, takes on the guise of a cosmic war with apocalyptic tones. The "helplessness of the present condition"[34] mirrors the anti-cosmic attitude of gnostic narratives, and the PLO's methods of waging war echoes the gnostic "antinomian strain. [...] No ethical standard limits the PLO method that includes bombing, killing, blackmailing, threatening to bring about the collapse of Western economic life, and forcing a US-USSR confrontation in the Mideast."[35] Mordechai Nisan also locates the gnostic character of the PLO in its alleged anti-Jewish sentiment[36] drawn, he says, from the original anti-Jewish attitude of Late-Antique gnostic systems.

In sum, Nisan's effort to identify a gnostic soul for the PLO is invalidated, or at least strongly weakened, because of his bias toward the Palestinian cause. He even goes so far as to say that the PLO's "political character is really a secondary identification"[37] compared with its mythic dream. But in reality, the Palestine Liberation Organization does not match the features of the gnostic pattern described in the previous chapter: the limited and partial scope of the group, which is founded on the idea of a nation, does not meet the global reach of each of the gnostic phenomena; iconoclasm is not even considered; the idea of a human transfiguration is absent; the salvific Gnosis is not there.

Lastly, the small contribution by Anastasia V. Mitrofanova is worth mention: talking of millenarian sects among modern terrorist organizations, she utters that they belong to Gnosticism (she mentions Hans Jonas above all). Two are the goals of such groups: the liberation from the individual body, on the one hand, and the destruction of the material world, on the other hand. Following this scheme, she traces a distinction among two kinds of millenarian gnostic sects: "Those that are more oriented to their own destruction, and those which tend more to destroy others."[38] It is definitely a curious perspective, but Mitrofanova does not elaborate on the

34 Ibid., p. 306.

35 Ibid., p. 307.

36 Nisan explicitly talks of an anti-Jewish attitude, surreptitiously combining this concept with anti-Zionism.

37 Nisan, 'PLO Messianism', p. 309.

38 Anastasia V. Mitrofanova, 'Religious Aspects of International Terrorism', *Age of Globalization*, no. 3 (2013): p. 106.

gnostic soul of contemporary terrorism, and she does nothing else other than pointing to Gnosticism as a useful explanatory notion.

3.2 *Framing the study of an ideology*

Before taking us a step further and trying to validate the thesis that Salafi-Jihadism is a gnostic phenomenon, it is important to define what Salafi-Jihadism is. Scholars and academics have employed the generic label of "Islamic fundamentalism" or "Islamist extremism" for too long. These names are confusing and even misleading due to the strong sentimental bias that today is ineradicably attached to them. Too often adopted by academics and journalists, they are nonetheless inappropriate for describing the true reality of the broader Islamist world. In fact, trying to prove the gnostic pattern on, say, Islamic fundamentalism *tout court*, would result in a generic study starting from the first intra-Islamic oppositions (e.g., the Khawārij of the first century of Islam) to the self-proclaimed Islamic State; or treating the Sudanese Mahdī, Muḥammad Aḥmad (d. 1885) and the 1979 Shiʿite Iranian revolution in the same way. The use of an accurate terminology is the first requirement for any scientific analysis.

As stated in the introduction, the present work intends to analyze the phenomenon from a philosophical point of view, which purpose brings about an important consequence: tackling a phenomenon like terrorism usually leads to adopt more applied and practical labels, whereas from a philosophical point of view what is central is to address the very ideology that lies behind all the different empirical manifestations. From the latter perspective, the labels "Islamism" and "fundamentalism", as well as "extremism" and "jihadism", become relevant only to the extent that they offer some differences in degree on the level of ideology, and therefore in the present work they will be considered only if their divergences reflect a just as relevant innovation on the level of thought.

Hence, the compass of the following research will be ideology rather than empirical evidence: the subject will not be fundamentalism or extremism as such but rather Salafi-Jihadism, the mature ideological construction of late violent Islamist militants. "Islamism" will be used as a synonym of "political Islam", that is to say, a rather extreme ideologization of the religion of Islam, or, which is the same, a manipulation of the spiritual tradition for political purposes. This statement is consistent with the claim that Salafi-Jihadism is a modern phenomenon – and in the following sections I will add that it is also a secular, and even atheist system of beliefs.

Salafi-Jihadism is a clear-cut ideology, a potent soteriology and an activist redemptive belief. As we will see, it is a somewhat new term and a novel ideological construction: many scholars and academics trace its origin back to the Second Gulf War (2003), others to the First Gulf War (1990-1991), albeit some oldest roots can be discerned among previous violent groups. Its genealogy is no doubt crucial to give reason to many otherwise enigmatic features of it, among which is the violent opposing attitude both against the so-called Far Enemy (the West, and especially the United States) and the Near Enemy (the deemed "infidel" secular Arab states), as well as the deep commitment to building an exclusively Islamic state that would prospectively tend to expand over the entire earth.

But before delving into the world of Salafi-Jihadism, we must first elaborate on each of the two terms singularly. "Salafi-Jihadism" is a composite name whose single terms ("Salafism" and "Jihadism") possess a proper and independent meaning from one another. The following two subsections will consider both names independently, exploring their eventual violent and extreme latent potential, and considering their multiple historical manifestations.

3.2.1 *The first term: Salafism*

The name "Salafism" (*salafiyya*) refers to the Islamic tendency that draws inspiration from, and sometimes aspires to go back to, the *al-Salaf al-Ṣāliḥ*, the "pious predecessors" or "righteous ancestors", who are generally identified with the first three generations of Muslims starting from the Prophet Muḥammad and whose proximity to him is believed to be the guarantee of their impeccability and flawlessness. These three generations are called *aṣ-Ṣaḥāba*, or the Companions of the Prophet; *at-Tābiʿun*, or the Successors; *atbāʿ al-tābiʿīn*, the Successors of the Successors. Parts of the *Ṣaḥāba* were the caliphs known as *al-Khulafāʾ al-Rāshidūn*, the "Rightly Guided" caliphs: Abū Bakr (573-634), ʿUmar (584-644), ʿUthmān (579-656) and ʿAlī (601-661), whose reign – taken together – is known as the golden age of Islamic history, "a concept […] that took a long time to mature and that in fact did not appear before the first half of the third century, when Aḥmad ibn Ḥanbal [the epynom of the Ḥanbalī school of jurisprudence, or *madhhab* (pl. *madhāhib*)] was one of the first to defend it."[39] And indeed, self-proclaimed Salafis give credit to a conception of the

39 Josef Van Ess, *L'alba della teologia musulmana* (1977; repr., Torino: Einaudi, 2008), p. 80.

flow of history that is rather degenerative: "It is assumed that after the third generation, who were still able to witness the lives of and learn from the *Ṣaḥāba*, corruption slowly crept into Islam."[40]

It is not simple to locate the birth of Salafism: some consider it a modern phenomenon, while others track its origin to the core of Islam – as I am going to briefly show. "Salafism" itself is a vague expression, for most Muslims does glorify the *Salaf*[41] which are "deemed unable to have made mistakes."[42] That is why Massimo Campanini has no doubt in asserting the existence of a "cross 'Salafi mentality' [...] in the Middle Ages as well as in the present day"[43], instead of arguing for the existence of a distinct tendency (-ism or *-iyya*).

In the wake of this interpretation, Salafism has been defined "not as a movement to adhere to, a party to vote for, but a method of dealing with the Sources,"[44] i.e., the Qur'ān and the Sunna. Yet, from a historical point of view that is incorrect because there have been, and still there are, people who self-identify as Salafis in the sense of being part of a specific movement or a distinct current – and that is why we can speak of Salafism as such. However, the earliest usage of the terms "Salaf" or "Salafism" was not associated with any religious party, as Massimo Campanini says when he talks of a mentality or an attitude. The Moroccan philosopher Mohammed Abed al-Jabri (d. 2010) considers Salafism in terms of "a type

40 Carmen Becker, 'Muslims on the Path of the Salaf Al-Salih', *Information, Communication & Society*, vol. 14, no. 8 (2011): p. 1188.

41 "The vagueness of the term 'Salafism' goes back to the fact that the attempt to return to an understanding of Islam in a kind of 'original form' as practiced by the righteous ancestors is not unique to Salafists, but arises from the special regard in which this period is held in the normative religious sources» (Sabine Damir-Geilsdorf, Mira Menzfeld, 'Who are "the" Salafis? Insights Into Lifeworlds of Persons Connected to Salafis(m) in North Rhine-Westphalia, Germany', *Journal of Muslims in Europe*, vol. 6, issue 1 [March 2017]: p. 47). And also: "In a tradition like Islam, defined by moments of divine intervention in human history in a sacred past, that past remains in some ways unsurpassable by definition" (Ovamir Anjum, 'Cultural Memory of the Pious Ancestors (*Salaf*) in al-Ghazālī', *Numen*, vol. 58 [2011]: p. 346).

42 Van Ess, *L'alba della teologia musulmana*, p. 10.

43 Massimo Campanini, 'Il salafismo e le sue fenomenologie', in *Quale Islam? Jihadismo, radicalismo, riformismo* (Brescia: La Scuola, 2015), p. 64.

44 Marco Di Donato, *Salafiti e salafismo. Religione e politica nell'Islam* (Brescia: La Scuola, 2018), p. 13.

of self-resistance to maladies of inner origin,"[45] a sort of self-immunizing reaction to deviations emerging from the same Islamic culture.

The today self-proclaimed Salafi is a Muslim who wants to get rid of all the interpretations produced by the four schools of law (Ḥanafī, Mālikī, Shāfiʿī, Ḥanbalī) and who aspires to recover and rediscover the pureness and innocence of the first three generations of Muslims by endorsing a strict literalist adherence to the Sunna – in his/her eyes, the *madhāhib* (schools of law) constitute a reprehensible innovation since they did not exist at the time of Muḥammad and thus constituted a barrier between the believer and the Revelation. Salafis "consider the text to be a source of strict imitation rather than a source of inspiration,"[46] an approach that results in "a strong opposition between two views: (Sunni) traditionalist vs. (Salafi) fundamentalism."[47] According to the latter view, all the schools of law have brought about innovations (*bidʿa*, pl. *bidaʿ*), shameful and disgraceful "novelties" that have polluted the *tawḥīd* ("oneness" of God) and the right practices of faith (*ibāda*). Sufism (*Taṣawwuf*), too, is considered a pernicious innovation that has led many Muslims to embrace polytheism (*shirk*) due to unorthodox practices such as the worshipping of "saint's" graves and making requests from the dead (*tawassul*) or asking for intercession to God (*tashaffuʿ*). Ultimately, even Shīʿa Islam, or Shiism, is harshly condemned due to the fact that it does not belong to Sunnism, the majority of the Muslim community, and that it denies the legitimacy of the four *Rāshidūn* caliphs – which accusations turn Shiism into a heresy.

Salafis leave no room for personal interpretation or for *taqlīd*, regarded as the "blind" following of one of the *madhāhib*: there is only one correct answer to any question – the past provides all the answers – and that answer can be found in the *ḥadīth*s,[48] accounts on the life or the sayings of the Prophet – eventually creating the paradox that "their [Salafis'] reverence for

---

45 Mohammed Abed al-Jabri, *Democracy, Human Rights and Law in Islamic Law* (London and New York: I.B. Tauris, 2009), p. 69. Al-Jabri, however, criticizes the rigid Salafism of these days because the model of the *Salaf* is ineffective by now. "That model was sufficient for us [Arab-Muslims] when history was of our own making. […] Recourse to identity as *al-salafiya* was sufficient and effective when we were alone in our own home" (ibid.)

46 Joas Wagemakers, 'Salafism or the Quest for Purity', *Oasis Center*, July 26, 2018. https://www.oasiscenter.eu/en/what.is.salafism-quest-for-purity (accessed July 27, 2018).

47 Ibid.

48 *Ḥadīth*, pl. *aḥādīth*, but given as *ḥadīths* in this study.

the practice of the forefathers is marked by literal and blind conformism"[49] that resembles the deprecated *taqlīd*. Independent interpretation or reasoning (*ijtihād*), not to be confused with personal interpretation or with relativism in the approach to the Scripture, is thus strongly endorsed, since it makes possible to escape from the too narrow and often misleading and inaccurate boundaries of the various schools of law. *Dalīl* (textual evidence) is often invoked as to reason Salafis' moral and practical claims: hence, a "scripturalist-based epistemology [...] or *dalīl*-based epistemology [... as well as] a frequent de-contextualization of the religious sources"[50] is at the basis of a complex set of procedures that allows Salafis to authenticate their beliefs and practices. In this sense, no *ʿulamāʾ* (sing. *ʿālim*), the religious scholars, have any privilege in the relationship with the Sacred[51]: Salafis believe to have an "unmediated access to the revelation"[52] just like the first three generations of Muslims. Implicit in this claim is that to counter Salafi view on practical and doctrinal issues, which is held as the pristine form of Islam, is to contradict and dispute the authority of the Qurʾān and of the Prophet himself.

In sum, "the ideologization of scriptural Islam, the rejection of post-Qurʾanic commentaries, the mythologization of the pious ancestors"[53] are all pillars of what is known as Salafism. Its quest for authenticity "is directly concerned with establishing unity with the idealized and divinized past, and thus with the divine commandments."[54] Salvation is evidently the final purpose of this strict code of conduct and this rigorous creed.

It is easy to understand why Salafism is judged by its adherents as the correct Islam: Salafis believe themselves to be the saved sect (*al-firqa al-nājiya*) and the victorious group (*al- ṭāʾifa al-manṣūra*), in accordance with an often quoted *ḥadīth* stating that "a group (*ṭāʾifa*) of people from my

---

49 Dario Tomasello, *Luci sull'Islam. 66 voci per un lessico* (Milano: Jouvence, 2018), p. 269.

50 Emin Poljarevic, 'In Pursuit of Authenticity: Becoming a Salafi', *Comparative Islamic Studies*, vol. 8, no. 1-2 (2012): pp. 159-160.

51 The figure of a Salafi *ʿālim*, which exists in the practice (Marco Di Donato talks of a "ulema-style approach" [Di Donato, *Salafiti e salafismo*, p. 52]), is highly problematic for it represents an irresolvable paradox within the Salafi assertion that scriptural egalitarianism should have priority, and should even override, the interpretative control owned by a particular class.

52 Becker, 'Muslims on the Path', p. 1187.

53 Lahouari Addi, 'Islam Re-Observed: Sanctity, Salafism, and Islamism', *The Journal of North African Studies*, vol. 14, no. 3/4 (September/December 2009): p. 342.

54 Poljarevic, 'In Pursuit of Authenticity', p. 147.

umma will always remain triumphant on the right path and continue to be triumphant (against their opponents)" (reported by Muslim.)[55] Salafis also refer to another prophetic tradition according to which the global Muslim community will split into seventy-three sects, one of which will be in the Paradise – that is of course the Salafi one – and the other seventy-two in Hell (reported by Ibn Māja.)[56]

A landmark in the studies on Salafism is an edited book by Roel Meijer (2013) entitled *Global Salafism. Islam's New Religious Movement.*[57] Several recognized scholars in the field of Islamic Studies contributed to the volume, eventually turning it in an essential handbook for the study of the phenomenon. In the introduction, Meijer recognizes that Salafism is not a homogeneous movement; its appeal is strong and deeply oppositional with respect to the surrounding world. Meijer writes:

> In a contentious age Salafism transforms the humiliated, the downtrodden, disgruntled young people, the discriminated migrant, or the politically repressed into a chosen sect (*al-firqa al-nājiya*) that immediately gains privileged access to the Truth. Salafis are therefore able to contest the hegemonic power of their opponents: parents, the elite, the state, or dominant cultural and economic values of the global capitalist system as well as the total identification with an alien nation which nation-states in Europe impose.[58]

Probably the most cited essay of the book is Bernard Haykel's "On the Nature of Salafi Thought and Action." Haykel says that the oppositional stance of Salafis is rooted in the well-established intent of purifying the Muslim community in accordance with what they believe the teachings

55 *Sahih* Muslim, book 33, *ḥadīth* 245, https://sunnah.com/muslim/33/245.

56 "The Jews split into seventy-one sects, one of which will be in Paradise and seventy in Hell. The Christians split into seventy-two sects, seventy-one of which will be in Hell and one in Paradise. I swear by the One Whose Hand is the soul of Muhammad, my nation will split into seventy-three sects, one of which will be in Paradise and seventy-two in Hell" (*Sunan* Ibn Māja, book 36, *ḥadīth* 67, https://sunnah.com/ibnmajah/36/67).

57 Roel Meijer, ed. by, *Global Salafism. Islam's New Religious Movement* (New York: Oxford University Press, 2013).

58 Roel Meijer, introduction to *Global Salafism. Islam's New Religious Movement*, ed. by Roel Meijer (New York: Oxford University Press, 2013), p. 13. In France, for example, "what has helped Salafism to gain adherents is the weakness of the allegiance, especially of Muslim youth, to the national community that is based on a social contract between the state and the citizen" (Mohamed-Ali Adraoui, 'Salafism in France. Ideology, Practices and Contradictions', in *Global Salafism. Islam's New Religious Movement*, ed. by Roel Meijer [New York: Oxford University Press, 2013], p. 366).

of the “pious ancestors” are. The same name “Salafism” is “heuristically useful because it is a marker of a distinctive form of engagement with the world.”[59] Salafis, Haykel argues, “believe that true belief in Islam is constituted by both inner faith and manifest action.”[60] Quite inevitably, therefore, whoever does not fulfill the appropriate deeds and does not perform the obligatory cult acts is liable to excommunication (*takfīr*) and becomes an unbeliever (*kāfir*, pl. *kuffār*). The Salafi style is engaged in a never-ending “boundary defence,”[61] demarcating the in-group fellows by actively isolating the out-group members.

Salafis are thus struggling for the dominance and predominance over the “Qur᾽ano-Sunnahic teachings.”[62] The Salafi worldview “is oppositional to, reactionary with, and even conflictual towards the (religious) Other.”[63] It is a Manichaean worldview indeed, based on a binary nature and on an antagonistic posture, “allowing for no civilizational cross-pollination and syncretism.”[64]

But where did Salafism come from? Is it possible to distinguish its historical roots? Or, conversely, is it a so blurred phenomenon that by now is impossible to determine its derivation?

Ovamir Anjum catalogues the *three genealogies* of Salafism that the academic literature proposes so far:

> [1] the medieval heritage culminating in Ibn Taymiyya and his followers and tapering off soon thereafter; [2] the early-20th-century liberal-reformist or modernist “Salafism” of ‘Abduh or, more precisely, of his cohort; [3] and the ultraconservative, Wahhabized Salafism that has been on the rise since 1970’s if not earlier.[65]

---

59 Bernard Haykel, ‘On the Nature of Salafi Thought and Action’, in *Global Salafism. Islam’s New Religious Movement*, ed. by Roel Meijer (New York: Oxford University Press, 2013), p. 35.

60 Ibid., p. 40.

61 Ibid., p. 41.

62 Adis Duderija, ‘Islamic Groups and Their World-Views and Identities: Neo-Traditional Salafis and Progressive Muslims’, *Arab Law Quarterly*, vol. 21, no. 4 (2007): p. 344. Adis Duderija justifies the use of the phrase “Qur᾽ano-Sunnahic” in the following manner: “[With it] I wish to emphasize the hermeneutically symbiotic relationship that existed between the two concepts during the formative period of Islamic thought” (ibid., p. 343).

63 Ibid., p. 363.

64 Ibid., p. 352.

65 Anjum, ‘Salafis and Democracy’, p. 450.

The scholarship identifies these three viable paths as the most probable perspectives from which to acknowledge the origins of Salafism. Nevertheless, these three genealogies often contrast each other, leaving the aspired global view on the subject in total chaos.

In accordance with the first proposed genealogy, an insightful analysis has been conducted by Jonathan Brown in *Is Islam Easy to Understand or Not?: Salafis, the Democratization of Interpretation and the Need for the Ulema* (2015). In the essay, the author takes into consideration the enduring debate within Islam between two tendencies: a Salafi iconoclastic stream, on the one hand, and the Sunni mainstream, on the other.

The ulema have been, and in a certain sense still are, indispensable for containing and limiting the spread of anarchic interpretations and the raining down of disordered and even dangerous readings of the Scripture, downplaying both religious extremism and the liberal diluting of orthodox teachings. Already during the late Umayyad Caliphate and the early Abbasid rule, Brown explains, the first encounter with other cultures made necessary relying on a caste of religious scholars to counter too risky innovations and dangerous hybridizations. The need for the ulema was even asserted by some *ḥadīth*s, one of which warned that the depriving of *ʿilm* (religious knowledge) would coincide with the disappearance of ulema.[66]

In the medieval period (12th-16th centuries)[67], the ulema strengthened and consolidated their privileged position even by adopting a precise distinctive dress code – the four schools of law (*madhāhib*) were at the time widely established and firmly rooted in centuries of practice and devotion. However, the monopoly of the ulema over religious interpretation started to be questioned by the early 14th century. Brown talks of a "strong iconoclastic resistance [...] stressing the egalitarian simplicity of pure Islam."[68] This movement, which was genuinely spontaneous and not at all

66 "The Prophet said, '(Religious) knowledge will be taken away (by the death of religious scholars), ignorance (in religion) and afflictions will appear; and Harj will increase'. It was asked, 'What is Harj, O God's Messenger?' He replied by beckoning with his hand indicating 'killing'" (*Ṣaḥīḥ* al-Bukhārī, book 3, *ḥadīth* 27, https://sunnah.com/bukhari/3/27).

67 It is problematic to talk of a medieval period in Islamic history, since the evolution of the Islamic civilization is different from the Christian one. However, in the present research the periodization is according to the Christian Era for the sake of clarity.

68 Jonathan A.C. Brown, 'Is Islam Easy to Understand or Not?: Salafis, the Democratization of Interpretation and the Need for the Ulema', *Journal of Islamic Studies*, vol. 26, issue (May 2015): p. 130.

organized, rejected *taqlīd* of the four schools but also speculative theology and any doctrinal innovations brought by Sufism.

In fact, "in the late Islamic Middle Ages, it was normal to associate the Sufi 'way' of purification with the common orthodox disciplines,"[69] and to the common believer it became standard to belong to any Sufi brotherhood as a completion of his/her religious achievement alongside the adherence to a school of law. In addition, the creativity and originality of Islamic culture halted due to the aforementioned hijacking of the law by the now established class of ulema: "Soon the jurisprudence ran aground in the shallows of an unbearable pedantry. [...] The greatest danger that Muslim law ran was the detachment from its original sources and from the dynamism of the first schools."[70]

The strong iconoclastic movement that emerged within Sunni Islam and that Alberto Ventura calls "proto-fundamentalism"[71] is what could be considered the proto-Salafi stream that would have led to contemporary Salafism. Its epicenter was the Damascus scholar Ibn Taymiyya (1263-1328), who criticized theosophical Sufism, speculative theology (*kalām*) and Hellenic-like philosophy (*falsafa*). Ibn Taymiyya's anti-esoteric and strongly egalitarian approach led him to adopt a quite literalist methodology in reading the sacred scriptures. Even more, "although he generally followed the Ḥanbalī school, Ibn Taymiyya pronounced legal rulings that broke not only with his own school but occasionally with all four schools of law."[72]

Eventually, in the 18th century revivalist and reformist movements from all over the Muslim world began to rise as a reaction to the excessive control of the schools over Islamic law. Jonathan Brown cites Muḥammad Ibn ʿAbd al-Wahhāb (d. 1792) in Arabia, Shāh Walī Allāh al-Dihlawī (d. 1762) in India, Muḥammad b. Ismāʻīl al-Amīr al-Ṣanʿānī (d. 1768) in Yemen, Abū l-Ḥasan al-Sindī (d. 1773) in Medina, Muḥammad al-Shawkānī (d. 1834) in Yemen. All these personalities disapproved and criticized *taqlīd*, the blind acceptance of another's ruling without knowing the evidence for this ruling. However, Brown points out that their intention was not to erase hierarchies or destroy the schools, but to challenge the

69 Fazlur Rahman, *La religione del Corano. Le radici spirituali di una grande civiltà* (Milano: NET, 2003), p. 197.

70 Paolo Branca, *Introduzione all'Islam* (Cinisello Balsamo: San Paolo, 1995), pp. 167-168.

71 Alberto Ventura, 'L'islām della transizione (XVII-XVIII secolo)', in *Islām*, ed. by Giovanni Filoramo (Roma-Bari: Laterza, 2007), p. 206.

72 Brown, 'Is Islam Easy to Understand or Not?', p. 131.

institutional rigidity by advocating acting reflexively on *ḥadīths* instead of just passively accepting legal elaborations. In other words, the target was "an excessive *madhhab* chauvinism that refuses to consider evidences from the *ḥadīth* corpus."[73] Hence, "the *taqlīd* problematic only applies to the scholarly elite, not the masses of Muslims."[74]

The proto-Salafi stream eventually turned into what is now known as Salafism, a generalized call to break the prison bars constituted by the four *madhāhib*.

On this latter point, Frank Griffel's account is quite remarkable. Griffel argues that Ḥanbalī legal tradition, Wahhabism and the new Muslim theological orientation known as *lā madhhabiyya* merged together in what is today Salafism.

Lā madhhabiyya, which literally means "non-schoolist" orientation, was initiated by Muḥammad al-Shawkānī in the early decades of the 19th century. His followers founded in India the movement of the *ahl-i ḥadīth* (people of *ḥadīth*), devoted to a critical approach to the religious sources and especially to the *ḥadīth* corpus, ceasing to follow uncritically the teachings of the four established schools, and adopting a critical attitude towards Ashʿarite theology[75] as well as Sufism. This tradition was developed and deepened by the work of the famous Salafi scholar Muḥammad Nāṣir al-Dīn al-Albānī (1914-1999), who had a strong influence over Salafi-Jihadism. Griffel's thesis is the following:

> Salafism today can be one of three attitudes: It can be (1) the strict application of *lā madhhabiyya* theology, such as in the work of al-Albānī [...]; it can be (2) the equally strict following of the Ḥanbalite school tradition, such as in the case of many Wahhābī scholars in Saudi Arabia [...]; or it can be (3) a combination of these two as we see it manifest in the contemporary *salafiyya* movement of Egypt and Sudan.[76]

In this respect, Griffel discerns two pedigrees of Salafism: the *lā madhhabiyya* theology, and the Ḥanbalī tradition, including Wahhabism.

73 Ibid., p. 143.

74 Ibid.

75 Ashʿarism is the most widespread theological school of Sunni Islam. It is considered to be the middle way between strict traditionalism and pure rationalist tendencies.

76 Frank Griffel, 'What Do We Mean By "Salafi"? Connecting Muḥammad 'Abduh with Egypt's Nūr Party in Islam's Contemporary Intellectual History', *Die Welt Des Islams*, vol. 55 issue 2 (September 2015): p. 210.

Jonathan Brown's and Frank Griffel's narratives belong to the first proposed genealogy as told by Ovamir Anjum, namely, "the medieval heritage culminating in Ibn Taymiyya and his followers" – even though Griffel also includes the *lā madhhabiyya* tradition which is just as important.

With regard to the second genealogy of Salafism (which originates from "the early-20th-century liberal-reformist or modernist 'Salafism' of 'Abduh or, more precisely, of his cohort"), the academic production is rather confused and puzzled due to the fact that for decades many scholars have talked, and still are talking, about a kind of modernist Salafism, or even enlightened Salafism – an expression that could seem an oxymoron, an insolvable paradox, a contradiction in terms. This story begins in 1798 during Bonaparte's campaign in Egypt. "The decadence of the Ottoman-Moghul Empires and the expansionist policy of the European powers forced Arab-Muslim countries to become aware of their 'delay' in many sectors and the urgency to remedy it."[77] The sense of crisis grew as the West advanced.

The only way to tackle the problem was to absorb what was deemed absorbable, or, in other terms, to try to become modern without losing the true Islamic identity. The reformist movement that commenced in Egypt and eventually spread from the Maghreb to the Mashrek

> assumed a twofold mission: containing the Western challenge by creating a synthesis between modern values and systems and what they perceived as eternal Islamic values and systems; and questioning the credibility, even the Islamicity, of the dominant traditional modes of religion by questioning their timelessness and their reality at the same time.[78]

What is important for the topic here addressed is the trio composed by Jamāl al-Dīn al-Afghānī (d. 1897), Muḥammad ʿAbduh (d. 1905) and Muḥammad Rashīd Riḍā (d. 1935). They belong to what has been dubbed the *Nahḍa*, that is, Islamic "renaissance" or "awakening", an intellectual current that was principally born from the realization of backwardness in the economic and technological fields, and was therefore a prevalently reactive theoretical construction.

77 Paolo Branca, 'From the Nahda to Nowhere?', in *The Struggle to Define a Nation. Rethinking Religious Nationalism in the Contemporary Islamic World*, eds. Marco Demichelis and Paolo Maggiolini (Piscataway, NJ: Gorgias Press, 2017), p. 476.

78 Basheer M. Nafi, 'The Rise of Islamic Reformist Thought and its Challenge to Traditional Islam', in *Islamic Thought in the Twentieth Century*, eds. Suha Taji-Farouki and Basheer M. Nafi (London-New York: I.B. Tauris, 2004), p. 40.

Al-Afghānī is regarded as the father of Islamic modernism. His personality was strongly pro-Islamic and pan-Islamic, and because of this deep sentiment he tried to find a solution for the harsh situation the Islamic world was living in at that time. His language register was directed to revive Islam; still, "no longer were the masses simply to be encouraged to follow their religion literally, but their religious loyalty was also to be used to bring about political goals: chiefly Muslim unity and resistance to Western encroachments."[79] Stated differently, his concern was not solely aimed at strengthening admiration for Islam, but rather at channeling Islamic sentiment in an anti-imperialist way and in the direction of a future political struggle. Also, he warned against Western science and technology, approving its use but being careful not to embrace the philosophy and the ethos underlying all these novelties.

In light of these few words, it is comprehensible why many scholars have defined al-Afghānī as the father of both modernism and radicalism: he inaugurated both Westernization and its rejection.

For the purposes of the present section, however, what is relevant is his cohort: Muḥammad ʿAbduh, his disciple, and Rashīd Riḍā, the disciple of the disciple. The standard scientific storyline sees in ʿAbduh the so-called *modernist* son and in Riḍā the *radical* son. ʿAbduh, in fact, stressed the importance of reason in dealing with traditional theological matters, bypassing the role of the ulema and striking up a deep relationship with Western developments in philosophical and technological fields. He was said to have resumed the spirit of the old rationalist school of theology of the Muʿtazila (8th-10th centuries). On the contrary, Rashīd Riḍā was the one who sought to go back to the golden era of Islamic times by reforming society in its entirety – here "reformism" means "re-form", to give again the form of the past, to reshape the whole in accordance with the imagine conceived about the Salaf, the pious ancestors. And therefore, Riḍā "follows the course that will be taken up later by Islamic fundamentalists starting from Ḥasan al-Bannā,"[80] the founder of the Muslim Brotherhood. The anti-colonial struggle, that was yet present in al-Afghānī, is taken to the extreme by Riḍā.

Now, Louis Massignon and Henri Laoust introduced in the debate an important element, the idea that this trio – al-Afghānī, ʿAbduh, and

79 Nikki R. Keddie, 'Islamic Philosophy and Islamic Modernism: The Case of Sayyid Jamāl al-Dīn al-Afghānī', *Iran*, vol. 6 (1968): p. 54.

80 Khaled Fouad Allam, 'L'islām contemporaneo', in *Islām*, ed. by Giovanni Filoramo (Roma-Bari: Laterza, 2007), p. 241.

Riḍā – would have inaugurated a movement called "*Salafiyya*" [81]. Khaled Fouad Allam rightly describes the *Salafiyya* current as both "a theological discourse and political project"[82] whose attitude towards the West was equally critical and enthusiastic. Mohammed Arkoun is aware of this evolution when he writes that "a close relationship is thus established between the success of the traditionalist reformist ideology – inspired by the *salafiyya*, partisans of a return to the ancestral Norm – and the growing pressure of the West."[83]

In light of this brief historical reconstruction (the second genealogical proposal according to Anijum),[84] Salafism (*Salafiyya*) was born from the encounter and the clash with the West. However, recently Henri Lauzière has challenged this account. First in a 2010 article and then in a 2016 book, Lauzière questions the same fact that Rashīd Riḍā or others from his group ever founded any current called *Salafiyya*. In fact, is it if possible that a reactionary movement like Salafism emerged from a modernist program? Lauzière is convinced that a profound confusion lies at the core of this idea, "the confusion between Salafi epithets and Islamic modernism"[85]: in the medieval period, being a Salafi

> meant abiding by the doctrine of the forefathers (*madhhab al-salaf*) in matters of dogma and theology (*uṣūl al-dīn*). Written sources make it clear that medieval scholars used the notion of *madhaab al-salaf* primarily in theological contexts, where it served as an authoritative and prestigious synonym for the Ḥanbali [ī] creed (*ʿaqīda*),[86]

81 Cf. Henri Laoust, 'Le Réformisme orthodoxe des "Salafiya" et les caractères généraux de son orientation actuelle', *Revue des Etudes Islamiques*, VI/2 (1932): pp. 385-434.

82 Fouad Allam, 'L'islām contemporaneo', p. 241.

83 Mohammed Arkoun, *La filosofia araba* (1975; repr., Milano: Xenia Edizioni, 1995), p. 96.

84 As reported above – but it is worth repeating it – Ovamir Anjum catalogues *three genealogies* of Salafism: "[1] the medieval heritage culminating in Ibn Taymiyya and his followers and tapering off soon thereafter; [2] the early-20th-century liberal-reformist or modernist "Salafism" of 'Abduh or, more precisely, of his cohort; [3] and the ultraconservative, Wahhabized Salafism that has been on the rise since 1970's if not earlier" (Anjum, 'Salafis and Democracy', p. 450).

85 Henri Lauzière, 'The Construction of *Salafiyya*: Reconsidering Salafism from the Perspective of Conceptual History', *International Journal of Middle East Studies*, vol. 42, no. 3 (August 2010): p. 376.

86 Ibid., p. 372.

and "neither al-Afghānī nor ʿAbduh [...] were Ḥanbalī in creed – quite the contrary."[87] Additionally, Lauzière claims that the association between al-Afghānī, ʿAbduh and Riḍā, with a movement called "*Salafiyya*" was a mistake made by the French scholar Louis Massignon in 1919 and, later, in 1925 – a mistake that has been transmitted through chains of transmission due to the prestige and stature of Massignon himself; as a consequence, Lauzière sees this putative connection as a pure Orientalist construction (Lauzière blames the "chain of academics who trusted each other's authority"[88]). Massignon made "a series of seemingly plausible but nonetheless untenable connections"[89] in order to support his idea.[90] Al-Afghānī, ʿAbduh and Riḍā never stated to be part of, let alone founders of, a movement called *Salafiyya*, and never claimed the label for themselves. For instance, in 1902 the same ʿAbduh wrote a short article in *al-Manār* magazine in which he mentioned the Salafis (*al-salafiyyīn*) without criticizing them, eventually presenting them as Muslims who distance themselves from the Ashʿaris on matters of theology – and Henry Lauzière wonders about the very fact that "ʿAbduh did not even expect his readers to know who the Salafis were."[91]

---

87 Henri Lauzière, 'What We Mean Versus What They Meant by "Salafi": A Reply To Frank Griffel', *Die Welt Des Islams*, vol. 56, issue 1 (April 2016): p. 90.

88 Henri Lauzière, *The Making of Salafism. Islamic Reform in the Twentieth Century* (New York: Columbia University Press, 2016), p. 43.

89 Lauzière, 'The Construction of *Salafiyya*', p. 380.

90 For the sake of completeness, Frank Griffel has criticized the claim that Massignon was wrong ("I must admit that I cannot see where Massignon's mistake lies" [Griffel, 'What Do We Mean By "Salafi"?', p. 201]) since al-Afghānī, ʿAbduh and Riḍā did refer to the rebirth of the very Islam of the *salaf*, a free, creative and unite Islam. To prove this point, Griffel quoted a part of ʿAbduh's autobiographical text that is highly significant. The quotation states: "I spoke on behalf of [...] the liberation of thought (*taḥrīr al-fikr*) from the shackles of blind emulation (*qayd al-taqlīd*), the understanding of religion according to the way of the *salaf* of the *umma* before the appearance of dissention, the return of religious learning to its original sources" (Muḥammad ʿAbduh, quoted in Griffel, 'What Do We Mean By "Salafi"?', p. 198). On the contrary, Joas Wagemakers concurs with Lauzière on this very point: "I have found no references to their [al-Afghānī and ʿAbduh] being Salafis. In fact, in a challenge to Griffel's claim, both men are actually consciously excluded from Salafism by the most prominent political Salafi writer in Jordan" (Joas Wagemakers, 'Salafism's Historical Continuity: The Reception of "Modernist" Salafis by 'Purist' in Jordan', *Journal of Islamic Studies* [October 2018]: p. 27).

91 Lauzière, 'The Construction of *Salafiyya*', p. 374.

Furthermore, "Massignon's conception of the *salafiyya* filtered back into the Middle East,"[92] and many Arab intellectuals started using this category and believing in the existence of a modernist *Salafiyya* (Lauzière mentions, for example, the antireformist scholar from al-Azhar, Yusuf al-Dijwi [d. 1946]; the Lebanese-Palestinian translator 'Ajjaj Nuwayhid [d. 1982]; and many 1930s Moroccan reformers who used the notion for indicating their own orientation). In other words, indigenous and exogenous uses of the term ended up validating each other, perpetrating the belief in a vague Salafi trend. And eventually, an endogenous use of the concept blurred even more the conceptual boundaries of the notion, and its lack of clarity prepared the ground for the hijacking of the term by a literalist and "Wahhabized" approach to the pristine sources.

Representing the (Ovamir Anjum's) third genealogy proposal (the one that believes Salafism to be "the ultraconservative, Wahhabized Salafism that has been on the rise since 1970s if not earlier"), Lauzière argues:

> The history of Salafism is much more recent than one might expect. [...] It's a phenomenon of the twentieth century. Contrary to popular belief, it dates neither from the medieval period nor from the late nineteenth century. [... It would] further helps us to notice the conspicuous absence of any discussion of a concept called Salafism in either Muslim or non-Muslim scholarship until about the 1920s.[93]

To sum up, the noun "Salafism" indicating a clear-cut movement did not exist in the Middle Ages, and when medieval Muslim scholars used the adjective "Salafi" they were only signaling the adherence to Ḥanbalī theology[94] – and the Ḥanbalī creed was tangentially fideist, meaning that it doubted any form of rationalist engagement with the sacred text or, to be more precise, it held that only a textual basis informs a believer's religion, nothing derived from sheer thought.

Secondly, the so-called *modernist Salafism* attributed to al-Afghānī, ʿAbduh and Riḍā is a total invention, and "it did not build on the medieval understanding of the doctrine of the forefathers (*madhhab al-salaf*) and had nothing to do with either theological fideism or the neo-Ḥanbalī interpretation of divine attributes."[95] It came out of nowhere – or rather

92 Ibid., p. 381.

93 Lauzière, *The Making of Salafism*, p. 20.

94 "In scholarly parlance, therefore, a Salafi was an adherent to Ḥanbali theology who could follow any school of Islamic law or none in particular. The term did not have a legal connotation" (Lauzière, *The Making of Salafism*, p. 28).

95 Ibid., p. 132.

it was completely invented by a false claim made by Louis Massignon. Eventually, it was in turn adopted by some Moroccan reformers in the 1930s, but it lost its strength when in the first years of the post-independence era the exponents of modernist Salafism were "politically domesticated [... and] became state employees and government officials"[96] of the new states based on socialist and Western models (e.g., the Baʿth Party in Syria, Nasser in Egypt, Bourguiba in Tunisia).

Lastly, the conception of a *purist Salafism* – the literalist and "Wahhabized" one, to be clear – derives directly from the misconception and polysemy of the so-called modernist Salafism. "The real change was the unambiguous application of the epithet 'Salafi' (historically a theological marker) to individuals who dealt with legal matters unencumbered by the canons of the traditional schools of Islamic jurisprudence"[97] – a tendency developed as a result of a Wahhabization of the same label "Salafism". After the abolition of the Caliphate in 1924, in fact, Riḍā became increasingly admired by the Saudi King ʿAbd al-ʿAzīz Āl Saʿūd[98], and sent to Saudi Arabia many of his disciples, ultimately drifting them toward religious purism. Moreover, during the postcolonial era purist Salafis, unlike modernist ones, did not change their aspiration, namely, the purification of Islam: their apolitical attitude protected them from insignificance and marginality, for they "did not run the risk of being defeated in the political arena"[99] and, on the contrary, preserved their prestige in the struggle against the galloping Westernization and against "three religious innovations they considered most dangerous: theological errors, legal partisanship, and Sufism."[100] Ultimately, "in the 1970s, the notion of purist Salafism came to overshadow the modernist version of the concept,"[101] and the label itself lost the theological-only distinctiveness and became a total and totalizing worldview encompassing both knowledge and practice.

To define this newborn concept, Lauzière adopts the term "ideology", a modern notion that distinguishes purist Salafism either from the medieval use of the label "Salafi" and from the modernist conception of Salafism.

---

96 Ibid., p. 163.
97 Ibid., p. 96.
98 It is worth noting that in 1929 the King recommended the use of the label "salafiyya" instead of the epithet "Wahhābī". Cf. Griffel, 'What Do We Mean By "Salafi"?', p. 218.
99 Lauzière, *The Making of Salafism*, p. 198.
100 Itzchak Weismann, 'New and Old Perspectives in the Study of Salafism', *The Middle East Book Review*, vol. 8, no. 1 (2017): p. 35.
101 Lauzière, *The Making of Salafism*, p. 199.

Purist Salafism should not be confused with religious conservatism, broadly conceived: rather, it is a comprehensive program for life. Henri Lauzière cites Mustafa Hilmi (d. 1932), an Egyptian professor of philosophy in Alexandria, who understood Salafism "as a civilizational worldview (*taṣawwur*) and a divine method (*manhaj rabbānī*) – two eminently Qutbist expressions. According to Hilmi", continues Lauzière, "this method contained all the necessary principles for organizing the social, economic, and political aspects of life."[102] A similar all-embracing program, that is,

> the idea of a distinctive Sunni methodology applicable to Islamic theology, law, and virtually all other aspects of the religious and human experience, was itself untraditional. [...] To say that it dates from the time of Ibn Taymiyya or Muhammad ibn 'Abd al-Wahhab not only is anachronistic but also obfuscates the development of modern Islamic thought. Although many of the ingredients of purist Salafism are old, the recipe and the final product (including the term *Salafism*) are not.[103]

Henri Lauzière's account on Salafism stands for the third genealogical proposal for Salafism that Ovamir Anjum listed.

All three have been taken into consideration (Salafism as a medieval heritage, Salafism as a modernist construction, Salafism as a Wahhabized branch of Islam). There is no correct answer, all of them are plausible historical reconstructions, and each of the three reveals something of the same nature of contemporary Salafism.

Now that the identity and history of contemporary Salafism has been defined and taken into account, and before turning to the study of jihadism, we must ask ourselves whether contemporary Salafism is always and everywhere the same, or whether it provides for diverse phenomenological manifestations. In other words, do contemporary Salafis belong to a uniform group?

A first answer is given by Tariq Ramadan in his book *Western Muslims and the Future of Islam* (2004). Here Ramadan recognizes the existence of a multileveled Salafism in contemporary Islamic community worldwide: Salafi literalism, Salafi reformism, and political literalist Salafism. The first group is composed by those who need textual references to justify their behavior, and thus forbid any interpretative reading of the Qur'ān and of the Sunna. The second group, while still concerned in bypassing the boundaries of the four juridical schools, is rationally committed to the

102 Ibid., p. 221.
103 Ibid., p. 236.

Text, that is to say, it "believe[s] that the practice of *ijtihād* [independent reasoning] is an objective, necessary, and constant factor in the application of *fiqh* [jurisprudence] in every time and place,"[104] and therefore it engages the new challenges of the current age and develops a dynamic and creative relation to the scriptural sources. The third group resembles the first one but adds a new flavor, namely, the political connotation that pushes its adherents to social, political and even revolutionary action.

A deeper, sharper and effective description of the Salafi types was conducted by Quintan Wiktorowicz in a study that has now become a milestone. It is entitled *Anatomy of the Salafi Movement*, it was published in 2006 and it is still quite influential. Wiktorowicz categorizes the Salafi factions into "purists", "politicos" and "jihadis"[105], considering their diversities as they appear from contextual analysis. In other words, the divergences among the three factions originate from the evaluation of the present world and the interpretation of context.

The "purists" are primarily concerned with preserving the integrity of Islam and transmitting the supposed "purity" of the pristine religion. They have three methods to convey and preserve the creed: "Propagation (*daʿwa*), purification (*tazkiyya*) and religious education or cultivation (*tarbiya*)."[106] "Purists", thus, do not envision themselves as a political movement but as a vanguard devoted to the protection of Islam from nefarious external influences and polluting Western values. It goes without saying that the main tendency of the "purists" groups is isolationism, in that any contact with non-Muslim entities, as well as misguided Muslims, could infect the "authentic" religious path. Additionally, any involvement in politics is deemed unacceptable: revolutionary approaches are traced to American, French and Marxist revolutions, and democratic involvement is a real commitment with the Western party politics model. "Politicos" and "jihadis", the "purists" believe, are more engaged with continuous utility calculation strategies rather than perpetrating the true message of Islam, which makes them rival factions in the struggle for the heart of

---

104 Tariq Ramadan, *Wester Muslims and the Future of Islam* (New York: Oxford University Press, 2004), p. 26.

105 In a previous study, Wiktorowicz had classified the Salafis in two categories, the moderates, or reformists, and the militants, or jihadis. See Quintan Wiktorowicz, 'The Salafi Movement. Violence and the Fragmentation of Community', in *Muslim Networks from Hajj to Hip Hop*, eds. Miriam Cooke and Bruce B. Lawrence (Chapel Hill and London: The University of North Carolina Press, 2005), pp. 215-216.

106 Quintan Wiktorowicz, 'Anatomy of the Salafi Movement', *Studies in Conflict & Terrorism*, vol 29, issue 3 (August 2006): p. 217.

Islam. Saudi Wahhabi clerical establishment and prominent personalities such as Muḥammad Nāṣir al-Dīn al-Albānī are among the exponents of the "purist" faction.

The "politicos" are politicized Salafis who emerged in the 1980s and 1990s in Saudi Arabia as the result of a hybridization between local Wahhabis and Muslim Brotherhood fellows from Egypt. The "politicos" argue that "they have a better understanding of contemporary issues and are therefore better situated to apply the Salafi creed to the modern context. They generally stop short of declaring revolution, unlike the jihadis, but are highly critical of incumbent regimes."[107] The lesson of Sayyid Quṭb was of great importance in shaping the "politicos" mindset. But there has been a particular event that triggered the movement, namely, the first Gulf War in 1990; after "purist" Saudi scholars permitted American troops to land on Arabic soil, the "politicos" denounced the religious establishment, warning that it was an offer for colonization.

> From the politico perspective, while the purists insisted on preaching about doomsday, how to pray, the heresy of saint worship, and other elements related to *tawḥīd*, corrupt regimes in the Muslim world repressed their people, the Israelis continued to occupy Islamic land, the Americans launched an international campaign to control the Muslim world, the Russian suppressed separatist aspirations in Chechnya and Dagestan, and the Indians slaughtered Kashmiri Muslims.[108]

Although "purists" insist that dealing with current affairs would produce emotional and irrational responses, the "politicos" are highly committed to international geopolitics and national governments. Among the "politicos" are influential Saudi scholars such as Salmān al-ʿAwda and Safar Ḥawālī.

Lastly, the "jihadis" are those Salafis who are confident that a violent action would resolve all problems that torment the Islamic community. They have emerged as a consistent group during the Soviet-Afghan war (1979-1989). Then, because of the 1990 Gulf War, Osama bin Laden revolted against the Saudi Kingdom, laying the foundation for the violent global jihadi turn. Finally, in 1994 the Saudi regime repressed the "politicos" and silenced both Ḥawālī and al-ʿAwda. It was only a matter of time before the "jihadis" denounced the senior clerical Saudi establishment of corruption and dependence upon the interests of the kingdom.

---

107 Ibid., p. 221.
108 Ibid., p. 223.

> The jihadi critique is thus based on judgments about the purists' inability of unwillingness to reveal the truth about context to the people. [...] The critique is not about belief; it is about the unwillingness of the purists to put this belief into practice by addressing the injustices of the regime and its American (and Zionist) masters.[109]

The battle cry of "jihadis" is *takfīr*, or, in Roman Catholic parlance, "excommunication", the declaration of other Muslims to be unbelievers (*kuffār*, sing. *kāfir*).

Recently, the division of Salafis into "purists", "politicos" and "jihadis" has been slightly revisited by Joas Wagemakers. The acknowledgement of a "degree of ideological and strategic fluidity"[110] within the Salafi community has convinced him that a scholar has to be more accurate and less rigid. To begin with, Wagemakers maintains that the label "purist" is ineffective because "all Salafis claim to be purists in their own way,"[111] and thus it would be more appropriate to refer to Wiktorowicz's first group as "quietists".

According to Wagemakers, the "quietists" do have political views but they do not express them in political and, so to speak, "profane" terms, but only in a religious way and exclusively in terms of discrete advices to the rulers. They do not engage in political activism nor do they participate in institutional politics.

The "politicos" (here the name is kept, as it is for the "jihadis") are influenced by the Muslim Brotherhood – and in this respect Wagemakers's reconstruction is consistent with Wiktorowicz's. "Some politicos are actually involved in parliamentary politics, while others [...] engage in contentious political debate and activism."[112] Yet, in Wagemakers's view, even "quietists" speak about politics and engage in political debates; yet, they generally do so in a religious way, whereas "politicos" adopt a secular stance, although their participation is always seen as an extension of their *daʿwa* commitment.

The "jihadis" "are, in a sense, perhaps the least understood of the three branches of Salafism."[113] Wagemakers distinguishes between classical

---

109 Ibid., pp. 227-228.
110 Joas Wagemakers, 'Revisiting Wiktorowicz. Categorising and Defining the Branches of Salafism', in *Salafism After the Arab Awakening: Contending with People's Power*, eds. Francesco Cavatorta and Fabio Merone (London: Hurst, 2017), p. 8.
111 Ibid., p. 11.
112 Ibid., p. 17.
113 Ibid., p. 18.

jihad, revolutionary jihad and global jihad, making the category more diverse and close to reality. In Wagemakers's own words: "Jihadi-Salafis' revolutionary jihad did not, as Wiktorowicz maintains, only emerge 'during the war in Afghanistan against the Soviet Union', but actually has ideological roots in the 1960s and 1970s."[114] The last remark on the "jihadis" is about their methodology: among the "jihadi" ranks there are both actual fighters and ideologues, who provide doctrinal justifications for violent and cruel actions.

3.2.2 *The second term: Jihadism*

"Jihadism" is a too often misinterpreted term. Today, in the West, it evokes the horror of 9/11 and the violence of suicide bombing attacks on European soil. In reality, however, it is a name with multiple meanings and, in particular, with several historical expressions. This section will review only modern types of jihadism, those dating from 18th century onwards, with the intent of contextualizing Salafi-Jihadism within a specific time and space, thus considering it one of the possible outcomes of a precise historical path.

To start with, there are *at least* four types of jihad in the modern era: (1) "'purification' jihad directed against other Muslims"[115] and aimed at restoring the integrity of Islam in traditionally Islamic territories – this kind of jihad occurred mainly in the 18th century; (2) anti-colonial jihad focused on countering the European presence in Islamic regions – this second type arose in the 19th century; (3) religious nationalist[116] jihad whose goal is to overthrown the despotic albeit indigenous (Arab and/or Muslim) rulers of Arab/Islamic countries – such jihad appeared in the 20th century; (4) global jihad, the most feared one from a Western perspective due to the fact that it is not confined into MENA region but its scope encompasses the whole world, and it is the type of armed struggle and radical worldview adopted by Salafi-Jihadi militants – this final jihad occurred in the 21st century.

This four-points list is not exhaustive, for there are kinds of jihad that do not uniquely coincide with one or the other of the classified

---

114 Ibid.

115 David Cook, *Understanding Jihad* (Berkeley and Los Angeles: University of California Press, 2005), p. 73.

116 The expression "religious nationalism" as linked to violent struggle against the so-called Near Enemy has been proposed by Fawaz A. Gerges in *The Far Enemy. Why Jihad Went Global* (New York: Cambridge University Press, 2010).

groups;[117] however, the above scheme provides a rather clear framework to investigate jihadism, preventing losing sight of the conceptual and historical coordinates of the various types of armed struggle, and showing a progression in the evolution of the modern ideology of jihad, that is, jihadism.

We will start with the first form of jihad. The most radical type of *purification jihad* is Wahhabism (*al-Wahhābiyya*), an Islamic religious orientation set up by Muḥammad ibn ʿAbd al-Wahhāb (1703-1792) in the province of Najd, in central Arabia, eventually spreading throughout the whole peninsula. Ibn ʿAbd al-Wahhāb forged an alliance with Muḥammad ibn Saʿūd (d. 1765), ancestor of the current reigning family. This alliance became famous, called the Pact of Najd.

> It was the first pact in the history of Islam in which spiritual power and temporal power were clearly separated: Ibn ʻAbd al-Wahhāb appointed the imams and judges and saw to the religious instruction. Ibn Saʻūd enjoyed the temporal power, which was limited, at that time, to appointing governors in the provinces and waging war. The pact was a verbal agreement by which Ibn Saʻūd undertook to follow Ibn ʻAbd al-Wahhāb's unitary (or Unitarian) doctrine – according to which there is no God outside God – on condition that the sheikh did not break the pact and that the prince reserved the levy of taxes on his subjects to himself. Ibn ʻAbd al-Wahhāb promised the prince that he would not leave the town and dangled the hope before him that, thanks to jihad, God would honour him with even greater blessings and resources. The emir swore loyalty to the sheikh in the name of God's religion, of God's prophet, of jihad, of the application of Islamic rules and of commanding right and forbidding wrong.[118]

The pact was the beginning of a long-term union that has been perpetrated to the present day. The strength of Muḥammad ibn ʿAbd al-Wahhāb and Muḥammad ibn Saʿūd's deal was so unbreakable and firm that it led to the unification of the Arabian peninsula under the banner of a reformed Islam – here "reformed" relates to the above mentioned 18th-century reformist movement that arose in many locations of the Islamic world against the four jurisprudential schools.

---

117 There are even examples of jihad that go beyond Muslims or Islam. For instance, in 1948 the Palestinians had their own fighting force called *al-Jihād al-Muqaddas* (the holy jihad) which included Arab Christians and whose aim was to rid Palestine of the Zionist takeover and occupation.

118 Hamadi Redissi, 'The Changing Face of Wahhabism', *Oasis*, no. 21 (June 2015): p. 35.

> Unlike the movements of the nineteenth and twentieth centuries, which arose in response to external aggressions, like European imperialism, or the desire for political independence, the movements of the eighteenth century arose largely in response to internal conditions. The most important of these was the perceived deterioration in Muslim beliefs and practices.[119]

Ibn ʿAbd al-Wahhāb, who was very sensitive to religious issues, felt the urgency to restore Islam to its former glory and to fight all the ungodly practices of the Muslims at that time.[120] The stringent adherence to the example of the Prophet Muḥammad became the compass of his actions. Fighting an actual jihad against the local tribes of Arabia (according to Ibn ʿAbd al-Wahhāb, "the purpose of jihad is the protection and aggrandizement of the Muslim community as a whole, not personal gain or glory"[121]), the Saʿūd family, backed by Ibn ʿAbd al-Wahhāb and his followers, unified what at the time was a politically blurred reality, giving birth to the First Saudi State (1744-1818) that evolved, through the Second Saudi State (1824-1891), in the actual Kingdom of Saudi Arabia (from 1902 onwards).

In an interesting paper, John O. Voll defines Wahhabism as a message-oriented type of renewal, as opposed to Mahdism which is a man-oriented renewal orientation. In fact, there has never been a great emphasis over the Wahhabi leader ("neither in this agreement [the Pact of Najd] nor in the teaching of the shaykh were there special charismatic claims made for the role of Muḥammad ibn ʿAbd al-Wahhāb"[122]), given that what needed to be implemented was the message of Islam – in this perspective, Mahdism, on the contrary, is a man-oriented orientation for the fact that strong emphasis is posed over the religious leader.[123]

---

119 Natana J. Delong-Bas, *Wahhabi Islam. From Revival and Reform to Global Jihad* (New York: Oxford University Press, 2004), p. 8.

120 For example, the "worship of tombs" of so-called saints, ending up destroying mausoleums of religiously relevant people like Khadīja, and the cupolas dedicated to ʿAlī in Mecca and Medina. The point was to avoid the veneration and worship of the people buried there, which would have violated the principle of *tawhīd*.

121 Ibid., p. 202.

122 John O. Voll, 'Wahhabism and Mahdism: Alternative Styles of Islamic Renewals', *Arab Studies Quarterly*, vol. 4, no. 1/2 (Spring 1982): p. 119.

123 Voll stresses the fact that there is a dialectical relation among the two kinds of renewals, for "the more legalistic, message-oriented *tajdīd* [renewal] always faces the danger of creating a justification for a more messianic style of renewal movement [… whereas] Mahdism may be suspected by other Muslims of already having departed from the limits of the faith in the direction of unacceptable, personalized innovation" (ibid., p. 121).

Another example of purification jihad is the struggle fought in Nigeria by Shehu Usman Dan Fodio (1754-1817), a Muslim mystic, philosopher and charismatic leader. Between 1804 and 1810 he engaged in a real jihad, uniting the ethnic group of the Fulani whose religion was Islam, and contrasting the dominant ethnic group of the Hausa whose religion was a form of Islam contaminated by local animistic traditions. The outcome of such jihad was the creation of the Sokoto Caliphate in what is now northern Nigeria, which lasted from 1804 to 1903. The main goal of Dan Fodio's jihad was exactly eradicating all pagan and animistic beliefs and cultual acts, and establishing a purer form of Islam. To pursue this objective, Dan Fodio never rejected the rumors that he himself was the Mahdi, even though he never claimed to be the Messiah: he "saw his mission as one of cosmic significance,"[124] since "no Muslim prior to Dan Fodio had conducted a jihad against the *bida*ʿ [innovations]."[125] Dan Fodio "went even further when he favored the abolition of the differences between four leading Muslim schools of law to have one single *madhhab*,"[126] adopting a Salafi orientation.

The second modern form of jihad is the *anti-colonial* one. With regard to this category, many are the cases of violent struggles fought against European powers that were occupying Islamic territories throughout the 19th century. In Algeria, for instance, the Sufi Islamic scholar ʿAbd al-Qādir (1808-1883) led a strenuous armed resistance against the French colonial invasion. The French invaded Algeria in 1830. From the very beginning, the French brutality was too much for the Algerian population, whose immediate response was to preserve its own way of life and its traditions as a response to the French attempt to destroy, or at least weaken, the colonized people's identity (religious, social and political), which was correctly considered a factor of indigenous unity. In this situation, ʿAbd al-Qādir tried vigorously to react by waging a jihad against the invaders. Jihad, indeed, was a particularly effective concept for the Algerian population, for it "legitimized his [ʿAbd al-Qādir's] state-building effort [...] and helped resolve matters of leadership and legitimacy"[127] in a diverse tribal environment as it was Algeria.

---

124 Cook, *Understanding Jihad*, p. 78.

125 Ibid., p. 77.

126 Peter Heine, 'I Am Not the Mahdi, But...', in *Apocalyptic Time*, ed. by Albert I. Baumgarten (Leiden: Brill, 2000), p. 74. Recalling John O. Voll's clarification, it is possible to assert that Dan Fodio's renewal is a man-oriented one.

127 Benjamin Claude Brower, 'The Amīr 'Abd al-Qādir ant the "Good Was" in Algeria, 1832-1847', *Studia Islamica, nouvelle édition*, no. 2 (2011): p. 46.

Another anti-colonial jihad was that fought in Libya against the Italian invaders. As early as 1910, Italy invaded Libya and conquered Tripoli in 1911. As a response, the Sanūsiyya *ṭarīqa* (brotherhood), a very popular Sufi order in Libya, began a rebellion against the Italians. The Sanusi Chief Sayyid Aḥmad al-Sharīf (1873-1933), grandson of the founder of the brotherhood, declared a jihad against the invaders in 1913, and that was the beginning of a long-term war between the Sanusi and the Italians which witnessed other jihad declarations such as in the 1930s. The war lasted until the formal end of the colonization period in 1947. For the Sanusi order, the fighting against the Italians was not seen as anti-Western, i.e., against a foreign philosophy or religion, but rather "the jihad was used as a tool to fight imperialism and heavy oppression,"[128] with a purely anti-colonial intent.

An additional famous anti-colonial jihad was fought in Sudan by Muḥammad Aḥmad ibn ʿAbd Allāh (1844-1885), the notorious self-proclaimed Mahdi. In 1881, the Sudanese Mahdi began a military campaign for the liberation of Sudan from the Anglo-Egyptian rule and a parallel campaign of revitalization of the Islamic religion against the religious facade of the Ottomans and the pagan traditions of indigenous Sudanese themselves – in this sense, the Mahdist jihad was a mixture of purification jihad and anti-colonial jihad.

In the siege of Khartoum (1885), the British Governor of Sudan, Charles George Gordon, lost his life, causing great stir in Europe. The victorious Mahdi was thus able to start a Mahdi state that lasted until 1898, but he himself, however, lost his life in the same year when Khartoum was taken, at the height of his glorious advance.

In his attempt to adhere strictly to the *sharīʿa*, Muḥammad Aḥmad and his followers, called the *Anṣār* (the companions) in remembrance of the Prophet's followers,[129] "ignore the 'ulama's work, and insist that they derive their Islamic legitimacy directly from the Qurʾan and the Prophet,"[130] invalidating the four Sunni canonical legal schools. The Salafi

128 Fait Muedini, 'Sufism and Anti-Colonial Violent Resistance Movements: The Qadiriyya and Sanussi Orders in Algeria and Libya', *Open Theology*, vol. 1, issue 1 (2015): p. 144.

129 The original *Anṣār* were the inhabitants of Medina who converted to Islam after the arrival in their city of the prophet Muḥammad. They are considered second only to the *Muhājirūn*, the very first Muslims who moved from their native Mecca to Medina.

130 Kazuo Ohtsuka, 'Salafi-Orientation in Sudanese Mahdism', *The Muslim World*, vol. 87, no. 1 (January 1997): p. 26.

orientation of the phenomenon is therefore clear, and the man-oriented character analyzed above is evident and preponderant.

Many others are the anti-colonial jihad cases (for instance, in Daghestan and in India[131]), and in all of them the religiously backed struggle served as the engine for the development of an identity- and/or nation-building process. However, "the implicit contradiction between nationalism and Islam was blurred during the anticolonialist struggle,"[132] for the common enemy put together religious and secular people, Islam and state, united under one and the same banner. It goes without saying that the discrepancy between both positions would have led to a break and to a recalibration of priorities, as we will see in a moment.

The third form of jihad that we have found at the beginning of this section is *religious nationalist jihad*, a prevalently 20th-century type of warfare. Such jihad is a form of violent struggle directed to overthrown the despotic rulers of Islamic countries in order to replace it with a true Islamic society. As noted above, there is no perfect break between all these forms of jihad; rather, it is possible – even necessary – to find the connection that runs between them, seeing them as communicating vessels and not as independent and isolated phenomena.

The expression "religious nationalist" was coined by Fawaz A. Gerges and it stands for a peculiar all-encompassing struggle directed against local rulers in the post-independent period. Actually, such a temporal positioning is not so correct, since the apex of religious nationalist jihad is in the second half of the 20th century. "Throughout the 1970s, 1980s, and the first half of the 1990s the dominant thinking among leading jihadis was that the ability of the international system, *dar al-harb*, or the House of War, to dominate and subjugate *dar al-Islam* depended on the collusion and submissiveness of

131 Quite peculiar is the case of the charismatic leader Khan Abdul Gaffar Khan (1890-1988), known as Badhah Khan, in the North West Frontier Province of India. He chose a non-violent method to counter the British colonial power. Civil disobedience and non-cooperation with the colonial authorities were justified on the background of Islamic teachings and profoundly grounded in the doctrine of jihad. "Jihad, he argues, has nothing to do with the spread of religion, and is instead war against oppression and exploitation [... since] the primary virtue recommended by the Quran [...] is the intolerance of injustice" (Mukulika Banerjee, 'Justice and Non-Violent Jihād: The Anti-Colonial Struggle in the North West Frontier of British India', *Études Rurales*, no. 149/150 [January-June 1999]: p. 195).

132 Emmanuel Sivan, *Radical Islam. Medieval Theology and Modern Politics* (New Haven and London: Yale University Press, 1985), p. 38.

local ruling 'renegades'."[133] The *near enemy* became the focal target of those willing to bring about a radical change in a finally freed Islamic world.

The starting point of this evolution dates back to the foundation of the Society of the Muslim Brothers (*Jamā'at al-Ikhwān al-Muslimīn*), better known as the Muslim Brotherhood, in 1928. The founder, Ḥasan al-Bannā (1906-1949), set up a powerful organization that quickly spread over the entire Muslim majority countries of the MENA region, becoming the most relevant Islamist organization in the world – a real mass movement indeed – and setting the conditions for further radical and/or moderate developments of political Islam.

According to al-Bannā's view, Islam is an all-embracing system:

> Islam is a comprehensive system which deals with all spheres of life. It is a state and a homeland (or a government and an *umma*). It is morality and power (or mercy and justice). It is a culture and a law (or knowledge and jurisprudence). It is a material and wealth (or gain and prosperity). It is jihad and a call (or army and a cause). And finally, it is true belief and worship[134].

In light of this conviction, "Islam is the solution"[135] (*al-islām huwa al-ḥall*) became the motto of the Muslim Brothers, and the need for a genuine Islamic government was the compass of all the activities the society organized.

The abolition of the Caliphate by Atatürk in 1924 was unquestionably a traumatic turnabout for the entire Islamic community and, at the same time, it was among the many reasons for the formation of the same group of the Muslim Brotherhood. Al-Bannā's opinion regarding the deterioration of the *umma* was surely spawned by the end of the Caliphal experience, yet it was also solicited by other causes such as the multiplication of sectarian clashes and the life of luxury of Muslim rulers. Moreover, "moral decadence, as well as economic bankruptcy and anti-religious education, was a deliberate

---

133 Fawaz A. Gerges, *The Far Enemy. Why Jihad Went Global* (New York: Cambridge University Press, 2010), pp. 43-44.

134 Ḥasan al-Bannā, 'Message of the Teachings', in *Majmū'at rasā'il al-imām al-shahīd Ḥasan al-Bannā,* by Ḥasan al-Bannā (Kuwait: International Islamic Federation of Student Organizations, 1996), p. 7.

135 In a 1939 epistle, al-Bannā defines Islam as a system providing a domestic policy, a foreign policy, a judicial system, a defense and military policy, an independent economic policy, a cultural and educational policy, a family policy, and a moral system.

design of European powers to weaken and dominate the Muslim world,"[136] al-Bannā believes. Freedom from Western subjugation in all aspects of life was thus the main goal of the Muslim Brotherhood. The secular system of government must also be replaced by a truly Islamic political structure with the Caliph as its head and with one single party – in fact, even though the Egyptian constitution contemplated Islam as the religion of the state, its laws neglected this nominal disposition. The submissive form of Islam at the outset of the 20th century needed to be neutralized by embracing a wide-ranging way of life imbued with true Islam.

Ḥasan al-Bannā was the man who indicated a viable solution for the people from all levels of society, from the lower classes to the upper-middle classes. He assumed a gradualist bottom-up approach to Islamization, meaning that the center of his action was the individual, and only by virtue of changing people's hearts could the critical mass be reached and the political system changed. Al-Bannā wrote:

> Our sincere brothers are requested to work according to the following steps: (1) reforming the self; […] (2) establishing an Islamic home. A Muslim should induce his family to respect his ideology; […] (3) instructing and guiding the society by spreading the call of righteousness, fighting atrocities and detestful things, encouraging virtue; […] (4) liberation of the homeland from all unislamic or foreign control, whether political, economic, or ideological; (5) reforming the government so that it may become a truly Islamic government; […] (6) rebuilding the international prominence of the Islamic *umma* by liberating its lands, reviving its glorious heritage, bringing closer the cultures of its regions, and uniting its countries so that one Islamic Caliphate may be established; (7) instructing the world about the Islamic ideology by spreading the call of Islam to all corners of the globe "until there is no more tumult or oppression and the Religion of Allah prevails". "Allah will not allow but that His Light should prevail".[137]

The length of this quotation is justified by its importance. Here the bottom-up approach involves the individual, society and, in the end, the whole world. In al-Bannā's opinion, jihad is a reasonable practice that every Muslim must perform at the end of a purification process: the urgency of foreign domination makes performing jihad a compelling defensive tool, whereas once the domination will be over, Muslims can wage jihad against the infidel powers of the world in order to spread the Islamic faith worldwide.

---

136 Ahmad Zein al-Abdin, 'The Political Thought of Ḥasan al-Bannā', *Islamic Studies*, vol. 28, no. 3 (Autumn 1989): p. 222.

137 Al-Bannā, 'Message of the Teachings', pp. 14-17.

Al-Bannā explains that "Allah ordained jihad for the Muslims not as a tool of oppression or a means of satisfying personal ambitions, but rather as a defence for the mission [of spreading Islam], a guarantee of peace."[138]

By 1940, Ḥasan al-Bannā established the so-called Special Apparatus (*al-niẓām al-khāṣṣ*), a militia organization within the Muslim Brotherhood, whose members were trained to use weapons and explosives and whose end was to fight colonialism and Zionism. But eventually, the Special Apparatus turned against the Egyptian ruling elites and killed several Egyptian public figures. Al-Bannā dissociated himself from the acts of violence and stigmatized all those hotheads that acted in such a ferocious way, but the reputation of the Muslim Brotherhood was slightly decreasing, and he himself was assassinated in February 1949 most probably by the Egyptian secret police.

What is important for the present section is emphasizing the national focus of al-Bannā and the Muslim Brotherhood. In a late writing entitled *Our Message in a New Phase*, that appeared in the 1940s, al-Bannā writes:

> Egyptian nationalism has a definite place in our call. It is its right that it should be defended. Surely we are Egyptians; the most honourable place on this Earth to us, we were born and raised up here. Egypt is the land, which has been an abode of belief. It gladly embraced Islam and gave it a new territory. […] This is only *a part of the entire Arab homeland*. Therefore, whatever effort we make for the welfare of Egypt, would in reality be for Arabia, The East and Islam.[139]

The designation of Egypt as "a part of the entire Arab homeland" is surprising, in that al-Bannā re-articulates nationalism from an Islamic point of view, without universalizing the single territory and, on the contrary, placing the nation in a broader perspective encompassing the whole *dār al-Islām* (house of Islam). In adopting this strategy, al-Bannā appropriates the language of modernity in order to replace its modern and

---

138 Ḥasan al-Bannā, 'On Jihad', in *Majmū'at rasā'il al-imām al-shahīd Ḥasan al-Bannā,* by Ḥasan al-Bannā (Kuwait: International Islamic Federation of Student Organizations, 1996), p. 254. In this text, al-Bannā quotes many prophetic traditions (*ḥadīths*) and Qur'anic verses to support his ideas. Among others, he reports the following one: "On the authority of Abu Hurayra (May Allah be pleased with him): A man said: 'O Apostle of Allah, what of a man who wants [to engage in] jihad in Allah's way, but desires the goods of this world?' He said: 'There is no reward for him'. And he [i.e., the man] repeated this [question] to him three times, but he said: 'There is no reward for him'. Published by Abu Da'ud" (ibid., p. 256).

139 Ḥasan al-Bannā, 'Our Message In A New Phase', *The Qur'an Blog*, https://thequranblog.files.wordpress.com/2008/06/_5_-our-message-in-a-new-phase.pdf (accessed March 20, 2019). Emphasis added.

Western meanings with Islamic ones. In other words, he set off a "counter-hegemonic process of re-signifying the space of modernity from a counter-hegemonic perspective."[140] According to his design, the progression towards an entirely Islamic government goes hand in hand with the Islamization of the nation-state structure and with the concern with national issues. "Egypt is a part of the Islamic land,"[141] al-Bannā stressed in 1939, and therefore the celebration of local nationalism is functional to the further universal spreading of the call (*daʿwa*) of Islam.

Jihad (in both and chronologically-progressive senses of spreading the *daʿwa* and actual warfare) must be waged internally, i.e., within the borders of a nation-state, for the sake of the future global Islamic society. In particular, after the 1936-1939 Arab revolt in Palestine, also known as the Great Revolt, and especially after the creation of Israel in 1948, "al-Bannā stressed that the '*daʿwa qawliyya*' (verbal call) of the first phase ought to give way to the '*jihād ʿamalī*' (practical jihad) of the second phase and invited all of his adherents to follow suit."[142]

However, his murder in 1949 halted this process. Only the personality of Sayyid Quṭb (1906-1966) was able to revamp the jihadist ideology, spurring Islamist militants in a very innovative and explosive way and conferring "upon the reestablished MB [Muslim Brotherhood] underground a sense of purpose it had lacked."[143] Quṭb witnessed the last phase of British colonization of Egypt, therefore his further-going criticism addresses less foreign invaders and more local rulers.

In the first stage of his life, Quṭb was a progressive intellectual: from the very beginning he received a quite modern education. When he was a child, he was enrolled in the Qur'anic institute of the village of Moshe, in Upper Egypt, but "he hated so much the unhygienic and unclean surroundings of the Qur'anic school that after his first day in the school, he went back to the state school."[144] Quṭb graduated in 1933

140 Andrea Mura, 'A Genealogical Inquiry Into Early Islamism: The Discourse of Hasan al-Banna', *Journal of Political Ideologies*, vol. 17, no. 1 (February 2012): p. 81.

141 Ḥasan al-Bannā, 'Oh Youth!', *The Qur'an Blog*, https://thequranblog.files.wordpress.com/2008/06/_9_-oh-youth.pdf (accessed 20 March, 2019).

142 Ran A. Levy, 'The Idea of *Jihād* and Its Evolution: Ḥasan al-Bannā and the Society of the Muslim Brothers', *Die Welt Des Islams*, vol. 54, issue 2 (2014): p. 151.

143 Sivan, *Radical Islam*, p. 31.

144 Ibrahim Olatunde Uthman, 'From Social Justice to Islamic Revivalism: An Interrogation of Sayyid Qutb's Discourse', *Global Journal of Human Social Science. Sociology, Economics & Political Science*, vol. 12, issue 11 (2012): p. 93.

in Arabic Literature and became immediately active as a supporter of the modernization of Egypt. He collaborated with many progressive newspapers such as *Al-ishtirākiyya* ("Socialism").

The event that changed his life and divided his intellectual activity into two distinct phases was his journey to America, where he lived for two years. He was sent there in 1948 by the Ministry of Education in order to study the modern educational system. He came back to Egypt after two intense years and, suddenly and surprisingly, he joined the Society of the Muslim Brothers. What has happened during this period?

The answer can be found in a short report of his stay in America entitled *Amrīkā allatī ra'āytu* ("The America I have seen"), a document written in the form of a diary where he took note of what he considered degenerate and immoral in the American society. Americans are "the case of a people who have reached the peak of growth and elevation in the world of science and productivity, while remaining abysmally primitive in the world of the senses, feelings, and behavior,"[145] Quṭb writes. He introduces the concept of *primitiveness*, the dominant theme of the work – a word that refers to spiritual backwardness and not to technical and material backwardness.[146] Every activity in America has this primitive imprinting, from sports to interpersonal relations, from sex ("the matter of sex is biological in America. The word 'bashful' has become a dirty, disparaging word in America"[147]) to art.[148] Americans "are enamored with muscular strength and desire it,"[149]

145 Sayyid Quṭb, 'The America I Have Seen: In the Scale of Human Values', in *America in an Arab Mirror. Images of America in Arabic Travel Literature. An Anthology 1895-1995*, ed. by Kamal Abdel-Malek (New York: St. Martin's Press, 2000), p. 11.

146 "Despite his advanced knowledge and superlative work, the American appears to be so primitive in his outlook on life and its humanitarian aspects that it is puzzling to the observer" (ibid., p. 14).

147 Ibid., p. 23. And also: "Human society has long struggled to build and forge sexual mores. It has regulated these relations, emotions, and feelings, and struggled against the coarseness of sensation and the gloominess of natural impulse, in order to let genuine relationships fly about, and free-ranging longings soar high unfettered, along with all the strong ties around these relationships, in the feelings of individuals, in the life of the family, and in society at large. This struggle was isolated from life in America at once" (ibid., pp. 21-22).

148 "Anything that requires a touch of elegance is not for the American" (ibid., p. 26). And also: "America's virtues are the virtues of production and organization, and not those of human and social morals. America's are the virtues of the brain and the hand, and not those of taste and sensibility" (ibid., p. 27).

149 Ibid., p. 14. And also: "The American by his nature is taken with grandeur in size and numbers. It is his first measure of the way he feels and evaluates" (ibid., p. 19).

and are completely absorbed by animal desires[150] – the American soul lacks of true spiritual life, people "go to church for carousal and enjoyment, or, as they call it in their language, 'fun'."[151] Quṭb concludes his report warning that "humanity makes the gravest of errors and risks losing its account of morals, if it makes America its example in feelings and manners."[152]

Once back in Egypt, Quṭb joined the Muslim Brotherhood. But his radicalization cannot be imputed solely to his contact with the "primitive" American way of life. In fact, between 1948 and 1950, three events shook his soul: "The formation of the state of Israel, the murder of Ḥasan al-Bannā (greeted with joy overseas) and a phase of hard confrontation in Egyptian domestic politics (a confrontation that later turns out to be pre-revolutionary)."[153]

Within the Muslim Brotherhood, Quṭb came into contact with the ideas of Abū l-Aʿlāʾ al-Mawdūdī (1903-1979), an Indian-Pakistani thinker who played an important role in the creation of Pakistan, and the founder of the Jamāʿat-i Islāmī, an Islamic party whose objective was to implement a strict political interpretation of Islam. The Muslim Brotherhood translated into Arabic many of Mawdūdī's books – *Towards Understanding Islam* (1932) and *Jihad in Islam* (1939) are two of the most know works of Mawdūdī that circulated among the Muslim Brothers – and widely disseminated his ideas, especially those related to the corruption of present days. It was from Mawdūdī that Quṭb borrowed the idea of *jāhiliyya* for describing the contemporary world; and in the thought of Quṭb it is possible to regard the notion of *jāhiliyya* as the natural evolution of that of "primitiveness" applied to American society.

Traditionally, *jāhiliyya* is the era of spiritual ignorance in Arabia that preceded the delivery of the Qurʾanic message.[154] In the formation period

---

150 With reference to sex, Quṭb writes that "controlling such desires is testament to freedom from slavery and to going beyond the first rungs of humanity's evolution, and that a return to the freedom of the jungle is a gripping slavery and a relapse to the first primitive levels" (ibid., pp. 13-14).

151 Ibid., p. 19. And also: "For this reason, each church races to advertise itself with lit, colored signs on the doors and walls to attract attention, and by presenting delightful programs to attract the people much in the same way as merchants or showmen or actors. [...] The minister does not feel that his job is any different from that of a theater manager, or that of a merchant" (ibid.)

152 Ibid., p. 26.

153 Davide Tacchini, *Radicalismo islamico. Con il diario americano di Sayyid Qutb* (Milano: ObarraO Edizioni, 2015), p. 69.

154 "The word *jahiliyya,* rendered as ignorance or barbarism, occurs several times in the Qurʾan (3:148; 5:55; 33:33; 48:26)" (Rizwi Faizer, 'Jahiliyya', in *Encyclopedia*

of the *ḥadīths* collections, the term *jāhiliyya* came to refer to the historical period prior to Muḥammad's prophetic mission, and thus a synonym of ignorance – the substantial ignorance of God and the Sacred. Mawdūdī for the first time applied the notion to contemporary societies, namely, the Western and the Communist worlds. "The word 'Jahiliyyat' [sic] is the antonym of Islam,"[155] he writes, making it a suitable description for social realities released from a specific time and space.

However, there is a difference between Mawdūdī's and Quṭb's understanding of the concept:

> Mawdūdī's definition of *jāhiliyya* mainly referred to the way of life and thought of the ruling classes, those leaders of Muslim India and not the person in the street. Furthermore, in al-Mawdūdī's view, there were two categories of *jāhiliyya*, namely pure *jāhiliyya* and mixed *jāhiliyya*. […] Quṭb, on the other hand, claimed that the whole world was living in a *jahili* society, which was pure *jāhiliyya.*[156]

Mawdūdī believes that the condition of Islamic societies is a situation of *mixed jāhiliyya*, a mixture of Islam and external influences, i.e., Western ideas and practices. In this view, colonialism has polluted the original Islamic way of life of traditionally Islamic countries. On the contrary, Quṭb is uncompromising: for him, there can be no halfway situation between Islam and *jāhiliyya*, and if even a drop of *jāhiliyya* contaminates the limpid waters of Islamic societies, then such Islamic societies become *jāhilī* environments: a society is either Islamic or *jāhilī.*[157]

He is very clear on this point in his most famous book, *Maʿālim fī aṭ-ṭarīq* ("Milestones"), first published in 1964. Here he writes:

> The *jāhilī* society is any society other than the Muslim society; and if we want a more specific definition, we may say that any society is a *jāhilī* society which does not dedicate itself to submission to God alone, in its beliefs and

---

of Islam and the Muslim World, vol. 1, ed. by Richard C. Martin [New York: Macmillan Reference USA, 2004], p. 370).

155 Abū l-Aʿlāʾ al-Mawdūdī, 'The Meaning of the Qurʾan', *Quran411.com*, https://www.quran411.com/quran/quran-tafseer-maududi.pdf (accessed 26 November, 2018).

156 Asyraf Hj. A.B. Rahman and Nooraihan Ali, 'The Influence of Al-Mawdudi and the Jama'at Al Islami Movement On Sayyid Qutb Writings', *World Journal of Islamic History and Civilization*, vol. 2, no. 4 (2012): p. 235.

157 According to Quṭb, "Islam knows only two kinds of societies, the Islamic and the *jāhilī*" (Sayyid Quṭb, *Milestones* [New Delhi: Islamic Book Service, 2002], p. 93).

ideas, in its observances of worship, and in its legal regulations. *According to this definition, all the societies existing in the world today are jāhilī.*[158]

To fully understand the nature of *jāhiliyya* we must introduce the concept of *ḥākimiyya*, usually translated as "sovereignty" and "authority",[159] which in Quṭb takes on the meaning of Sovereign of sovereignty, that is, God's maximum sovereignty over all things. Consequently, "this concept of *ḥākimiyya* is the prism through which Quṭb viewed the political system of the world, dividing it into Islam and *jāhiliyya*:"[160] what is not under God's control, is *jāhilī* – that is to say, what does not follow God's commandments and precepts, is un-Islamic. Man has to co-operate in accordance with *ḥākimiyya*, taking the place that is his own within the harmonious system of the created universe, and obeying the sacred norms disclosed by the prophet Muḥammad in what is deemed to be the last and final Revelation – which implies that *jāhiliyya* breaks with the same human nature. A true Islamic system is based on God alone as the Legislator, whereas "other systems rest on the principle that *ḥākimiyya* (absolute sovereignty) belongs to man and he legislates for himself."[161] Or, formulating this concept otherwise and in a more straightforward manner, "*jāhiliyya* is the *ḥākimiyya* of humans; Islam is the *ḥākimiyya* of God."[162] In fact, Quṭb maintains that *jāhiliyya* "transfers to man one of the greatest attributes of God, namely sovereignty, and makes some men lords over others"[163] – which implies that an Islamic system will free men from the servitude to other men, bringing forth universal freedom.[164]

This is to say that religious nationalist jihad is part of a more comprehensive system of thought that tends to delegitimize the actual

158 Quṭb, *Milestones*, p. 80. Emphasis added.

159 "The word is derived from the Arabic root '*ḥ-k-m*,' which appears in various forms about two hundred times in the Qur'an, with a range of different meanings: to judge, to decide, to rule, and so forth" (Stéphane Lacroix, 'Ḥākimiyya', in *Encyclopedia of Islam, Three*, eds. Kate Fleet, Gudrun Krämer, Denis Matringe, John Nawas, Everett Rowson. Accessed 28 March, 2019, https://referenceworks.brillonline.com/entries/encyclopaedia-of-islam-3/hakimiyya-COM_30217).

160 Sayed Khatab, 'Hakimiyyah and Jahiliyyah in the Thought of Sayyid Qutb', *Middle Eastern Studies*, vol. 38, no. 3 (July 2002): p. 147.

161 Ibid., p. 158.

162 William E. Shepard, 'Sayyid Qutb's Doctrine of *Jāhiliyya*', *International Journal of Middle East Studies*, vol. 35, no. 4 (November 2003): p. 525.

163 Quṭb, *Milestones*, p. 11.

164 Sayyid Quṭb describes Islam as "a universal declaration of the freedom of man from servitude to other men and from servitude to his own desires, which is also a form of human servitude" (Quṭb, *Milestones*, p. 57).

rulers of Islamic countries by resorting to a more articulated theoretical observation than a mere dissatisfaction with the policies implemented in a specific moment by a specific person. Quṭb blames "what we consider to be Islamic culture, Islamic sources, Islamic philosophy and Islamic thought"[165] as *jāhilī* constructs. It is the first time that such a radical consideration was ever expressed. Renzo Guolo recognizes the extraordinary significance of this statement by saying that for Quṭb "the West is now inner West,"[166] and the domestic nature of this insidious enemy requires a total response, hence not a speculative reaction only, but an active, operational and vigorous struggle. The Islamic system confronting the *jāhilī* one "should come into the battlefield as an organized movement and a viable group"[167] without distinctions based on gender, race, language and country: Islam is *the* nationality, and no other considerations should be taken into account in the effort of building the alternative to *jāhiliyya.*

Basing his considerations on the life of the Prophet, Quṭb insists there is a distinction between the Meccan and the Medinan periods: the Meccan period aims at removing all *jāhilī* influences, thus adopting education, preaching and persuasion for reforming beliefs and ideas ("Our aim is first to change ourselves to that we may later change the society"[168]); the Medinan period, that follows chronologically, will witness the actual fight, or *jihād*, designed to abolish all the authorities and organizations of the *jāhilī* systems. In this sense, he is talking of a period yet to come, projecting the classical historical periodization (Meccan and Medinan periods) into an enlarged temporal horizon, and making it the compass for the next turning point of civilization.

Jihad is not at all a defensive practice, Quṭb clearly states,[169] thence describing the reasons for the militant struggle: "To establish God's authority in the earth; to arrange human affairs according to the true guidance provided by God; to abolish all the Satanic forces and Satanic systems of life; to end the lordship of one man over others."[170] Jihad will be

165 Quṭb, *Milestones*, p. 20.

166 Renzo Guolo, *Avanguardie della fede. L'islamismo tra ideologia e politica* (Milano: Guerini e Associati, 1999), p. 26.

167 Quṭb, *Milestones*, p. 47.

168 Ibid., p. 21.

169 "If we insist on calling Islamic jihād a defensive movement, then we must change the meaning of the word 'defense' and mean by it 'the defense of man' against all those elements which limit his freedom" (ibid., p. 62).

170 Ibid., p. 70.

but "an eternal state,"[171] a permanent condition, an endless effort that will only end on Judgment Day.

To begin with, true Muslims forming the vanguard (*ṭal'ia*)[172] need to free the homeland of Islam, namely, the so-called Islamic world, the territories where Islam was dominant in the past centuries. However, this action is not the ultimate objective of the vanguard: the finally emancipated Islamic world will become "the headquarters for the movement of Islam, which is then to be carried throughout the earth to the whole of mankind."[173] In saying so, Sayyid Quṭb, willing or not, sets a priority: he gives a national imprint to his jihad.

Therefore, when Quṭb became "not only the president of the propaganda section, but also the most influential ideologist of the entire movement [of the Muslim Brotherhood],"[174] the purpose of the organization became making Egypt a real Islamic state. The battle to fight was that against the *ṭāghūt,* the transgressor ruler who refuses to enforce the *sharī'a.* The Arab ruling élite are Westernized and must be overthrown. In fact, "the enemy is no longer 'out there'"[175], and muscular action is thus required.

On July 23, 1952, the Free Officers Movement organized a coup and overthrew King Fārūq (r. 1936-1952), finally ending the British occupation of the country. At the beginning the Muslim Brothers had good relations with the Free Officers and with Jamāl 'Abd al-Nāṣir (known in English as Nasser), hoping that the conditions to finally create an Islamic state had arrived. Sayyid Quṭb was appointed the contact person between the Muslim Brothers and the Free Officers. Nonetheless, something went wrong: the Free Officers gave a socialist, nationalist and secular turn to their government, and Quṭb dismissed himself from all public offices.[176]

---

171 Ibid., p. 65.

172 "It is necessary that there should be a vanguard which sets out with this determination and then keeps walking on the path, marching through the cast ocean of *jāhiliyya* which has encompassed the entire world" (ibid., p. 12).

173 Ibid., p. 72.

174 Margherita Picchi, 'Sayyid Qutb: biografia di un pensatore militante', in *La battaglia tra islam e capitalismo*, by Sayyid Qutb (Venezia: Marcianum Press, 2016), p. 24.

175 Yvonne Yazbeck Haddad, 'The Qur'anic Justification for an Islamic Revolution: The View of Sayyid Qutb', *Middle East Journal*, vol. 37, no. 1 (Winter 1983): p. 28.

176 In *Milestones*, Sayyid Quṭb attacks the ideology of Arab nationalism when, talking of history of Islamic world, he writes that "in this great Islamic society Arabs, Persians, Syrians, Egyptians, Moroccans, Turks, Chinese, Indians, Romans, Greeks, Indonesians, Africans were gathered together – in short, peoples of all nations and all races. […] This marvelous civilization was not an 'Arabic civilization' even for a single day; it was purely an 'Islamic civilization'" (Quṭb,

Following a clash between some Muslim Brotherhood students and regime members, Nasser outlawed the Brotherhood in January 1954, and Quṭb was imprisoned. Ten years later, Quṭb was released, but when the Brotherhood was accused of planning the assassination of Nasser, once again Quṭb was arrested with the charge of plotting to overthrow the state. It was the year 1965. On August 29, 1966, he was executed by hanging with six other members of the Brotherhood.

Sayyid Quṭb's experience with prisons of the regime helps one to understand his thinking: behind the bars he matured awareness that society must be totally redone and that the condition of *jāhiliyya* had by then penetrated the deepest folds of society, given that the military and the police tortured, mocked and brutalized many prisoners, particularly those who belonged to the Muslim Brotherhood, the only social and political force that promoted the full application of the *sharīʿa*.

However, Quṭb was an advocate of *daʿwa* (preaching), and he stressed the importance of consciousness raising before any actual implementation of Islamist ideology. He did not disdain violence, but

> as to whether he was engaged in a plot to overthrow the Egyptian government at the time of his last arrest, the evidence of his writings suggests that he would have considered this quite premature but would not have eschewed violence when the time came. He gives no clear indication, however, of when the revolution would come.[177]

The extent of Quṭb's influence over Egyptian radical groups is huge. Quṭb was very influential particularly in the years following his death. Groups such as al-Takfīr wa-l-Hijra and Tanẓīm al-Jihād, also known as Jihad Group or Egyptian Islamic Jihad, owe much to his system of thought. William Shepard stresses that all these organizations learned from Quṭb "the idea that the most immediate danger comes from within the Islamic society, not from without."[178] This means that religious nationalist jihad in Egypt[179] reached

Milestones, pp. 49-50). In his vision, Arab nationalism implies division and represents a form of *jāhiliyya*, opposing the universality of Islam. The nation-state is compared to a tribal society, which in turn contradicts *tawḥīd*. In short, Quṭb is against both Pan-Arabist ideology and Egyptian nationalism, which stem from the *jāhilī* tendency to divide rather that unite.

177 Shepard, 'Sayyid Qutb's Doctrine of *Jāhiliyya*', p. 531.

178 Ibid., p. 536.

179 The cases cited are Egyptian, but it must be considered that the importance they have had for the rest of the Islamic world is exemplary, and their evolution has influenced all subsequent religious nationalist jihadi groups.

its maturity in the second half of the 20th century, at a moment when the death of Quṭb made clear that the government was opposing all Islamist attempts to implement *sharīʿa* in a country that was finally freed from the colonial power: if the British were no more, the only obstacle for the full application of Islam as a system became the ruling class, namely, Nasser and his successor, Muḥammad Anwar al-Sādāt (r. 1970-1981).

But in particular, there was one event that gave a decisive boost to the Islamist cause: the Six-Day War between Israel and a number of Arab countries. The 1967 defeat of the Arab coalition changed the way Arab countries as well as radical organizations perceived themselves. All of a sudden, the nationalist pride of Egypt fell apart, pan-Arab nationalism seemed farther away and a sentiment of moral inferiority took up their empty spaces. Then, another mutation occurred: someone started to think that for too long society had been far from true Islam, in contrast to the Israeli population and its (supposed) religious disposition. The spark for a religious outburst was lit.

The group known as al-Takfīr wa-l-Hijra was formed in the early 1970s by Shukrī Muṣṭafā (1942-1978). A member of the Muslim Brotherhood, Muṣṭafā was arrested in 1965 in the wake of the general repression of the Society in Egypt. He spent much of his time in prison reading Quṭb's writings. Upon his release in 1971, al-Takfīr wa-l-Hijra took shape.

The idea of *hijra* (here meaning exodus from an impious society and its separation from the rest of the *jāhilī* world) pretends to replicate Muḥammad's migration from Mecca to Medina in the year 622. Quṭb did talk of a degree of separation from *jāhiliyya* (the vanguard "should keep itself somewhat aloof from this all-encompassing *jāhiliyya,*"[180] he wrote), but in Muṣṭafā's mind, and later in al-Takfīr wa-l-Hijra's practice, the degree of withdrawal was greater than what Quṭb intended it, as we will see soon.

The other term definying the group is *takfīr*. *The Encyclopedia of Islam. Second edition* states that "from earliest Islamic times onwards, this was an accusation hurled at opponents by sectarians and zealots, such as the Kharijites, but a theologian like al-Ghazālī held that, since the adoption of *kufr* was the equivalent here of apostasy, entailing the death penalty, it should not be lightly made."[181] The use of this term has thus been discouraged throughout Islamic history: the memory of the Kharijites (al-Khawārij)

180 Quṭb, *Milestones*, p. 12.

181 John Owen Hunwick, 'Takfīr', in *Encyclopedia of Islam, Second edition*, ed. by P.J. Bearman et al., vol. 10 (Leiden: Brill, 1997), p. 122.

has always been alive in the mind of the global Islamic community.[182] Accusing someone of *takfīr* is declaring him/her a *kāfir* (infidel), which means that a Muslim charged with this allegation is a *murtadd* (apostate). It goes without saying that the abuse of *takfīr* breaks down the unity of the *umma* – that is why it has always been limited and contained.

The group led by Shukrī Muṣṭafā, known as al-Takfīr wa-l-Hijra, elaborated an all-encompassing and exclusive worldview based on *hijra* (separation from the rest of the corrupted and sinful world) and *takfīr* (excommunication of all Muslims outside of the radical organization). Muṣṭafā rejected the four traditional Sunni schools of law, which he accused of being syncretistic innovations and not part of the pure Islamic teaching. All members of this sect-style group were forced to spend time only with people who were already part of the organization. And according to the idea of *hijra*, they built parallel communities in low-rent districts in Cairo and in mountains outside of the city of Asyūṭ. They "viewed themselves as the *exclusive* inheritors of the prophetic tradition to the degree that they rejected 1,300 years of Islamic thought and practice."[183]

At the beginning, al-Takfīr wa-l-Hijra constituted no threat for the government since it did not participate in the political life of the country. But in July 1977, some members of the group kidnapped and executed Muḥammad Ḥusayn al-Dhahabī, a former Minister of Waqf and Professor at al-Azhar University, because he was a critic of militant jihadist movements in the country and especially of al-Takfīr wa-l-Hijra itself. His murder was followed by a violent crackdown, and Shukrī Muṣṭafā was arrested and executed the following year, in March 1978.

The gradualist approach of al-Takfīr wa-l-Hijra, despite the last act of violence that betrayed some rush to purify the world, was similar to what Quṭb had described: first preaching, then expanding – or, that is the same, first *da'wa*, then jihad.

The other group that drew inspiration from Sayyid Quṭb, Tanẓīm al-Jihād, embraced a more radical method. Its target was not society as a whole, which was regarded as essentially religious and broadly Islamic, but the ruling élite and its alleged anti-Islamic behaviors and decisions. Contrary to al-Takfīr wa-l-Hijra, which adopted a passive, separatist ideology and

182 The Kharijites are a group of schismatic Muslims of the 1st century of Islam. They broke with the fourth Caliph, 'Alī ibn Abī Ṭālib, following the battle of Ṣiffīn (657), where 'Alī accepted Mu'āwiya's arbitration. After the battle of Nahrawān (659), a Kharijite murdered 'Alī (661).

183 Jeffrey B. Cozzens, 'Al-Takir wa'l Hijra: Unpacking an Enigma', *Studies in Conflict & Terrorism*, vol. 32, no. 6 (2009): p. 494.

a long-term approach, the al-Jihad Group "followed an activist, militant ideology that committed it to immediate and violent action against the regime."[184] Eventually, the al-Jihad Group was successful in assassinating the President of Egypt, Muḥammad Anwar al-Sādāt, on October 1981, seeking to spark a total revolution that should have led to an Islamic state. But history tells a different story: Egyptians did not rebel, and the repression of many Islamist organizations, as well as imprisonment and execution of proper al-Jihad's members, took place throughout the entire country.

The ideologue of the group was Muḥammad ʿAbd al-Salām Faraj (1954-1982), whose 1981 book entitled *al-Farīḍa al-Ghāʾiba* ("The Absent Obligation" or "The Neglected Duty") became the manifesto of operative Islamism. Faraj was executed for his role in planning and coordinating the assassination of Sādāt.

In the manifesto, Faraj describes jihad as "the peak of Islam"[185] and "the only way to bring Islam back,"[186] although today forgotten ("This is an obligation denied by some Muslims and neglected by others, despite that the evidence concerning its obligation is crystal clear in the book of Allah"[187]). He draws inspiration from Sayyid Quṭb's theoretical elaboration on the perversion of society and the restoration of God's rule. The main difference between the two ideologues is based on the judgment about society at large: Quṭb regards Egyptian society as *jāhilī*, whereas Faraj is more optimistic about it, believing it to be essentially Muslim. "According to Faraj's optimistic worldview, getting rid of the rulers would be enough in order to return Islam to this nation and establish an Islamic state. After their removal, nobody will have an aversion to Islam".[188] Faraj's optimistic enthusiasm was nevertheless a false move, if we take into consideration the ruinous end of the group and the inactivity of the Egyptian population after al-Sādāt's death.

Al-Farīḍa al-Ghāʾiba is a clear policy document on how to carry forward an effective Islamist revolutionary action. The final goal of jihad is the return of the Caliphate, as Faraj plainly states at the beginning of the book

---

184 David Zeidan, 'Radical Islam in Egypt: A Comparison of Two Groups', *Middle East Review of International Affairs*, vol. 3, no. 3 (September 1999), http://meria.idc.ac.il/journal/1999/issue3/zeidan.pdf (accessed December 2, 2016).

185 Muḥammad ʿAbd al-Salām Faraj, *Jihad. The Absent Obligation* (Birmingham: Maktabah Al Ansaar Publications, 2000), p. 38.

186 Ibid., p. 14.

187 Ibid., p. 19.

188 Danny Orbach, 'Tyrannicide in Radical Islam: The Case of Sayyid Qutb and Abd al-Salam Faraj', *Middle Eastern Studies*, vol. 48, no. 6 (November 2012): p. 970.

– but before countering the West and its Zionist allies, the duty for Muslims is to fight and depose all the false rulers of Islamic countries.[189] The national character of Faraj's jihad is evident. "If the [Islamic] state can only be established by fighting, then it is compulsory on us to fight,"[190] he writes. And also: "The present rulers have apostatized from Islam."[191] These rulers are to blame for their links with the colonial powers, which invalidate their adherence to Islam. And if "one of the necessary conditions of the Islamic state is that Islamic laws must govern it,"[192] as Faraj vehemently maintains, all the present rulers are apostates because they are acting like the Tartars, that is, they adopt laws laid by the Western powers and borrowed from foreign legal systems. The Damascus scholar Ibn Taymiyya (1263-1328) is lengthily cited in the book, and, with reference to the Tartars, Faraj relies on his harsh words against the invasion of the Mongols in his time.[193] The Western mentality and values have penetrated Islamic society by means of those apostate (*murtaddūn*) rulers, and there is no doubt that "the entire

---

189 To justify this claim, Faraj quotes a famous prophetic tradition on the progression of various forms of government – that same *ḥadīth* that will be reclaimed by the self-proclaimed Islamic State. "The Messenger of Allaah said: 'The Prophecy will remain among you for as long as Allaah wills it to remain, then He will lift it when He wills to; then there will be Khilaafah on the method of Prophecy, and it will remain for as long as Allaah wills it to remain, then He will lift it when He wills to; then there will be hereditary reign, and it will remain for as long as Allaah wills it to remain, then He will lift it when He wills to; then there will be tyrannical reign. And it will remain for as long as Allaah wills it to remain, then He will lift it when He wills to, then there will be Khilaafah on the method of Prophecy, which shall govern people by the Sunnah of the Prophet, and Islaam will encounter on earth an audacity, which the inhabitants of the Heavens and Earth will be pleased with and the Heaven shall pelt down (by Allaah's Leave) all the vegetation and blessed things to emerge' (Collected by al-Haafidh al-Iraqi through Ahmad and classified it saheeh). The hereditary reign was indeed over. As for the tyrannical one it occurs by means of coup d'etats, which enable those who are behind them to rule despite the will of the people. This *ḥadīth* gives us glad tidings about the return of Islam in our age and provides the Islamic resurgence with hope and informs them (the Muslims) that they will have a brilliant future in terms of economy and agriculture" (Faraj, *Jihad. The Absent Obligation*, pp. 17-18).

190 Faraj, *Jihad. The Absent Obligation*, p. 20.

191 Ibid., p. 24.

192 Ibid., p. 20.

193 The capture of the capital Baghdad of the Abbasid Caliphate by the Mongols in 1258 becomes here a strong metaphor suggesting that a traumatic event is occurring even today.

mentality of the Westerner has been carefully designed to be hostile to Islam,"[194] Faraj asserts.

Muḥammad ʿAbd al-Salām Faraj presents three situations in which jihad becomes obligatory: (1) when the Muslim army and an infidel army meet to fight; in this situation, no one should leave and all Muslim fighters must take part to the battle; (2) when disbelievers invade an Islamic country; in this case, jihad is carried forward as a defensive effort; (3) when the legitimate Muslim leader orders the community of the believers to embrace weapons and set off a jihad. Today, what renders jihad an obligatory duty is the second point:

> The enemies are these rulers who have snatched the leadership of the Muslims. Thence jihad against them is *farḍ al-ʿayn* [individual duty]. Besides, the Islamic jihad is now in need of the effort of very Muslim. And it should be borne in mind that when jihad is *farḍ al-ʿayn*, it is not required to seek permission from one's parents for the to march forth as scholars said: "it becomes like praying and fasting".[195]

In transforming jihad in a *farḍ al-ʿayn*, or individual duty, Faraj is saying that jihad is as important as the five pillars of Islam – actually, he makes it the *sixth* pillar of Islam.

In sum, Muslims must take action and conquer a portion of territory for establishing the Islamic state, in a defensive effort designed to free their homeland from corrupt rulers.

However, jihad is not for defense only: "Fighting in Islam is to raise Allah's word highest, either offensively or defensively,"[196] Faraj states. Hence, "when an Islamic state is set up, and there is no threat to its borders, jihad is carried out offensively against the enemies of Allah, and in order to propagate the religion."[197] Expanding the state will be only the further step: internal liberation and emancipation is the primary and foremost duty of the revived Muslim community. "Establish the state and remove the tyrants"[198] becomes the motto of jihadists and their primary objective.[199] This elaboration led Faraj to "coin the terms 'near

194 Faraj, *Jihad. The Absent Obligation*, p. 41.
195 Ibid., p. 59.
196 Ibid., p. 49.
197 Ibid., p. 45.
198 Ibid., p. 64.
199 "The priority for the Muslims right now, the minimum for their religion, is the establishment of an Islamic state, where they can establish and secure the rule of Allah" (ibid., p. 47) And also: "It is obligatory upon the Muslims to raise their

enemy' and 'far enemy' and [to] assign the highest priority to militarily confronting the former"[200] – such terminology has entered the rhetoric of radical Islamists and is by now still very useful for the classification of these groups.

The murder of al-Sādāt was justified as the first move toward a total revolution. Such an extreme action was also a reaction to some incendiary events: to the Camp David Accords of 1978-79 aiming at recognizing the state of Israel in what was once Muslim territory; to the new economic orientation known as the *infitāḥ*[201]; and to the 1979 Iranian Revolution, which has undeniably inspired the Egyptian radicals.

The nationalist blueprint of the groups and personalities studied in relation to the category of religious nationalist jihad derives from "a repulsion for and rejection of the moral decadence that is prevalent in society [and not from] concern for foreign policy:"[202] this attitude accords a recognizable and distinguishable identity to many Muslim Brotherhood's offshoots, and especially to Sayyid Quṭb's direct or indirect disciples.

The shift of target, from the internal enemy to the external enemy, was a slow and gradual process. Two are the chief personalities that conveyed the new direction of the jihadi mission and projected the jihadist movement into the global arena: Ayman al-Ẓawāhirī (b. 1951) and Osama bin Laden (1957-2011). Therefore, *global jihad*, which is the last type of jihad that we have classified at the beginning of this section, flourished from the ashes of the failure of actually changing the secular regimes within the Arab world – in fact, failing to achieve its objectives due to the strong resilience of the military and secular regimes, the religious national jihad ended up giving itself other objectives, drastically changing its structure and giving life to the global jihad program.

Following this line of reasoning, let us elaborate somewhat on al-Ẓawāhirī, leader of today's al-Qāʿida and second in command during Bin Laden's leadership, and how his thinking was influenced by Quṭb's ideas. In this sense, it is not incorrect to state that al-Ẓawāhirī is the very link between religious nationalist jihad and global jihad.

---

swords against the rulers who are hiding the truth and manifesting falsehood" (ibid., p. 49).

200 Gerges, *The Far Enemy*, p. 44.

201 The *infitāḥ* policy is a liberalization program based on the free market: it combines a solid state sector, incentives for foreign investment and private companies, and significantly reduces the power of the military, giving space to a new class of capitalists.

202 Gerges, *The Far Enemy*, pp. 45-46.

In his most famous book entitled *Knights Under the Prophet's Banner* (*Fursān Taḥt Rāyat al-Nabī*), written in 2001, he traces his intellectual formation and operational training, and justifies the shift from focusing on the domestic enemy to targeting the United States and its allies. In the book, al-Ẓawāhirī explains that his involvement in the jihad movement in Egypt began in the mid-1960s, when Nasser banned the Muslim Brotherhood and arrested many of its members, including Sayyid Quṭb. Soon al-Ẓawāhirī's group, the Egyptian Islamic Jihad, took as ideological reference the same Quṭb, whose personality "was the spark that ignited the Islamic revolution,"[203] he writes. However, the death of al-Sādāt led to a strong crackdown on Islamist groups in Egypt, and eventually al-Ẓawāhirī was arrested. He spent three years in prison, and instead of changing his mind about the issue of jihad, he increasingly identified himself with the suffering and the dedication of Sayyid Quṭb – in other words, he became even more radicalized, developing the deep impression that the Egyptian government had become one of the harshest enemies of the Islamic religion. His active participation in the underground life of the Egyptian Islamic Jihad after the three years in prison made him a leading personality within the movement, and his intellectual standing allowed him to impose himself on the scene of the so-called religious national jihad.[204]

---

203 Ayman al-Ẓawāhirī, 'Knights Under the Prophet's Banner', in *His Own Words. A Translation of the Writings of Dr. Ayman al Zawahiri*, ed. by Laura Mansfield (Old Tappan: TLG Publications, 2006), p. 48. Al-Ẓawāhirī also says: "Sayyid Quṭb became an example of sincerity and adherence to justice. He spoke justice in the face of the tyrant (Jamal Abd-al-Nasir) and paid his life as a price for this" (ibid., p. 49). The connection between al-Ẓawāhirī and Sayyid Quṭb is important in that it is the main ingredient for the creation of the Salafi-Jihadi ideological construct along with Wahhabism – the latter will be later introduced by Osama bin Laden, as we will see in a moment.

204 During the day of the trial, on December 4, 1982, in front of the court, the journalists and the other three hundred defendants, he was filmed saying: "Now we want to speak to the whole world! Who are we? Who are we? Why they bring us here, and what we want to say? About the first question, we are Muslims! We are Muslims who believe in their religion! We are Muslims who believe in their religion, both in ideology and practice, and hence we tried our best to establish an Islamic state and an Islamic society! […] We are not sorry, we are not sorry for what we have done for our religion, and we have sacrificed, and we stand ready to make more sacrifices! We are here – the real Islamic front and the real Islamic opposition against Zionism, Communism, and imperialism! […] And now, as an answer to the second question, Why did they bring us here? They bring us here for two reasons! First, they are trying to abolish the outstanding Islamic movement […] and, secondly, to complete the conspiracy of evacuating the area in preparation for the Zionist infiltration. […] We are here – the real Islamic front and the real

However, the evolution in the direction of a global perspective started one year before his arrest, when he was asked to go to Afghanistan in order to take part in a relief project. From the very beginning, the Afghan resistance against the Soviet invasion was estimated by al-Ẓawāhirī to be a golden opportunity to relaunch the jihadi movement and to breathe new life into the tired and disillusioned ranks of militants. As al-Ẓawāhirī narrates, "the opportunity to go to Afghanistan was a gift handed on a gold platter. I was always searching for a secure base for jihadist activity in Egypt because the members of the [Egyptian] fundamentalist movement were the target of repeated security crackdowns."[205]

In 1980, he spent four months in Peshawar, Pakistan, before returning to Egypt where he was arrested in 1981; then, he was released in 1984 and in 1986 he left Egypt and rejoined the jihad in Afghanistan. The Afghan war had another peculiarity that made it the jihadi war *par excellence*: it was truly and explicitly Islamic. In al-Ẓawāhirī's words:

> The Muslim youth in Afghanistan waged the war to liberate Muslim land under purely Islamic slogans, a very vital matter, for many of the liberation battles in our Muslim world had used composite slogans, that mixed nationalism with Islam and, indeed, sometimes caused Islam to intermingle with leftist, communist slogans.[206]

The need of having an arena that would act like an incubator for other jihadi soldiers was, for al-Ẓawāhirī, another reason for attaching so much importance to Afghanistan. That is why "the Afghan resistance sees its struggle more in terms of a 'holy war' than as a war of national liberation."[207]

Armed with passionate enthusiasm, al-Ẓawāhirī "opened the Islamic Jihad bureau in Peshawar to serve both as a liaison point for new Mujahedeen [sic] and a recruitment agency."[208] But he was not the only leader to have had such an idea: the Afghan war was a golden opportunity for whoever wanted to offer a longer-term perspective for the jihad. And,

---

Islamic opposition against Zionism, Communism, and imperialism!" (Quoted in Lawrence Wright, 'The Man Behind Bin Laden. How and Egyptian Doctor Became a Master of Terror', *New Yorker*, September 16, 2002, https://www.newyorker.com/magazine/2002/09/16/the-man-behind-bin-laden).

205 Al-Ẓawāhirī, 'Knights Under the Prophet's Banner', p. 26.

206 Ibid., pp. 35-36.

207 Olivier Roy, 'Islam in the Afghan Resistance', *Religion in Communist Lands*, vol. 12, no. 1 (1984): p. 55.

208 Nimrod Raphaeli, 'Ayman Muhammad Rabi' Al-Zawahiri: The Making of an Arch-Terrorist', *Terrorism and Political Violence*, vol. 14, no 4 (Winter 2002): p. 7.

in fact, in Afghanistan al-Ẓawāhirī came into contact with a network built by ʿAbd Allāh Yūsuf Muṣṭafā al-ʿAzzām (often referred to as ʿAbdallāh ʿAzzām) and Osama bin Laden.

ʿAbdallāh ʿAzzām (1941-1989) can be considered the leading jihadi figure of the Afghan resistance and the grandfather of the organization known as *al-Qāʿida*. His effort for internationalizing the jihad is well known: born in the village of Sīlat al-Hārithiya, about eight kilometers northwest of the city of Jenin in the West Bank, Palestine, he was traumatized when Israeli tanks occupied his village in 1967. He took part in the resistance against Israeli occupation, but he was soon disillusioned by the secular and socialist stances of the Palestine Liberation Organization (PLO). After finishing his PhD in the Principles of Islamic Jurisprudence at al-Azhar University in Cairo in 1973, he moved to Jordan, taught Islamic law for six years at the University in Amman, and grew in importance within the local Muslim Brotherhood organization. In the mid-1980s, ʿAzzām "moved to Saudi Arabia. There he joined Muhammad Quṭb [Sayyid Quṭb's brother] on the faculty of King Abdul Aziz University. At the university, Quṭb and ʿAzzām shared a young Saudi student named Osama bin Laden."[209] However, there is no mention by either ʿAzzām or Bin Laden that they met at Jidda. Finally, in 1981 ʿAzzām moved to Islamabad, Pakistan. From that moment on, his life was completely absorbed by the Afghan resistance movement, and his efforts changed the face of the global jihadi movement. His energy was directed to arbitrate between the local commanders and to work as an intermediator between Afghan *mujāhidūn* (sing. *mujāhid*) and Arab and non-Arab Muslims volunteers from other Islamic countries. For these reasons, he wrote two books that became immediately influential among militants, *The Defense of the Muslim Lands* in 1984, and *Join the Caravan* in 1987.

In these works, his intent is "to popularize the idea of a universal and international Islamic jihad, rather than the existing condition of each national Muslim group concentrating on a narrow area of concern related to their own circumstances"[210] – clearly this is the way out from the religious national jihad towards the global jihad.

From the first pages of *Join the Caravan*:

> We then are calling upon the Muslims and urging them to proceed to fight, for many reasons, at the head of which are the following:

209 Dore Gold, *Hatred's Kingdom: How Saudi Arabia Supports the New Global Terrorism* (Washington: Regnery Publishing, 2004), chap. 6, Kindle.

210 Andrew McGregor, 'Jihad and the Rifle Alone: 'Abdullah ʿAzzām and the Islamist Revolution', *The Journal of Conflict Studies*, vol. 23, no. 2 (Fall 2003): p. 98.

1. In order that the Disbelievers do not dominate;
2. Due to the scarcity of men;
3. Fear of Hell-fire;
4. Fulfilling the duty of Jihad, and responding to the call of the Lord;
5. Following in the footsteps of the Pious Predecessors;
6. Establishing a solid foundation as a base for Islam;
7. Protecting those who are oppressed in the land;
8. Hoping for martyrdom;
9. A shield for the Ummah, and a means for lifting disgrace off them;
10. Protecting the dignity of the Ummah, and repelling the conspiracy of its enemies;
11. Preservation of the earth, and protection from corruption;
12. Security of Islamic places of worship;
13. Protection of the Ummah from punishment, disfiguration and displacement;
14. Prosperity of the Ummah, and surplus of its resources;
15. Jihad is the highest peak of Islam;
16. Jihad is the most excellent form of worship, and by means of it the Muslim can reach the highest of ranks.[211]

ʿAzzām also stresses the importance for the entire Muslim community of engaging in jihad, and speaks of it as a *farḍ ʿayn*, or individual duty: "According to our modest experience and knowledge, we believe that jihad in the present situation in Afghanistan is individually obligatory (*farḍ ʿayn*)."[212] And also: "So, everyone not performing jihad today is forsaking a duty, just like the one who eats during the days of Ramadhan without excuse, or the rich person who withholds the Zakat from his wealth. Nay, the state of the person who abandons jihad is more severe."[213]

In Afghanistan, ʿAzzām met the young Osama bin Laden, and together they founded the Maktab al-Khadamāt (MAK), or the Afghan Services

211 'Abdullah ʿAzzām, *Join the Caravan* (London: Azzam Publications, 2001), pp. 5-6. All these reasons for joining the fight in Afghanistan can be put into three different categories (pragmatic reasons, theological reasons, non-theological reasons) in order to understand the peculiar and composite strategy for legitimizing the fight: this, at least, is the work done by Sebastian Schnelle in an interesting essay where he argues that the pragmatic reasons are those strictly linked to the same situation on the Afghan camps; the theological reasons are Islamic justifications for a legitimate jihad; and the non-theological reasons are those that can be accepted across faiths and cultures (like the self-defense against an act of aggression, which is also in agreement with the Charter of the United Nations). See Sebastian Schnelle, 'Abdullah Azzam, Ideologue of Jihad: Freedom Fighter or Terrorist?', *Journal of Church and State*, vol. 54, no. 4 (January 2012): pp. 625-647.

212 ʿAzzām, *Join the Caravan*, p. 20.

213 Ibid., p. 11.

Office, the purpose of which was to facilitate the arrival of Muslim volunteers and to coordinate the distribution of recruits on the different battlefields and training camps. A huge amount of money was raised by the effort of ʿAzzām and the generosity of Bin Laden, whose family was one of the richest of Saudi Arabia: "There is no certain figure, but the estimates are of several hundred million dollars that would have flowed to Peshawar [the basis of MAK] between 1985 and 1989."[214]

Osama bin Laden (1957-2011), whose family is still one of the wealthiest of Saudi Arabia, moved to Afghanistan in 1980 when he was only 23 years old, and instantly became a reference point thanks to his charisma and not in the least due to his capital. He managed to supervise the flow of Muslim volunteers in collaboration with ʿAzzām. Some years after he broke with ʿAzzām and joined al-Ẓawāhirī, giving shape to al-Qāʿida and supervising the so-called Arab-Afghans. "What made Bin Laden attractive to Ẓawāhirī was his financial status as the heir to a multi-billion dollar construction company in Saudi Arabia, while Bin Laden was impressed by Ẓawāhirī's organizational skills and superior jihadist credentials."[215] However, the two agreed that the two organizations (al-Ẓawāhirī's Egyptian Islamic Jihad and Bin Laden's newborn al-Qāʿida) had to keep their own identity and operate each within its own sphere.

In February 1989, the war in Afghanistan came to an end when the Soviet forces withdrew. Now al-Qāʿida needed to find another enemy to fight. "It appears that some fighters wanted to attempt to free India-controlled Kashmir, while others wanted to fight against 'infidel' Arab regimes. Interestingly, little evidence suggests that the Afghan fighters wanted to attack the United States"[216]. At this very stage, global jihad was still intertwined with religious national jihad.

Meanwhile, on November 24, 1989, ʿAbdallāh ʿAzzām was killed in an assault that is still shrouded in mystery. The chaos that followed the withdrawal of the Soviet Union and the emergence of warlords, bandits and drug lords, as well as the brutal civil war between rival *mujāhidūn* groups in Afghanistan forced al-Ẓawāhirī and Bin Laden to emigrate in Sudan, a safe space for jihadi forces thanks to the June 1989 coup d'état that had led

214 Thomas Hegghammer, "Adballah ʿAzzām, l'imam del jihad', in *Al-Qaeda. I testi*, ed. by Gilles Kepel (Roma-Bari: Laterza, 2006), p. 102.

215 Siddharth Ramana, 'The Road Ahead for Al-Qaeda: The Role of Aymaan Al Zawahiri', *International Institute for Counter-Terrorism*, June 17, 2011, https://www.ict.org.il/article.aspx?id=1101#gsc.tab=0. (accessed 14 February, 2018).

216 R. Kim Cragin, 'Early History of Al-Qa'ida', *The Historical Journal*, vol. 51, no. 4 (December 2008): p. 1056.

to power Omar al-Bashīr (b. 1944), whose influential counselor was Ḥasan al-Turābī (1932-2016), a leading Islamist ideologue.

In the following year (1990), the first Gulf War erupted as a bolt from the blue. Promptly, Osama bin Laden offered his support to Saudi Arabia for the mission of liberating Kuwait from the Iraqi invasion because, after the end of Soviet-Afghan war, the many Arab-Afghans, who had had real training and were thus skilled soldiers, were in search of a new mission. The answer, however, was negative, and Saudi Arabia preferred to ask for protection from the United States. This choice was decisive for the future of al-Qāʿida: at that very same moment, Bin Laden "chooses Saudi Arabia as his main enemy."[217] The sacred soil of Arabia has been trumped by infidels' feet, he argued, and the reigning family was guilty of having let the "head of the *kuffār*", the USA, arriving in and stationing on the holy land of Islam. The rejection of the help the Arab-Afghans could have given under those circumstances, moreover, made Bin Laden believe that the Saʿūd family had betrayed the Islamic religion. Bin Laden became disillusioned with the Saudi regime, whose religious credibility was reduced to zero – in fact, for Bin Laden this move represented "a double *vulnus*: the confirmation that the West was driving a neo-colonial policy of aggression against the territories of Islam; and the disrespect of the sacredness of the soil of Arabia, occupied by unbelieving armed powers."[218]

In a letter addressed to the *ʿulamāʾ* of Saudi Arabia and written around late 1995 and early 1996, Bin Laden denounces this aggression as "a calamity unprecedented in the history of our *umma*"[219] because it is "the first, the biggest, and the most dangerous Crusader invasion of Saudi Arabia."[220] He adds: "All this happened on the watch of the region's rulers, and with their active participation."[221] And, finally, he makes an appeal to the *ʿulamāʾ*: "Honorable and righteous scholars, the divine punishment afflicting the *umma* is due to the neglect of its religion and the abandonment of jihad for the sake of God Almighty."[222]

217 Omar Saghi, "Osama bin Laden, l'icona di un tribuno", in *Al-Qaeda. I testi*, ed. by Gilles Kepel (Roma-Bari: Laterza, 2006), p. 14.

218 Massimo Campanini, 'Breve storia di Al-Qaeda', in *Quale Islam? Jihadismo, radicalismo, riformismo*, ed. by Massimo Campanini (Brescia: Editrice La Scuola, 2015), p. 45.

219 Osama bin Laden, 'The Invasion of Arabia', in *Messages to the World. The Statements of Osama bin Laden*, ed. by Bruce Lawrence (London and New York: Verso, 2005), p. 15.

220 Ibid., p. 17.

221 Ibid., p. 16.

222 Ibid., p. 18.

During the years 1990-1995, in which al-Qāʿida sought a new enemy and fluctuated between Saudi Arabia and the United States, al-Ẓawāhirī devoted himself almost exclusively to the reorganization of the Egyptian Islamic Jihad from Sudan, launching a series of attacks on the nearby Egyptian soil to encourage what we have called the religious national jihad. Things changed in the year 1995, when a failed attack on the life of the Egyptian President Ḥusnī Mubārak at Addis Ababa caused another harsh repression of Islamist groups in Egypt and drew the attention of the United States to the presence of al-Qāʿida in Sudan. On May 1996, both al-Ẓawāhirī and Bin Laden were forced to fly away from the country.[223] They decided to go back to Afghanistan, where they began to establish training camps for *mujāhidūn*, setting up the new headquarters of al-Qāʿida. In the year after, the Taliban took power in Afghanistan and willingly gave them protection.[224]

What is decisive in the shape of the identity of a now mature al-Qāʿida is the *Declaration of Jihad against the Americans Occupying the Land of the Two Holy Sanctuaries* issued after Sudan requested Bin Laden to leave Khartoum. Here Bin Laden addresses Muslims across the world and blames "the blatant imperial arrogance of America, under the cover of the immoral United Nations,"[225] calling for an active and tenacious resistance against these Satanic forces. In it, Osama bin Laden orders two kinds of actions.

First, he points out that Saudi Arabia is the biggest trading partner in the Middle Eastern region – a situation that is regrettable and unjustifiable, in that Americans are occupying the sacred soil of Arabia and are helping the Zionist state against the Palestinians. He suggests that "depriving these

223 The attack on Mubārak made clearer to the world Bin Laden's true ambitions. And even though Bin Laden's investments in the country were consistent, Sudan needed international economic cooperation – something that it could have not reached without expelling a famous terrorist from its territories.

224 The Taliban, namely, the "(madrasa) students", emerged in Afghanistan in 1994 as a new force that fostered stability and promoted peace in a very unstable country. In September 1996, the Taliban entered Kabul and declared the Islamic Emirate of Afghanistan. Once in charge, the Taliban started to impose their own strict religious vision. Their Islamic view, in fact, was influenced by the Deobandi Islam, a revivalist form of Sunni Islam that developed as a reaction to the British colonial rule in India. However, Saudi Arabia's funding to the Taliban during the Afghan civil war produced a transformation in their core doctrine, to the point that Juan R.I. Cole talks of a "neo-Deobandi school, influenced by Wahhabi ideas from Saudi Arabia" ('The Taliban, Women, and the Hegelian Private Sphere', in *The Taliban and the Crisis of Afghanistan*, ed. by Robert D. Crews and Amin Tarzi [Cambridge: Harvard University Press, 2008], p. 142).

225 Osama bin Laden, 'Declaration of Jihad', in *Messages to the World. The Statements of Osama bin Laden*, ed. by Bruce Lawrence (London and New York: Verso, 2005), p. 25.

occupiers of the huge returns they receive from their trade with us is a very important way of supporting the jihad against them, and we expect you to boycott all American goods."[226]

Secondly, he turns to the global community of believers commanding them to engage in a jihad against the infidel West. In his own words:

> I say to our Muslim brothers across the world: your brothers in Saudi Arabia and Palestine are calling for your help and asking you to share with them in the *jihad* against the enemies of God, your enemies the Israelis and Americans. They are asking you to defy them *in whatever way you possibly can*, so as to expel them in defeat and humiliation from the holy places of Islam.[227]

Thus, the target of al-Qāʿida gradually shifted from Saudi Arabia to the United States, as the following sentence, written by Bin Laden in 1997, shows: "Our main problem is the US government, while the Saudi regime is but a branch or an agent of the US. By being loyal to the US regime, the Saudi regime has committed an act against Islam."[228]

Once back in Afghanistan after the five years spent in Sudan, the metamorphosis from religious national jihad to global jihad was apparently complete. The same Ayman al-Ẓawāhirī changed the strategy of his group, the Egyptian Islamic Jihad: either for operational necessity or for ideological conversion, the fact is that al-Ẓawāhirī embraced the global perspective fostered by Bin Laden. "The struggle for the establishment of the Muslim state cannot be considered a regional struggle,"[229] al-Ẓawāhirī declares in his *Knights Under the Prophet's Banner*. He speaks of "a new awareness"[230] that was spreading among the believers, a sense of an imminent liberation that will arrive only if the whole *umma* will come together and fight the infidels. "A fundamentalism coalition is taking shape,"[231] al-Ẓawāhirī continues, "the struggle against the external enemy cannot be postponed. It is clear […] that the Jewish-Crusade alliance will not give us time to defeat the domestic enemy."[232]

---

226 Ibid., p. 29.
227 Ibid., p. 30. Emphasis added.
228 Osama bin Laden, 'From Somalia to Afghanistan', in *Messages to the World. The Statements of Osama bin Laden*, ed. by Bruce Lawrence (London and New York: Verso, 2005), p. 45.
229 Al-Ẓawāhirī, "Knights Under the Prophet's Banner", 201.
230 Ibid., p. 205.
231 Ibid., p. 204.
232 Ibid., pp. 220-221.

The Afghan war played a central role in this evolution – it was perceived, seen and lived as a real founding myth, since for the first time *mujāhidūn* from different parts of the world fought side by side, all sharing the same goal. Both Bin Laden and al-Ẓawāhirī started to believe that the victory over the Soviet army demolished the idea of a superpower, preparing the *mujāhidūn* to wage war against the United States.[233]

The document that confirms the global stretch of the jihadi movement is *The World Islamic Front's Declaration to Wage Jihad Against the Jews and Crusaders* and it was issued on February 23, 1998. Under the banner of this World Islamic Front (another name for al-Qāʿida), Bin Laden gave a renewed start to his organization. Signed by other four personalities,[234] the document, written in the form of a *fatwā* (legal opinion), asserts that

> the ruling to kill the Americans and their allies – civilians and military – is an individual obligation [*farḍ al-'ayn*] incumbent upon every Muslim who can do it and in any country – this until the Aqsa Mosque [Jerusalem] and the Holy Mosque [Mecca] are liberated from their grip, and until their armies withdraw from all the lands of Islam, defeated, shattered, and unable to threaten any Muslim.[235]

The statement represented the official fusion of the Egyptian Islamic Jihad with al-Qāʿida. These words set the war against "the Devil's army – the Americans."[236] The *'ulamā'* have lost their power of persuasion in the eyes of the *mujāhidūn*; in the document it is written: "We also call on Muslim ulema, leaders, youths, and soldiers to launch the raid on Satan's U.S.,"[237] which demonstrates the lack of community driving force generally exerted by the *'ulamā'*. Now *mujāhidūn* "see themselves as the arbiters of what is right and what is wrong in jihad, and feel that their position as the

---

233 Al-Ẓawāhirī: "The jihad battles in Afghanistan destroyed the myth of a superpower in the minds of the Muslim mujahideen young men" ('Knights Under the Prophet's Banner', p. 38). Bin Laden: "What we benefited from most was that the myth of the superpower was destroyed not only in my mind but also in the minds of all Muslims" ('From Somalia to Afghanistan', p. 48).

234 Ayman al-Ẓawāhirī; Abū Yāsir Rifāʿī Aḥmad Ṭāhā, representative of the Egyptian al-Jamāʿa al-Islāmiyya; Sheikh Mir Ḥamza, secretary of the Jamiat Ulema-e-Pakistan; Fazlur Rahman, amīr of the Jihad Movement in Bangladesh.

235 World Islamic Front, 'Al-Qaeda's Declaration of War Against Americans', in *The Al Qaeda Reader. The Essential Texts of Osama Bin Laden's Terrorist Organization*, ed. by Raymond Ibrahim (New York: Broadway Books, 2007), p. 13.

236 Ibid.

237 Ibid., p. 14.

staunchest defenders of Islam gives them the authority that the 'court' of *'ulama* have abdicated."[238]

The *mujāhidūn* became so involved in a twofold struggle: on the one hand, the war against the United States and its allies, and on the other, the struggle against the inner enemies, namely, the puppet governments and the facade *ʿulamāʾ* who had hijacked Islam with their pointless formalisms and dependence on political considerations.

On August 7, 1998, al-Qāʿida attacked the US embassies in Tanzania and Kenya, and on October 12, 2000, it bombed the USS Cole, an American guided missile destroyer ship. Finally, al-Qāʿida succeeded in conducting the most spectacular attack until now, the destruction of the Twin Towers in New York City on September 11, 2001. Notwithstanding future developments (the birth of the self-proclaimed Islamic State in Syria and Iraq and other doctrinal evolutions promoted by new radical theoreticians), "the transition from the phase of jihadist guerrillas to the phase of sensational terrorism"[239] has taken place, and global Salafi-Jihadism was officially born.

238 David Cook, 'Islamism and Jihadism: The Transformation of Classical Notions of Jihad into an Ideology of Terrorism', *Totalitarian Movements and Political Religions*, vol. 10, no. 2 (June 2009): p. 186.

239 Gilles Kepel, 'The Origins and Development of the Jihadist Movement: From Anti-Communism to Terrorism', *Asian Affairs*, vol. 34, no. 2 (July 2003): p. 104.

CHAPTER 4
IS SALAFI-JIHADISM AN ADDITIONAL GNOSTIC CHAPTER?

4.1 *What is Salafi-Jihadism?*

The end of ideology and the exhaustion of utopia may be appropriate diagnoses for the West, where the post-modern condition – defined using Jean-François Lyotard's words as "incredulity toward metanarratives"[1] – has cast a deep shadow on any possibility of reorganizing the political around a shared narrative. But the paradigm of the end of ideology does not apply to the Islamic world: the failure of pan-Arab nationalism, the 1967 Six-Day War, and the 1978 Camp David Accords opened the door for another ideological metamorphosis. This time, however, the ideology was indigenous in its nature: Islam took on the burden of giving a new chance to the frustrated Arab population, adopting an alternative rhetoric to the ones imbued with Western models. Political Islam was more attuned to the majority of the peoples living in the MENA region. And finally, the 1979 Iranian revolution ignited the spark that would have provoked the fire of Sunni jihadism – all the more so during the Soviet-Afghan war, when the delusion of national jihadists turned into a never seen before solidarity and body spirit among all militants galvanized by a new mission.

Salafi-Jihadism is the ideological outcome of this long historical path – a new ideology[2] that draws on religious lines and that is more likely to be absorbed by the local population. Interestingly however, Salafi-Jihadism had, and still has, a strong appeal on the Western youth too, a phenomenon that requires new conceptual instruments to be fully understood, but that

---

1 Jean-François Lyotard, *The Postmodern Condition: A Report on Knowledge* (Minneapolis: University of Minnesota Press, 1984), p. xxiv.

2 Even President George W. Bush in September 2006 recognized the ideological nature of al-Qā'ida's doctrine: "The terrorists who attacked us on September the 11th, 2001, are men without conscience – but they're not madmen. They kill in the name of a clear and focused ideology, a set of beliefs that are evil, but not insane" ('President Discusses Global War on Terror', September 5, 2006, available at https://georgewbush-whitehouse.archives.gov/news/releases/2006/09/20060905-4.html).

reveals also the deep influence over the global population, overcoming the boundaries of traditionally Islamic countries, showing an unexpected vitality and a surprising degree of adaptation to several cultural environments.

To be clear, Salafi-Jihadism is the ideology shared by the today two main jihadist groups competing for the leadership of the anti-Western struggle, al-Qāʿida and the self-proclaimed Islamic State (IS), including of course their local allies such as al-Shabāb and Boko Haram.[3] Salafi-Jihadism is among the last strong and solid ideologies today. Its impact on everyday life is enormous even in the West, where the recent terrorist attacks have caused many causalities and have raised the level of alertness. It is difficult to say when groups like al-Qāʿida and IS will cease to exert their influence and to organize violent actions – many times in the past the two groups have been declared dead or moribund, but promptly something has happened, turning the situation in favor of the violent Islamists, to the extent that counter-terrorism analysts are now more cautious in their judgments over the grip of the jihadi organizations.

In order to effectively counter the appeal of Salafi-Jihadism, the first thing to do is to study its doctrinal content and its theoretical apparatus. In this sense, do we know what Salafi-Jihadism is? In the previous chapter, I have made a perhaps too schematic but I believe effective distinction between four types of jihad: "purification" jihad, anti-colonial jihad, religious nationalist jihad, and global jihad. This classification shows a progression in the evolution of jihadism, pointing out that the targeting of the "far enemy", i.e., the West and, in particular, the United States, is a rather recent innovation. Salafi-Jihadism stems from the historical succession of these four kinds of jihad, but at the same time *it includes them all*, or at least some elements of each: it is impossible to imagine Salafi-Jihadism without the effort of purifying Islam from heterodox acts of devotion and liberal innovations; or without the idea of freeing Muslim lands from foreign powers; or without the conviction that Arab states are governed by fake Muslim leaders who do not apply the *sharīʿa*, instead preferring secular laws inspired by Wester codes.

The present section will try to answer to the question about the very nature of Salafi-Jihadism, addressing straightforwardly the problem on what is *al-salafiyya al-jihādiyya*. The first thing to say is that this very term, "according to Abū Muḥammad al-Maqdisī, is an exonym, rather

3 Al-Shabāb is a radical Islamist group active in East Africa and born in 2006; it is an ally of al-Qāʿida. Boko Haram is an extremist organization based in Nigeria; it was founded in 2002, and in 2015 its leader pledged allegiance to the so-called Islamic State.

than a name the school chose for itself. He does not oppose it per se, but only warns against the implication it carries that the salafi-jihadis are just a subset of salafis, and their rivals, the quietist salafis, also deserve the name."[4] It is self-evident that a group of Muslims who proclaims itself the pure vanguard of Islam would refuse any label other than Sunnis or Salafis. The Western label "Salafi-Jihadism" is nevertheless useful to identify those militants that adopt jihad as an effective act of devotion along the lines of the pillars of Islam.

Thomas Hegghammer notes the fact that the term is of recent use but its origins are still unclear. It gained popularity in the early 1990s in England, in those London districts where the Islamist community used to gather and live in. The London Jihadist magazine *al-Ansar* adopted the term "Salafi-Jihadism" in several occasions during the 1990s, for example in a 1994 interview with Ayman al-Ẓawāhirī, when he admitted the existence of a "Salafi-Jihadi movement" (*ḥaraka al-salafiyya al-jihādiyya*). But "it was only from 2003 onward that its use proliferated and entered Western discourse,"[5] probably because of the huge impact of Gilles Kepel's deeply influential book *Jihad* (2000) on the academic debate.[6] Equally, an example of the use of the label by the same jihadi theoreticians and militants can be found in the strategist Abu Bakr Naji (d. 2008), head of media and propaganda of al-Qāʿida, who made an explicit reference to Salafi-Jihadism in his most famous work, *The Management of Savagery* (*Idārat at-Tawaḥḥush*), published online in 2004.[7]

4 Daniel Lav, *Radical Islam and the Revival of Medieval Theology* (New York: Cambridge University Press, 2012), p. 120.

5 Thomas Hegghammer, 'Jihadi-Salafis or Revolutionaries? On Religion and Politics in the Study of Militant Islamism', in *Global Salafism. Islam's New Religious Movement*, ed. by Roel Meijer (New York: Oxford University Press, 2013), p. 252.

6 Gilles Kepel identifies a distinct wave within the ongoing jihadist movement and that he calls "jihadist-Salafism" (Gilles Kepel, *Jihad: The Trail of Political Islam* [Cambridge: Harvard University Press, 2002], p. 219). In talking of a similar concept, probably Kepel was influenced by an essay of Quintan Wictorowicz published in the year 2000, where the author identifies two factions in the Salafi world, the jihadis and the non-jihadis. See Quintan Wictorowicz, 'The Salafi Movement in Jordan', *International Journal of Middle East Studies*, vol. 32, no. 2 (May 2000).

7 See Abu Bakr Naji, *The Management of Savagery* (Harvard: Institute for Strategic Studies, 2006), p. 80: "From all of the sections and topics of the study, we conclude that the movements of *salafiyya jihad* are ahead of others in their understanding of the religion of God, exalted be He – an understanding of sharia and universal laws. They are the hope (for the Muslim community) if God, exalted be He, so wills it."

The second introductory point, which is self-evident but needs to be underlined as often as possible, is that Salafi-Jihadism is an ideological strain born from the combination and the encounter of Salafism, on one side, and jihadism, on the other side. As we have previously studied, Salafis seek to restore the golden age of Prophet Muḥammad and of the first generations of believers, strictly sticking on the rules of *sharīʿa*. This does not mean that Salafism produces jihadism, or that a non-Salafi cannot be a jihadi. Mark Sedgwick notes that jihadism alone – without any Salafi connotations – "is generally used in an attempt to promote major political change. This may be the fall of a local regime, or the liberation of a territory from foreign, non-Muslim rule, or even to bring about the retreat of American global power. Jihadism, then, is primarily about means, not ends."[8] The union of jihadism and Salafism, on the contrary, is about means *and* ends – the definition of Gnosis as a *diagnosis-therapy* of human alienation is of some help to understand this very point.

Salafi-Jihadis are not simply those Salafis who share a propensity for violent actions, but those Salafis who aspire to *restore the golden era of Islam by means of violence*. This definition will return in the entire following discussion, given that some scholars have sometimes proposed different nomenclature for the Salafi-Jihadi ideology, losing sight of this essential definition. There are certainly other features that mark out different aspects of Salafi-Jihadism, and there are also other definitions of it, but the fundamental aspect of what is today known as Salafi-Jihadism is the program of restoring the golden era of Islam by means of violence.

Following this intuition, the British scholar Shiraz Maher, in an essay that has become a landmark among the studies on the subject, defines Salafi-Jihadism as "a potent soteriological programme,"[9] the attempt of achieving personal and collective salvation through a political-religious ideological construction.

Maher has no doubt in considering Salafi-Jihadi creed to have an ideological nature: he grounds this remark in the observation that Salafi-Jihadism is "based around an idea, rather than a particular leader or personality,"[10] "it does not belong to a particular group or movement,"[11] as jihadists' statements have lengthily demonstrated (an example is al-

8 Mark Sedgwick, 'Jihadism, Narrow and Wide: The Dangers of Loose Use of an Important Term', *Perspectives on Terrorism*, vol. 9, issue 2 (April 2015): p. 39.

9 Shiraz Maher, *Salafi-Jihadism. The History of an Idea* (London: Hurst & Company, 2016), p. 207.

10 Ibid., p. 21.

11 Ibid., p. 16.

Qāʿida's response to the death of Bin Laden: "Are the Americans able to kill what Sheikh Osama lived and fought for, even with all their soldiers, intelligence, and agencies? Never! Never! Sheikh Osama did not build an organization that would die with him, nor would end with him.")[12] Shiraz Maher goes further and compares Salafi-Jihadism with Eric Voegelin's concept of political religion, stating: "Salafi-Jihadism […] can be considered Islam's latest – and perhaps most successful – political religion,"[13] that is, the last and desperate attempt to find an all-encompassing meaning by building it with arms and violence on earth. Salafi-Jihadism's resilient nature is based on this assumption – which also reveals that Eric Voegelin's philosophy is effective even for a very modern phenomenon that originated outside the Western world. The adoption of the concept of revolutionary Gnosticism, therefore, appears as a legitimate move, especially after having investigated Voegelin's late rejection of the concept of political religion in favor of that of Gnosticism. Following this line of reasoning, the definition of Salafi-Jihadism as "Islam's latest political religion" opens the door for another statement (to be investigated), that is, Salafi-Jihadism as a revolutionary gnostic construction.

But for the moment let us go back to the definition of this peculiar ideology and ask ourselves what are its historical and doctrinal roots.

Scholars are rather unanimous in stating that Salafi-Jihadism is a *hybrid ideology* born from the encounter of a politicized form of Islam developed by the Muslim Brotherhood, and especially the radical kind of Sayyid Quṭb, with Saudi Wahhabism. The persecution of the Muslim Brotherhood at the hands of socialist military regimes that occurred in the post-independence period in Egypt, Syria and other MENA countries (notably Nasser's crackdown of the Islamists launched in 1954) led to a strong radicalization within the same organization (the case of Sayyid Quṭb is illustrative), but it resulted also in a massive flow of radicalized Muslims into a self-proclaimed Muslim state, the safe Saudi Arabia. To counter the socialist tendencies of rival neighboring countries and to gain more and more weight in the region, the Saudi government welcomed those Muslims who felt marginalized and persecuted in their own states. Muslims with Salafi tendencies and Islamists inspired by Quṭb's theories began living in close

12 May 3, 2011 al-Qāʿida's statement, quoted in Shiraz Maher and Amany Soliman, 'Al-Qaeda confirms death of bin Laden', *ICSR Insight*, May 6, 11, https://icsr.info/2011/05/06/icsr-insight-al-qaeda-confirms-death-of-bin-laden/ (accessed May 9, 2017).

13 Maher, *Salafi-Jihadism*, p. 27.

contact with the rigorous Wahhabi community. Furthermore, King Fayṣal's policy of modernization and reform harnessed those Muslim Brothers who could have been a resource for the country: the idea was to counter Nasser's revolutionary socialist rhetoric and the appeal emanating from the Islamic Revolution in Iran in 1979, while at the same time strengthening the position of Saudi Arabia in the region.

For these reasons, Muslim Brothers, who were particularly well-versed in Western concepts and knew the functioning of a modern state – we shall not forget the modernist imprinting given by al-Bannā to the movement – were given high teaching positions in newly established universities and schools, "where they helped form a new generation of conscious Saudi Islamists engaged in their society's social and political realities. […] The Wahhabi students fell under the spell of their foreign mentors."[14]

The outcome of this hybridization was a movement known as the Islamic Awakening (*al-ṣaḥwa al-islāmiyya*), or simply *Saḥwa*, which "quickly established itself as a counter-culture to the religious establishment in Saudi Arabia over the course of only a few decades, starting in the mid-1950s."[15] The transplantation of Muslim Brothers into the rigorous Wahhabi environment of Saudi Arabia, thus, resulted in the creation of a true underground movement, a cluster of university-educated clerics who combined conservative Wahhabism with political activism, which opposed the quietist stances of the religious Saudi establishment. In fact, the Islamic activism embraced by the Saḥwa movement was of an unknown form for the Arabia of that time. The words of Stéphan Lacroix are enlightening in providing a relevant sketch of the anatomy of the Saḥwa movement:

> The Sahwi [sic] counterculture was defined by adherence to an ideology and to certain practices that ran, at the time of their emergence, against the preponderant social norms. The ideology of the Saḥwa is located at the juncture of two distinct schools of thought with different views of the world: the Wahhabi tradition and the tradition of the Muslim Brotherhood. Like the Muslim reformist tradition from which it derives, the tradition of the Muslim Brotherhood is primarily political and was constructed, in its Bannaist version, against the "imperialist West," and in its Qutbist version, against the "godless

14 Itzchak Weismann, 'A Perverted Balance: Modern Salafism between Reform and Jihād', *Die Welt Des Islams*, vol. 57, issue 1 (2017): p. 53.

15 Mike Kelvington, 'Importing the Muslim Brotherhood: Creation of the Saḥwa in Saudi Arabia', *The Havok Journal*, April 27, 2019, https://havokjournal.com/world/middle-east/importing-muslim-brotherhood-creation-Saḥwa -saudi-arabia/ (accessed May 1, 2019).

> regimes" of the Middle East. The Wahhabi tradition, in contrast, is primarily religious and was constructed against the *bidaʿ*, that is, the impurities that were supposed to have emerged around the original dogma of the pious ancestors. Historically, its principal enemy was not the West nor the political authorities but the non-Wahhabi groups within Islam, beginning with the Shiites and the Sufis. The concerns and priorities of the two traditions were thus totally distinct. This made them formally complementary and laid the groundwork for the emergence of the Saḥwa through the intermediary of the educational system that, though dominated by the methods and thinking of the Muslim Brotherhood, maintained creed as a Wahhabi preserve. Ideologically, the Saḥwa could be described as a hybrid of Wahhabism and the ideology of the Brotherhood. On theological questions connected to creed and on the major aspects of Islamic jurisprudence, the Sahwis adhered to the Wahhabi tradition and considered themselves its faithful heirs. But on political and cultural questions, their view of the world tended toward that of the Muslim Brotherhood, although it was partly reformulated in terms derived from the Wahhabi tradition.[16]

The length of the quotation is justified by its importance.

The main target of the Sahwis were those Muslims that Quintan Wiktorowicz calls the "purists", the Saudi religious establishment, and in particular the Senior Council of *ʿUlamāʾ*, obsessed with preserving and propagating a pure understanding of Islam at the expense of a direct involvement in the political arena, so producing a strong tendency toward isolationism. The Sahwis, on the contrary, were prone to confront the Saudi government, yet not with violent means or with a revolutionary attitude but through public advices – recommendations about a true divine legislation, instructions for the expulsion of liberal agents on Arabic soil, and so on.

The politicized form of Salafism embraced by the Sahwis was a new type of non-violent political activism in the Saudi landscape.

The eruption of the First Gulf War (1990-1991) was a watershed for the Saḥwa movement. Ṣaddām Ḥusayn's invasion of Kuwait in August 1990 pushed the Saudi rulers to invite American troops to help defend the kingdom. The Senior Council of *ʿUlamāʾ* issued a *fatwā* in order to justify this move – for a state founded on an austere interpretation of Islam, the decision to rely on the non-Muslim United States was not a simple one. The *fatwā* had the intention of religiously approving an unprecedented geopolitical move, the presence of non-Muslim soldiers in

16 Stéphane Lacroix, *Awakening Islam. The Politics of Religious Dissent in Contemporary Saudi Arabia* (Cambridge, Mass. and London: Harvard University Press, 2011), p. 52.

the land of the two holy places – Mecca and Medina. "The theoreticians and guardians of the movement slowly came to understand the high cost of ideological purity and the value of realism in domestic and foreign affairs."[17] In the *fatwā*, the *ʿulamāʾ* validated this decision because it was "dictated by necessity."[18]

Soon, prominent leaders of the Saḥwa movements such as Salmān al-ʿAwda and Safar Ḥawālī criticized this resolution, challenging the senior clerical Saudi establishment by sound reproaches and the distribution of cassettes among the population. The Memorandum of Advice addressed to King Fahd (r. 1982-2005) and issued on September 1992 was the apex of the Saḥwa criticism towards the kingdom, a strong demand for reforms. With a similar document, the Sahwis

> had no intention to overthrown the ruling family; rather, they intended only to ensure that the Saudi project of modernization remain within the legal and moral bounds of the *sharīʿa*, that it serve the broad interests of the national and transnational Muslim community, and that they themselves be given a central role in directing and supervising the process.[19]

In doing so, "as Wahhabis, the Saḥwa *ʿulamāʾ* substituted the rationalist and liberal openness of the early [Egyptian] *salafiyya* with rigid literalism and exclusivism, while as radical Islamists they demanded not merely to direct but eventually to control and supervise the state's adoption of Western measures."[20] The lethal cocktail of Salafi-Jihadism was already there but contained and limited.

Meanwhile, the jihadi movement born in the context of the Soviet-Afghan conflict was knocking on the door of Saudi Arabia. Osama bin Laden insisted in offering the kingdom the Afghani veterans for the defense of the country, deploring the choice of relying on a non-Muslim army, particularly the one belonging to the United States. But the situation was about to become explosive: in 1995, the Saudi government repressed the Saḥwa movement. Many leaders of the opposition were arrested, including

---

17 Abdulaziz H. al-Fahad, 'From Exclusivism to Accommodation: Doctrinal and Legal Evolution of Wahhabism', *New York University Law Review*, vol. 79, no. 2 (May 2004): p. 487.

18 Senior Council of *'Ulamā'*, 'Statement by the Council of Senior *'Ulama* Supporting Actions Taken by the Leader Inviting Qualified Forces to Respond to the Aggression Against this Country', fully reported in al-Fahad, 'From Exclusivism to Accommodation', p. 518.

19 Weismann, 'A Perverted Balance', p. 57.

20 Ibid., p. 58.

Salmān al-ʿAwda and Safar Ḥawālī. As shown in the previous chapter, bin Laden, by now disenchanted with the Saʿūd family, immediately became a strong opponent of Saudi Arabia.

Actually, bin Laden, "often cites al-Hawali and al-ʿAwda to justify his pronouncement against the United States."[21] The influence of the Saḥwa movement on bin Laden was enormous. His strong Wahhabi culture soon intertwined with the Muslim Brotherhood posture, the more so in Afghanistan, where he had met ʿAbdullāh ʿAzzām and Ayman al-Ẓawāhirī, both chief figures of the radical and Quṭbist offshoot of the organization.

Salafi-Jihadism is therefore a sort of evolution of the Saḥwa dissent, with the difference that the latter had a reformist approach, whereas the former adopts a more revolutionary style and does not come to terms with any ruler, for all rulers are infidels (*kuffār*) and liable to excommunication (*takfīr*).

Both forms of Salafi activism draw their political consciousness and vocabulary from the Muslim Brotherhood. This is particularly evident in *Al-Qāʿida's Creed and Path*, a document first published online in 2003: composed of 41 points that consist of as many ideological assumptions, the document states at point 5:

> We believe that all rule and legislation belong to God alone, and that His rule constitutes absolute justice and all that opposes it constitutes oppression that must be rejected. [We also believe] that one of the foundations of faith and conditions for its validity is to refer matters to God's rule and legislation, and that all who refer matters to other than God's rule and legislation, and who do not rule on the basis of God's revelation, have adhered to an arbitrary legislation, which God has not permitted. And because of this, such a person(s) is an infidel who has abandoned the Muslim community and has followed the rule of the age of pre-Islamic ignorance (*jāhiliyya*).[22]

This quotation includes all the main ideological features that encompass both Wahhabism and the Quṭbist conceptual arsenal, namely, *jāhiliyya*, *takfīr*, and *ḥākimiyya*. Furthermore, in the document it is clearly stated that *takfīr* is "a legal act,"[23] that the leaders who do not rule in accordance with the *sharīʿa* "are infidel apostates,"[24] that secularism (*ʿilmāniyya*) and

---

21 Peter L. Bergen, *Holy War, Inc. Inside the Secret World of Osama bin Laden* (New York: The Free Press, 2001), p. 78.

22 'Al-Qaeda's Creed and Path', translated and published in Bernard Haykel, 'On the Nature of Salafi Thought and Action', in *Global Salafism. Islam's New Religious Movement*, ed. by Roel Meijer (New York: Oxford University Press, 2013), p. 52.

23 Ibid.

24 Ibid., p. 53.

democracy are "tribulations of this age,"[25] that Islamic groups that decide to participate in elections are "reprehensible innovators (*ahl bid'a*),"[26] that any factionalism other than Islam constitutes an act of apostasy, including "pan-nationalist, nationalist, communist, Baathist and socialist parties,"[27] that the aim of the revolutionary action is to "establish a rightly-guided Caliphate on the prophetic model,"[28] and that the most honest and righteous people were the Companions of the Prophet and the so-called Followers (*at-tābi'īn*) of the 2nd and 3rd centuries, and "after this lying will spread and loyalty will weaken."[29]

The hybridization of Wahhabism with Quṭbism is evident and manifest. This combination is actually the theoretical basis of Salafi-Jihadism, which stems from a mixture of historical circumstances, doctrinal affinities, disillusionment toward other ideological solutions, and genuine quest for authenticity in an increasingly modern world. Joas Wagemakers says that Salafi-Jihadism is "directly or indirectly influenced by the revolutions in Egypt and Iran in 1952 and 1979 respectively, the wars in Afghanistan and the Persian Gulf, as well as by ideological trends such as the spreading of Wahhabism and the ideas of Qutb."[30] Stated differently, Salafi-Jihadism refers to a conceptual construction "mixing Wahhabi-inspired Sunni fundamentalism with a revolutionary program of overthrowing unjust and un-Islamic regimes in the Muslim world, as well as irredentism aiming at expelling non-Muslim military presence and influences from Muslim lands."[31]

Alongside the Afghan war, the Iranian Revolution, the First Gulf War and the Saḥwa movement, there were other historical circumstances that pushed for a more lethal evolution of Salafi-Jihadism. After 9/11, the Americans invaded Afghanistan, overthrew the Taliban regime and forced

---

25 Ibid.

26 Ibid., p. 54.

27 Ibid.

28 Ibid., p. 55. This statement will be analyzed later in this study, being it the doctrinal claim of the self-proclaimed Islamic State. In fact, the territorial context of Iraq and Syria, that blurred territory often called "Syraq", was propitious for the establishment of a Caliphate based on the prophetic model – an assertion that brings with it many apocalyptical meanings and eschatological prophetic reminiscences.

29 Ibid. Strong is here the Salafi orientation and the backward-looking posture.

30 Joas Wagemakers, *A Quietist Jihadi. The Ideology and Influence of Aby Muhammad al-Maqdisi* (New York: Cambridge University Press, 2012), p. 18.

31 Petter Nesser, 'Abū Qatāda and Palestine', *Die Welt Des Islams*, vol. 53, no. 3-4 (2013): p. 417.

the al-Qāʿida leadership to loosen the grip on the organization. The result was a less hierarchical and pyramidal structure in favor of a more fluid, unpredictable and articulated configuration.

Bruce Hoffman traces the structure of al-Qāʿida in the post-9/11 situation, which has evolved in an amorphous entity working through local proxies and "lone-wolf" independent actors. Hoffman distinguishes between al-Qāʿida Central, al-Qāʿida Affiliated and Associates, al-Qāʿida Locals, and al-Qāʿida Network.[32]

Al-Qāʿida Central, also known as Senior Leadership (AQSL), comprises the historic leaders of the movement, including Osama bin Laden and Ayman al-Ẓawāhirī. It is the central command and control apparatus, which from 2001 onward acts more as a giver of advices and a provider of political incitement and religious backing, forced underground due to the fierce American "War on Terror."

Al-Qāʿida Affiliates and Associates are those insurgent groups "who over the year have benefited from bin Laden's largesse and/or spiritual guidance and/or have received training, arms, money and other assistance"[33] from the central structure. This category includes the Groupe Salafiste pour la Prédication et le Combat, which in 2007 became al-Qāʿida in the Islamic Maghreb (AQIM); al-Qāʿida in the Arabian Peninsula (AQAP); Jamāʿat al-Tawḥīd wa al-Jihād, that in 2004 transformed into al-Qāʿida in Iraq (AQI), and others. In other words, al-Qāʿida acts like a franchise, offering its name to as many local branches as possible, multiplying its presence and strengthening its formal leadership over a number of groups.

Al-Qāʿida Locals are those groups and factions that do not have a constant link with al-Qāʿida Central and which are more likely to have had a tenuous link prior to 9/11; today, Bruce Hoffman states, they are disconnected from the central apparatus.

Finally, al-Qāʿida Network includes all those home-grown radicals, the sympathizers, from the MENA region and from Europe as well. They are able to prepare and carry out attacks "in solidarity with or support of al-Qaeda's radical jihadi agenda,"[34] representing a permanent basin for any potential attack.

The increasing use of the Internet and the growing debates on online forums offers to this vast and fluid network the effective means to

32 Bruce Hoffman, *Combating Al Qaeda and the Militant Islamic Threat* (Santa Monica, CA: RAND Corporation, 2006), https://www.rand.org/pubs/testimonies/CT255.html (accessed March 26, 2016).

33 Ibid.

34 Ibid.

communicate and coordinate in a way unthinkable until a few years earlier. Being deprived of their physical headquarters, the interactions between al-Qāʿida Central and the other (formal or informal) affiliates are transferred on the virtual space: "The tolerant, virtual environment of the Internet offers them a semblance of unity and purpose. [...] These forums, virtual marketplaces for extremist ideas, have become the 'invisible hand' that organizes terrorist activities worldwide."[35] In this new situation, the Internet has truly globalized the jihadist message, allowing bin Laden and al-Ẓawāhirī to be heard in every corner of the earth.

But at the same time, the innovation of the Internet has had a huge impact on the ideology of Salafi-Jihadism. We should not underestimate the direct and indirect effect of free online discussions on the same understanding of the jihadi ideology. Once the US degraded the capability of al-Qāʿida Central, numerous new real or self-proclaimed scholars, as well as normal people without any religious legitimacy, autonomously began discussing high-priority topics of Islam, "favoring the creation of a sort of 'neo-*umma*' in a jihadist key, with its own imaginary made up of martyrs and fighters, progressively drawing a new 'tradition' completely based on its own interpretation of jihad and its claimed originality and purity."[36] The direct interactions between online users favored a new symbolism and a collective memory made up of grievances, shared feelings, scattered photographs taken from various wars in the Middle East, and Qurʾānic textual references for armed struggle without an appropriate religious exegesis. Paolo Maggiolini unequivocally utters: "The relationship between contemporary jihadism and armed jihad in its classical sense seems to take on the contours of a distant echo rather than of its most original re-proposal."[37]

On this point, Hamadi Redissi believes that the decentralized form of jihadism that inhabits the virtual space is what he calls the third form of fundamentalism, an original evolution in the history of Islamist violence. According to Redissi's perspective, the first fundamentalism was that of the *Nahḍa*, the Islamic renaissance launched by Jamāl al-Dīn al-Afghānī, which "fluctuates between jihad and *ijtihād* [effort of interpretation];"[38]

35 Marc Sageman, 'The Next Generation of Terror', *Foreign Policy*, no. 165 (March-April 2008): pp. 39, 41.

36 Paolo Maggiolini, 'Dal jihad al jihadismo: militanza e lotta armata tra XX e XXI secolo', in *Jihad e terrorismo. Da al-Qaʿida all'Isis: Storia di un nemico che cambia*, ed. by Andrea Plebani (Milano: Mondadori, 2016), p. 41.

37 Ibid., p. 43.

38 Hamadi Redissi, *Islam e modernità. L'incontro dell'Islam con l'Occidente* (Verona: Ombre Corte, 2014), p. 82.

the second fundamentalism consisted of the struggle against the "tyrants" (*ṭāghūt,* pl. *ṭawāghīt)* ruling over the post-colonial states in the MENA region and which was commenced by the Muslim Brotherhood; the third fundamentalism is like "a spiderweb, a series of web sites linked together in a network, […] an Islamic international […] where al-Qāʿida, instead of getting lost in the confused multitude of such groups, tends to use each of them to weave its own network."[39]

The last evolution of Salafi-Jihadism occurred in 2003, when the United States led the multination invasion of Iraq to overthrow President Ṣaddām Ḥusayn. The new focal point of the worldwide jihadi movement became Iraq, a country that has always been essential for the geopolitical balance of the region and for the Islamic religion *tout court*, having been the base of the Abbasid Caliphate for many centuries. Soon al-Qāʿida Central denounced the act of violence perpetrated by the US invaders with the following statement: "The campaign against Iraq has aims that go beyond Iraq into the Arab Islamic world. […] Its first aim is to destroy any effective military force in the proximity of Israel. Its second aim is to consolidate the supremacy of Israel."[40] The occupation of Baghdad, "a former capital of Islam,"[41] as bin Laden referred to it, was of great preoccupation and concern for the Salafi-Jihadi militants, because it was done "in preparation for the creation of Greater Israel."[42] And even though Ṣaddām Ḥusayn was leading the Arab Socialist Baʿth Party, bin Laden exhorted and urged all *mujāhidūn* to fight alongside the Iraqi government, for "despite our firm belief in the infidelity of socialism, […] this current battle and the fighting that will take place in the coming days are reminiscent of the battles that Muslims engaged in previously."[43]

It was only a matter of time before the Iraq War turned into a new Afghan conflict, a struggle that caught the attention of the whole jihadist movement. Now, however, it was time to destroy the last remaining superpower, the

---

39 Ibid., pp. 92-93.

40 Ayman al-Ẓawāhirī, cited in Thomas Hegghammer, "Global Jihadism after the Iraq War", *Middle East Journal*, vol. 60, no. 1 (Winter 2006): p. 18.

41 Osama bin Laden, 'To the Muslims of Iraq. 2003', in *The Al Qaeda Reader. The Essential Texts of Osama Bin Laden's Terrorist Organization*, ed. by Raymond Ibrahim (New York: Broadway Books, 2007), p. 243.

42 Ibid. With the expression "Greater Israel" the jihadi rhetoric refers to belief that Israel secretly seeks to conquer the portion of territory promised by God to Abraham in Genesis 15:18, a country stretching from the Nile, in Egypt, to the Euphrates, in Iraq.

43 Ibid., p. 248.

United States, which was leading "the international alliance of evil"[44] waging a "Crusade" against the very religion of Islam. The Iraqi conflict assumed quite soon symbolic and eschatological tones.

A radical transformation took place on the battlefield. First, a huge mass of people decided to travel to the country, with the same spirit as the foreign fighters who went to Afghanistan to help counter the Soviet army. In this case, however, the migration was justified using the idea of replicating the *hijra* Muḥammad undertook from Mecca to Medina in 622. In other words, the true involvement in the fight for the defense of Islam needed a degree of separation from the rest of the world: the engagement had to be total and complete.

A second evolution that caused a certain amount of debate was the increased brutalization of the methods used on the battlefield by the Islamist militants, including decapitations of civilians, unrestrained violence, and kidnappings. Thomas Hegghammer says that "with a few exceptions,[45] these methods had not previously been used by radical Sunni groups before the Iraq War."[46]

Hence something must have happened; and in fact, a new, more deadly actor appeared on the scene. It was Abū Muṣʿab al-Zarqāwī (1966-2006), a Jordanian jihadist who is today infamous for being the grandfather of the so-called Islamic State. In 1999, he founded Jamāʿat al-Tawḥīd wa al-Jihād (Organization of Monotheism and Jihad), a group that played a relevant role during the Iraqi insurgency that followed the fall of Ṣaddām Ḥusayn. From the very beginning, it did not go unnoticed in the eyes of other actors of the war, nor in the eyes of the global jihadist community. The series of attacks carried out by al-Tawḥīd wa al-Jihād were designed to increase media exposure, resulting in an ever-greater popularity of the group. The strategy of the group was about exploiting the context of a failing state unable to provide basic services to its citizens. But at the same time, many remarks and criticisms arose from the Iraqi population and even from the scholarly representatives of Salafi-Jihadism.

---

44 Ibid., p. 246.

45 Thomas Hegghammer lists these exceptions: "The Shiʿite Islamist group Hizbullah carried out many high-profile kidnappings of Western citizens in Lebanon in the 1980s. Some of the hostages were killed, though not by decapitation. The Algerian group GIA kidnapped and decapitates seven French monks in Algeria in the spring of 1996. In January 2002, the American journalist Daniel Pearl was abducted and beheaded by Sunni militants in Pakistan" (Hegghammer, 'Global Jihadism after the Iraq War', p. 26).

46 Ibid.

In this respect, a mention on the so-called Zarqāwī-Maqdisī debate is needed.

Abū Muḥammad al-Maqdisī (b. 1959) is a Salafi-Jihadi religious scholar, though not part of the al-Qāʿida leadership. He is considered "the most influential living jihadi theorist."[47] He is mentor and spiritual father of al-Zarqāwī, whom he met in Afghanistan in the early 1990s. After the Afghan experience, they both went to Jordan, their country of origin, and set up a group of militant Islamists, *Bayʿat al-Imām*, more focused on *daʿwa* (preaching) rather than on violent activities. Despite this inclination, they arranged an armed action against Israel, and both al-Maqdisī and al-Zarqāwī were imprisoned in 1994 by the Jordanian authorities. In goal, they continued to spread the call, being successful in recruiting new followers among their fellow-prisoners. Nonetheless, something was about to break. "While [al- Maqdisī], despite his explicit message, spread his ideas in a friendly and kind manner, al-Zarqāwī was much harsher, blunter and more direct to those he considered his enemies."[48] The different attitude of the two – al-Zarqāwī's confrontational behavior and al-Maqdisī's more gentle style – provoked the first break: al-Zarqāwī took over the leadership of *Bayʿat al-Imām*. In 1999, once out of prison, al-Zarqāwī moved to Afghanistan and later to Iraq, whereas al-Maqdisī preferred to remain in Jordan, where he continued to write books, trying to go back to a normal life again. Arrested and arrested again on several occasions on charges of conspiracy to commit terrorist acts against Western tourists and US soldiers, early in 2003 al-Maqdisī began to look with concern toward Iraq. He believed that young radicals fighting in the Iraqi scenario were going too far in their actions committed in the name of jihad. He wrote numerous treatises, volumes and articles against the extreme jihadi practices adopted by his former pupil al-Zarqāwī, who became by now a significant actor in the Iraqi insurgency. In a tract specifically referred to him, al-Maqdisī advised al-Zarqāwī to stop the violence directed at the Shiites living in Iraq, who along with the Western aggressors were now the targets of al-Zarqāwī's jihadist fury.

Indeed the Islamist movement has always emphasized pan-Islamism in the face of the external threat represented by the West and the "infidel" Arab rulers or deemed unorthodox groups such as the Shiites. For the first time, thus, an internal conflict was breaking the unity among Muslims, and it was al-Zarqāwī's fault. In this situation al-Maqdisī, though without

47 William McCants and Jarret Brachman, *Militant Ideology Atlas* (West Point, NY: Combating Terrorism Center, 2006), p. 8.

48 Wagemakers, *A Quietist Jihadi*, p. 43.

rejecting jihad, reproached his former pupil, in the hope he would have changed his mind and stopped his extreme practices. But instead, in 2005 al-Zarqāwī attacked al-Maqdisī, expressing surprise about his former teacher's criticisms, saying that al-Maqdisī's words could harm the Iraqi jihad, and decided to go further in his project of destabilizing the country without any moral and practical constraints.

It was the birth of a new movement within the Salafi-Jihadi ranks, the *neo-Zarqawist*, which introduced sectarian warfare and unrestrained violence as regular actions to be implemented in the global jihad. "This movement is less predictable and potentially more violent"[49] and, besides, "the neo-Zarqawists are not scholars or clerics. [...] They criticize al-Maqdisī's lack of 'jihadist credentials' since, unlike al-Zarqāwī, he has never been involved in actual combat."[50]

Eli Alshech has dubbed this more radical movement as "neo-Takfirism" in that it is more prone to adopt *takfīr* as a flexible weapon against everyone and everything deemed un-Islamic by its own arbitrary standards. Alshech notes: "Neo-Takfiris consider uncompromising zeal to constitute perfect piety. For them, a person who is not zealous lacks religiosity and authority. Indeed, al-Zarqāwī's followers considered his piety as a legitimate and sufficient basis for religious authority. Erudition and scholarship were secondary."[51]

In a 2001 article, Quintan Wiktorowicz notes that a reformist Salafi-Jihadi approach does exist, and he believes that "several prior phases are necessary before a jihad is permissible,"[52] e.g., *tarbiya* (education) and *taṣfiya* (purification), or, in other terms, changes at the level of individuals. Wiktorowicz warnes the West that "highly visible American military action may inadvertently provide empirical credibility for jihadi framings and tip the balance of power within the Salafi movement away from the reformist counter-discourse."[53] The US invasion of Iraq realized these dark expectations, and the neo-Zarqawist, or neo-Takfirist group, was thus able to come to light.

49 Murad Batal al-Shishani, 'The Dangerous Ideas of the Neo-Zarqawist Movement', *CTC Sentinel*, vol. 2, issue 9 (September 2009): p. 18.

50 Ibid., p. 19.

51 Eli Alshech, 'The Doctrinal Crisis within the Salafi-Jihadi Ranks and the Emergence of Neo-Takfirism. A Historical and Doctrinal Analysis', *Islamic Law and Society*, vo. 21, issue 4 (September 2014): p. 431.

52 Quintan Wiktorowicz, 'The New Global Threat: Transnational Salafis and Jihad', *Middle East Policy*, vol. 8, no. 4 (December 2001): p. 30.

53 Ibid., p. 35.

However, coming back to the historical discourse, Abū Muḥammad al-Maqdisī's suspicions, dilemmas and uncertainties about Abū Muṣʿab al-Zarqāwī's Iraqi group Jamāʿat al-Tawḥīd wa al-Jihād were shared also by al-Qāʿida Central. In the first stages of the conflict there was no official merger between al-Tawḥīd wa al-Jihād and al-Qāʿida due to al-Zarqāwī's extreme views and *modus operandi*, since he was harshly anti-Shiʿa, whereas al-Qāʿida leadership, on the contrary, was more prudent, believing that, to drive out the Western powers from the occupied Islamic countries, the support of all the Muslim world would have been necessary, without making any sectarian distinctions. At this stage of the war against the West, al-Qāʿida believed, insisting on theological differences was only an obstacle for the success of the mission. As a response, al-Zarqāwī wrote a letter to Osama bin Laden in 2004 replying that "if we succeed in dragging them [the Shiites] into the arena of sectarian war, it will become possible to awaken the inattentive Sunnis as they feel imminent danger and annihilating death."[54]

Eventually, on October 2004 al-Qāʿida accepted al-Zarqāwī's oath of allegiance, and al-Tawḥīd wa al-Jihād joined bin Laden's global network: it was the birth of al-Qāʿida in Iraq (AQI). Even though they were aware of the problem arising from the implicit endorsement of such an extreme violence, bin Laden and al-Ẓawāhirī had decided to reconsider anyway an alliance with al-Zarqāwī because by then he had become too important on the Iraqi scene. "It was a marriage of convenience".[55]

Notwithstanding the new situation, al-Zarqāwī continued to foment violence and to generate instability, "perfectly aware that his success would have mainly depended on the instability of the new Iraq and on the support of the Arab-Sunni community at large."[56] By provoking and repressing the Shiites, he aimed at igniting a sectarian civil war and at creating a fragile security environment to exploit and where to thrive.

On June 7, 2006, the United Stated killed al-Zarqāwī. On June 12, Abū Ayyūb al-Maṣrī, also known as Abū Ḥamza al-Muhājir, was appointed new leader of AQI, and after few months, on October 15, the Islamic

---

54 Abū Muṣʿab al-Zarqāwī, *Letter to bin Laden*, available at https://2001-2009.state.gov/p/nea/rls/31694.htm (accessed July 3, 2018).

55 Andrea Plebani, 'From Terrorist Group to Self-Proclaimed State: The Origins and Evolution of IS', in *Daesh and the Terrorist Threat: From the Middle East to Europe*, ed. by Hedwig Giusto (Brussels: Foundation for European Progressive Studies, 2016), p. 36.

56 Andrea Plebani, 'Origini ed evoluzione dell'autoproclamato Stato Islamico', in *Jihad e Terrorismo. Da al-Qaʿida all'Isis: Storia di un nemico che cambia*, ed. by Andrea Plebani (Milano: Mondadori, 2016), p. 48.

State of Iraq (ISI) was officially founded. The media spokesman of the new organization, Muḥārib al-Jubūrī, identified a certain Abū ʿUmar al-Baghdādī as the "Commander of the Faithful", and al-Maṣrī became his deputy and war minister of ISI. It was the beginning of a new era.

The proclamation of ISI was made without any consultation with bin Laden or, more generally, with al-Qāʿida Central, and many among the central leadership were complaining about this unusual and unexpected evolution.

At any rate, ISI turned out to be a total disaster, not even taken seriously by other jihadists: as a matter of fact, within the jihadi community itself there were many discontents and doubts about ISI's legitimacy. Finally, on April 18, 2010, Abū ʿUmar al-Baghdādī and Abū Ayyūb al-Maṣrī were killed in a joint raid by American and Iraqi forces. A new leader was about to be appointed, driving ISI toward a fatal evolution: on May 2010, Abū Bakr al-Baghdādī assumed the leadership of the group. The first decision he made was to replace ISI's leaders suspected of disloyalty with people nearer to him, especially former Ṣaddām Ḥusayn's officials. In this way, he consolidated his position and strengthened the group.

"The Islamic State does not recognize synthetic borders, nor any citizenship besides Islam," declared al-Baghdādī in July 2012.[57] Then, on April 9, 2013, he announced that *Jabhat al-Nuṣra* (JN), al-Qāʿida's Syrian affiliate, was absorbed into ISI: the Islamic State of Iraq and the Levant (ISIL) was born. From this moment on, the Islamic State became a fluid entity, spread over two countries, in the geographical area often called "Syraq". This decision created attrition between al-Baghdādī and Abū Muḥammad al-Jawlānī, leader of *Jabhat al-Nuṣra*, who publicly rejected the merger and immediately pledged an oath of allegiance to al-Ẓawāhirī, who had meanwhile become the leader of al-Qāʿida after Osama bin Laden's death on May 2, 2011. The clash between ISIL and al-Qāʿida started at this very moment, with al-Baghdādī publicly rejecting al-Ẓawāhirī's role and denying any connection with al-Qāʿida. As a response, on February 2, 2014, al-Qāʿida Central officially disassociated itself from ISIS, referring to it "as the group that calls itself a state."[58] And, in June,

57 Quoted in Tim Lister, 'What does Isis really want?', *Cnn*, December 11, 2015, http://edition.cnn.com/2015/12/11/middleeast/isis-syria-iraq-caliphate/ (accessed March 11, 2017).

58 Nelly Lahoud, 'The Islamic State and al-Qaeda', in *Jihadism Transformed. by Al-Qaeda and Islamic State's Global Battle of Ideas*, eds. Simon Staffell and Akil N. Awan (London: Hurst & Company, 2016), p. 27.

after having conquered Mosul, al-Baghdādī changed the name from ISIL into the sole "Islamic State" (IS), declaring the long-awaited Caliphate.

The conflict between the two parties of the Salafi-Jihadi ranks, the "Maqdisiyyūn" – who are prone to consider spiritual and scholarly guidance of more value than jihad only – and the "Zarqawiyyūn" – who take al-Zarqāwī as their model and emphasize combat experience as the primary source of legitimacy – was revived by the rise of IS; and, besides, the establishment of a self-proclaimed Caliphate "has also caused a split among the former [the Maqdisiyyūn], with al-Maqdisī and several others siding with Jabhat al-Nuṣra/Jabhat Fath al-Sham [sic], while some others who had previously been close to al-Maqdisī now chose IS, partly because it seemed to represent exactly the type of goal that al-Maqdisī had long called for: an Islamic state."[59]

Yet, there is also another central development to be pointed at (and which will be discussed later in this chapter), namely, the apocalyptic fervour of a new generation of jihadists, persuaded they were leading the world to its end, fulfilling ancient prophecies and waging a cosmic war against absolute enemies. The Islamic State possessed this eschatological mindset from its very beginning, and the self-proclaimed Caliph used extensively symbols pertaining the Islamic apocalyptic imaginary to exhort and encourage the many militants on the ground and to call other jihadists from abroad. After all, the Islamic State

> shifted the jihadist movement from an abstract future eschatology to one realized in the here and now, claiming that 'the signs of victory have appeared'. In doing so, they tend not to engage in detailed political commentary or explorations of ideological subtleties, instead focusing on how the material facts of conquering territory, securing loyalty and support and amassing wealth bear out the realization of divine prophecy.[60]

Nonetheless, the differences between the two groups (al-Qāʿida and the Islamic State) do not invalidate the definition of Salafi-Jihadism given above, that is, an ideology that plans to restore the golden era of Islam by means of violence – and as we will see, the eschatological framework of the two groups, their belief in the end of the world, does not contradict the

---

59 Joas Wagemakers, 'Jihadi-Salafism in Jordan and the Syrian Conflict: Divisions Overcome Unity', *Studies in Conflict & Terrorism*, vol. 41, no, 3 (2018): p. 200.

60 Simon Staffell and Akil N. Awan, introduction to *Jihadism Transformed. by Al-Qaeda and Islamic State's Global Battle of Ideas*, eds. Simon Staffell and Akil N. Awan (London: Hurst & Company, 2016), p. 17.

state-building effort and the determination of reestablishing the flawless Islamic era. The divergences among them pertain to the operational aspect, on the one hand, and affect some ideological segments, on the other, but they do not abrogate the very goal at the basis of Salafi-Jihadism, preserving its ideological core intact.

4.2 *Essential Salafi-Jihadi features*

It is Shiraz Maher in his already classic book *Salafi-Jihadism. The History of an Idea* (2016) who stresses the unity of Salafi-Jihadism, notwithstanding potential divisions and dissimilarities among the various jihadi actors. What Maher does is to present a set of conceptual aspects as constituting essential features of Salafi-Jihadism. He thus registers five essential characteristics: *tawḥīd, ḥākimiyya, al-walāʾ wa-l-barāʾ*, jihad, and *takfīr*. "Whilst all of these ideas exist within normative Islamic traditions, and there is nothing particularly unique or special about them, what makes them relevant in this context is that the contemporary Salafi-Jihadi movement has interpreted and shaped them in unique and original ways."[61]

Speaking about moderate Islam, Osama bin Laden himself once declared: "The Islam preached by the advocates of interreligious dialogue does not contain [the doctrine of] Loyalty and Enmity [*al-walāʾ wa-l-barāʾ*]; nor does it contain [offensive] jihad; nor boundaries established by the *sharīʿa* – since it is these very doctrines that worry the West most."[62] Similarly, Ayman al-Ẓawāhirī said: "There is a firm bond between loving the Lord, befriending the believers, and waging jihad in the path of Allah."[63] This means that bin Laden and al-Ẓawāhirī are highly critical of any other Muslim who do not accept and believe in all of the five points that Maher lists.

> The five defining characteristics are therefore principally concerned with two things – protection and promotion. Protection of the faith comes through jihad, *al-walāʾ wa-l-barāʾ*, and *takfīr*; while its promotion is linked to *tawḥīd*

---

61 Maher, *Salafi-Jihadism*, p. 14.

62 Osama bin Laden, 'Moderate Islam is a Prostration to the West', in *The Al Qaeda Reader. The Essential Texts of Osama Bin Laden's Terrorist Organization*, ed. by Raymond Ibrahim (New York: Broadway Books, 2007), p. 25.

63 Ayman al-Ẓawāhirī, 'Loyalty and Enmity: An Inherited Doctrine and a Lost Reality', in *The Al Qaeda Reader. The Essential Texts of Osama Bin Laden's Terrorist Organization*, ed. by Raymond Ibrahim (New York: Broadway Books, 2007), p. 100.

> and *ḥākimiyya*. […] The doctrine of *al-walāʾ wa-l-barāʾ* establishes lines of loyalty and disavowal; *takfīr* delineates Islam against everything else and protects it against insidious corruption from within; *tawḥīd* and *ḥākimiyya* explain what legitimate authority should look like and who it should serve; and jihad prescribes the method for this particular revolution.[64]

Another example of the effectiveness of Maher's understanding is the exposition given by Abū Muṣʿab al-Zarqāwī in al-Qāʿida in Iraq's *Creed and Methodology* published on March 2005. The text is brief and very explicit: "We believe in defending *tawḥīd* and eliminating polytheism. […] The Almighty has absolute authority. […] Those who commit atheism in their heart, with their tongue, or by their actions will be excommunicated. […] Every believer should initiate jihad against the enemy. […] Muslims are one nation."[65] In these few sentences we can recognize all five elements that Maher deems essentials for the Salafi-Jihadi thought. Hence, in the Salafi-Jihadi ideological blend, "these principles are turned into the pillars of a totalitarian system, reaching into the private lives, […] and are used as disciplinary measures of control."[66]

Let us study briefly each of these five features.

The first characteristic of Salafi-Jihadism that Maher lists is *jihad*, too often erroneously translated as "holy war"; but in reality,

> the semantic meaning of the Arabic term *jihad* has no relation to holy war or even war in general. It derives, rather from the root *j.h.d.,* the meaning of which is to strive, exert oneself, or to take extraordinary pains. *Jihad* is a verbal noun of the third form of the root verb *jahada*, which is defined classically as exerting one's utmost power, efforts, endeavors, or ability in contending with an object of disapprobation.[67]

Most of the early collections of *ḥadīth*s of the 9th century, where the traditions on war were numerous, "contain extensive discussions of jihad, which in most collections are located immediately after the sections

---

64 Maher, *Salafi-Jihadism*, pp. 15-16.

65 Abū Muṣʿab al-Zarqāwī, 'Our Creed and Methodology', *DSpace -Digital Repository Unimib*, April 13, 2005, https://scholarship.tricolib.brynmawr.edu/bitstream/handle/10066/5026/AQI20050321.pdf?sequence=3&isAllowed=y (accessed 13 January, 2015).

66 Roel Meijer, 'Salafism and the Challenge of Modern Politics. A Comparison Between ISIS and the Al-Nour Party', *Orient – German Journal for Politics, Economics and Culture of the Middle East*, vol. 57, issue 2 (2016): p. 22.

67 Reuven Firestone, *Jihad: The Origin of Holy War in Islam* (New York: Oxford University Press, 1999), p. 16.

devoted to the 'five pillars of Islam.'"[68] The six canonical collections of Sunni Islam – those of al-Bukhārī, Muslim, al-Tirmidhī, Abū Dāwūd, Ibn Māja, and al-Nasāʿī – "accord a prominent place to jihad."[69] And the more the theoretical and doctrinal elaboration was refined, the more jihad was regulated by a legal process. David Cook considers the intellectual elaboration on jihad as commenced by the systematic thought of al-Shāfiʿī (d. 820), architect of Islamic law and the eponym of one of the four Islamic schools of law, who established the legal foundation for jihad, which was completed by the Ḥanafī 11th-century jurist al-Sarakhsī. "From this point forward, although individual points continued to be debated, the Muslim method of warfare was set."[70] And it goes without saying that "no one writing in the jihad tradition thinks that indiscriminate or total war can be justified,"[71] meaning that rules concerning both *jus ad bellum* and *jus in bello* were fixed.

However, once this process came to an end, the world order changed. The presence of a multiplicity of Islamic political entities, despite the nominal central authority of the Caliphate, caused the proliferation of multiple interpretations of jihad; finally the League of Nations era, preceded by the end of the Caliphal institution (1924), was the final step towards the (formal) dismissal of offensive jihad on the basis of a global convention. Now all member states were, and still are, bound by the Charter of the United Nations, which expressly stipulates that "armed force shall not be used, save in the common interest."

Ayman al-Ẓawāhirī without a hint of a doubt defines the United Nations as "a hegemonic organization of universal infidelity,"[72] adding that a true Muslim "is not permitted to join or have recourse to it."[73] In other words, the new world order is totally ignored, and even attacked, by Jihadi-Salafi militants, on the belief that *kuffār* (disbelievers, infidels) have arranged an oppressive global Jewish-Christian system with the sole objective of assaulting and harming the same religion of Islam. As a consequence, for Salafi-Jihadis the possibility of waging jihad is open again. But what is particularly noteworthy is that, at this stage, non-state actors, and

---

68 David Cook, *Understanding Jihad* (Berkeley and Los Angeles: University of California Press, 2005), p. 14.

69 Ibid., p. 17.

70 Ibid., p. 22.

71 John Kelsay, 'Just War, Jihad, and the Study of Comparative Ethics', *Ethics & International Affairs*, vol. 24, no. 3 (2010): p. 233.

72 al-Ẓawāhirī, 'Loyalty and Enmity', p. 102.

73 Ibid.

specifically al-Qāʿida affiliates and the so-called Islamic State, claim the monopoly of violence for themselves – from which the problem regarding the actual target of the "War on Terror."

More importantly, the real legitimacy for the Salafi-Jihadi claim originates directly from the intrusion of Western powers into the inner affairs of Arab states. Stated differently, the "state of peace" proclaimed by the United Nations does not meet the reality of the MENA region. As such, "there may arise disagreements among Muslims regarding the obligation to wage jihad, not over whether or not jihad remains an obligation even under a 'state of peace', but over whether or not an actual 'state of peace' exists."[74] Which credibility has the presumption of a generalized "state of peace" when Afghanistan, Sudan, Lebanon, Iraq, Libya and other Islamic-majority countries are being constantly destabilized? In this widespread situation of chaos and betrayed promises, the jihadi message proliferates. Both al-Qāʿida and the Islamic State have proved capable of manipulating the misfortunes of the Arab peoples on their behalf.

Jihad returns on the international scene in a transfigured shape: no longer as an instrument in the hands of Islamic majority governments, but as a weapon adopted by unpredictable "glocal" movements. In this innovative environment, Jihadi-Salafism is the declaration that jihad is the only means by which Islam will thrive, leading to the re-establishment of the golden era and the victory over the forces of evil. According to bin Laden, jihad becomes "a rite […] that shall never fail or diminish, till the Day of Judgment."[75] "Jihad is the most excellent work a servant Muslim can render,"[76] writes al-Ẓawāhirī. According to this sensibility, jihad is not only a means to an end, that end being a fully Islamic political entity, but it becomes an eschatological vehicle "irrespective of any state, or of any material end-goal."[77] This implies that strategical considerations intertwine with the pursuit of universalist goals, provoking the transformation of indiscriminate violence into a redemptive means – and violence as a magic tool that redeems humankind recalls to mind the idea of gnostic self-salvation, as will be argued in the next sections. In Osama bin Laden's own words:

74 Jackson, 'Jihad and the Modern World', p. 20.

75 Bin Laden, 'Moderate Islam is a Prostration to the West', p. 33.

76 Al-Ẓawāhirī, 'Loyalty and Enmity', p. 81.

77 Gilbert A. Ramsay and Sarah V. Marsden, 'Leaderless Global Jihadism: The Paradox of Discriminate Violence', *Journal of Strategic Studies*, vol. 38, no. 5 (2015): p. 598.

> Oh people of Afghanistan, you know that *jihad* is of the utmost value in Islam, and that with it we can gain pride and eminence in this world and the next. You know that it saves our lands, protects our sanctity, spreads justice, security, and prosperity, and plants fear in the enemies' hearts. Through it kingdoms are built, and the banner of truth flies high above all others. Oh people of Afghanistan, I am convinced that you understand these words of mine more than anyone else, since throughout the ages no invader ever settled in your lands, since you are distinguished for your strength, defiance and fortitude in the fight, and since your doors are open only to Islam. That is because Muslims never came as colonizers or out of worldly self-interest, but as missionaries bringing us back to God.[78]

A theological explanation of jihad can be found in *Dābiq*, the online magazine published by the Islamic State for propaganda purposes. In number 15 issued on July 2016, it is stated that "waging jihad – spreading the rule of Allah by the sword – is an obligation found in the Qur᾽ān, the word of our Lord, just as it was an obligation sent in the Torah, the Psalms, and the Gospel."[79] According to Islamic tradition, the sacred texts of Judaism and Christianity were corrupted and manipulated over time, causing the distortion of the true religious message and making it necessary for God to intervene one last time through the person of Muḥammad. Being the message of God the One, all the revelations (which are but reflections of the same truth) convey the same content, including jihad. "In the remnants of the Torah, it is found that 'the Lord is a person of war' (Exodus 15:3),"[80] it is stated in the magazine. And also: "Even Jesus, whom the Christians have titled the 'Prince of Peace,' is recorded in their scripture as saying, 'Do not think that I have come to bring peace to the earth. I have not come to bring peace, but a sword' (Matthew 10:34)."[81]

The Qur᾽ānic foundation for jihad is found in the well-known "sword verses":

> And when the sacred months have passed, then kill the polytheists wherever you find them and capture them and besiege them and sit in wait for them at every place of ambush. But if they should repent, establish prayer, and give *zakāt*, let them [go] on their way. Indeed, God is Forgiving and Merciful. (Qur᾽an 9:5)

---

78 Osama bin Laden, 'To the People of Afghanistan', in *Messages to the World. The Statements of Osama bin Laden*, ed. by Bruce Lawrence (London and New York: Verso, 2005), p. 159.

79 *Dābiq*, n. 15 (July 2016): p. 78.

80 Ibid.

81 Ibid., p. 79.

> Fight those who do not believe in Allah or in the Last Day and who do not consider unlawful what Allah and His Messenger have made unlawful and who do not adopt the religion of truth from those who were given the Scripture – [fight] until they give the *jizya* willingly while they are humbled. (Qur'an 9:29)

By putting a strong emphasis on these and other similar verses, Jihadi-Salafi militants tend to downplay other Qur'ānic injunctions (for instance, "Fight in the way of Allah those who fight you but do not transgress. Indeed, Allah does not like transgressors." [Qur'an 2:190]) in the interest of the broader global jihadi cause. And therefore, the often proclaimed defensive jihad (it is more al-Qāʿida than the Islamic State to give prominence to the defensive nature of its effort) ultimately turns into an offensive jihad. Protecting the Islamic community and preserving centuries-old traditions could seem to be noble causes worthy of defense, indeed; however, "these types of defensive postures are easily manipulated to form offensive justification for war or revolution,"[82] giving form to a military struggle "with the goals of reshaping Islamic society by ridding it of Western influence and presence, economically and politically."[83] Offensive attacks are justified as defensive measures, and the idea of a Western conspiracy to contain Islam fuels the offensive actions against the United Nations members guilty of intervening into the MENA inner affairs.

The discourses of bin Laden and al-Ẓawāhirī are full of calls for reciprocity (*qiṣāṣ*), a measure that justifies even the targeting of civilians. The Qur'ānic source is 5:45 which states: "And We ordained for them therein a life for a life, an eye for an eye, a nose for a nose, an ear for an ear, a tooth for a tooth, and for wounds is legal retribution." Interestingly, however, *qiṣāṣ* "is traditionally restricted to cases where the aggressor is known. Retribution is carried out only against the specific individual guilty of having inflicted the original harm;"[84] in the case of Salafi-Jihadism, the principle is expanded to the point of embracing entire populations deemed guilty of being supportive of "infidel" governments. In this way, *qiṣāṣ* becomes an instrument of international law, placing Salafi-Jihadism at odds with Islamic theology which holds to be unlawful to kill non-combatants. In January 2004 bin Laden announced:

---

82 Brek Batley, *The Justifications for Jihad, War and Revolution in Islam* (Canberra: Strategic and Defence Studies Centre, 2003), p. 6.

83 Bashir Abdul-Raheem, 'The Concept of Jihad in Islamic Philosophy', *American International Journal of Social Science*, vol. 4, no. 1 (February 2015): p. 146.

84 Maher, *Salafi-Jihadism*, p. 50.

> We do not differentiate between those dressed in military uniforms and civilians. [...] American history does not distinguish between civilians and military, not even women and children. They are the ones who used bombs against Nagasaki. Can these bombs distinguish between infants and military?[85]

Salafi-Jihadism also downplays the difference between the "greater" and the "lesser" jihad, a nowadays widespread understanding that distinguishes a purely spiritual striving (the "greater" jihad) from the actual militarily struggle (the "lesser" jihad) and that accords to the former a bigger importance than to the latter. This interpretation firstly flourished in the nascent *Taṣawwuf*, or Sufism, which accorded a strong value to a now famous *ḥadīth*:

> A number of fighters came to the Messenger of God, and he said: "You have done well in coming from the 'lesser jihad' to the 'greater jihad.'" They said: "What is the 'greater jihad'?" He said: "For the servant [of God] to fight his passions."[86]

This *ḥadīth*, however, is not contained in any of the six canonical books of *ḥadīths*, and therefore is highly criticized by its detractors and by violent Islamic groups, especially Salafi-Jihadis: the idea the "greater" jihad tries to portray is an image of religious struggle in terms of a spiritual action, the fight against one's own lower passions, intended to be more important than the actual fight against infidels. David Cook explains that the above-mentioned *ḥadīth*

> can be dated to the first half of the ninth century, when the ascetic movement in Islam was beginning to coalesce into Sufism, the mystical interpretation of Islam. Traditions indicating that jihad meant spiritual warfare, however, are entirely absent from any of the official, canonical collections (with the exception of that of al-Tirmidhi, who cites "the fighter is one who fights his passions"); they appear most often in the collections of ascetic material or proverbs.[87]

85 Quoted in John Miller, 'Greeting, America. My name is Osama bin Laden', *Esquire*, September 9, 2016, https://www.esquire.com/news-politics/a1813/osama-bin-laden-interview/ (accessed January 15, 2018).

86 This *ḥadīth* is reported by Ahmad ibn al-Husayn al-Bayhaqi (d. 1066) in the book *Al-Zuhd al-Kabīr* (Grand Asceticism), and the translation is provided by David Cook in *Understanding Jihad*, p. 146.

87 Cook, *Understanding Jihad*, p. 35.

Salafi-Jihadis tend to ignore such interpretation and any other readings that depict jihad as a non-violent fight. In *Dābiq* it is clearly affirmed that, "Do not be taken in by claims that the 'real jihad' is giving *da'wa* – rather, the real *da'wa* is waging jihad!"[88] Sayyid Quṭb and Muḥammad ʿAbd al-Salām Faraj have explicitly held the same position in their writings.

Takfīr is the second feature of Salafi-Jihadism according to Shiraz Maher. We have already dealt with this issue in relation to the rise of the Islamic State (IS), whose use of *takfīr* (excommunication, declaration of apostasy) was, and still is, preponderant. The advice given on the propaganda magazine *Dābiq* to all fellow *mujāhidūn* is: "Be wary very wary of allying with the Jews and Christians, and whoever has slipped by a word, then let him fear Allah, renew his faith, and repent from his deed. [...] *Even if he supported them just by a single word.* He who aligns with them by a single word falls into apostasy – extreme apostasy."[89] In *Rumiyah*, another propaganda magazine of IS, it is written that

> the Islamic State has continued to have a firm policy against *kufr* [unbelief] and *riddah* [apostacy]. It hasn't hesitated to make *takfīr* despite the blame of any critics. […] Therefore, it is essential to mention one of the very nullifiers that have cost so many individuals the price of losing their religion: refusing to make *takfīr* of the *kuffār* [unbelievers] and doubting their *kufr*, and this applies to anyone who refuses to make *takfīr* of any *murtadd* [apostate] who has fallen into one of the nullifiers. So as an example, anyone who denies that a so-called "Muslim" Member of Parliament is a *murtadd kāfir* – as he has committed *shirk* [idolatry, polytheism] with Allah in legislation – is himself a *murtadd.* And anyone who denies that a so-called "Muslim" in the military service of the *kuffār* is a *murtadd kāfir* – as he has supported the cause of *ṭāghūt* [tyrant] – is himself a *murtadd.* And anyone who refuses to make *takfīr* of those who consider the *sharīʿa* of Allah to be unsuitable for this era, or refuses to make *takfīr* of those who are fighting to establish democracy, is himself a *murtadd.* And whoever reads this article can no longer say, "I was never told."[90]

This long passage illustrates quite distinctly the intransigent position of the Islamic State on the issue of *takfīr*, which portrays the image of a more sectarian group than al-Qāʿida. Such is the real difference between the two groups: for al-Qāʿida, declaring other Muslims as *murtaddūn* (apostates) and *kuffār* (unbelievers) is rather problematic, in that intra-Muslim

---

88 *Dābiq*, n. 15 (July 2016): p. 28.

89 *Dābiq*, n. 4 (October 2014): p. 44. Italics added to emphasize the strict and demanding position on *takfīr* issue.

90 *Rumiyah*, n. 7 (March 2017): pp. 19-20.

sectarian warfare would distract from fighting the non-Islamic West and would also alienate potential Muslim allies; for IS, on the contrary, the purity of the Sunni message should be defended at all costs, at the expense of the inclusiveness of the *umma* and even at the cost of killing all minorities from the "Caliphal" territories, from Shiites to Yazidis ("Their creed [of Yazidis] is so deviant from the truth that even cross-worshipping Christians for ages considered them devil worshippers and Satanists"[91]). Consequently, "accusation of takfirism, which come together with the Kharijite label, are levelled against IS not only by prominent mainstream scholars and Muslim organizations all over the world[92], but also by jihadist circles such as leaders of al-Qaeda."[93]

To make it clearer, the main discrepancy between al-Qāʿida and the Islamic State lies on the method (*manhaj*) and not on the ideology or doctrine. It is a question of priorities: al-Qāʿida does level *takfīr* at the Arab regimes who are deemed to have colluded with the West, but prioritizes the fight against the West, believing that the defeat of the Far Enemy would result in the end of its support to local regimes ("Once the American enemy has been defeated, our next step would be targeting the region's leaders who had been the pillars of support for that American hegemony."[94]) The Islamic State, on the contrary, prioritizes the fight against the Near Enemy and the Shiites, called with

91 *Dābiq*, n. 4 (October 2014): p. 14.

92 In this respect, it is worth mentioning the "Letter to Baghdadi" issued on September 2014 and signed by 122 Muslim scholars from all over the world. The intent of the letter was to display the erroneous and dangerous positions of the Islamic State, denouncing its extremism and condemning the very claim of the Caliphate. On the matter of *takfīr*, in the letter, available at the website www.lettertobaghdadi.com, it is written that "disbelief requires the intention of disbelief, and not just absentminded words or deeds. It is not permissible to accuse anyone of disbelief without proof of the intention of disbelief. Nor is it permissible to accuse anyone of being a non-Muslim without ascertaining that intention." Mainstream Islamic position on *takfīr*, in fact, relies heavily on a famous *ḥadīth* stating "If a man says to his brother 'O *kāfir*!' then surely one of them is such [i.e., a *kāfir*]" (*Ṣaḥīḥ* al-Bukhārī, book 78, *ḥadīth* 130, https://sunnah.com/bukhari/78/130). The *ḥadīth* wants to highlight the impossibility of denouncing one's own faith, in that if the accused Muslim was not a *kāfir*, then the accuser would be undoubtedly a *kāfir*, at least because of the very fact of having caused a scandal within the *umma*, breaking its unity and internal solidarity.

93 Muhammad Haniff Hassan, 'The Danger of Takfir (Excommunication): Exposing IS' Takfiri Ideology', *Counter Terrorist Trends and Analyses*, vol. 9, no. 4 (April 2017): p. 7.

94 Osama bin Laden, quoted in Aron Heller, 'The Lost Dakota Fighters of Israel's War of Independence', *Tablet Magazine*, May 28, 2019, https://www.tabletmag.

the pejorative appellation of *rāfiḍa* ("rejector" or "rejectionists"),[95] without, however, disdaining sporadic attacks on the West. From the very beginning, the result of this strategy was a real state of terror in the zones under the Caliphal influence, but this tension was unsustainable in the long term, running the risk of alienating the local population. Al-Qāʿida has always been aware of this danger, and Ayman al-Ẓawāhirī himself once declared that the so-called Islamic State was more extremist than the Khawārij because "the Khawārij made *takfīr* on sinners, but [...] IS would even make up sins when they want to legitimize the killing of someone."[96]

In an interesting article on *Arab Law Quarterly* written by three scholars of Islamic issues, the authors retrace the historical evolution of radical *takfīr* listing four important moments: the Khawārij, or Kharijites, who represent the first occurrence in Islamic history of someone declaring *takfīr* against other fellow Muslims; the Mongol invasion in the 13th century, a period when the Islamic scholar Ibn Taymiyya condemned the newly converted Mongols because they did not succeed in implementing *sharīʿa* law; the purification movements in the 18th century, whose protagonist was Muḥammad ibn ʿAbd al-Wahhāb and his rejection of the many traditions that had emerged within the Islamic community after the first generation of Muslims; and the reaction against the West in the 20th century, with particular reference to Abū l-Aʿlā al-Mawdūdī and Sayyid Quṭb.[97]

Interestingly, the authors point out that

---

com/jewish-life-and-religion/285229/dakota-fighters-of-israels-war-of-independence (accessed June 2, 2019).

95 See, for example, the 2005 declaration of Abū Muṣʿab al-Zarqāwī: "The *rāfiḍa* are an evil sect that left the fold of Islam and fight the *ahl al-sunna wa-l-jamāʿa*. [...] During their whole history, the *rāfiḍa* have never made enemies with anyone except the people of Islam." ('Script of the Dialogue with Sheikh Abu Musab Al-Zarqawi', *Al-Furqan Media*, https://www.cia.gov/library/abbottabad-compound/B6/B6B68BAC05F26E830E97B9A252942EBE_cricket.pdf [accessed May 13, 2019]). The term *rāfiḍa* was originally used by (proto-)Sunnites as a pejorative definition for Twelver Shiites, those who refuses to recognize the authority of the first three well-guided Caliphs.

96 Christina Hartmann, 'Who Does (Not) Belong to the Jihadis' Umma? A Comparison of IS's and al Qaida's Use of Takfīr to Exclude People from the Muslim Community', *Journal of Deradicalization*, no. 13 (Winter 2017/18): p. 230.

97 Mohammed Badar, Masaki Nagata and Tiphanie Tueni, 'The Radical Application of the Islamist Concept of Takfir', *Arab Law Quarterly*, vol. 31, no. 2 (June 2017): pp. 142-148.

> there is no Qur'anic support for the earthly punishment of apostacy by man. This is not the case for sins or crimes such as theft or fornication, which are dealt with by prescribed punishments. Capital punishment for turning away from Islam thus pertains to a human creative endeavor aimed at criminalizing a sin which, by definition, is only accountable for in the hereafter.[98]

In jihadi discourse, on the contrary, "the consequence of *takfīr* is not only punishment in the afterlife (*'ākhira*), but can also mean that a person can be legitimately killed and their property can be confiscated in this life (*dunyā*)."[99] Declaring someone a *kāfir* is dangerous for his/her (immanent more than transcendent) safety.

The subjectivity with which Salafi-Jihadi militants adopt *takfīr* as a weapon against other Muslims is clear from the following statement made by the al-Qāʿida member Anwar al-ʿAwlaqī (d. 2011): "We do not judge by what is in the hearts. We judge by what is apparent."[100] This statement is a clear denunciation of *irjāʿ* (to defer, to postpone), the basic concept of the early Islamic theological position known as *Murjiʾa*, whose adherents, the Murjiʾites, preferred to leave the judgment of one's faith to God in order to preserve the Islamic community from lacerating divisions on a doctrinal basis. Salafi-Jihadi theorists "reject the very premise on which *irjāʾ* is established. They argue that conviction and testimony are necessary prerequisites of *īmān* (faith) but that these aspects of faith are meaningless unless they are accompanied by acts (*ʿamal*)."[101]

In particular, the nonchalant and insolent use of *takfīr* by the Islamic State is indiscriminate and radical, ending up with the targeting of four broad categories of people: "Muslim rulers, who do not rule according to the *sharīʿa*; Islamist parties that take part in democratic elections; Muslim rebels questioning the authority of a ruler; and other jihadis coming to the defense of Sunnis who are declared apostates by IS."[102] After all, "Islam is the religion of the sword, not pacifism,"[103] is said on *Dābiq*. And elaborating on this statement, the magazine continues: "One of the biggest *shubuhāt* [wrong arguments][104] propagated by

98 Ibid., p. 139.
99 Hartmann, 'Who Does (Not) Belong to the Jihadis' Umma?', p. 219.
100 Anwar al-'Awlaqī, 'Tawfique Chowdhury's Alliance with the West', *Anwar al-Awlaki blog* February 12, 2009, https://archive.org/stream/Anwar.Awlaki.Audio.Archive/Tawfique.Chowdhury.Alliance.with.the_djvu.txt (accessed August 1, 2018).
101 Maher, *Salafi-Jihadism*, pp. 80-81.
102 Hartmann, 'Who Does (Not) Belong to the Jihadis' Umma?', p. 220.
103 *Dābiq*, n. 7 (February 2015): p. 20.
104 In Islamic law, *shubuhāt* are illicit acts that resemble licit ones but are nonetheless illegal.

the heretics is the linguistic root for the word 'Islam'. They claim it comes from the word *salām* (peace), when in actuality it comes from words meaning submission and sincerity sharing the same consonant root."[105] Submission, then, is a word that has the double meaning of "submission to God" and "submission to the central authority of the Caliphate", and which eventually translates into the following statement: "Anyone who rebels against its [of the Caliphate] authority inside its territory is considered a renegade, and it is permissible to fight him."[106] This extremist consequence is based on the belief that *tawḥīd*, the oneness of God, is embodied in the state, and that anyone who does not join it is considered a *kāfir*: "This is what ISIS leadership believes in as they see the Islamic state they lead as having a monopoly over religious truth, and thus those who disobey the state have renounced their faith."[107]

Takfīr promotes a deadly tendency to fratricide and fosters a dangerous intra-confessional struggle, carrying with it the specter of *fitna*, an Arabic term that is a constant threat, a pending menace for the *umma*:

> It means 'seduction', an internal war within Islam, a centrifugal force that brings destruction, implosion and ruin to the community. [...] It is a permanent threat that weighs on the perpetuity of Muslim society, that disturbs the conscience of the *ʿulamāʾ* and the doctors of the law, and pushes them to precaution and prudence.[108]

The third feature of Salafi-Jihadism in Shiraz Maher's definition is *al-walāʾ wa-l-barāʾ*, an Islamic theological concept that has been used as a weapon by Salafi-Jihadi militants. "O you who believes in *walāʾ* and *barāʾ*,"[109] urges the magazine *Dābiq* – revealing its importance in the radical worldview. Indeed this doctrine, *Dābiq* continues, is said to be "a fundamental cornerstone of Islam."[110]

What is it and what does it refer to? Its literal translation is "loyalty and disavowal", suggesting loyalty to God, to His laws and to Muslims, and disavowal of everything else. It is an advice to all Muslims – beware of everything lying outside Islam – which eventually becomes an injunction, a commandment. It could also be translated as "allegiance

---

105 *Dābiq*, n. 7: p. 22.

106 *Dābiq*, n. 1 (July 2014): p. 27.

107 Bader Al-Ibrahim, 'ISIS, Wahhabism and Takfir', *Contemporary Arab Affairs*, vol. 8, no. 3 (2015): p. 414.

108 Gilles Kepel, *Fitna. Guerra nel cuore dell'Islam* (2004; repr., Rome-Bari: Laterza, 2006), p. 273.

109 *Dābiq*, n. 4 (October 2014): p. 9.

110 *Dābiq*, n. 12 (November 2015): p. 34.

and disassociation", or "love and hatred," pointing in either case at the dangerousness of anything deemed un-Islamic. This is to say that a Muslim should direct his/her devotion to God only and his/her loyalty exclusively to fellow Muslims. To be avoided and even fought against, that is, what pertains the side of *barāʾ*, are *kufr* (unbelief), *shirk* (idolatry or polytheism), *bidʿa* (pernicious innovations in the realm of faith), *kuffār* (disbelievers), and any political system developed outside of an Islamic framework such as democracy and nationalism.

"According to this line of thinking, the only relationship between Muslims and disbelievers is that of active enmity or passive hatred."[111] In a certain sense, the concept of *al-walāʾ wa-l-barāʾ* divides the world into two separate domains, creating the condition for demarcating the identity of the good in-group as opposed to the evil out-group – it enhances cohesion within the *umma*, promotes homogeneity and encourages solidarity among the Muslims facing the "others".

Many are the Qurʾānic verses that form the foundation of this doctrine. For instance, "O you who have believed, do not take the Jews and the Christians as allies. They are allies of one another. And whoever is an ally to them among you – then indeed, he is [one] of them" (5:51); "Let not believers take disbelievers as allies [*awliyāʾ*, people to whom one shows *walāʾ*] rather than believers" (3:28); "You will not find a people who believe in Allah and the Last Day having affection for those who oppose Allah and His Messenger, even if they were their fathers or their sons or their brothers or their kindred" (58:22); "And never will the Jews or the Christians approve of you until you follow their religion. Say, 'Indeed, the guidance of Allah is the [only] guidance.' If you were to follow their desires after what has come to you of knowledge, you would have against Allah no protector or helper" (2:210).

From a historical perspective, Joas Wagemakers traces the roots of the concept back to the pre-Islamic Arabian Peninsula, where the different tribes were often at war with one another. As is known, it was a duty of each tribe to protect its members against attacks from outsiders. However, the tribes

> sometimes decided to expel one of their own so as not to jeopardize relations with another tribe they were allied with. Such a person was referred to as a

111 Joshua Gilliam, 'Why They Hate Us. An Examination of *al-wala' wa-l-bara'* in Salafi-Jihadist Ideology', *Military Review Online Exclusive* (February 2018): 2, https://www.armyupress.army.mil/Journals/Military-Review/Online-Exclusive/2018-OLE/Feb/They-Hate/ (accessed January 22, 2019).

> *khali'* (outcast) and the act of expulsion was, apart from *khal'* [separation], also called *tabarru'*. The latter term is linguistically related to *bara'* and denotes that a particular tribe declares itself innocent (*bari'*) of the fate of its former member.[112]

The concept was subsequently adapted to the needs of the newborn Islamic religion. The first group to use *al-walāʾ wa-l-barāʾ* in a confrontational way was the uncompromising sect of the Kharijites. The subsequent evolution occurred in the writings of the famous Hanbali scholar Ibn Taymiyya: he stressed the importance of avoiding excessive close contacts with other religious groups such as the Jews and the Christians. Muslims have their own identity, rituals, religious festivals and even clothing, he said, and they must avoid external influences so as not to fall into the temptation to produce religious innovations (*bidʿa*).

The next step in the evolution of *al-walāʾ wa-l-barāʾ* occurred in Wahhabism: Sulayman ibn 'Abdallah Āl Shaykh (d. 1818), a grandson of Muḥammad ibn ʿAbd al-Wahhāb, dealt with the topic and used it "not just as a means to fight *bidʿa* but as a tool against *kufr*."[113] He thus added a political dimension to the concept: if until Wahhabism *al-walāʾ wa-l-barāʾ* was a tool to separate Muslims from non-Muslims, it now became "an instrument that does the same but also distinguishes 'real' Muslims from their 'apostate' fellow-believers."[114] And so, people who traditionally were part of the in-group were now included in the broader out-group of the enemies of Islam. In a sense, Wahhabism added an inquisitorial approach to the meanings of *al-walāʾ wa-l-barāʾ*.

Another step towards the radicalization of the same concept was made by Juhaymān al-ʿUtaybī (d. 1980), a Saudi militant who in 1979 organized the "Grand Mosque seizure", the takeover of the *al-Masjid al-Ḥarām* in Mecca to protest against the Saʿūd family. The righteous Muslim, al-ʿUtaybī believed, should show enmity to the enemies of Islam – disavowal, then, should take the form of visible behaviors, from the withdrawing from the supposedly deviant Saudi society to the point of fighting (*qitāl*). Juhaymān al-ʿUtaybī has greatly influenced Abū Muḥammad al-Maqdisī, the former teacher of Abū Muṣʿab al-Zarqāwī,

---

112 Joas Wagemakers, 'The Transformation of a Radical Concept: *al-wala' wa-l-bara'* in the Ideology of Abu Muhammad al-Maqdisi', in *Global Salafism. Islam's New Religious Movement*, ed. by Roel Meijer (New York: Oxford University Press, 2013), p. 83.

113 Ibid., p. 87.

114 Wagemakers, *A Quietist Jihadi*, p. 153.

who further developed *al-walāʾ wa-l-barāʾ* into a revolutionary tool in the hand of the *mujāhidūn*.

In the discussion of the concept, Abū Muḥammad al-Maqdisī often quotes Qurʾan 5:51: "O you who have believed, do not take the Jews and the Christians as allies. They are allies of one another. And whoever is an ally to them among you – then indeed, he is [one] of them. Indeed, Allah guides not the wrongdoing people." Yet, the most mentioned *sūra* is the sixtieth, verse 4:

> There has already been for you an excellent pattern in Abraham and those with him, when they said to their people, "Indeed, we are disassociated from you and from whatever you worship other than Allah. We have denied you, and there has appeared between us and you animosity and hatred forever until you believe in Allah alone" except for the saying of Abraham to his father, "I will surely ask forgiveness for you, but I have not [power to do] for you anything against Allah. Our Lord, upon You we have relied, and to You we have returned, and to You is the destination."

In his most famous book, *Millat Ibrāhīm* ("The Religion of Abraham") published in 1988, al-Maqdisī states: "The *Millat* of Ibrāhīm is: (1) Sincerity of worship to Allāh alone, with everything that the phrase 'the worship' (*al-'ibāda*) encompasses in meanings; and (2) the disavowal (*barā')* from the *shirk* and its people."[115] By expanding the scope of the word "worship", al-Maqdisī transfers the denunciation of *al-walāʾ wa-l-barāʾ* to every legislation other than *sharīʿa*. Man-made laws are considered to be idols along the lines of false deities of polytheistic cults. He distinctly denounces as *ṭawāghīt* (the great pre-Islamic Arabian deities) all the "idols made from stone, or the sun, or the moon or a grave or a tree or legislations and laws from the invention of man."[116]

Consequently, Muslims living in secular countries, including by now even Muslim-majority states, are actually being loyal to non-Islamic laws. What al-Maqdisī suggests is to wake up all Muslims from the state of *jāhiliyya* and to wage jihad against the idolatrous regimes. "If Allāh has ordered us with jihad, and has clarified that there is no hardship in it," al-Maqdisī writes, "and that that is the *millat* of Ibrāhīm – then know that this fundamental. Waging jihad with the life, and following the religion of Ibrāhīm – it is this that differentiates the truthful one from the pretending

115 Abū Muḥammad al-Maqdisī, *Millat Ibrāhīm*, (n.p.: at-Tibyān Publications, n.d.), pp. 34-35.

116 Ibid., p. 52.

claimant."[117] As a conclusion, jihad "is the highest level of openly showing the enmity and hatred towards the enemies of Allāh,"[118] al-Maqdisī maintains.

> By thus connecting *walā'* towards "un-Islamic" laws with worship, and its alternative – *barā'* – with jihad, while at the time stressing the necessity of disavowal for all Muslims, al-Maqdisī has turned *al-walā' wa-l-barā'* from a quietist tool to purify the religion into an instrument for revolution. [...] He shifted the separating element of *al-walā' wa-l-barā'* not just partially but entirely from the Muslim/non-Muslim divide to the "true" Muslim/"apostate" Muslim one.[119]

This understanding of *al-walā' wa-l-barā'* was eventually transmitted to Abū Muṣ'ab al-Zarqāwī and then to the self-proclaimed Islamic State.

On the al-Qā'ida side, it was Ayman al-Ẓawāhirī who gave centrality to this concept in the 2002 book *Al-Wala' wa-l Bara': Aqidah Manqulah wa Waqi' Mafqud* ("Loyalty and Disavowal: An Inherited Doctrine and a Lost Reality"). According to al-Ẓawāhirī, "the primary way for Muslims to distinguish themselves from the non-Muslims is the former complete adherence and practice of *sharī'a* laws. [... And] Muslims can never love or befriend infidels in anyway until the latter submit to Islam."[120]

In his treatise, al-Ẓawāhirī lengthily quotes several Qur'ānic passages (3:28, 4:144, 5:51-58, 5:80-81, 60:13, 2:120-121) to warn Muslims that the only reason why the infidels are kind with the believers is to turn them back into a state of infidelity. Basing his conclusions on Ibn Taymiyya's rigor – especially the idea that close relations with infidels is a sign of a lack of faith – al-Ẓawāhirī lists a number of prohibitions that Muslims must abide by: against taking non-Muslims as intimates and sharing the secrets of Muslims with them; against appointing infidels to dignified and important positions; against glorifying the infidels' religious ceremonies and customs; and against aiding infidels against fellow Muslims. With regard to the last point, al-Ẓawāhirī enumerates the occurrences in contemporary history when Arab states have helped the West and when Muslims have fought each other: the First Gulf War (the US troops were dispatched to Saudi

117 Ibid., p. 7.

118 Ibid., p. 106.

119 Wagemakers, *A Quietist Jihadi*, pp. 173-174.

120 Mohamed Ali, 'Al-Wala' Wal Bara' (Loyalty and Disavowal) in Modern Salafism: Analysing the Positions of Purist, Politico and Jihadi Salafis', in *Terrorist Rehabilitation. A New Frontier in Counter-Terrorism*, ed. by Rohan Gunaratna and Mohamed Bin Ali (New Jersey: Imperial College Press, 2015), p. 172.

Arabia to strike Muslims in Iraq), the Afghan jihad (Pakistan was used as the Western base to kill *mujāhidūn* in Afghanistan), the Palestinian cause (a conflict where by now everyone seems to be safeguarding Israel's security only, ignoring the Palestinian population).

What a true Muslim should do, al-Ẓawāhirī continues, is to wage jihad against three types of enemy: the infidels, i.e., those who never submitted to Islam; the apostates, or Muslims that have derailed from the straight path of Islam, and especially the apostate rulers; and the hypocrites.

"Allah Exalted has forbidden us from taking infidels as friends and allies, and aiding them against the believers, by either word or deed. Whoever foes this is an infidel like them,"[121] al-Ẓawāhirī writes. And he continues: "This hostility toward infidels, which is a pillar of faith according to Allah, cannot be achieved except by [first] renouncing the idolatrous [tyrants]."[122] By saying so, al-Ẓawāhirī sets the priority of al-Qāʿida. And ultimately: "Failure to uphold this fundamental pillar [i.e., *al-walāʾ wa-l-barāʾ*] leads to the dissolution of a Muslim's creed."[123]

In *Inspire*, the propaganda magazine published by al-Qāʿida in the Arabian Peninsula (AQAP), it is reported that

> Allah says that every Muslim will be tested for his loyalty. A believer will not be left to claim belief without that belief being verified, and part of that verification is by testing where does the loyalty of the believer lie. [...] Today loyalty of Allah and His Messenger and the believers is manifested in defending Islam and the Muslims, and failure in that test is having ones loyalty towards America and its allies and the agents of America – the rulers of the Muslim world. Those who do not disavow the rulers have not practiced the *ʿaqīda* [creed] of *walāʾ* and *barāʾ*.[124]

Therefore, the doctrine of *al-walāʾ wa-l-barāʾ* surely is one of the central features of Salafi-Jihadism. This is apparent also in the case of the Islamic State: on the magazine *Dābiq* much space is dedicated to the clarification of such doctrine. On number 10, for instance, are reported four *ḥadīths* that validate the centrality of *al-walāʾ wa-l-barāʾ* for the jihadi

---

121 Ayman al-Ẓawāhirī, 'Loyalty and Enmity: An Inherited Doctrine and a Lost Reality', in *The Al Qaeda Reader. The Essential Texts of Osama Bin Laden's Terrorist Organization*, ed. by Raymond Ibrahim (New York: Broadway Books, 2007), p. 99.

122 Ibid., p. 111.

123 Ibid., p. 112.

124 *Inspire*, n. 2 (October 2010): pp. 61-62.

struggle.[125] On number 11, furthermore, an entire article is entitled "*Walā'* and *barā'* versus American racism". Racial hatred has no place in Islam, it is argued, since "a Muslim's loyalty is determined, not by his skin color, his tribal affiliation, or his last name, but by his faith."[126] *Walā'*, thus, pertains only to the adherence to the Islamic religion. In the supposedly established Islamic state, all national and racial affiliations are null and void. "The only acceptable line of division is that which separates between a Muslim and a *kāfir*, whereas any other course of division would only be a source of weakness."[127] The lesson of Abū Muḥammad al-Maqdisī is quite evident in the following declaration:

> So let every Muslim who wishes to taste the sweetness of *walā'* and *barā'* follow the example of Ibrāhīm and declare enmity towards the *kuffār* amongst his own people – whether black, white, Arab, or non-Arab – and then march forth and wage war against them with whatever means are available to him.[128]

The confessional identity becomes the only marker of this transnational Islamic brotherhood, and faith converts into the sole basis of citizenship. *Al-walā' wa-l-barā'* takes on the contours of a political tool used against all power structures that differ from a pure Islamic system; basically, *barā'* is declared against the whole world outside of the borders of the self-proclaimed state of Iraq and Syria. *Barā'*, then, requests action, or physical confronting those who are not part of the ranks of the *mujāhidūn*. It commands Muslims to completely withdraw their support from any established state-authority, from the government as such to the judiciary and the military. By doing so, al-Qāʿida and the Islamic State are demanding for themselves the leadership over the whole *umma*, presenting their leaders and their statements as expressions of a pure, unadulterated form of Islam.

The fourth defining category of Salafi-Jihadism that Shiraz Maher considers is *tawḥīd*. This word, which "stems from the Arabic origin of '*waḥāda*' (to unify), or '*wahīd*' (one),"[129] is often translated as "monotheism", and is "in the true sense of the term, the act of believing and

---

125 See *Dābiq*, n. 10 (July 2015): pp. 38-39.

126 *Dābiq*, n. 11 (August 2015): p. 19.

127 Ibid., p. 20. The Muslim "loves those whom Allah loves and hates those whom Allah hates. He forges alliances for the cause of Allah and breaks relations for the cause of Allah" (ibid., p. 19).

128 Ibid., p. 21.

129 Abdurezak A. Hashi, 'Between Monotheism and Tawhid: A Comparative Analysis', *Revelation and Science*, vol. 3, no. 2 (2013): p. 25.

affirming that God is one and unique (*wāḥid*)."[130] It denotes the Oneness and Unity of God, the pillar of Islam. The Qur'an presents this doctrine quite distinctly and explicitly, most eminently in *sūra* 112: "Say, 'He is Allāh, [who is] One, Allāh, the Eternal Refuge. He neither begets nor is born, Nor is there to Him any equivalent.'" Qur'an 21:22 tries to demonstrate that the co-existence of two gods would be impossible: "Had there been within the heavens and earth gods besides Allāh, they both would have been ruined." And Qur'an 2:255 affirms Allāh's omnipotence:

> Allah – there is no deity except Him, the Ever-Living, the Sustainer of [all] existence. Neither drowsiness overtakes Him nor sleep. To Him belongs whatever is in the heavens and whatever is on the earth. Who is it that can intercede with Him except by His permission? He knows what is [presently] before them and what will be after them, and they encompass not a thing of His knowledge except for what He wills. His Throne extends over the heavens and the earth, and their preservation tires Him not. And He is the Most High, the Most Great.

Hence, the Qur'ānic perspective of monotheism is uncompromising, as Allāh is said to be one, unbegotten, omnipotent, unique and unequalled.

What does this have to do with Salafi-Jihadism? The doctrine of *tawḥīd* has been widely debated throughout Islamic history in its entirety. And Salafi-Jihadism is no exception. For Salafi-Jihadi ideologues, *tawḥīd* should not only be believed in, but rather entirely realized in one's own full life. Everything must adhere to the doctrine of monotheism.

Muḥammad ibn 'Abd al-Wahhāb wrote an important book on the topic, *Kitāb al-Tawḥīd*, which goes into detail about the issue. Its content has been summarized by the former Grand Mufti of Saudi Arabia, 'Abd al-'Azīz bin Bāz (d. 1999), who explains that Ibn 'Abd al-Wahhāb identified three aspects of *tawḥīd*: *tawḥīd al-rubūbiyya* (Oneness of Lordship), *tawḥīd al-ulūhiyya* (Oneness of worship), *tawḥīd al-asmā' wa-l-ṣifāt* (Oneness of names, qualities and attributes). The first denomination refers to God's actions, from the same initial creation to the control over all universe ("Allāh is the Creator, the Provider, the One Who brings benefit, and the Only One Who can harm, the One Who brings to life, to One Who causes death, the King of the entire dominion.")[131] It is the recognition of his omnipotence. *Tawḥīd al-ulūhiyya* is the acknowledgement that Allāh only deserves to be worshiped

130 Daniel Gimaret, '*Tawḥīd*', in *Encyclopedia of Islam, Second edition*, vol. 10 (Leiden: Brill, 1997), p. 389.

131 'Abd al-'Azīz bin Bāz, *Explanation of Important Lessons for Every Muslims* (Riyadh: Darussalam Publishers, 2002), p. 213.

and obeyed, and that what God has legislated should be strictly respected. Finally, *tawḥīd al-asmā' wa-l- ṣifāt* is the acceptance of all Allāh's names and attributes that are found in the Islamic revelation, as Ibn Bāz explains: "Under this category, we affirm for Allāh all that He affirmed about Himself and all that His Messenger Muḥammad affirmed about Him – all of His Beautiful Names, and all of the Attributes that those Names indicate, without resembling them to the attributes of creatures."[132]

Muḥammad ibn ʿAbd al-Wahhāb "believed that *tawḥīd* was going unrealized because people only understood one or two aspects of it."[133] Accordingly, faith alone in the doctrine of *tawḥīd* is insufficient. Faith should be coupled with action, and *tawḥīd* has to be individually and socially realized to be really effective.

The Wahhabi version of *tawḥīd* strongly influenced the jihadi doctrine.[134] The grandfather of al-Qāʿida, ʿAbdullāh ʿAzzām, even wrote a treatise on the topic, *The Tawḥīd of Action*. The same unambiguous title presents both the theoretical and practical aspects united into one single notion. In the book, ʿAzzām explains that *tawḥīd al-rubūbiyya* and *tawḥīd al-asmā' wa-l-ṣifāt* represent the theoretical aspects of *tawḥīd*, and for this reason they "can be understood by attending a lecture or two."[135] And he continues:

> So this, everyone of us memorizes it! You've memorized, right? Or no? This is something easy. Do you know why? Because this is the theoretical aspect of *īmān* (which does not require action)... It is a matter of knowing it and affirming it. And never was a single Prophet sent for this reason, ever. Rather, the only reason they were sent, was to establish *tawḥīd al-ulūhiyya*, the *tawḥid* of action.[136]

Tawḥīd al-ulūhiyya is therefore "only affirmed through stances taken in life,"[137] which he believes to be jihad and *tawakkul* (reliance on God in all matters)[138] – and, as Ibn ʿAbd al-Wahhāb maintains, "to have trust

---

132 Ibid., p. 218.

133 Maher, *Salafi-Jihadism*, p. 147.

134 To give just one example, the distinction of these three aspects of *tawḥīd* is also reported in IS's magazine *Rumiyah*: "The testimony of *tawḥīd* [...] encompasses *tawḥīd* of worship, *tawḥīd* of lordship, and *tawḥīd* of names and attributes." (*Rumiyah*, n. 1 [September 2016]: p. 6).

135 'Abdullah ʿAzzām, *The Tawḥīd of Action* (n.p.: at-Tibyān Publications, n.d.), p. 5.

136 Ibid., p. 6.

137 Ibid.

138 "O mujahid! O you who left in order that the word of Allāh be supreme and that the word of those who disbelieve be low, and O you who sacrificed everything so that *tawḥīd* prevails all over the world: do not be of those who would reduce or

(tawakkul) in Allah is a religious duty. Trust upon Allah *(tawakkul)* is a condition of faith *(īmān).*"[139] *Tawakkul* leads also to "a liberation of the human soul from *khawf* (fear)... fear of death and position..."[140] The open battle against the "forces of infidelity" should not worry the *mujāhid*, for "fear is a great form of worship, and the only one worthy of it is God."[141] Hence, "what could you ever fear, other than Allāh?"[142]

ʿAzzām writes that "as a basic rule, you will not be able to understand many verses [of the Qurʾan], except when it is a reality you are going through – a reality of jihad."[143] Practice is needed in order to understand *tawḥīd* and to settle it in the world, making Islam a living ideal. Faith should be coupled with action. In the book, ʻAbdullah ʿAzzām also quotes Sayyid Quṭb by saying that "Sayyid Quṭb (may Allāh have mercy upon him) said: 'Verily, this *dīn* does not reveal its hidden beauties to a cold sitting *faqīʾ* who does not struggle to establish this *dīn* upon this earth."[144] Going through the battlefield is the best way to realize *tawḥīd* and to have a deeper understanding of the same concept of monotheism, ʿAzzām believes.

In a quite unequivocal form, Abū Muḥammad al-Maqdisī states that "*tawḥīd* is the first purpose and the basic of the fundamentals [of Islam], and jihad is the true method to establish it on earth."[145] Analogously, Abū l-Aʿlā al-Mawdūdī "identified the intimate relationship between *tawḥīd* and

break their *tawḥīd*. Instead, rely on Allāh appropriately, for He manages affairs and brings about the necessary means by His command." (*Rumiyah*, n. 7 [March 2017]: p. 13).

139 Muḥammad ibn ʻAbdul-Wahhāb, "Kitāb at-Tauhid", *IslamBasic.com*, http://www.islambasics.com/book/kitab-at-tauhid-the-oneness-of-allah (accessed June 11, 2019).

140 ʿAzzām, *The Tawḥīd of Action*, p. 7.

141 Muḥammad Atta, 'Suicide Note', in *Anti-American Terrorism and the Middle East*, eds. Barry Rubin and Judith Colp Rubin [New York: Oxford University Press, 2002], p. 235.

142 Azzam, *The Tawḥīd of Action*, p. 9. On October 2002, Osama bin Laden defined the Islamic community "the *umma* of *tawḥīd*, which puts complete trust in Allāh alone and fears none other than Him" ('Why We Are Fighting You', in *The Al Qaeda Reader. The Essential Texts of Osama Bin Laden's Terrorist Organization*, ed. by Raymond Ibrahim [New York: Broadway Books, 2007], p. 207).

143 ʿAzzām, *The Tawḥīd of Action*, p. 10. *Tawḥīd al-ulūhiyya* "cannot be brought up inside the soul – meaning, it cannot become rooted firmly inside the soul – except by jihad" (ibid., p. 9).

144 Ibid., p. 10.

145 Abū Muḥammad al-Maqdisī, 'Monotheism and Jihad – The Distinguished Title', *Pulpit of Monotheism and Jihad*, July 24, 2009, https://muwahhidmedia.files.wordpress.com/2013/06/abu-muhammad-asim-maqdisi-montheism-and-jihad-the-distinguished-title.pdf (accessed April 12, 2019).

state. So nothing can be left out of His Lordship."[146] By saying so, ʿAzzām, al-Maqdisī and al-Mawdūdī suggest that "any Muslim who refrained from jihad was [is] suffering from deficiencies in their faith,"[147] as the Islamic State writes in *Rumiyah* magazine: "Whoever does not single out Allāh with *ilahiyya* (the right to be worshiped) in all forms of worship and obedience has nullified the *shahāda* of *tawḥīd* and – through his action – has belied what he claims of belief in the *tawḥīd* of *rubūbiyya* and *al-asmāʾ wa-l-ṣifāt*."[148]

Al-Qāʿida and the self-proclaimed Islamic State constantly work for the political realization of *tawḥīd*, linking this doctrine to a program of revolutionary change. Ayman al-Ẓawāhirī, for example, exhorts to

> rely on your Lord, *renew your tawḥīd*,[149] rise up with your true faith, follow the revealed religion of Allāh, and stand with it in the face of the arrogant criminals, as your truthful and trustworthy Prophet (peace be upon him), his righteous companions, and his purified family (Allah was pleased with them all) stood in the face of the world, inviting, giving the good news, warning and performing jihad in order that Allāh's Word be made the highest and the word of the infidels the lowest. And there is no third choice.[150]

In al-Qāʿida's discourse, *tawḥīd* is used as a banner to unite the whole *umma* and direct it towards a common end. In Osama bin Laden's words: "[Our] top priority is uniting opinions under the word of monotheism [*tawḥīd*] and defending Islam, its people and countries, and urging Muslims to prepare for and carry out jihad."[151] Likewise, the Islamic State always considered the self-proclaimed Caliphate as the implementation of *tawḥīd* upon earth:

> the *umma*'s unity was not beyond reach, as long as it was pursued on the basis of the *tawḥīd* of Allāh. It was this form of unity to which the Islamic

146 Asma Kounsar, 'The Concept of *Tawhid* in Islam: In The Light of Perspectives of Prominent Muslim Scholars', *Journal of Islamic Thought and Civilization*, vol. 6, issue 2 (Fall 2016): p. 107.

147 Maher, *Salafi-Jihadism*, p. 158.

148 *Rumiyah*, n. 3 (November 2016): p. 16.

149 Similarly, in the first number of the magazine *Dābiq* it is stated that the Caliphate's "most important goal would be to revive *tawḥīd*." (*Dābiq*, n. 1 [July 2014]: p. 34).

150 Ayman al-Ẓawāhirī, 'Realities of the Conflict Between Islam and Unbelief', *As-Sahab Media*, December 2006, https://www.cia.gov/library/abbottabad-compound/67/67BD026383A5C82BEBB2AD11BB31A1E9_Dr_Aiman_Reality_of_the_Conflict_En.pdf (accessed June 6, 2019).

151 Osama bin Laden, 'Resisting the New Rome', in *Messages to the World. The Statements of Osama bin Laden*, ed. by Bruce Lawrence (London and New York: Verso, 2005), p. 230.

> State called the *mujāhidūn* – a form of unity that gave *tawḥīd* its proper due, as opposed to sacrificing it for the sake of temporary political gain. […] The *mujāhidūn* were being mobilized to unite upon *tawḥīd* and to form a unified front against every *mushrik* [idolater] in every corner of the earth.[152]

In this sense, the doctrine of *tawḥīd* assumes a double function: on the one hand, to unite the Muslim community under the same banner, as a reflection of divine unity on human society; and on the other hand, to trust God only (*tawakkul*) and, as a consequence, to become free from *khawf* (fear) in the battlefield, waging a more effective jihad. The result will be the full application of *sharī'a* in the future Islamic state (for al-Qā'ida) or in the actual Caliphate (for the Islamic State).

The last feature of Salafi-Jihadism that Shiraz Maher lists is *ḥākimiyya*, which is usually translated as "God's sovereignty". I have already introduced the concept with regard to Sayyid Quṭb, therefore here I will place *ḥākimiyya* within the broader Salafi-Jihadi framework.

When spoken about, *ḥākimiyya* is referred to as the establishment of God's absolute authority on earth. In this perspective, the Caliphate is commonly said to be the only political form that fits the divine requirements.

The Indian-Pakistani thinker Abū l-A'lā al-Mawdūdī is generally considered to be the one who coined the term *ḥākimiyya*. In his thought, *ḥākimiyya* comprises both the legal and the political domination, and therefore

> both the active (*rubūbiyya* [lordship, supremacy]) and the passive (*ulūhiyya* [divinity, hence to be worshiped]) aspects of Allāh's divinity manifest themselves through the so-called "divine domination" (*ḥākimiyya*) over the human world. This domination essentially amounts to an unlimited divine authority over the humankind.[153]

The securing of political sovereignty for God is a quite new concept: it stems from the Islamist activism of the 20th century, having Mawdūdī and Quṭb as its theoretical fathers. The need for this concept is deeply rooted in the colonial environment, and in a way it is possible to say that *ḥākimiyya* was born from the encounter with the modern West and as a quest for a genuine identity. Its genesis is concomitant with "the creation of an

---

152 *Rumiyah*, n. 8 (April 2017): p. 39.

153 Valerii V. Pugachev, 'Abul A'la Mawdudi's Concept of *Hakimiyya* and its Critical Assessment in Islamic Legal-Political Thought', *Vestnik of Saint Petersburg University Law*, vol. 9, issue 2 (2018): p. 234.

imagined unitary Islam, the Islam *par excellence*,"[154] "as if it were a unitary entity capable of overcoming sectarian and denominational differences and a long history of Islamic ramification and pluralism."[155] The downfall of the Ottoman Caliphate pushed the whole *umma* to find a way to express its proper Islamic identity *face à* the overwhelmingly military strength and cultural influence of Europe.

Mawdūdī writes:

> Today there are many countries whose Muslim population is, after attaining independence, naturally eager to base its polity on those principles and traditions of Islam which are a demand of its faith and conscience. But, unfortunately, in almost all such countries the reins of power have been in the hands of those persons who not only did not have even an elementary understanding of Islamic Law and Constitution, but had all their education and training for the running of Godless secular states.[156]

The grievances of the Muslim population in those countries fed the growing request for a political system that would reflect Islamic requirements. Secularism and *laïcité* were feared and strongly opposed by the champions of the Islamic authenticity. "Islam, speaking from the viewpoint of political philosophy, is the very antithesis of secular Western democracy,"[157] Mawdūdī continues. "Islam [...] altogether repudiates the philosophy of popular sovereignty and rears its polity on the foundations of the sovereignty of God [*ḥākimiyya*] and the viceregency [*khilāfa*] of man."[158]

These words show the fact that "the elements coming from the Western culture were not able to completely undermine the traditional ones, nor were they able to amalgamate with them in a final synthesis."[159] Exploitation of men by other men and moral decay in public standards, both deemed Wester-imported vices, paved the way for the belief that Islam is the sole basis for a full renaissance of Islamic civilization.

154 Sherif Younis, 'How 'Abduh's Caftan Brought Forth Today's Islamic Ideologies', *Oasis*, no. 21 (June 2015): p. 21.

155 Ibid., p. 16.

156 Abū l-A'lā al-Mawdūdī, *The Islamic Law and Constitution* (Lahore: Islamic Publications, 1960), pp. v-vi.

157 Ibid., p. 138.

158 Ibid., p. 139.

159 Paolo Branca, 'Il califfato tra storia e mito', in *Il marketing del terrore*, eds. Monica Maggioni and Paolo Magri (Milano: Mondadori, 2016), pp. 35-36.

"*Jāhiliyya* is the *ḥākimiyya* of humans; Islam is the *ḥākimiyya* of God"[160] was the idea of both Mawdūdī and Quṭb. Accordingly, the entire world is divided into two blocs, the one that is *jāhilī* and the other that is grounded on the will of God.

Democracy belongs to the first block for the very fact that in a democratic system the will of the people is formally superior to the will of God and to divine legislation (*sharīʿa*). Democracy, considered a true blasphemy by every Islamist and especially Salafi-Jihadis, is strongly and firmly rejected by almost every ideologue. Abū Muḥammad al-Maqdisī even wrote a treatise entitled *Democracy: A Religion*, stating that the democratic way of conducting political affairs is a form of apostasy.[161] The implicit corollary is that democracy is a real religion: "Be careful not to limit the word 'religion' just to Christianity, or Judaism and so on, because you may follow the other void religions and go astray. *It includes every religion, method, judgment system, and law* that the creatures follow and adhere to,"[162] al-Maqdisī writes. And which kind of freedom does democracy support? Al-Maqdisī has no doubts: a freedom of disbelief: "This is the freedom of democracy: to be free from Allah's religion and His legislation and the exceeding of His limits."[163] Who are the priests of democracy? The elected people. "These representatives, in fact, are erected, engraved images and worshipped idols, and claimed gods that are set up and fixed in their temples, at their heathen sanctuaries (the parliaments)."[164] The choice is between the true Islamic religion and the false democratic religion: "So, you must choose the religion of Allah and His pure legislation, His brilliant light, His straight road. Or the religion of democracy, and its polytheism, disbelief, and its closed, misguided path. You must choose the judgement of Allah, the One, or the judgement of the man-made deity."[165]

---

160 William E. Shepard, 'Sayyid Qutb's Doctrine of *Jāhiliyya*', *International Journal of Middle East Studies*, vol. 35, no. 4 (November 2003): p. 525.

161 Al-Maqdisī writes that "democracy originated in the land of the disbelief and the apostasy. It grew in the hotbeds of polytheism and corruption in Europe, where there was a separation between the religion and the life. Through this expression was established an atmosphere that carried all of its poisons and imperfections, whose routes have no relation with the belief's earth or the irrigation of the doctrine and the good-will" (Abū Muḥammad al-Maqdisī, *Democracy: A Religion* [Sprinvale South: Al Furqan Islamic Information Centre, 2012], p. 72).

162 Al-Maqdisī, *Democracy: A Religion*, p. 25. Emphasis added.

163 Ibid., p. 32.

164 Ibid., p. 33.

165 Ibid., p. 35.

Hence, securing God's rights and providing temporal empowerment for *sharīʿa* is the theoretical basis for Salafi-Jihadis. For example, the heated debate between al-Qāʿida and the Muslim Brotherhood was based on the concept of democratic participation itself. In the widely circulated book *The Bitter Harvest* published around 1991, Ayman al-Ẓawāhirī criticizes the Muslim Brothers' softening of tones in their consideration of democracy; in fact, they accepted to be prudently part of that political system, and this choice is considered by al-Ẓawāhirī on the same level of apostasy. By countering democratic participation, al-Ẓawāhirī recalls al-Maqdisī by saying that democracy is an actual religion in that "religion [...] means the regularization and ordering of people's lives."[166] "Obedience is a form of worship,"[167] al-Ẓawāhirī maintains, and democracy "is a new religion that deifies the masses by giving them the right to legislate without being shackled down to any other authority."[168] As a conclusion, al-Ẓawāhirī points to the same dichotomy of al-Maqdisī: "Whoever claims to be a 'democratic-Muslim' or a Muslim who calls for democracy, is like one who says about himself 'I am a Jewish Muslim' or 'I am a Christian Muslim' – the one worse than the other. He is an apostate infidel."[169]

The only political engagement that a "pure" Muslim should embrace is the establishment of *ḥākimiyya* on earth. In al-Ẓawāhirī's own words, the Muslim must bring about "a Muslim government that will protect rights, defend sanctities, institute justice, spread [the principle of] consultation, raise the banner of jihad, and confront the invaders, the foes of Islam."[170] Here jihad is connected with *ḥākimiyya*, and it cannot be otherwise. "It is unimaginable that the Muslims could create a government in Palestine or elsewhere based on the rule of other than the *sharīʿa*, and whose authority doesn't come from the *sharīʿa*,"[171] al-Ẓawāhirī argues. And to lay the

166 Ayman al-Ẓawāhirī, 'Sharia and Democracy' in *The Al Qaeda Reader. The Essential Texts of Osama Bin Laden's Terrorist Organization*, ed. by Raymond Ibrahim (New York: Broadway Books, 2007), p. 130. And he continues: "The very first prerogative of godhood is the right to be obeyed by the people: the right to establish order, guidelines, laws, regulations – the right to establish values and standards, to say what is good and what is evil" (ibid., p. 132).

167 Ibid., p. 132.

168 Ibid., p. 130.

169 Ibid., p. 136.

170 Ayman al-Ẓawāhirī, 'Ayman al-Zawahiri Interview Four Years After 9/11', in *The Al Qaeda Reader. The Essential Texts of Osama Bin Laden's Terrorist Organization*, ed. by Raymond Ibrahim (New York: Broadway Books, 2007), p. 187.

171 Al-Ẓawāhirī, 'Realities of the Conflict'.

foundations for such a system, the overthrowing of "infidel" governments is the principal prerequisite.

It goes without saying that the theoretical foundation of the Islamic State, or IS, is the doctrine of *ḥākimiyya* – a *ḥākimiyya* finally achieved and yet to be protected and expanded to include the entire world. The total and totalitarian change towards a worldwide *ḥākimiyya* will follow the revolutionary transformation of the world by means of global jihad.

4.3 *Salafi-Jihadism in light of the gnostic pattern*

Salafi-Jihadism is an effective and persuasive ideology that stems from the Islamic background of disenfranchised and alienated peoples from Morocco to Southeast Asia, deluded by the end of the Caliphal experience and willing to give new strength to a weakened and dangerously undermined *umma* facing the immense power of the West. In the effort of shaping Salafi-Jihadism, numerous personalities have contributed over a period of several decades. The last two most lethal heirs of this poisonous doctrine are al-Qāʿida and the Islamic State (IS), whose nefarious actions are sadly well-known to us all.

The aim of the present research is to demonstrate the possibility of framing Salafi-Jihadism using the philosophical concept of revolutionary Gnosticism. The success of this task would reveal that Salafi-Jihadism adopts a gnostic mindset and a non-Islamic framework. In this way, the inconsistency of this ideology with the very religion of Islam will become evident, despite the heavy application of traditional Islamic ideas, though in a distorted way, by its ideologues and militants.

As already stated in the first part, this research is not a theological work nor a doctrinal treatise: rather, it is a philosophical analysis of an Islamic ideological production – and it employs and tries to implement a notion, i.e., revolutionary Gnosticism, which is an analytical concept to study revolutionary phenomena.

After having presented the meaning of revolutionary Gnosticism in Chapter 1 and Chapter 2, and following the clarification of the historical evolution and the ideological content of Salafi-Jihadism in Chapter 3 and in part of Chapter 4, the present section deals with the possibility of applying revolutionary Gnosticism to Salafi-Jihadism. Is Salafi-Jihadism an additional gnostic chapter after the past experiences of the radical Anabaptists in Münster, of the Puritanism of Oliver Cromwell in England, of the Jacobin Terror in France, and of the two totalitarian experiments of Nazism and Bolshevism?

4.3.1 *The inescapable background: the secularization*

To start with, let us stress the cultural background in which Salafi-Jihadism flourished. In explaining the emergence of revolutionary Gnosticism, in fact, one element proved extremely important for the entire process, that is, secularization. Previously in this work I have said that the story of revolutionary Gnosticism is contiguous to the issue of secularization: when God ceases to be the only trusted authority, man does not hesitate to take His place, and politics, along with violent means, supplants the actual acts of devotion and pious deeds. This is not to say that secularization has made violent revolutionary groups appear; however, the decline of the public role of religion as well as the radical undermining of local traditions, coupled with the wider process of modernization, created a strong resentment among the disoriented masses, which then chose to take the reins of collective salvation, confusing the two plans of the spiritual and the temporal right at the time when these two spheres were about to be separated.

Eric Voegelin's concept of the In-Between is useful here: the confluence of the two spheres (the transcendent and the immanent) is the most visible symptom of Gnosticism – it is a sign that the traditional faith in the trustworthy and supreme Beyond is inexorably cracked. Man has to rely on his own forces. In a certain sense, the assumption of responsibility for salvation could have only emerged in a secular society, where the traditional authority of the Sacred is eroded and where people immanentize the idea of a lost earthly paradise, placing it in a far past. Revolutionary Gnosticism is a structure of thought that does not belong to traditional societies, even in the peculiar cases of religious revolutions; instead, it is typical of secular societies, or societies in the process of secularization.

> The existence of many links, albeit reactive and polemical, between modernization and fundamentalism indicates the existence of a series of common points with the horizon of secularization: even if these phenomena are at first glance antithetical, they develop in the same historical context and have common causes.[172]

It was the very separation of politics and religion, coupled with the decreasing of public relevance of religion, that created the condition for religions to act as ideologies and for ideologies to assume the character

172 Agostino Giovagnoli, *Storia e globalizzazione* (Rome-Bari: Laterza, 2010), p. 211.

of religions.[173] As a matter of fact, among all its various meanings, secularization also stands for "the relocation of some fundamental models of Christian theology to political theory, such as the attributes of sovereign power or the idea of representation."[174] Therefore, "religion is no longer an indispensable component of the political order."[175] And the legislator becomes free from the regulatory constraints of tradition.

Many academic studies show that Muslims began to live similar processes starting from the encounter with the West, especially during the colonial period. But what diverges in the Islamic world with respect to the European experience is that all these innovations in the fields of politics, economics, culture and religion were not part of an indigenous decision or of a local development within the homegrown tradition. Quite the contrary, modernization and secularization were elaborations imported from an alien culture.

Stated differently, Muslims have not lived all those little evolutions that gradually would have led to the creation of secular societies – instead, they found themselves to be secular against their will and out of the blue.

On the Islamic disorientation caused by European modernity, Dāryush Shāyegān, a prominent Iranian philosopher, published in 1989 a helpful book, *Le regard mutilé. Schizophrénie culturelle: pays traditionnels face à la modernité* ("The Mutilated Gaze. Cultural Schizophrenia: Traditional Societies Confronting Modernity"). With great lucidity and clarity of mind, Shāyegān is aware of the troubles that the Islamic world has lived for assimilating the Western culture. In a sense, the Muslim community has never fully absorbed all modern paradigms, causing several cracks in its collective consciousness. Tensions between new ideas and traditional patterns soon arose. "Within my culture, nothing prepared me for a change of this kind, nor announced it to me,"[176] Shāyegān writes. Outside of the West, modernity is out of context. Today Islam has "a mutilated

---

173 "The 20th century ended with the collapse of ideologies that had assumed the character of religions. The 21st century seems to have opened with the affirmation of a religion that acts as an ideology" (Jean Daniel, 'La modernità, l'Islam e l'assoluto', in *Islam e Occidente. Riflessioni per la convivenza*, ed. by Andrea Riccardi [Rome-Bari: Laterza, 2002], p. 3).

174 Graziano Lingua, *Esiti della secolarizzazione. Figure religiose nella società contemporanea* (Pisa: Edizioni ETS, 2013), p. 30.

175 Ernst-Wolfgang Böckenförde, *Diritto e secolarizzazione. Dallo Stato moderno all'Europa unita* (1991; repr., Rome-Bari: Laterza, 2010), p. 44.

176 Dāryush Shāyegān, *Lo sguardo mutilato. Schizofrenia culturale: paesi tradizionali di fronte alla modernità* (1989; repr., Milan: Edizioni Ariele, 2015), p. 17.

gaze because it remains in break with the archaeology of [modern] knowledge."[177]

Modernity is defined as "the shifting of the gaze from top to bottom,"[178] the passage from metaphysics to history, the cluster of concepts that comprises individualism, critical thought, scientific method, disenchantment, and the adoption of efficiency criteria (utility and productivity). The Islamic world before the confrontation with the West lived in a "pre-Galilean world [... that] was immune to the three shocks – cosmological, biological and psychological – which, according to Freud, have forged the consciousness of modern man."[179] Once that the two worlds – modern West and Islamic culture – came into contact, all kinds of hybridization and intersection took place. But "the two paradigms,[180] the old and the new, intersecting with each other, ended up deforming reciprocally."[181] The deformations and distortions in the fragile consciousness of a wounded Islamic civilization inevitably culminated in the phenomenon of Islamization – an agitated rejection of the exogenous and an idiosyncratic recovery of the endogenous.

"Extra-western civilizations live in the era of two paradigms: their own and that produced by the great scientific revolutions,"[182] Shāyegān observes. This situation of staggered worlds living within a same culture creates an intolerable situation, and indigenous groups progressively develop a language full of resentment and based on "the colonizer-colonized dialectic [and on] the underlying and moralizing idea that everything that is exogenous is necessarily bad and what is endogenous is necessarily good."[183]

But in such a condition, modernity is not at all avoided or denied:

> Subtly internalized in the perceptive apparatus, by virtue of the planetary network that is behind it, [modernity] is, whether we want it or not and often

---

177 Ibid., p. 69.

178 Ibid., p. 46.

179 Ibid., p. 193.

180 Resorting on philosopher of science Thomas Kuhn, Dāryush Shāyegān defines a "paradigm" in terms of "the set of beliefs, of recognized values and of techniques which are common to the members of a given group. The paradigm is a certain worldview to which members of a community of scientists and thinkers adhere. When it changes due to scientific developments, the world in which scientists live also changes, and they see things differently, that is, from a new perspective" (ibid., p. 61).

181 Ibid., p. 69.

182 Ibid., p. 64.

183 Ibid., p. 102.

> without our knowledge, the a priori form of our gaze. […] It presents itself as an unconscious westernization. […] This new paradigm is always present, even when we believe that we have definitively gotten rid of it.[184]

In this light, Shāyegān defines the Islamist phenomenon same as "placing an old (traditional) discourse in a new (modern) context."[185] In fact, "behind all these arguments there is a great illusion, i.e., the profound conviction of having transformed the linear time of history into a cyclical time, of having restored the point of return and, in so doing, *of having bypassed modernity*."[186]

The analysis of Shāyegān overlaps with the reflections of Ian Buruma and Avishai Margalit in the work *Occidentalism: The West in the Eyes of Its Enemies* (2004). In a certain sense, Buruma and Margalit carry on the conclusions of Shāyegān by delving into a concept for which they coined the neologism "Occidentalism". The word mimics Edward Said's "Orientalism", meaning the essentialist attitude of reducing all Eastern societies to some fixed and usually underdeveloped elements, denying the differences between Middle Eastern, Asian and African cultures. A corollary of this discourse is the idea that the West is superior and rational, whereas the omni-comprehensive East is inferior and irrational.

Likewise, "Occidentalism" is an essentialist and comprehensive vision of modern West, a reductive view that eventually converts into an attitude of challenge. Occidentalism "simply turns the Orientalist view upside down. To diminish an entire society or a civilization to a mass of soulless, decadent, money-grubbing, rootless, faithless, unfeeling parasites is a form of intellectual destruction."[187]

Islamists are full of Occidentalist prejudices. The lenses through which they look at Europe and America are those of Occidentalism. "The West in general, and America in particular, provokes envy and resentment more among those who consume its images, and its goods, than among those who can barely imagine what the West is like."[188] Jihadists, in this respect, are those who eminently possess a secular mindset, and they cannot do anything about it.

---

184 Ibid., p. 95.

185 Ibid., p. 94.

186 Ibid., p. 138. Emphasis added.

187 Ian Buruma and Avishai Margalit, *Occidentalism: The West in the Eyes of Its Enemies* (New York: The Penguin Press, 2004), p. 10.

188 Ibid., p. 15.

> No Occidentalist, even the most fervent holy warrior, can ever be entirely free of the Occident. [...] What makes their [of Islamist revolutionaries] terror so lethal is not just the religious hatred borrowed from old texts, which is in any case often based on distortions, but the synthesis of religious zealotry and modern ideology, of ancient bigotry and modern technology.[189]

As a consequence, all symbols of the modern West turn into as many targets for their destructive action. The metropolis, new Babylon, becomes the source of moral decadence,[190] and trade converts into a Satanic tool to implement the obscure plan of the West. It is not by chance that the World Trade Center was chosen by al-Qāʿida as the target for the most spectacular terrorist attack ever.

Ian Buruma and Avishai Margalit give a name to the much-hated essence of the West, that mixture of greed, sensuality, materialism, rationalism,[191] atheism, relativism and individualism: *Komfortismus*. It is a word first used by the German social scientist Wener Sombart (1863-1941) in his document *Händler und Helden* ("Merchants and Heroes") published in 1915.

> Sombart begins his book by describing the [First World] war as an existential battle, not just between nations, but between cultures and worldviews, or *Weltanschauungen*. England, the land of shopkeepers and merchants, and republican France represent "West European civilization"; "the ideas of 1789"; "commercial values"; Germany is the nation of heroes, prepared to sacrifice themselves for higher ideals. [...] It is about the 'merchant *Weltanshauung'* that Sombart waxes most eloquent. The typical merchant, he says, is interested only in "what life can offer him" in terms of material goods and physical comfort. Sombart uses the term *Komfortismus* for the bourgeois mentality.[192]

Komfortismus is contagious and treacherous, in that it destroys the possibility of living a traditional and heroic life. "Better to die gloriously for an ideal than to live in *Komfortismus*,"[193] is believed by Occidentalist people. Material comfort and individual freedom are the worst threats to a

---

189 Ibid., p. 144.

190 "The commercial metropolis was where singular cultures, rooted in blood and soil, broke down, and an urban civilization was forged out of cosmopolitan diversity" (ibid., p. 31).

191 "The arrogant West, in Occidentalist eyes, is guilty of the sin of rationalism, of being arrogant enough to think that reason is the faculty that enables humans to know everything there is to know" (ibid., p. 95).

192 Ibid., pp. 52-53.

193 Ibid., p. 72.

life of religious purity.[194] Corruption is spread by means of a mindset based on *Komfortismus*. Indeed, "more corrosive even than military imperialism is the *imperialism of the mind*."[195]

The secularization experienced by the Islamic world is thus imported from the outside and is experienced as a shock for the socio-cultural background of countries from Morocco to India.

Arnold Toynbee finds that two are the alternatives a society faces *vis-à-vis* a stronger civilization: "Zealotism" and "Herodianism". The former is defined as "archaism evoked by foreign pressure,"[196] and it is typical of a man "who takes refuge from the unknown in the familiar;"[197] the latter is a mimetic reaction for which "the most effective way to guard against the danger of the unknown is to master its secret,"[198] learning from it and courageously facing the novelties. Toynbee recognizes Wahhabism as a form of Zealotism, and Mustafa Kemal Atatürk to be the best representative of Herodianism.

Luciano Pellicani continues and prolonges Toynbee's discourse. He acknowledges the "radioactive power"[199] of the West and identifies a new kind of ongoing colonization over the East, since "the process of political decolonization has in no way stopped the cultural colonization."[200] To Toynbee's discussion, Pellicani adds the elements of today's global market[201] and instantaneous communication, two elements that in his view are capable of "attacking the genetic code of other cultures."[202] In describing Zealotism, Pellicani gives the better example of Salafi-Jihadism, which embodies the

---

194 "The Occident, as defined by its enemies, is seen as a threat not because it offers an alternative system of values, let alone a different route to Utopia. It is a threat because its promises of material comfort, individual freedom, and the dignity of unexceptional lives deflate all utopian pretensions. The anti-heroic, antiutopian nature of Western liberalism is the greatest enemy of religious radicals, priest-kings, and collective seekers after purity and heroic salvation" (ibid., p. 72).

195 Ibid., p. 95. Emphasis added.

196 Arnold J. Toynee, 'Islam, the West, and the Future', in *Civilization on Trial*, by Arnold J. Toynee (London, New York and Toronto: Oxford University Press, 1946), p. 188.

197 Ibid.

198 Ibid., p. 193.

199 Luciano Pellicani, *Jihad: le radici* (Rome: Luiss University Press, 2004), p. 15.

200 Ibid., p. 27. "Permanent cultural aggression has been a feature of relations between the West and the East for centuries now" (ibid., p. 58).

201 "Modernity is a constructively imperialistic civilization, whose central institution is the market. The market, *ex definitione*, knows no borders: it is an institution with a planetary vocation" (ibid., p. 57).

202 Ibid., p. 19.

intransigent reaction against the foreign presence in all spheres of life. It is the last "zealous response to Western cultural aggression, dominated by the idea that the spiritual integrity of the peoples of Islam is threatened by the 'Godless civilization,' centered on the binomial secularism-individualism."[203] In one word, what is strongly opposed is *Komfortismus*.

Besides a psychological reaction to Western-imported values, Islamic countries have actually experienced a radical shift of paradigm in institutional life and in social environment. Beginning in the 19th century, in the Ottoman lands the sphere of law underwent a process of hybridization with codes and constitutions along European models.[204] This meant that the field of jurisprudence divorced from religious logics, and the *ʿulamāʾ* were progressively marginalized. Also, modern education entered Islamic schools and universities, and religion became a subject alongside many others: "In country after country since the 1950s, access to higher education has rapidly expanded. [...] There is now a critical mass of educated people who are able to read and think for themselves, without relying on state and religious authorities."[205] The rise of the press first, radio broadcasting and television after, and finally the diffusion of the Internet, created a free public space unthinkable until then. "In this process, religion becomes part of plural political and ideological field, thus further diminishing its sanctity and authority."[206] Additionally, the secularization of the popular mind happened because of the widespread fascination for cinema stars and television shows. All the more so, modern ideologies soon spread out in all Islamic countries, leading Marxists and Socialists, Fascists and all kind of nationalists to contribute to political life. Rural depopulation and rapid urbanization were other two phenomena that affected this period of precipitous changes. Therefore, Sami Zubaida's following statement is not so odd: "Religious revival, 'fundamentalism' and 'political Islam' are phenomena of secularization. They are ideological

---

203 Ibid., p. 66. But this doesn't mean that Zealotism is pernicious while Herodianism is advantageous or even beneficial. Arnold Toynbee warns against such a remark. He says that even Herodianism is a dangerous game due to the sudden change of paradigm within a culture it causes, and because it is a mimetic, and not a creative, solution.

204 The Tanẓīmāt was a period of intense reform in the Ottoman Empire. It occurred in the 19th century and it aimed at modernize the empire.

205 Dale F. Eickelman, 'Islam and the Languages of Modernity', *Daedalus*, vol. 129, no. 1 (Winter 2000): p. 124.

206 Sami Zubaida, 'Islam and Secularization', *Asian Journal of Social Science*, vol. 33, issue 3 (September 2005): p. 443.

and cultural reactions against the *fait accompli*."[207] The Muslim world was already secularized at the time of the birth of Islamic radicalism – either on the psychological side and on the institutional one. It is not by chance that the radical understandings of Islam "spread particularly between the mid-1970s and the late 1980s among urbanized and educated young people who had no chance of social growth and among representatives of the religious bourgeoisie, both critical of the new political and socio-economic elites in power after the independence."[208] Hence, Salafi-Jihadism "appears to be the result of experiences of uprooting, abandonment or rejection of traditional social networks."[209]

The mutual dependence of the two terms (secularization and Islamic radicalism) is apparent from the birthplace of the Muslim Brotherhood: "The city of Ismailiye, in which the Brotherhood was founded, was at the time considered one of the most Europeanized cities in 1920s Egypt (and was administered by the British army.)"[210]

In the light of all these elements, it is possible to assert that

> the major paradox of Islamism is that it is a modern phenomenon that emerged as a reaction to Western penetration of the Islamic world. [...] Modern totalizing claims to provide a worldview and a complete social, economic and political system embodied in an "Islamic state" should be regarded as a reaction to Western colonial rule.[211]

This quotation emphasizes two elements: that the social and cultural background against which Islamist arose was already secular; and that the same ideology that aspires at establishing an Islamic state is profoundly modern. The secular worldview that encompasses the Islamist ideology is, as a consequence, common to Salafi-Jihadism, the latter being the ripe fruit of what Toynbee calls Zealotism. In this respect, John Gray brilliantly

---

207 Ibid., p. 445.

208 Valentina Fedele, *L'Islam mediterraneo. Una via protestante?* (Acireale and Rome: Bonanno Editore, 2012), p. 65.

209 Fabio Dei, *Terrore suicida. Religione, politica e violenza nelle culture del martirio* (Rome: Donzelli Editore, 2016), p. 128.

210 Ali Kaya and Muhammed Hüseyin Mercan, 'Rethinking Islamism Through Political', in *Transformation of the Muslim World in the 21st Century*, ed. by Muhammed Hüseyin Mercan (Newcastle Upon Tyne: Cambridge Scholars Publishing, 2016), p. 2.

211 Roel Meijer, 'The Problem of the Political in Islamist Movements', in *Whatever Happened to the Islamists? Salafis, heavy Metal Muslims, and the Lure of Consumerist Islam*, eds. Amel Boubekeur and Olivier Roy (London: Hurst/Columbia University Press, 2012), p. 27.

makes the point by recognizing that Salafi-Jihadism is modern not only because it uses recent technologies – a similar explanation would be poor and simplistic. Rather, the ideological foundation of Salafi-Jihadism itself is "a typical modern hybrid,"[212] or better

> a highly syncretic construction. Azzam took from Qutb the idea of a revolutionary vanguard – a notion whose affiliations are more with Bolshevik ideology that with any Islamic source. His attack on rationalism contains echoes of Nietzsche. Modern Western influences are fused with Islamic themes.[213]

According to Slavoj Žižek, "instead of considering IS as an extreme case of resistance to modernization, we should rather conceive it as a case of perverse modernization."[214] And in the words of Bassam Tibi, "the prototype of the fundamentalist is a political man, a *homo politicus*, and not, as erroneously supposed, a *homo religiosus*, a religious man."[215] As a corollary, Massimo Borghesi maintains that radical Islamism, "for which the theological component is fully identified with the political one, is not a moment of purification of the faith but the phase of its completed secularization."[216]

All these considerations validate the previous assumption that Salafi-Jihadism was born following a process of secularization, though externally induced. There is, thus, a parallel with the other experiences listed above and belonging to the story of revolutionary Gnosticism: if this concept is contiguous to the issue of secularization, Salafi-Jihadism is no exception. On this line of reasoning, and drawing on Michael Walzer's theory (for whom Puritanism is an "ideology of transition" because it represents a response to the disorder of a period of transition from a traditional to a modern society), Nader A. Hashemi maintains that "political modernization in the Muslim world has produced a similar form of radical politics akin to English Puritanism, French Jacobinism,

212 John Gray, *Al Qaeda and What It Means to be Modern* (London: Faber and Faber, 2007), p. 77.

213 Ibid., p. 79.

214 Slavoj Žižek, *L'Islam e la modernità. Riflessioni blasfeme* (Milan: Ponte alle Grazie, 2015), p. 28.

215 Bassam Tibi, *Il fondamentalismo religioso alle soglie del Duemila* (Turin: Bollati Boringhieri, 2001), p. 36. In the same page, Tibi argues that "fundamentalism wants to fight Western modernity but it is completely imprisoned by it".

216 Massimo Borghesi, *Critica della teologia politica. Da Agostino a Peterson: la fine dell'era costantiniana* (Genova: Marietti, 2013), p. 333.

and Russian Bolshevism"[217] – which are three examples of the gnostic revolutionary mindset.

This statement leads us to one conclusion: Salafi-Jihadism could have only emerged in a secular environment, at a time when trust in God was diminishing and humankind, suddenly set loose from old certainties, felt authorized to take His place, as a reaction to uncertainty and social dislocation.

Let us now move on to the six points forming the gnostic pattern to investigate more closely whether Salafi-Jihadism is a gnostic construction or not.

4.3.2 *The world is evil: anti-cosmism*

In a revolutionary gnostic perspective, the world is corrupted, degraded, wicked and sinful. The starting point of the gnostic worldview is a pessimistic understanding of the context in which one finds oneself living. The surrounding world is a place of exile, a prison. Anti-cosmism is the first incitement for a total revolution: the actual situation should be turned upside down, the gnostic thinks.

The question we are now going to answer is the following: is this same awareness present in Salafi-Jihadi ideology? Is the sentiment of extraneousness to the world part of the Salafi-Jihadi conception of reality?

There are two categories that meet this condition: *jāhiliyya* and *gharbzadagi*. They are both related to each other, despite the fact that the former is an Arabic word and the latter a Persian term.

Gharbzadagi could be translated as "Westoxification" or "Occidentosis", a clinical metaphor that denounces the Western influence as a disease. The concept was first coined by the Iranian philosopher Ahmad Fardīd (1910-1994), but it was then popularized by his disciple Jalāl Al-I Ahmad (1923-1969) in the book *Occidentosis: A Plague from the West* published in 1962. If for Fardīd "Westoxification" means principally the hegemony of ancient Greek philosophy over the whole Western-imported thought and the deficiency of the West to understand the spiritual constitution of the East, for Jalāl Al-I Ahmad the concept assumes on a more polemical tone. He writes:

217 Nader A. Hashemi, 'Islamic Fundamentalism and the Trauma of Modernization: Reflections on Religion and Radical Politics', in *An Islamic Reformation?*, ed. by Michaelle Browers (Lanhan, Maryland: Lexington Books, 2004), p. 172.

> I speak of 'Occidentosis' as of tuberculosis. But perhaps it more closely resembles an infestation of weevils. Have you seen how they attack wheat? From the inside. The bran remains intact, but it is just a shell, like a cocoon left behind on a tree. At any rate, I am speaking of a disease: an accident from without, spreading in an environment rendered susceptible to it.[218]

"Westoxification" is used to denounce the affection of Iranians for the Western technology and for a type of thought, both philosophical and practical, that is completely alien from Iran and its history. Following this reasoning, it seems that the Easterners do not run the risk of absorbing the alien culture coming from the West; rather, *they are in danger of being absorbed* by it.[219] As this process goes on, "the Westoxified culture generally forgets about the originality of its traditional symbols."[220] Hence, "Westoxification" describes "the aggregate of events in the life, culture, civilization, and mode of thought of a people having no supporting tradition, no historical continuity, no gradient of transformation, but having only what the machine brings them."[221]

The West is seen as the reign of what Al-I Ahmad calls "Mechanosis," the governing of the inexorable logic of technology and capitalism. The risk is that the educational system of non-Western countries adapts to this model, creating a youth "corrupted and stupified by corporeal pleasures."[222]

What is interesting is that Jalāl Al-I Ahmad is not a reactionary in the Salafi-Jihadi sense. He is not a nativist nor a Zealot. Quite the contrary, he trusts the educational system and encourages democratization: "I speak of a democratization of the nation leadership, that is, of removing it from the monopolistic grasp of this or that person or family."[223]

---

218 Jalāl Al-I Ahmad, *Occidentosis: A Plague From the West* (Berkeley: Mizan Press, 1984), p. 27.

219 "To remain only consumers of the machine, to submit utterly to this twentieth-century juggernaut, is the road we have followed thus far. This road has led us to our present circumstances – Occidentosis" (ibid., p. 78).

220 Jalal Farzaneh Dehkordi and Mohammed Amin Mozaheb, 'Escaping from Orientalized Orientals: Studying *Occidentosis* as a Methodological Polemic for Regaining Eastern Identity versus West', *English Language, Literature & Culture*, vol. 2, no. 4 (2017): p. 33.

221 Al-I Ahmad, *Occidentosis*, p. 34.

222 Ibid., p. 133. On the topic of technology and Islam, the Italian philosopher Emanuele Severino wrote a book on the risk that Islam runs in adapting to Western technology. He writes: "The forces that today make use of the technology are *destined* to serve it" (*Dall'Islam a Prometeo* [Milan: Rizzoli, 2003], p. 23).

223 Al-I Ahmad, *Occidentosis*, p. 132.

What is relevant for the present section is that the idea of the East sick of the West is an "apocalyptic vision [that] can feed a form of terrorism like that of Bin Laden or others,"[224] as Khaled Fouad Allam warns while explicitly referring to Jalāl Al-I Ahmad. It is also true that the author of *Occidentosis* is Iranian and has nothing to do with the genesis of Salafi-Jihadism. However, it is true that after the Iranian Revolution the conviction that the Islamic world needs to get rid of the West started to circulate among the élite and the masses. Jalāl Al-I Ahmad's cautious opening to democracy was about to be outclassed by the jihadi option.

Interestingly, "Westoxification" refers to a vision of the world that in many respects overlaps with the idea of *jāhiliyya*. Already taken into account in the previous chapter, this concept was intensively used by Sayyid Quṭb to designate the present reality of widespread disbelief and distance from God. Currently, there are no Islamic societies nor political systems that adhere to *sharīʿa*, he believes. And if traditionally *jāhiliyya* stands for the polytheistic society of pre-Islamic Arabian Peninsula, Quṭb makes a meta-historical use of it, that is to say, he decontextualizes *jāhiliyya* and applies it to all kind of social realities that are distant from Islam. In this way, *jāhiliyya* becomes a synonym of the ignorance of God's Revelation. "All the societies existing in the world today are *jāhilī*,[225] Quṭb believes. For that reason, from an Islamist perspective the current situation is critical, deeply critical, almost incurably critical. The plague of "Westoxification" affects all societies in the world and it is up to a handful of militants, the vanguard (*ṭaliʿa*) of *mujāhidūn*, to restore humankind to health.

Without any doubt anti-cosmism is the pre-condition for Salafi-Jihadism. The description of today's world made by jihadists is always negative and pessimistic. For example, interviewed by the American sociologist Mark Juergensmeyer, Mahmud Abouhalima, one of the members of the team that carried out the attack on the World Trade Center in 1993,

> compared a life without religion to a pen without ink. "An ink pen," he said, "a pen worth two thousand dollars, gold and everything in it, it's useless if there's no ink in it. That's the thing that gives life," Abouhalima said, drawing out the analogy, "the life in this pen... the soul." He finished his point by saying, "the soul, the religion, you know, that's the thing that's revived the whole life. Secularism," he said, looking directly at me, "has none, they have none, you

224 Khaled Fouad Allam, *L'Islam globale* (Milan: Rizzoli, 2002), p. 46.
225 Quṭb, *Milestones*, p. 80.

> have none." And as for secular people, I asked, who do not know the life of religion? "They're just moving like dead bodies," Abouhalima said.[226]

The world is full of zombies and, just like in the worst B-movies, the plague spreads through bites or through contact. The Westerners are killers – they murder the reign of the spirit, they spread impurity, they pollute the crystal-clear water of the Sacred. Today's world is poisoned and infested. Impurity is the atmosphere that covers the whole earth – hence the obsession with purity that characterizes the attitude of every jihadist. Fethi Benslama notes that "the jihadist discourse tries to persuade young men that the world in which they live is corrupt, unjust, wrapped in lies: an obscene world."[227] "In reviving the ways of the Salaf, they tend to view the present world as a fallen one,"[228] is the judgement of Graeme Wood. And David Cook says that "for the contemporary Muslim the present world is a world turned upside down. Everywhere his faith has lost ground."[229]

In the wake of these considerations, Andrea Plebani has an intuition:

> The impression is that beyond the rhetoric linked to the figure of the 'great American Satan' and the undoubted responsibilities of the Western world, at the base of the anger that moves the actions of the jihadist militants there is the rejection of the present reality – a corrupt reality marked by new and old forms of slavery.[230]

The Salafi-Jihadi individual feels alien to the present world where Islam is a religion next to other religions. He or she has the impression that something in the order of the cosmos is no longer as it used to be. The first reaction he or she has is to get rid of all the rules imposed by the outside. "As for the rest of the world [non-Western countries], you impose upon them

---

226 Mark Juergensmeyer, *Terror in the Mind of God. The Global Rise of Religious Violence* (Berkeley, Los Angeles and London: University of California Press, 2000), p. 69.

227 Fethi Benslama, *Un furioso desiderio di sacrificio. Il supermusulmano* (Milan: Raffaello Cortina Editore, 2017), p. 47.

228 Graeme Wood, *The Way of the Strangers* (New York: Random House, 2011), chap.1, Kindle.

229 David Cook, *Islam and Apocalyptic* (Boston: Center for Millennial Studies, 2005), http://www.mille.org/scholarship/papers/cookabs.html (accessed November 24, 2017).

230 Andrea Plebani, *Jihadismo globale. Strategie del terrore tra Oriente e Occidente* (Florence: Giunti, 2016), p. 118.

your monstrous, destructive policies,"[231] Ayman al-Ẓawāhirī said once to the Americans. And he warned: "Today the world is given over to the tyrants."[232] So, what Salafi-Jihadi militants should do is "to save the *umma* from its painful reality,"[233] "until all chaos ceases."[234]

The theme of anti-cosmism is fairly present in the Salafi-Jihadi narrative and that is reasonably predictable: without the persuasion that the world is evil, there would not be any need for a revolution. We can easily assert that the first feature of revolutionary Gnosticism is present in Salafi-Jihadism.

4.3.3 *The glorious past: tripartition of history*

The second element of the gnostic pattern is a peculiar conception of history which places in the past a glorious golden era that is by now completely lost but that could be recovered in the future. The previous feature of anti-cosmism is justified by this very historical understanding – the present is a time of corruption, the past was a state of perfection, and the future will be a restored time of excellence.

As explained in Chapter 2, this tripartite scheme is borrowed from the Late-Antique gnostic belief in an original pure divine unity, the *Pleroma*, which was eventually destroyed following some sort of "original sin", and from which the creation of the world (the present condition) was derived – and the world, i.e., the whole cosmic system, will finally be overcome in the future thanks to the presence in humankind of a divine spark. These three phases (an original pure divine unity, a primordial disruption, the final dissolution that coincides with the reconstitution of unity) are completely immanentized in the mentality of revolutionary Gnosticism.

At this point, let us try to answer the question on whether Salafi-Jihadism shares a similar tripartition of history. Was there a golden age in the past? Is this golden age irremediably lost, or is there the hope for a restauration?

Talking of a golden age in Islam is easier than in Christianity, indeed. I have went into this very idea when I dealt with Salafism: the *al-Salaf al-Ṣāliḥ*, the "pious predecessors" or "righteous ancestors", are generally

231 Ayman al-Ẓawāhirī, 'Letter to the Americans: Why Do We Fight and Resist You?', in *His Own Words. A Translation of the Writings of Dr. Ayman al Zawahiri*, ed. by Laura Mansfield (Old Tappan: TLG Publications, 2006), p. 300.

232 Ayman al-Ẓawāhirī, 'Jihad, Martyrdom, and the Killing of Innocents', in *The Al Qaeda Reader. The Essential Texts of Osama Bin Laden's Terrorist Organization*, ed. by Raymond Ibrahim (New York: Broadway Books, 2007), p. 150.

233 Al-Ẓawāhirī, 'Loyalty and Enmity', p. 113.

234 Al-Ẓawāhirī, 'Jihad, Martyrdom', p. 144.

identified with the first three generations of Muslims, the *al-Ṣaḥāba*, or the Companions of the Prophet; the *al-Tābiʿūn*, or the Successors; the *ʿatbāʿ al-Tābiʿīn*, the Successors of the Successors. Some *Ṣaḥāba* were actually the *Rāshidūn* Caliphs (632-661), Abū Bakr, ʿUmar, ʿUthmān and ʿAlī. And here lies the space for talking of a perfect past: the reign of the *Rāshidūn* Caliphs is traditionally known as the golden age of Islamic history. "The society of the companions of Allah's Messenger is the best society to have ever existed on the earth,"[235] as IS's *Rumiyah* magazine puts it.

To put it better, in the words of Alberto Ventura, "the last year of Prophet's life coincides with the end of a cycle and, at the same time, it opens a new cycle, which is nothing more than the re-actualization of the primordial time, that originated from the creation of the heavens and the earth."[236] The Prophet Muḥammad, thus, brought the time to a close by delivering the full divine message to humankind, paving the way for a new era of divine participation and adherence to the true human nature (*fiṭra*). The first generations of Muslims are believed to have followed carefully, rigorously and with great faith all the sacred prescriptions; but after those pious men, history witnessed a slow but inescapable decline. Again in Ventura's words:

> Islam has a vision of history that is more involutional than evolutionary. Had the Prophet not warned that Islam would end up in exile (*gharīb*), just as it had begun? And had he not also remembered that the best generations were his own and those immediately following, to be replaced gradually by communities increasingly aloof from the original spirit of revelation?[237] And had he not pointed out that, given such decadence, in the last times in order to being saved it will be enough to observe only one tenth of the law, whereas at the beginning the non-fulfilment of only one tenth led to damnation? In such a framework, it can certainly not be assumed that time brings with it an intrinsic improvement in the spiritual quality of men. The only allowed aspiration is at best to put a stop to the physiological decadence of the world, to limit the failures that the corrosive work of time exerts on the community of believers. This is the deepest reason why in traditional Islam an idea similar to that of

---

235 *Rumiyah*, n. 12 (August 2017): p. 7. On the following page, as a mantra to be repeated constantly, it is written that "the society of the Sahabah was the purest of societies and the furthest of them from immorality."

236 Alberto Ventura, *Sapienza sufi. Dottrine e simboli dell'esoterismo islamico* (Rome: Edizioni Mediterranee, 2016), p. 193.

237 "The Prophet said, 'Near the establishment of the Hour there will be days during which religious ignorance will spread, knowledge will be taken away, and there will be much *al-harj*, and *al-harj* means killing'" (*Ṣaḥīḥ* al-Bukhārī, book 92, *ḥadīth* 14, https://sunnah.com/bukhari/92/14).

> utopia, understood as the collective renewal of society, has never appeared – only in modern times, and always under the influence of Western culture, the idea of utopia has been able to assert itself.[238]

This is a conception of the flow of history that is rather degenerative: "It is assumed that after the third generation, who were still able to witness the lives of and learn from the *Ṣaḥāba*, corruption slowly crept into Islam."[239] The idea of a golden era was coined to preserve the myth of the impeccability of the first generations. Idealizing and romanticizing the time of Muḥammad and of the early Muslims serves as a model for new believers. Many are the elements that flow into the idealized image of that period: the strong devotion of the first Muslims, who were even able to remember all the verses of the Qur'an perfectly; the overemphasized accounts of the lives of some of the early Muslims; and the idea that the conquest of other territories were not violent and that the conversions to Islam of new people were slow, due to the status of "protected minorities" given to most of the conquered inhabitants. Hence, this regressive nature of history "is encapsulated by the idea of the imperative of going back to an ideal model of the Prophet's Sunna that only existed in the past."[240]

On the other hand, the idealization of early Islam carries within it a danger, namely, that "the community becomes so obsessed with recreating something past that it fails to see and deal with the real challenges and problems of the present."[241] As a result, it is not about an *idealization* but a real *idolization* of the past. "So sanctified, the first generations entered into the Faith more than into History."[242]

There is no parallel with the Western idea of a golden age of freedom and innocence. Patricia Crone acknowledges that "all medieval Muslims envisaged life in what Westerners call the state of nature as nasty, brutish,

238 Alberto Ventura, 'L'islām della transizione (XVII-XVIII secolo)', in *Islām*, ed. by Giovanni Filoramo (Roma-Bari: Laterza, 2007), pp. 204-205.

239 Carmen Becker, 'Muslims on the Path of the Salaf Al-Salih', *Information, Communication & Society*, vol. 14, no. 8 (2011): p. 1188.

240 Adis Duderija, 'The Salafi Worldview and the Hermeneutical Limits of Mainstream Sunni Critique of Salafi-Jihadism', *Studies in Conflict & Terrorism*, DOI: 10.1080/1057610X.2018.1529359.

241 William Montgomery Watt, *Islamic Fundamentalism and Modernity* (London and New York: Routledge, 1988), p. 22.

242 Fazlur Rahman, *La religione del Corano. Le radici spirituali di una grande civiltà* (1979; repr., Milano: NET, 2003), p. 313.

and short."[243] Besides, "there is no Arabic term for 'the state of nature'. It is evoked with statements like 'if people were left on their own' (i.e. without divine intervention), or 'If God left them alone with their natures.'"[244] Crone continues:

> Medieval Muslims did not write utopias in the sense of imaginary travel accounts or other descriptions of ideal societies which do not exist, such as Iambulus' *City of the Sun* or Thomas More's *Utopia*, nor did they often use exotic peoples or noble savages to illustrate social and political ideals.[245] As noted before, they were not given to seeking ideals outside their own civilization at all. But they did place a golden age right at the beginning of their own history, and their numerous accounts of this age add up to a detailed utopia of great emotive power. It was a *primitivist utopia*, both in the sense that it presented the earliest time as the best and in the sense that it deemed a simple, society to be the most virtuous [...] the patriarchal Medina.[246]

Massimo Campanini prefers to use the expression of "retrospective utopia", that is,

> the tendency, widespread especially in traditionalist Islam, to look at the past, at the indefectible age of the Prophet and (at least for the Sunnis) at the well-guided Caliphs, as the golden age of Islam – an age that must be implanted, imitated and, if possible, reproduced also in the present and in the future. The retrospective utopia implies a distortion of the historical time for which, on the one hand, the evolutionary parable of humanity from the golden age onwards has been of irrecoverable progressive decadence and involution, while, on the other hand, the planning of the construction and realization in the future of the best state for the good of humanity cannot depart from the distinctive characteristics of the era of the Prophet.[247]

In Campanini's historical and philosophical account, the Islamic political elaboration passed through five stages: (1) the accomplishment of utopia during the *Rāshidūn* Caliphs; (2) the time of the absence of a true political theory during the Umayyad Caliphate and the early Abbasid one;

243 Patricia Crone, *Medieval Islamic Political Thought* (Edinburgh: Edinburgh University Press, 2004), p. 262.
244 Ibid.
245 It is interesting, however, Ibn Ṭufayl's (d. 1185) allegorical tale *Ḥayy ibn Yaqẓān* (c. 1175), a philosophical romance in which the author describes the life of Ḥayy, a self-taught philosopher who grows up alone on an equatorial and uninhabited island.
246 Crone, *Medieval Islamic Political Thought*, p. 318. Emphasis added.
247 Massimo Campanini, 'Il salafismo e le sue fenomenologie', in *Quale Islam? Jihadismo, radicalismo, riformismo* (Brescia: La Scuola, 2015), p. 68.

(3) the period of the conceptualization of an Islamic state in 11th century starting from al-Māwardī (d. 1058); (4) the end of the centralized Caliphal experience and the rise of rival Caliphates (the Fatimids, the Almohads) and of local dynasties; (5) the absence of the Caliphate and the beginning of a new theorization of utopia.[248] This last phase is dominated by Islamist radicalism, which "cultivates the utopia of a new Islamic state, but topples it backwards, aiming to recover and reproduce – completely unrealistically – the perfect society of Medina."[249]

Here we get to the point. "Modern Islam, in its reformist tendencies as well as in its fundamentalist currents, is inspired by a vision of history that privileges the beginning over the end, the past over the future. Without any doubt, it is a utopia that we could define as 'of the ideal beginning.'"[250] For that reason, the gnostic division of history is fully present in Salafi-Jihadism: the Salafi side of the ideology wants to go back to the *al-Salaf al-Ṣāliḥ* ("Salafism is a philosophy that believes in progression through regression,")[251] whereas the jihadi side is ready to fight for achieving it. "We believe that the best people in terms of good deeds after the century of the Prophet and his Companions are the Followers of the second and third centuries. After this lying will spread and loyalty will weaken:"[252] this is what *al-Qā'ida's Creed and Path* document states.

According to a similar historical perspective, history has passed through an era of perfection and is now in the phase of estrangement from it; but the golden age is not irremediably gone, being the future the time of restauration.

Another element that supports this thesis can be found in *Dābiq* magazine soon after the declaration of the Caliphate. In an article entitled *From Hijra to Khilafah*, a famous *ḥadīth* is reported that follows the scheme of a past perfection, an unavoidable decline and, again, a restauration:

> There will be prophethood for as long as Allah wills it to be, then He will remove it when He wills. Then there will be Khilafah on the prophetic methodology and it will be for as long as Allah wills, then He will remove it when He wills. Then there will be harsh kingship for as long as Allah wills,

248 Massimo Campanini, 'L'utopia nel pensiero politico dell'Islam. A proposito del *Medieval Islamic Political Thought* di Patricia Crone', *Oriente Moderno*, vol. 84, no. 3 (2004), pp. 679-682.

249 Ibid., p. 683.

250 Josef Van Ess, *L'alba della teologia musulmana* (1977, repr., Torino: Einaudi, 2008), p. 79.

251 Maher, *Salafi-Jihadism*, p. 7.

252 'Al-Qaeda's Creed and Path', p. 55.

then He will remove it when He wills. Then there will be tyrannical kingship for as long as Allah wills, then He will remove it when He wills. Then there will be Khilafah on the prophetic methodology (reported by Ahmad).[253]

Today's world is experiencing a progressive shift away from the perfection of the past, like a ship adrift. "For Islamists, modernity is simply a sign of how far people can move away from the true faith."[254] "Westoxification" is only the ultimate sign of this wicked condition. But eventually, one day the perfect society will rise again against the modern *jāhiliyya*. For al-Qāʿida, the Caliphate will come after a long struggle against the Satanic forces; for the Islamic State, the time has finally come and the *mujāhidūn* need only to manage the situation.

As said earlier, from the tripartition of history derive two consequences: iconoclasm and apocalypticism.

I defined *iconoclasm* as the fury against everything that pertains to the present state of corruption. All things that have been created in the ignorance of the true faith deserve to be destroyed. Luciano Pellicani's idea of a "tabula rasa policy" exhibits the real essence of gnostic iconoclasm. The past constantly reminds the gnostic of his/her wicked condition. The earthly paradise must be built from the ruins of previous sinful and impious civilizations. For Salafi-Jihadis, "everything that is pre-Islamic, immersed in the *jāhiliyya* [...] or everything that is idolatrous and departs from the *sharīʿa* [...] must be thrown down."[255]

A curious analysis has been conducted by Ernest Tucker. He compares the radical Anabaptists in Münster with the Taliban in the 1990s, finding out that both "emphasized the symbolic destruction of existing religious and cultural treasures with an intensity that far transcended their fellow religious reformers,"[256] even leading to the burnings of books (the Taliban devastated the cultural center of Naser-e Khosrow, ending up with the destruction of 55000 books; the Anabaptists burnt every book in the city with the exception of the Bible). "Both groups view the destruction of longstanding cultural and religious symbols as part of their relentless

253 Quoted in *Dābiq*, n. 1: p. 34.

254 Hamed Abdel-Samad, *Fascismo islamico* (Milan: Garzanti, 2017), p. 16.

255 Luca Nannipieri, *Arte e terrorismo. Sulla distruzione islamica del patrimonio storico artistico* (Soveria Mannelli: Rubbettino, 2015), p. 30.

256 Ernest Tucker, 'Primitivism as a Radical Response to Religious Crisis: The Anabaptists of Münster in the 1530s and the Taliban of Afghanistan in the 1990s', in *An Islamic Reformation?*, ed. by Michaelle Browers (Lanhan, Maryland: Lexington Books, 2004), p. 149.

campaigns to define in a theatrical way their conflict with all existing norms save the scriptures they recognizes."[257]

Although Tucker's goal is to demonstrate that Muslims and Christians react in similar ways to similar periods of change, the comparison between the Taliban and the radical Anabaptists is not so relevant for our purposes – the Taliban are only a local and national response with no interest in expanding beyond Afghanistan's borders, whereas Salafi-Jihadism is a global ideology. A better comparison should be made between the radical Anabaptists and Salafi-Jihadis in their most radical forms, i.e., al-Qāʿida and the Islamic State. This section is elaborating just on this topic.

As a matter of fact, numerous are the archaeological heritages that have been destroyed by radical Islamists. In Iraq and Syria the self-proclaimed Islamic State raided all the archaeological sites, destroyed museums and burned books. Similar actions were carried out also in Lebanon, Mali, Egypt, Indonesia, Afghanistan and Pakistan.

It is said that Islam itself is against any figurative representation, and in part it is true, since there are many *ḥadīths* that clearly oppose any form of art.[258] However, Silvia Naef notes that there are many other *ḥadīths* that permit the exhibition of pictures according to the place they are located in,[259] and others that allow images to be painted as long as they do not imitate human or animal life.[260] "There are no Islamic treaties on images. [...] It would be difficult to find [in Ghazālī] as well as in other authors, a 'theory of the image,'"[261] Naef realizes. And after a long excursus on the history of Islamic art, Naef concludes that, though in different forms

257 Ibid., p. 154.

258 For example, "The Prophet said, 'Angels do not enter a house that has either a dog or a picture in it'" (reported by al-Bukhārī, book 59, *ḥadīth* 128, https://sunnah.com/bukhari/59/128); and "The people who will receive the severest punishment from Allah will be the picture makers" (reported by al-Bukhārī, book 77, *ḥadīth* 166, https://sunnah.com/bukhari/77/166).

259 "ʿĀʾisha said: 'I covered a small room closet of mine, meaning, from the inside, with a curtain on which there were images. When the Prophet came, he tore it down, so I made two pillows from it, and I saw the Prophet reclining on one of them'" (reported by Ibn Māja, book 32, *ḥadīth* 3784, https://sunnah.com/urn/1279050).

260 "Ibn ʿAbbās said: 'I heard him say: All the painters who make pictures would be in the fire of Hell. The soul will be breathed in every picture prepared by him and it shall punish him in the Hell', and he (Ibn ʿAbbās) said: 'If you have to do it at all, then paint the pictures of trees and lifeless things'" (reported by Muslim, book 37, *ḥadīth* 152, https://sunnah.com/muslim/37/152).

261 Silvia Naef, *La questione dell'immagine nell'Islam* (Milan: ObarraO Edizioni, 2011), pp. 24-25.

and circumstances, "the image has always existed throughout Islamic history."[262]

The passage *from a genuine aniconism to a fanatic iconoclasm* has been a constant in Islamic history, so much so that "we know nothing about the centuries-old pre-Islamic architecture, although it is likely that the wealthy merchants of Mecca lived in well-built palaces."[263] Nonetheless, the form of Salafi-Jihadi iconoclasm has something new: it is blind and justified by a plan to recreate the perfect society.[264] All evidences of past peaceful coexistence and of cultural heterogeneity are to be destroyed. The Middle Eastern cultural landscape composed by many religions living side by side is to be reshaped and remodeled to comply with the new totalizing narrative. The stated rationale of this blind violence is formally the rejection of *shirk* (idolatry, polytheism), in compliance with the destruction of the idols carried out by Abraham/Ibrāhīm and by the Prophet Muḥammad in the Ka'ba after the conquest of Mecca – as the official IS magazine *Dābiq* stresses by reporting that

> [w]ith the *kuffār* up in arms over the large-scale destruction at the hands of the Islamic State, the actions of the *mujāhidūn* had not only emulated Ibrāhīm's (*'alayhis-salām*) destruction of the idols of his people and Prophet Muhammad's (*sallallāhu 'alayhi wa sallam*) destruction of the idols present around the Ka'bah when he conquered Makkah, but had also served to enrage the *kuffār*, a deed that in itself is beloved to Allah.[265]

Yet, the novelty of this blind violence lies in the selective prohibition of images, which reveals the will to have a *tabula rasa* of certain specific images and not to forbid them all. Finbarr Barry Flood stresses that with the diffusion of videos, photographs and other multimedia contents of the devastations and demolitions of museums and archaeological sites (e.g., the Buddhas of Bamyan, in Afghanistan, blown up by the Taliban in March 2001, and whose video was broadcasted by al-Qā'ida for propaganda purposes; and the Mosul museum in Iraq, looted and brutally destroyed by the Islamic State, whose images were released in a terrible propaganda video in February 2015), Salafi-Jihadi groups fall into the contradiction of prohibiting images while, at the same time, producing other images.

262 Ibid., p. 63.

263 Maria Bettetini, *Distruggere il passato. L'iconoclastia dall'Islam all'Isis* (Milan: Raffaello Cortina Editore, 2016), p. 66.

264 Not to mention the income IS made from the black market of ancient artefacts.

265 *Dābiq*, n. 8 (March 2015): p. 22.

> [T]he stills and videos of IS are, therefore, necessarily underwritten by an implicit claim that they violate no injunction. In this sense, they are comparable to the didactic images produced by many Islamist groups for educational or polemical purposes. Paradoxically, such usage is premised on the very distinction between educational and idolatrous images that 'progressive' jurists have made use of since the nineteenth century to argue the need to protect pre-Islamic antiquities.[266]

As a matter of fact, Muḥammad ʿAbduh, Jamāl al-Dīn al-Afghānī's disciple and great Egyptian modernist, issued a *fatwā* that allowed the use of images for scientific and pedagogical purposes, though keeping the ban for religious functions.

What does this observation tell us? That Salafi-Jihadis do not have a problem with images *per se*; on the contrary, it is about specific vestiges in particular territories: violence is directed against the ancient traces found in the space of the restauration (Afghanistan for al-Qāʿida prior to 9/11, and Iraq and Syria for the Islamic State prior to the field defeat). To be cancelled are all those traces of civilizations that have lived before and after the divine revelation in Mecca and outside of Islamic influence. Humanity must forget everything but Islam: only then will it be possible to erase *jāhiliyya* once and for all. Salafi-Jihadis

> use such a sacred past to affirm the one true pattern of Islamic history compared to which all others are heretical and morally contaminating: it is from this standpoint that classical and pre-Islamic ruins such as those at Palmyra can be destroyed in a cleansing iconoclasm that confirms, at the same time, the true moral worth of ISIL and its own historical lineage.[267]

In a recent book, Olivier Roy realizes the importance of such a dimension in the Salafi-Jihadi theory and practice:

> Not only are human beings destroyed, but statues, places of worship, and books as well. Memory is annihilated. […] As a British convert to ISIS wrote, "When we descend on the streets of London, Paris and Washington the taste will be far bitterer, because not only will we spill your blood, but we will also demolish your statues, erase your history and, most painfully, convert

266 Finbarr Barry Flood, 'Idol-Breaking as Image-Making in the "Islamic State"', *Religion and Society: Advances in Research*, no. 7 (September 2016): p. 120.

267 Paul B. Rich, 'How Revolutionary Are Jihadist Insurgencies? The Case of ISIL', *Small Wars & Insurgencies*, vol. 27, no. 5 (2016): p. 780.

your children who will then go on to champion our name and curse their forefathers."[268]

Other than iconoclasm, there is an additional consequence that stems from the tripartition of history: *apocalypticism*. In the gnostic vision of the succession of the three eras, history is considered to be fulfilling its cycle. Reaching the last stage, nothing else is to be achieved. Iconoclasm, i.e., the destruction of everything that is linked to the present state of corruption, will lead to the third stage of time, the ultimate moment of human history. The reestablishment of the past in the future will make history running out all the possibilities, delivering humanity to its true and final destination.

The obsession with the apocalypse is a constant of all gnostic movements. The End of Time is declined both in religious terms and in atheistic terms depending on the identity of the group (radical Anabaptists and Puritans on the one side, and Jacobins, Bolsheviks and Nazis on the other side). It goes without saying that Salafi-Jihadis see apocalypticism through the lenses of a religious worldview. Yet, a question should be answered first: does Salafi-Jihadism share an apocalyptic vision? Does the belief in an approaching final era play a role in the theory and in the practice of such militants?

There is much evidence that shows the authentic apocalyptic fervor of both al-Qāʿida and the Islamic State. In a sense, the awakening of apocalypticism within contemporary Islam is due to contingent historical events. We can list three episodes, all three revolving around the year 1979. The first one is the *Iranian revolution*. It was a turning point for the whole Middle East, indeed. Yet, it was not free from messianic inclinations, and there were many tendencies to call the Āyatollāh Khomeini the long awaited Mahdī, the Islamic savior.[269]

---

268 Olivier Roy, *Jihad and Death. The Global Appeal of Islamic State* (New York: Oxford University Press, 2017), p. 3.

269 Jean-Pierre Filiu, in his very interesting book *L'Apocalypse dans l'Islam* (2008) writes: "The rumor spread of the appearance of the Āyatollāh's face on the Moon, on the night of 27 November 1978, and millions of believers claimed to have actually seen the facial features of the imām in the image of the satellite. Khomeinist networks built the messianic metaphor to better feed popular passions. Thus the Āyatollāh-Moon becomes the sun rising from the West, therefore a sign of the Hour." (*L'apocalisse nell'Islam* [2008; repr., Milan: ObarraO Edizioni, 2011], pp. 98-99). However, "the leaders of the Islamic Republic of Iran have generally sought to proscribe, or to at least deter, political messianism within their realm" (Jean-Pierre Filiu, "The Return of Political Mahdism", *Current Trends in Islamist Ideology*, vol. 8 [May 2009], p. 29).

The second event is the messianic revolt in Mecca, also known as the *Grand Mosque seizure*, "the biggest violent resistance the regime had been met with since the creation of Saudi Arabia."[270] On November 20, 1979, a group of about three-hundred extremists succeeded in occupying the Great Mosque, calling for the end of the House of Saʿūd's rule. The leader, Juhaymān al-ʿUtaybī, announced that Muḥammad bin ʿAbd Allāh al-Qaḥṭāni, his brother-in-law, was the long-awaited Mahdī. Soon the Saudi regime mobilized the armed forces, creating a siege that lasted two weeks, from 20 November to 4 December. The fight ended with the intervention of French commandos of the GIGN (*Groupe d'Intervention de la Gerdarmerie Nationale*) and with the consequent death of all the insurgents and even of the supposed Mahdī. And yet, "in certain millenarian circles of Arabia it remained for a long time the conviction that the Mahdi had not been killed in Mecca, but that he was hiding to escape the forces of Evil."[271]

The third event occurred in 1979 is the *Soviet invasion of Afghanistan*, which was a traumatic experience for the entire Islamic world and which soon became the beginning of global jihad.

This triple shock – the Iranian revolution, the Grand Mosque seizure, and the Soviet invasion of Afghanistan – triggered the apocalyptical imagination, shaping al-Qāʿida's belief in a cosmic war between the good and the bad.

But it was a fourth event that created the conditions for the birth of the Islamic State's toxic apocalyptical ideology: the 2003 war in Iraq. Anticolonial thoughts, eschatological feelings, jihadi approach and Caliphal reminiscence are the elements that flow into IS, preparing a lethal cocktail of a "mix of apocalypticism, puritanism, sectarianism, ultraviolence, and promises of a Caliphate."[272]

Both al-Qāʿida and the Islamic State have confidence in the approaching End of Time, giving credit to the imminent coming of the Mahdī after whom the world would approach its slow and ineluctable conclusion. Still, the two groups have different positions concerning the apocalypse: al-Qāʿida has always been more prudent and, apart from stressing the metaphysical importance of global jihad, it has prevalently downplayed apocalyptic zeal. Just call to mind al-Qāʿida's letter to Abū Ayyūb al-Maṣrī,

---

270 Simon Mabon and Grant Helm, *Da'ish, the Ikhwan and Lessons from History* (London: The Foreign Policy Centre, 2016), https://fpc.org.uk/wp-content/uploads/2016/06/1765.pdf (accessed June 14, 2016).

271 Filiu, *L'apocalisse nell'Islam*, p. 106.

272 William McCants, *The Isis Apocalypse* (New York: St. Martin's Press, 2015), p. 153.

the former leader of AQI (al-Qāʿida in Iraq) and, later, of the Islamic State of Iraq (ISI). In the letter, AQ's leadership states that apocalyptic thinking "is very dangerous and corrupts policy and leadership"[273] – actually, in this first mutation of the Islamic State, apocalypse was taking the place of strategy, and everything was falling apart.

Nonetheless, it is undeniable that apocalypticism is part of al-Qāʿida's mindset as well. Many members of al-Qāʿida have been shaken by the trembling of the End of Time, excited for the advent of the Mahdī, worried about the final battles. "Bin Laden's 'perception of time' could in the most likely way be characterized as a turning point in which God gives His people clear signs that promise a drastic improvement in their situation. [It is an] optimistic perception of living in a charismatic turning point in times."[274] The cosmic battle against the corrupt and corrupting West is definitive and conclusive for the fate of the world. The escalation of catastrophic events such as the war in Iraq, in Afghanistan, the revolution in Iran, the attack on the Twin Towers, the involvement of an increasing number of actors in the so-called "War on Terror", is a sign that something essential is changing, that metaphysical realities are at work, and that a radical transformation is about to take place. "The more catastrophic history becomes, the closer the Kingdom of God is to us,"[275] writes Bruno Étienne with reference to radical Islamism. "Bin Laden lives in a symbolic universe which he reads apocalyptically."[276] Each event is transfigured through the lenses of those who look at the world with the eyes of a redeemer. "Bin Laden represents a passage to a revolutionary form of millenarianism: al-Qāʿida wants the return to the golden age with the prospect of the imminent end of the world."[277] As a confirmation of what has been said, in the document *Al-*

---

273 Quoted in Bill Roggio, Daveed Gartenstein-Ross, Tony Badran, *Intercepted Letters from al-Qaeda Leaders Shed Light on State of Network in Iraq* (Washington, DC: Foundation For Defense of Democracy, 2008), http://www.defenddemocracy.org/media-hit/intercepted-letters-from-al-qaeda-leaders-shed-light-on-state-of-network-in/ (accessed April 22, 2016).

274 Thomas Scheffler, 'Svolta epocale e la lotta per la liberazione: la diagnosi del presente di Usāma bin Lādin', in Te*rrore al servizio di Dio. La "guida spirituale" degli attentatori dell'11 settembre 2001*, eds. By Hans G. Kippenberg and Tilman Seidensticker (Macerata: Quodlibet, 2007), p. 107.

275 Bruno Étienne, *L'islamismo radicale* (Milan: Rizzoli, 1988), p. 270.

276 Richard Landes, *Apocalyptic Islam and Bin Laden* (Boston: Center for Millennial Studies, 2005), http://www.mille.org/people/rlpages/Bin_Laden.html (accessed November 11, 2017).

277 Silvia Scaranari, *Jihād. Significa e attualità* (Milan: Paoline, 2016), p. 111.

Qaeda's Creed and Path it is possible to read that "jihad will last until judgement day."[278]

The most renowned apocalypticist of al-Qāʿida is Abū Muṣʿab al-Sūrī (b. 1958), who "incorporated apocalyptic narratives [...] and predictions in his writings."[279] He writes: "Jihad is an obligation until the advent of the Hour. The community that fights for what is true and just will be victorious [...] and will persevere until the last of its members fight against the Antichrist."[280] In this reading, "the apocalyptic exegesis becomes a guideline for action,"[281] and the jihadi effort is stretched over time to the arrival of the Antichrist.

But it was the self-proclaimed Islamic State of Abū Bakr al-Baghdādī to have brought this apocalyptic and eschatological reasoning to its extreme and destructive consequences. Islamic doomsday prophecies have deeply shaped IS's identity and strategy. The so-called Islamic State was built on the same idea of the approaching End of Time: the Day of Judgement is near, the world, already corrupted and morally perverted, is about to be destroyed, and the Mahdī, the Muslim saviour, is about to come. Armed with these ideas, the Jordanian militant Abū Muṣʿab al-Zarqāwī gave birth to a plan directed to establish a Caliphate, the *last* Caliphate, the Caliphate "according to the prophetic method", after which there would be the end of history.

The same banner of the Islamic State has a potent eschatological meaning. As an anonymous affiliate of IS explained on 2007: "We are certain that it will be the flag of the people of Iraq when they go to aid [...] the Mahdī at the holy house of Allāh."[282] Many are the Islamic traditions (*ḥadīths*) that consider the black flag as the indication of the approaching Mahdī.[283] For example,

---

278 'Al-Qaeda's Creed and Path', p. 55.

279 Jessica Stern and J.M. Berger, *ISIS: The State of Terror* (Manhattan: Ecco Publisher, 2015), p. 223.

280 Quoted in Filiu, *L'apocalisse nell'Islam*, p. 243.

281 Ibid., p. 244.

282 'A Religious Essay Explaining the Significance of the Banner in Islam', English translation published on Combating Terrorist Center website, www.ctc.usma.edu/post/a-religious-essay-explaining-the-significance-of-the-banner-in-islam-english-translation-2 (accessed November 18, 2015).

283 Legends on black banners and the Mahdī circulated for the first time during the last years of the Umayyad caliphate (661 – 750 CE). Many *ḥadīths* telling about soldiers fighting under black standards that would overthrow the Umayyad reign widely circulated among the Muslim population. The Abbasid anti-Umayyad propaganda was exploiting – probably creating *ex novo* – Prophetic traditions to

> The people of my Household will face calamity, expulsion and exile after I am gone, until some people will come from the East carrying black banners. They will ask for something good but will not be given it. Then they will fight and will be victorious, then they will be given what they wanted, but they will not accept it and will give leadership to a man from my family. Then they will fill it with justice just as it was filled with injustice. Whoever among you lives to see that, let him go to them even if he has to crawl over the snow (reported by Ibn Māja).[284]

In another *ḥadīth*, the reference to the Mahdī, "the Rightly Guided One", is clearer:

> Three will fight one another for your treasure, each one of them the son of a caliph, but none of them will gain it. Then the black banners will come from the east, and they will kill you in an unprecedented manner. [...] When you see them, then pledge your allegiance to them even if you have to crawl over the snow, for that is the caliph of Allah, Mahdi (reported by Ibn Māja).[285]

The man from Muḥammad's family, in the first *ḥadīth*, and the Mahdī, in the second *ḥadīth*, are one and the same person; after all, another *ḥadīth* states that "The Mahdī will be one of the descendants of Fāṭima" (reported by Ibn Māja).[286] As is recited in another prophetic tradition: "If only one day of this time (world) remained, Allāh would raise up a man from my family who would fill this earth with justice as it has been filled with oppression" (reported by Abū Dāwūd).[287]

The Islamic State believes that the Muslim community will confront a huge coalition of *kuffār* (unbelievers, infidels). The amount of *kuffār* would account for eighty, meaning eighty countries. Such precision is due to many *ḥadīths* prophesizing the final battle between the Muslims and the Byzantines, today interpreted as the modern crusaders, i.e., the Western coalition. The following *ḥadīth* is reported by al-Bukhārī and it is the main source for this prediction:

> Count six signs that indicate the approach of the Hour: my death, the conquest of Jerusalem, a plague that will afflict you (and kill you in great

back its cause, "ratifying the link between the black color, the Prophet and their [the Abbasid] dynasty." (Chiara Pellegrino, *Perché la bandiera dello Stato Islamico è nera* [Milan: Oasis Foundation, 2016], https://www.oasiscenter.eu/it/perche-la-bandiera-dello-stato-islamico-e-nera [accessed 12 July, 2016]).

284 *Sunan* Ibn Māja, book 36, *ḥadīth* 157, https://sunnah.com/ibnMāja/36/157.

285 *Sunan* Ibn Māja, book 36, *ḥadīth* 159, https://sunnah.com/ibnMāja/36/159.

286 *Sunan* Ibn Māja, book 36, *ḥadīth* 161, https://sunnah.com/ibnMāja/36/161.

287 *Sunan* Abū Dawūd, book 38, *ḥadīth* 5, https://sunnah.com/abudawud/38/5.

> numbers) as the plague that afflicts sheep, the increase of wealth to such an extent that even if one is given one hundred Dinars, he will not be satisfied; then an affliction which no Arab house will escape, and then a truce between you and Bani Al-Asfar (i.e. the Byzantines) who will betray you and attack you under eighty flags. Under each flag will be twelve thousand soldiers.[288]

In this context, the black flag is the symbolical representation of the oneness of God (*tawḥīd*), the indivisibility of the truth, which is opposed to the fragmentation of the opposite side, the camp of *kufr* (disbelief). The bigger the anti-IS coalition becomes, the more the prophecy is fulfilled. "Supporters of the State counted the number of nations that had signed up for 'Rome's' coalition against it. 'Thirty states remain to complete the number of eighty flags that will gather in Dābiq and begin the battle' tweeted one."[289]

Abū Bakr al-Baghdādī traces his own genealogy to the Prophet himself through the lineage of the tenth imām, and, as a consequence, to ʿAlī.[290] Turkī ibn Mubārak al-Binʿalī (d. 2017), the ablest apologist of the Islamic State, used this information to prove the newborn Caliphate was fulfilling eschatological prophecies. The following *ḥadīth* has been used to endorse such claim:

> I heard the Messenger of Allah say: Islam will continue to be triumphant until there have been twelve Caliphs. Then the Prophet said something which I could not understand. I asked my father: What did he say? He said: He has said that all of them (twelve Caliphs) will be from the Quraysh (reported by Muslim).[291]

Obviously there have been far more than twelve Caliphs from the Quraysh tribe, so "Bin'alī sided with those who interpreted the prophecy as requiring twelve *just* Caliphs. There had already been five, six, or seven, so only a handful more were destined to appear,"[292] Binʿalī says, and Abū Bakr al-Baghdādī was believed to be one of them. After this chain of twelve just Caliphs, the world will witness the triumph of Islam over the

288 *Ṣaḥīḥ* al-Bukhārī, book 58, *ḥadīth* 18, https://sunnah.com/bukhari/58/18.
289 McCants, *The Isis Apocalypse*, p. 104.
290 It is curious to note that once he became leader of ISI, and even before, when he adopted the revolutionary Salafi-Jihadi attitude, he turned against the Shiites. But anyhow, this element – the descent from the Prophet – has played a central role in making him the new leader of the Islamic State, and it soon became an important justification for his role as the Caliph.
291 *Ṣaḥīḥ* Muslim, book 33, *ḥadīth* 8, https://sunnah.com/muslim/33/8.
292 McCants, *The Isis Apocalypse*, p. 116.

unbelievers, and so the End of Time. Abū Bakr al-Baghdādī is (was) on the path towards the Hour.

In light of this message, William McCants recognizes that, at this stage of evolution, it is "the Caliphate the locus of the group's apocalyptic imagination rather than the Mahdī. That does not mean the Mahdī will not appear soon – only a handful of just caliphs need to rule before the Mahdī arrives. But for the moment, the Caliphate is a greater priority than doomsday."[293]

In April 2014, two months before the "restoration" of the Caliphate, the new Islamic State's official spokesman, Abū Muḥammad al-ʿAdnānī (d. 2016), speaking in exquisite classical Arabic, made the announcement of the possible revival of such important Islamic political institution: "A state of Islam rules by your Book and by the tradition of your Prophet and fights your enemies. So reinforce it, honor it, aid it, and establish it in the land. Make it a Caliphate in accordance with the prophetic method."[294] Even before, in August 2013, he said: "Our goal is to establish an Islamic state that does not recognize borders, on the Prophetic methodology."[295]

These declarations allude to a prophecy of the Caliphate's return. The *ḥadīth* is the following:

> "There will be Prophethood for as long as Allah wills it to be, then He will remove it when He wills. Then there will be Khilāfa on the Prophetic methodology and it will be for as long as Allah wills, then He will remove it when He wills. Then there will be harsh kingship for as long as Allah Wills, then He will remove it when He wills. Then there will be tyrannical kingship for as long as Allah wills, then He will remove it when He wills. And then there will be Khilāfa upon the Prophetic methodology" And then [the Prophet] fell silent. (Reported by Aḥmad ibn Ḥanbal).[296]

This *ḥadīth* is even reported in the first number of the magazine *Dābiq* to justify the establishment of the Caliphate. In this view, the Islamic State asserts to represent the *last* and *just* – because prophetically justified –

293 Ibid., p. 143.

294 Cited in William McCants, *Islamic State Invokes Prophecy to Justify Its Claim to Caliphate* (Washington, D.C.: Brookings Institution, 2014), https://www.brookings.edu/blog/markaz/2014/11/05/islamic-state-invokes-prophecy-to-justify-its-claim-to-caliphate/ (accessed 2 July, 2017).

295 Cited in Graeme Wood, "What ISIS Really Want", *The Atlantic*, March 2015, http://www.theatlantic.com/magazine/archive/2015/03/what-isis-really-wants/384980/ (accessed 20 June, 2017).

296 This very translation of the *ḥadīth* is reported in *Dābiq*, n. 1: p. 34.

Islamic political construction before the End of Time. "This new condition opens the path for the complete unification of all Muslim peoples and lands under the single authority of the Khalīfa,"[297] it is written in *Dābiq*.

The two prophecies – the one about the twelve Caliphs, and the other about the prophetic methodology – have been put in mutual relation, so that one completes the other in an inseparable knot.

The declaration of the Caliphate was issued in June 2014 by al-ʿAdnānī, who said: "The flag of the Islamic State, the flag of monotheism, rises and flutters. [...] It is a dream that lives in the depths of every Muslim believer. [...] It is the caliphate. It is the caliphate – the abandoned obligation of the era... Now the caliphate has returned. We ask God the exalted to make it in accordance with the prophetic method."[298] The fight had assumed eschatological tones.

Even the expansion in Syria followed a prophetical path. As is well known, in Syria the Christian monk Baḥīrā recognized Muḥammad as the prophet when Muḥammad was a child or perhaps an adolescent. This story has baptized Syria as the space of prophecy, and such a title endured over centuries until today. Syria is "the space of the fulfillment. Everything, strategically and eschatologically, will coincide in that territory of sand and lions,"[299] writes Pietrangelo Buttafuoco.

The belief on the centrality of Syria transformed the current war in a "unique conflict, full of political and religious meanings [... that] promote the flows of foreign fighters."[300] The Islamic State exploited the reputation of Syria to make itself the prophetical subject intended to fulfill the prophecies.[301] In this view, the choice to call the propaganda magazine with

297 Ibid., p. 40. Furthermore, in the magazine *Rumiyah* the Islamic State insisted on this concept by saying that "in future segments, we will present – by Allah's permission – examples of the paths followed by the people of misguidance in their endeavor to supposedly establish the religion, implement the Shari'ah, and bring back the khilafah, in order to show the difference between these paths and the prophetic methodology, which the Islamic State adhered to – by Allah's grace – until Allah granted it consolidation in the land" (*Rumiyah*, n. 7 [March 2017]: p. 9).

298 Citen in McCant, *The ISIS Apocalypse*, pp. 121-122.

299 Pietrangelo Buttafuoco, *Il feroce Saracino* (Milan: Bompiani, 2015), p. 33.

300 Renzo Guolo, *L'ultima utopia* (Milan: Guerini e Associati, 2015), p. 12.

301 There is one prophecy that has been accurately avoided by the Islamic State – it is something that could have provoked many troubles to the legitimacy of the self-proclaimed Caliphate, which stretched from Iraq to Syria in that spaces re-baptized "Syraq". The prophecy talks about the emersion of the Antichrist in that very space: "He [the Dajjāl, the Deceiver] will appear from what is between ash-Shām and al-Iraq, causing devastation toward the right and toward the left. O

the name of "Dābiq" is not accidental. The magazine was first published in July 2014 in many languages including English, and its aim was to frame and to give shape to the apocalyptic jihad of IS.

In the first page of *Dābiq* there is a quotation by Abū Muṣʿab al-Zarqāwī: "The spark has been lit here in Iraq, and its heat will continue to intensify – by Allah's permission – until it burns the crusader armies in Dābiq."[302] Dābiq is a town in the northern countryside of Aleppo that plays a central role in the Islamic apocalyptic narration. The magazine also mentions a famous *ḥadīth* that gave birth to the belief that one of the final battles will be fought in Dābiq:

> The Hour will not be established until the Romans land at al-A'maq or Dābiq. Then an army of the best people on the earth at that time will leave from al-Madinah for them.
>
> When they line up in ranks, the Romans will say: "Leave us and those who were taken as prisoners from amongst us so we can fight them". The Muslims will say, "Nay, by Allah, we will not abandon our brothers to you". So they will fight them.
>
> Then one third of them will run away; Allah will never forgive them. One third will be killed; they will be the best martyrs with Allah. And one third will conquer them; they will never be afflicted with fitnah. Then they will conquer Constantinople.
>
> While they are dividing the war booty, having hung their swords on olive trees, Shaytan [Satan] will shout, "The false Messiah [Dajjal] has taken your place among your families". So they will leave [for their families], but Shaytan's claim is false.
>
> When they arrive to Sham [Syria] he comes out. Then while they are preparing for battle and filing their ranks, the prayer is called. So 'Isa Ibn Maryam [Jesus son of Mary] will descend and lead them.
>
> When the enemy of Allah sees him, he will melt as salt melts in water. If he were to leave him, even then he would melt until he perished, but he kills him with his own hand, and then shows them his blood upon his spear. (Reported by Muslim).[303]

The centrality of Dābiq is so essential in the apocalyptic schedule that the Islamic State conquered the little town from Sunni rebels in summer 2014 even though it was strategically irrelevant. On November 16, 2014, the Islamic State killed an American hostage, Peter Kassig, beheading him

worshippers of Allāh! Hold fast!" (Reported by al-Tirmidhī, book 33, *ḥadīth* 83, https://sunnah.com/tirmidhi/33/83).

302 *Dābiq* n. 1: p. 2.

303 *Ṣaḥīḥ* Muslim, book 54, *ḥadīth* 44, https://sunnah.com/muslim/54/44.

precisely in Dābiq. "And here we are, burying the first crusader in Dābiq. Eagerly awaiting for the remainder of your armies to arrive," said the murderer of Kassig in the video of the execution broadcast on the web.[304]

In conclusion, the so-called Islamic State used[305] a wide range of prophecies to make its message more appealing, rooting its legitimacy in the doctrine, quoting the Qur'an and the Sunna, fulfilling the forecasts, even with violence, to prove its message. "The apocalyptic revanchism of the organization that promised divine justice had an influence on disillusioned Muslim youth both in the Middle East and in other regions."[306] Conquering Dābiq and using black flags are two central decisions for IS's goal, having a symbolic importance for the foreign fighters and making them sure of the party they are fighting with. In other words, the militants "want verification that they are on the right path,"[307] and they can obtain it by comparing the reality they are living in with the prophecies about the return of a victorious and powerful Islam. "Each specific conflict is a metaphor for an age-old conflict that will end only in a final battle,"[308] writes Olivier Roy.

---

304 The debate whether attacking Dābiq or not had long since influenced the international coalition's decisions about the tactic to adopt. This fact clearly shows the power and force of the Islamic State's apocalyptic message. In an article on *The New York Times* published on December 7, 2015, for instance, talking about a possible invasion on Syrian and Iraqi soil, the journalist writes: "Should that invasion happen, the Islamic State not only would be able to declare its prophecy fulfilled, but could also turn the occurrence into a new recruiting drive at the very moment the terrorist group appears to be losing volunteers" (Rukmini Callimachi, 'U.S. Seeks to Avoid Ground War Welcomed by Islamic State', *The New York Times*, December 7, 2015, http://www.nytimes.com/2015/12/08/world/middleeast/us-strategy-seeks-to-avoid-isis-prophecy.html?_r=0). In the same article, Jean-Pierre Filiu says that "because of these prophecies, going in on the ground would be the worst trap to fall into," and, thus, "to break the dynamic, you have to debunk the prophecy."

305 The use of the past tense is mandatory because the failure of the Caliphal project in the territory of "Syraq" caused an initial loss of confidence in the possibility of creating the last and ultimate Caliphate. Nevertheless, the sense of adaptability of the radical group is strong, to the extent that the loss of territories did not completely downplayed the faith in the fulfilling of the prophecies. "ISIS, like other apocalyptic groups, changes its understanding of prophecy's fulfillment based on circumstances" (William McCants, 'Apocalypse Delayed', *Jihadica* [blog], October 16, 2016, http://www.jihadica.com/apocalypse-delayed/ [accessed 18 October, 2016]).

306 Nukhet Sandal, 'Apocalypse Soon. Revolutionary Revanchism of ISIS', in *The Future of ISIS. Regional and International Implications*, eds. by Feisal al-Istrabadi and Sumit Ganguly (Washington, DC.: Brookings Institution Press, 2018), p. 24.

307 David Cook, *Contemporary Muslim Apocalyptic Literature* (New York: Syracuse University Press, 2005), p. 11.

308 Roy, *Jihad and Death*, p. 45.

Bringing about the messianic age – this is the self-assigned task of Salafi-Jihadis – "is the unveiling of *the* meaning and its fulfillment, the final triumph, certainly melancholic but not without an anticipated enjoyment for the final victory of Islam. It is a total purification, thanks to the disappearance of the world."[309]

Salafi-Jihadism stretches from the past to the future (the eschatological time), constantly looking behind and further, but not focusing on the present, being the present a *not-anymore golden era* and a *not-yet eschatological era*. The present is only considered in function of the final collapse, and it does not stand by itself.

Bob de Graaff positions al-Qāʿida and the Islamic State among the group of apocalyptists he labels "the fanatics", placing Salafi-Jihadism alongside the radical Anabaptists, the Puritans, Robespierre, Bolshevism and Nazism – exactly those names that are the representatives of revolutionary Gnosticism, as given above. De Graaff defines the fanatics as those "convinced that God must be given a helping hand or that the course of history should be accelerated. Consequently, fanatics are voluntarists: they do not want to wait, but instead impose their will on history and others."[310] These jihadists "must be willing to give up everything, even actively desire to give it all up, in order to bring about the messianic age."[311]

The question of the apocalypse is thus patently present in the Salafi-Jihadi discourse. Moreover, the secular way Salafi-Jihadis interpret the eschatological narrations is at odds with more traditional exegesis. By exploiting religious materials for strategical concerns, they break any link with the orthodoxy. In this way, "the apocalyptist constantly seeks new interpretations of ancient material to bolster his convictions, an approach diametrically opposite that of the conservative religious scholar."[312] In continuity with what is said above, it is possible to assert that such behavior is bizarrely a form of secularization, since the tradition is put in brackets and personal interpretations prevail.

In conclusion, both al-Qāʿida and the self-proclaimed Islamic State are "constantly poised between a mythical past reread in the light of the present conditions and a future halfway between the apocalypse and the

309 Benslama, *Un furioso desiderio di sacrificio*, p. 48.

310 Bob de Graaff, 'IS and its Predecessors: Violent Extremism in Historical Perspective', *Perspectives on Terrorism*, vol. 10, issue 5 (October 2016): p. 97.

311 David Cook, 'Muslim Apocalyptic and Jihad', *Jerusalem Studies in Arabic and Islam*, vol. 20 (1996): pp. 77-78.

312 Cook, *Contemporary Muslim Apocalyptic Literature*, p. 3.

new golden age"[313] – which is another way of referring to the tripartition of history.

4.3.4 *An Islamic humankind: the immanentization of the* eschaton

Persuaded that reality is degraded and corrupted, and that the world has passed through a state of perfection and will again reach the same excellence in the future, the revolutionary gnostic believes that the last stage – the third age – will be permanent and stable, freezing historical evolution into an ultimate and perpetual society. This restored flawless society is the immanent (and not supernatural) destination of all humanity, the revolutionary gnostic thinks. As described in Chapter 2, revolutionary Gnosticism revolves around the idea of an "immanentist eschatology" (the expression is coined by Eric Voegelin), meaning that the *eschaton*, i.e., the "last things", will be reached *in* history and not *beyond* history.

What is extremely important here is that humanity will be transfigured to the point that no violence, no envy, no jealousy, no poverty, no need and no lust will be more. The spiritual structure of humankind is destined to be radically transformed. Therefore, the transfiguration of humanity is what characterizes more this third point of the gnostic pattern.

It is legitimate to ask ourselves whether Salafi-Jihadism contains what Voegelin calls the immanentization of the *eschaton*. To some extent, the answer has already been given in the previous subsection; however, it is worth making this very point more explicit.

Barry Cooper elaborates on this idea:

> Modern Islamist thinkers such as Quṭb or bin Laden easily combine jihadist and apocalyptic traditions in the expectation that a final and ecumenic conquest requires a pure society, which in turn is a bridge to the end time, an essential element in a grandiose redemptive event prior to the end of the world.[314]

The pure society that will come into being at the end of a long process (the fifth point of the gnostic pattern clarifies that this process is a cosmic war) will be the final political construction of humankind before the final collapse – which makes sense of the apocalyptic fury combined with the state-building effort common to the Islamic State and al-Qāʿida. The future society, which will be fully Islamic and will exist under an unmediated

313 Plebani, *Jihadismo globale*, p. 77.

314 Barry Cooper, *New Political Religions, or An Analysis of Modern Terrorism* (Columbia and London: University of Missouri Press, 2004), p. 116.

divine sovereignty, will never witness oppression nor coercion, for the wills of all people will be coincident with Islamic morality and naturally consistent with *sharīʿa*: this perfect social order will mirror divine truth. The Salafi-Jihadi project is articulated around the idea of "creating a new type of *homo islamicus*, removed from all national, tribal, racial and ethnic, even family and affective attachments, a man truly uprooted in order to create a new society from scratch."[315] And because of this, Olivier Roy says, "the Caliphate is a fantasy [... based on a] strategic impossibility [... for which] there is no political perspective."[316] Salafi-Jihadis are thus animated by the intention of "(re)making the Islamic *homo novus*."[317]

Here is how Abū l-Aʿlā al-Mawdūdī describes the idealized Islamic golden age at the time of the Prophet:

> Arabia had the most singular government of the time, based as it was on the principle of the sovereignty of God and the viceregency of man. The law of the land was Islam. The administration of the state lay in the hands of the honest and pious people. *The country had no trace of violence, oppression injustice or immorality. Peace, justice, truth and honesty reigned supreme everywhere.* Many of the people of the country had come to possess highest moral attributes because they were honest in worshipping God and obeying Him.[318]

From these words it is apparent that when one speaks of an Islamic *eschaton*, it is always about *ḥākimiyya*, the establishment of God's absolute authority on earth. Under these circumstances, man-made laws are abhorred, being a violation of God's legislation – and so, with reference to Salafi-Jihadism, *antinomianism* plays a role just like in other gnostic experiences, but on a different level, since laws *per se* are not rejected but only are man-made laws: "The literal interpretation [of Qurʾānic verses] according to the Jihadi-Salafis is the supremacy of divine legislation over un-Islamic laws or secular political ideologies,"[319] to the point that Salafi-Jihadis believe to be "above the law in the name of the law,"[320] the latter being considered superior to all other legislations.

---

315 Roy, *Jihad and Death*, p. 26.

316 Ibid., p. 4.

317 Plebani, *Jihadismo globale*, p. 14.

318 Abū l-Aʿlā al-Mawdūdī, *Islam: An Historical Perspective* (Birmingham: U.K.I.M. Dawah Centre, 1996), p. 4. Emphasis added.

319 Abdulbasit Kassim, 'Defining and Understanding the Religious Philosophy of jihādī-Salafism and the Ideology of Boko Haram', *Politics, Religion & Ideology*, vol. 16, nos. 2-3 (2015): p. 179.

320 Benslama, *Un furioso desiderio di sacrificio*, p. 75.

For the militants of the Islamic State, the administrative experiment in the land of Syria and Iraq is (was) identified with the restauration of *ḥākimiyya* and with the advent of the last political institution before the apocalypse. As Alessandro Orsini reports in his book, Maria Giulia Sergio, the young Italian woman who fled to Syria to live in the Islamic State, once said: "The Islamic State is the perfect state."[321] In his *The Way of the Strangers*, Graeme Wood collects several stories of jihadists or people close to the Salafi-Jihadi universe. It is worth reporting some of these accounts:

> In May 2015, twelve members of the Mannan family of Luton, England, traveled together to Raqqah, Syria, the de facto capital of the Islamic State. They ranged in age from one to seventy-five, and an open letter from the family rebuked anyone who suspected they had been tricked into going. "Don't be shocked when we say that none of us were forced against our will," they wrote. "It is outrageous to think that an entire family could be kidnapped and made to migrate like this." They had made their journey "by the command of the Khalifah [caliph] of the Muslims." And they found what they wanted – "*a land that has established the Shariah, in which a Muslim doesn't feel oppression [...], in which a parent doesn't feel the worry of losing their child to the immorality of society [...], in which the sick and elderly do not wait in agony.*"[322]

> Three generations of conservative Muslims from outside London, a skirt-chasing bachelor from South Australia, and tens of thousands of others had all drunk their inspiration from the same fountains. In addition to the physical caliphate, with its territory and war and economy to run, there was a caliphate of the imagination to which all these people had already emigrated long before they slipped across the Turkish border. They believed the state that awaited them would purify their lives by forbidding vice and promoting virtue. Its leader, Abu Bakr al Baghdadi, would unify the world's Muslims, restore their honor, and allow them iniquities they had suffered due to differences of race, wealth, or nationality in the countries of their birth.[323]

Wood also reports a conversation with the Salafi Egyptian Hesham Elashry, a jihadist-sympathizer.

> "I've seen pictures," he said wistfully. He meant the Islamic State propaganda. "They have enough food, enough everything. If you live under their protection, it's beautiful." Seeds that once yielded a single stalk of wheat now, under the

321 Alessandro Orsini, *ISIS. I terroristi più fortunati del mondo e tutto ciò che è stato fatto per favorirli* (Milan: Rizzoli, 2016), p. 21.
322 Wood, *The Way of the Strangers*, prologue, Kindle.
323 Ibid.

> Islamic State's care, gave three or four. Miracles were happening. "The *Dawlah Islamiyyah* [Islamic State] came to save people from terror and find protection and freedom," he continued. They were Sunni saviors. He considered them the possible fulfillment of prophecy: a caliphate that would arise out of nowhere, as Muhammad foretold, and clear away the rule of Muslims by tyrants. "You can't fight *'aqida* [creed]," Hesham said. "What's wrong in what they're doing?"[324]

The para-state that the Islamic State built in "Syraq" is always described in utopian and idealistic terms by its sympathizers and militants. The truly Islamic political construction is seen as the exact opposite of the West, "for practically everything valued by the immoral West is condemned under *sharīʿa* law."[325] In fact, "the ability to connect the past with the future to legitimize its cause has been the most prominent factor in spreading the Salafi-Jihadi message and challenging the West in a conflict of ideas."[326]

An Islamic state, whether IS's or al-Qāʿida's, will defeat poverty and will promote healthcare, as issue 9 of *Dābiq* magazine shows.[327] Everything will be perfect and flawless, and no war will ever be born from a reconciled humanity anymore. "A Muslim government [...] will protect rights, defend sanctities [and] institute justice."[328] Salafi-Jihadis "believe that such a government is the sole remedy for the ills of Islamic nations, that it will purify society, promote cultural progress, provide justice and exalt God's word."[329]

The *eschaton* will be of course a shared reality, that is to say, it will encompass the whole world, leaving nothing outside its reach: the regeneration and transfiguration of humankind will be total. "Islam would flourish and regain its rightful place at the head of the world,"[330] and the ontological nature of reality will be altered, or, in a gnostic perspective, fixed and restored to health. In a message directed to the youth of the *umma*, Osama bin Laden says that jihad should be aimed to counter infidels "until

---

324 Ibid., chap 2.

325 Bin Laden, 'Moderate Islam is a Prostration to the West', p. 37.

326 John Turner, 'From Cottage Industry to International Organisation: The Evolution of Salafi-Jihadism and the Emergence of the Al Qaeda Ideology', *Terrorism and Political Violence*, vol. 22, no. 4 (September 2010): p. 555.

327 *Dābiq*, n. 9 (May 2015): pp. 24-26.

328 Al-Ẓawāhirī, 'Ayman al-Zawahiri Interview Four Years After 9/11', p. 187.

329 Muhammad Sa'id al-'Ashmawy, *Against Islamic Extremism* (Gainesville: University Press of Florida, 2001), p. 79. A few pages after the author says that "many Muslims see an Islamic government as the only defense against what they see as Western degeneracy" (ibid., p. 87).

330 Mark Stout, 'In Search of Salafi Jihadist Strategic Thought: Mining the Words of the Terrorists', *Studies in Conflict & Terrorism*, vol. 32, issue 10 (October 2009): p. 879.

these forces are crushed to naught, all the anti-Islamic forces are wiped off from the face of this earth, and Islam takes over the whole world and all the other false religions."[331]

The path towards the *eschaton* will witness a progressive reduction of *kufr* (unbelief) in the world until a total Islamic rule. The announcement of the self-proclaimed Caliphate brought "the grayzone to the brink of permanent extinction... by reviving the great body of Islam and so no Muslim had any excuse to be independent of this entity embodying them and waging war on their behalf in the face of *kufr*,"[332] as *Dābiq* magazine explains. The scope of the perfect society is widening more and more until the moment it incorporates everything – which observation reveals a gradual and growing *eschaton*, in view of the fact that the already-existing Caliphate of IS (no longer on the ground, though) should first embrace the whole earth before the Mahdī comes and rules with his divine wisdom; yet, the IS's Caliphate is believed to be the Caliphate "in accordance with the prophetic methodology," and for the Islamic State's militants it is already the last and ultimate Caliphate before Judgment Day.

What is important, though, is the immanent nature of this transfiguration. William Shepard cannot ignore it: "The social and political activism of radical Islamists bespeaks a much more worldly orientation than has been usual among pious Muslims in the past, and they are strikingly characterized by what Max Weber called 'inner worldly asceticism'."[333] Salafi-Jihadism is at odds with traditional Islam, which has always been much more concerned for otherworldly needs compared to this-worldly problems. In this sense, the liberation Salafi-Jihadism envisions and pursues is immanent and empirical rather than transcendent and metaphysical, and the desired and sought *eschaton* is, and cannot but be, immanent.

Sayyid Quṭb gives an example of such an aspiration when he writes that "it is about building the kingdom of God on earth."[334] The stress is placed on "on earth". Khaled Fouad Allam maintains that

> radical Islam does not imply a discourse of faith: [rather] it builds a new ideology, centered on the concept of state. It follows that most of the political

---

331 Osama bin Laden, 'The Youth of Islam', in *The Al Qaeda Reader. The Essential Texts of Osama Bin Laden's Terrorist Organization*, ed. by Raymond Ibrahim (New York: Broadway Books, 2007), p. 269.

332 *Dābiq*, no. 7 (February 2015): p. 55.

333 William E. Shepard, 'Islam and Ideology: Towards a Typology', *International Journal of Middle East Studies*, vol. 19, no. 3 (August 1987): p. 316.

334 Quoted in Paolo Branca, V*oci dell'Islam moderno. Il pensiero arabo-musulmano fra rinnovamento e tradizione* (Genova: Marietti, 1997), p. 198.

> language of radical Islam concerns the economy and the government; it poses from the top the problems of the definition of an Islamic state or republic and of the Islamization of society, and from the bottom those of the family, of the woman, of Islamic education: all components of an ideological vulgate strongly inspired by the Marxist vulgate.[335]

This is to say that the attention of Salafi-Jihadism is paid to immanent concerns only and that the perfect and final stage of history here to come will involve merely material issues.

In brief, in the closing period of time that will precede the end of days, humankind will not be able to hurt anyone due to its transfigured nature in accordance with Islamic revelation. As Bruno Étienne cleverly says, "The purpose of radical Islamism is entirely terrestrial. […] Radical Islamism is the need of the Kingdom, and the Kingdom that is of this world is actually a different world."[336] What is envisioned by Salafi-Jihadism is a different world, which embraces not only a different political structure but also, and above all, a different humanity. The same spiritual structure of humankind will be altered and made unable to exert violence, for God's will shall fill earth and the whole universe. The implicit consequence is that the *eschaton* will not have an effect on humankind only but also on the empirical world *tout court*, and everything will act in line with the Revelation. The same Islamic apocalyptic narrative upholds that after the devastation brought forth by the demonic populations of Gog and Magog, God will send a purifying rain that will make earth sparking like a mirror. In *Ṣaḥīḥ* Muslim it is narrated that after the rain,

> the earth would be told to bring forth its fruit and restore its blessing and, as a result thereof, there would grow (such a big) pomegranate that a group of persons would be able to eat that, and seek shelter under its skin and milk cow would give so much milk that a whole party would be able to drink it. And the milk camel would give such (a large quantity of) milk that the whole tribe would be able to drink out of that and the milk sheep would give so much milk that the whole family would be able to drink out of that, and at that time Allah would send a pleasant wind which would soothe (people) even under their armpits, and would take the life of every Muslim.[337]

The immanent *eschaton* foreseen by Salafi-Jihadis is a combination of this prophetic tradition and of the golden age that was established in the

335 Fouad Allam, 'L'islām contemporaneo', p. 256.
336 Étienne, *L'islamismo radicale*, p. 267.
337 *Ṣaḥīḥ* Muslim, book 54, *ḥadīth* 136, https://sunnah.com/muslim/54/136.

first period of Islam – exactly like in the project of radical Anabaptists, who were planning on restoring the primitive Church while, at the same time, propitiating the advent of the New Jerusalem and the Messiah.

Again, the Caliphate/*eschaton* that will replicate the past golden age will precede the End of Time, leading to the Day of Judgment and, in the meantime, it will guarantee peace, prosperity, wealth and religiosity. The circle of history thus comes to an end, exhausting all its meaning and leading humanity to its highest.

4.3.5 *The ultimate knowledge: the Gnosis*

The fourth point of the gnostic pattern is the Gnosis. With this term I refer to the complete knowledge of the mystery of evil and of the mystery of history. The gnostic professes to know everything, especially *why* the world is as it is and *how* humankind can change its course. The exhaustive comprehension of human alienation aims at changing the current degraded situation. Besides holding an anti-cosmic disposition and believing in a past golden era and in a future immanentized *eschaton*, the gnostic claims to possess the key to resolve the damaged and decayed human condition. Luciano Pellicani's definition, which is also given above, is meticulous and comprehensive: Gnosis is

> a total complete knowledge (descriptive and normative) [that] contains a diagnosis-therapy of human alienation. Thanks to the Gnosis, the gnostic knows the matrix of the (temporary) unhappiness of man – the catastrophe that overturned and degraded the world, filling it with horrors of all kinds – and the way to the Promised Land. In other words, those in possession of the gnosis know what humanity has been and has become because of the fall, as well as when and how redemption will take place. This knowledge is therefore a veritable soteriology, a liberating science, since, along with the awareness of degradation, it gives humanity the certainty of restoration of original being.[338]

Gnosis is both descriptive (a diagnosis) and normative (a therapy), a total and ultimate liberating science. It involves the *why* and the *how* – why the world is full of evil and how to free it from evil.

To ask ourselves if a Gnosis with these implications really exists in Salafi-Jihadism, it is vital not to be misled by the religious character of this ideology. The radical Anabaptists in Münster and the Puritans in England

338 Luciano Pellicani, *Revolutionary Apocalypse. Ideological Roots of Terrorism* (Westport and London: Praeger, 2003), p. 152.

were both gnostic *and* Christian, and in such cases their religious character did not prevent the assimilation of the gnostic *Weltanschauung*. Their interpretation of the Holy Scriptures was deemed superior, conclusive and irrevocable, whereas the old world of priests, hierarchy and rules was considered to be a detour, an error in the straight path towards the full application of God's will. The apocalyptic feeling was common to Anabaptists and Puritans, being the world – in their beliefs – on the brink of the final collapse, just before the Second Advent of Christ.

Is there a similar presumption in Salafi-Jihadism?

To a certain extent, the solution to the mystery of history (which is one of the meanings of Gnosis) is already present in the credence of the tripartition of history and in the confidence in a future immanent *eschaton*. Salafi-Jihadis believe in the present (for the Islamic State) or future (for al-Qāʿida) Caliphate "according to the prophetic methodology," in the forthcoming advent of the Mahdī, and in the degraded nature of present-day reality. They are able to unmistakably place in history all these ages they say to believe in, creating a calendar and giving to their gnostic fellows the possibility to follow that exact schedule. In fact, the future is no longer obscure for the "enlightened", so that the fear of death is replaced by courage, bravery and fortitude. Nothing is hidden for them: the last stage of history will come soon and the West will fall because of historical (and divine) necessity – the assertion of which significantly recalls the Communist *petitio principii* concerning the capitalist system. "The idea of a culmination of history […] follows logically from the premise of absolute knowledge."[339]

Salafi-Jihadis do not possess only the knowledge regarding the mystery of history, but also that of the mystery of evil. *Why* humankind derailed from the straight path ordered by God is clear in their mind; *how* to fix the situation and to cure modern *jāhiliyya* is as much evident. As a matter of fact, the notion of an absolute knowledge "also leads to the temptation to attain global revolution as its logical corollary. […] The legitimate existence of any contending standpoints must be eliminated."[340]

Michele Martelli recognizes in the jihadists the "crazy presumption of being the messengers, trustees, delegates, imitators and representatives of God on earth"[341] thanks to the divine knowledge they believe to possess.

339 Shiujun Cui and Joshua Glinert, 'Jihadi-Salafi Ideology: The Suspension of Dialectic and Radicalization of Thought', *Journal of Middle Eastern and Islamic Studies (in Asia)*, vol. 10, no. 4 (2016): p. 104.

340 Ibid.

341 Michele Martelli, *Teologia del terrore. Filosofia, religione e politica dopo l'11 settembre* (Rome: Manifestolibri, 2005), p. 76.

These fighters are animated by "the arrogant, fanatical and irreverent activism of those *who know*, or presume to know, even though they do not know and cannot know."[342] Martelli recognizes here distinct gnostic influences. With the same tone, Donatella Di Cesare says that Salafi-Jihadi militants are "convinced that they belong to an initiatory vanguard in possession of the key to deciphering the hidden meaning that eludes the sight of others."[343] Such is the gnostic attitude.

Sayyid Quṭb, Osama bin Laden, Ayman al-Ẓawāhirī, Abū Muṣʿab al-Zarqāwī, Abū Bakr al-Baghdādī and all the other Salafi-Jihadi personalities believe their interpretation of the Scriptures is the same as Prophet Muḥammad's, and this is enough for them. Westoxification and *jāhiliyya*, two aspects of the same disease that affects the world, must be eradicated once and for all. Islam is the cure and jihad the means for administering the treatment: "We believe that the victorious faction is a faction of knowledge and jihad,"[344] al-Qāʿida once declared. Salafi-Jihadis are in possession of a divine knowledge reserved for the chosen people, a knowledge that is accessible to them thanks to their pious devotion and abiding by the wisdom of the *al-Salaf al-Ṣāliḥ*. They know when and where the final battles and the advent of the Mahdī will take place, and they act accordingly without doubting. For example, "in al-Ẓawāhirī's operational code, the long-term eventual prospects for the creation of an Islamic Caliphate and for rule by sharia law are certain. […] The political future is, in al-Ẓawāhirī's operational code, completely predictable."[345] Islam is finally being understood in its entirety, they say, and Salafi-Jihadis are confident that the *umma* is awakening from the torpor of sin and distance from God. The "ethical authenticity"[346] is recovered from earliest times, when the Prophet's companions were still alive and the first community was firmly anchored in the divine norms. And those who are legitimate representatives of God, those who are holders of a superior knowledge, are only the *mujāhidūn*, the fighters. "It is only those who participate in the jihad personally […] that are legitimate sources of religious authority."[347]

342 Ibid., p. 81. Emphasis added.

343 Donatella Di Cesare, *Terrore e modernità* (Turin: Einaudi, 2017), p. 113.

344 'Al-Qaeda's Creed and Path', p. 55.

345 James D. Jacquier, 'An Operational Code of Terrorism: The Political Psychology of Ayman al-Zawahiri', *Behavioral Sciences of Terrorism and Political Aggression*, vol. 6, no. 1 (2014): pp. 27-28.

346 Guolo, *L'ultima utopia*, p. 26.

347 Elisa Giunchi, *Nel nome di Allah. L'autorità religiosa nell'Islam* (Milan: Jouvence, 2017), p. 221.

An insightful article written by Eli Alshech delves into this very argument. Alshech notes that from 9/11 onward there has been a big debate among Salafi-Jihadi circles centered on who is the most reliable religious authority. Drawing on the charisma-based concept of authority elaborated by Max Weber and following Quintan Wiktorowicz's classification of the Salafi factions into "purists", "politicos" and "jihadis," Alshech explains that having the politicos (i.e., the Saudi Saḥwa movement) a specific grasp of modern geopolitical issues, the jihadis started to rely more on another form of knowledge to gain ground within the Salafi community and in the *umma* in general. Three are the personalities that Alshech analyzes to explain this new form of knowledge: Yūsuf al-ʿUyayrī (1973-2003), first leader of al-Qāʿida in the Arabian Peninsula (AQAP); Abū Muḥammad al-Maqdisī; and Ḥusayn ibn Maḥmūd, pseudonym of an al-Qāʿida leader and popular writer on online jihadi forum.

Yūsuf al-ʿUyayrī asserts that only the *mujāhidūn* have a deep and complete knowledge of reality due to their involvement in the battlefield; in his vision, the *mujāhidūn* are "the only legitimate source of information on matters of jihad."[348] Even Roel Meijer distinguishes this peculiarity in al-ʿUyayrī's thought by writing that "truth (*haqq*) can only be discerned in action, which is jihad. [...] Only the *mujāhidūn* as the vanguard can have true knowledge for they have acquired this unique experience. In this activist sense Jihadi-Salafism is truly transformative."[349] Al-Maqdisī goes way beyond this statement: recalling Qurʾan 29:69 ("And those who strive for Us, We will surely guide them to Our ways. And indeed, Allah is with the doers of good"), he writes that the *mujāhidūn* "possess *superior insight*. [...] Allāh grants him insight as a reward for his jihad... (and as a result,) his comprehension, knowledge, and grasp of the truth are much greater that (those of) other people."[350] But the peak of these declarations is reached by Ḥusayn ibn Maḥmūd, who describes the jihadi

348 Eli Alshech, *The Emergence of the 'Infallible Jihad Fighters' – The Salafi Jihadists' Quest for Religious Legitimacy* (Washington: MEMRI, 2008), http://www.memri.org/publicdocs/InfalliableJihadists_final.pdf (accessed December 22, 2015).

349 Roel Meijer, 'Re-Reading al-Qaeda Writings of Yusuf al-Ayiri', *International Institute for the Study of Islam in the Modern World (ISIM) Review*, no. 18 (Autumn 2006): p. 17.

350 Abū Muḥammad al-Maqdisī, quoted in Alshech, *The Emergence of the 'Infallible Jihad Fighters'*. Italics mine. See also Joas Wagemakers, 'Reclaiming Scholarly Authority: Abu Muhammad al-Maqdisi's Critique of Jihadi Practices', *Studies in Conflict & Terrorism*, vol. 34, issue 7 (June 2011): p. 532: "Al-Maqdisī [...] praises jihad fighters as having superior knowledge about jihad because of their experiences."

fighter as infallible. "Whoever devotes his soul to Allāh, Allāh will render him immune to the lies of the deceitful,"[351] he states. In his view, thus, the *mujāhid* possesses a privileged access to the truth thanks to the willingness to sacrifice his/her own life for the sake of God in the battlefield. With Ḥusayn ibn Maḥmūd we are undoubtedly in the realm of Gnosticism in that the supernatural knowledge is given from the above to the chosen ones and it is salvific in so far as it leads to individual and collective redemption.

In conclusion, in all these three authors "the *mujāhid*'s authority [...] is not based on his scholarship or intellectual credentials, but is essentially metaphysical,"[352] attributing the *inability to err* exclusively to the Salafi-Jihadi enlightened.

The Salafi-Jihadi doctrine shines like a true Gnosis – diagnosis-therapy of human alienation, solution for any problem, cure for any disease, relief from oppression, salvation for humankind. And the enlightened, the *mujāhidūn*, are those in possession of the salvation for themselves and for the whole world, bringing forth the effort of spreading the same awareness in the *umma* and among the most indolent Muslim ("For the first time, the *umma* is waking up,"[353] said an IS sympathizer), in the wait for the End of Time. The compass to follow is that of a perfect and flawless society, the immanent *eschaton*, which can be reached only through the application of Gnosis, defined as "knowledge of the method of transforming being."[354]

But how to apply such a Gnosis? Let us move to the following point of the gnostic pattern in an attempt to answer this question.

4.3.6 *Redemption anyway: political-revolutionary self-redemption*

Once the revolutionary gnostic knows the key to fix what he/she deems wrong with the world, all he/she needs to do is act. No one but him/her can fix things. Applying the salvific knowledge is the only chance for redemption. Driven by the anti-cosmic attitude that grips his/her soul, the gnostic is now focused on turning the world upside down, which will make all sufferings disappear and society thrive as in the golden age. The objective is the transfiguration of the nature of humankind, and everything he/her does is justified on the basis of such a goal – the end justifies the

351 Hossein Ibn Mahmoud, quoted in Alshech, *The Emergence of the 'Infallible Jihad Fighters'*.

352 Alshech, *The Emergence of the 'Infallible Jihad Fighters'*.

353 Wood, *The Way of the Strangers*, chap. 3, Kindle.

354 Eric Voegelin, 'I movimenti gnostici di massa del nostro tempo', in *Il mito del mondo nuovo*, by Eric Voegelin (Milan: Rusconi, 1970), p. 27.

means. As Augusto Del Noce once said, revolution takes the place of grace. The meaning of history is reached following voluntaristic action and thus the will of God is *done* by human beings, in the sense that God is ousted and excluded from the scope of action and thought. Salvation is not provided by the divine but by humankind itself, hence humankind save itself alone. In Eric Voegelin's own words: "The forces of the world-immanent human creatures blend with the transcendental forces of the divinity in an ineffable manner so that the action of man is no longer the action of man but the effectiveness of divine energy working through the human form."[355] God is no more, absorbed as He is by the body of gnostic people.

The application of the Gnosis takes the form of a revolution – a total, complete, devastating revolution that will flip the world, using a degree of violence that knows no restrain. Violence is magic, in the sense that it is rooted in the belief that nature can change its structure following an activist and transformative performance. A gnostic revolution, in fact, is based on a truly magical expectation, that is, the transformation of the nature of society and of the nature of humankind; and certainly such a magic faith has very little of traditional and orthodox.

The last era, the golden age that will precede the end of the world, will result from an entirely human effort, as John Gray writes: "In secular version of the Apocalypse, the new age comes about through human action."[356] A similar proposition reveals, if there were any more need, the secular and, in a more extreme way, the atheist character of any revolutionary gnostic experience, being such position rooted in "the pretension [...] that the historical process necessarily curves in this direction"[357] as a result of a human decision and action.

As a consequence of this mentality, gnostic revolutionaries want to force and compel times, hastening the apocalypse and building here and now the perfect society. Why wait if there is an actual recipe for happiness and for the end of all wars? If history will necessarily go in that direction, why not accelerate and hurry that course, reducing the time humankind lives in the age of total corruption? A gnostic revolution is compassionate and liberating.

355 Eric Voegelin, 'The People of God', in The Collected Works of Eric Voegelin, vol. 22, ed. by David L. Morse and William M. Thompson (Columbia and London: University of Missouri Press, 1998), p. 174.

356 John Gray, *Black Mass. Apocalyptic Religion and the Death of Utopia* (London: Penguin Books, 2008), p. 13.

357 Gianfranco Miglio, *Lezioni di politica. Storia delle dottrine politiche* (Bologna: Il Mulino, 2011), p. 341.

Consequently, gnostic revolutionary politics is the prosecution and the definite fulfillment of God's redeeming act – humanity saves itself, redemption becomes a self-redemption, politics takes on the role of a "soteriological practice,"[358] and the revolution turns in the *last* violence that will put an end to any other violence, for in the third age humankind will be incapable of hurting anyone.

In a Salafi-Jihadi perspective, it is jihad that plays the main role and that dresses the clothes of the soteriological practice *par excellence.* "Revelation in the interests of revolution"[359] is the foundation of Salafi-Jihadism. Reuven Paz writes that

> the Jihadi-Salafis have turned the jihad into a dynamic that purifies Muslim society through a small elitist fighting group. [...] There is a kind of Marxist-Leninist revolutionary touch with the signs of the destruction of the "old society" in favour of building a new type of Muslim and a new Muslim society.[360]

Paz also recognizes the "'magic touch' of violent jihad,"[361] distinguishing its transformative nature that puts it at odds with the classical understanding of the concept.

For the Egyptian radical ideologue Muḥammad ʿAbd al-Salām Faraj, author of *al-Farīḍa al-Ghāʾiba* ("The Neglected Duty",) "the ultimate triumph of Islam has been prophesied, and all that remains is for Muslims to fulfill this prophecy,"[362] to the point that "he comes the closest to seeing jihad as a salvific action, even to the point of reducing Islam to the question of whether or not Muslims fight."[363] In brief, what Faraj comes to believe is that jihad is the sole vehicle for salvation and that whoever participates in this cosmic struggle against the unbelievers is automatically redeemed. The apocalyptic scenario is the natural background of this belligerent thought, and Faraj does not *believe* but actually *knows* the future – history is written

358 Pellicani, *Revolutionary Apocalypse*, p. 20.

359 Hamadi Redissi, *Islam e modernità. L'incontro dell'Islam con l'Occidente* (Verona: Ombre Corte, 2014), p. 90.

360 Reuven Paz, 'Debates Within the Family. Jihadi-Salafi Debates on Strategy, Takfir, Extremism, Suicide Bombings, and the Sense of the Apocalypse', in *Global Salafism. Islam's New Religious Movement*, ed. by Roel Meijer (New York: Oxford University Press, 2013), p. 270.

361 Ibid.

362 David Cook, *Understanding Jihad* (Berkeley: University of California Press, 2005), p. 108.

363 Ibid., p. 110.

and Muslims must fulfill the prophecy. As said in the previous subsections and as David Cook brilliantly summarizes, "dramatic and cataclysmic events are expected to occur – indeed, the believers should *want* them to occur because they herald the passing of the old non-Muslim order and the beginning of the new."[364]

By the same token, Anwar al-ʿAwlaqī (d. 2011), former leader of al-Qāʿida in the Arabian Peninsula (AQAP), writes that

> we know from the *aḥadīth* of the Prophet that disbelief will carry on until the Day of Judgment. Therefore Jihad will also carry on until the Day of Judgment since we are told to wipe out *kufr* from the world. On a side note, Jihad will end when ʿĪsā rules the world. Why's that? Because 'Īsā will fight *kufr* and there will be no more disbelief whatsoever. And after 'Īsā's death, there will be no more Jihad because Allah will take away the souls of the believers and leave all the *kuffār* left on earth to go through the Last Hour. In addition, there is no Jihad against Yāʾjūj and Māʾjūj because there is no capability of fighting them; they will be destroyed by a miracle.[365]

Jihad will lead directly to the Day of Judgment. On this topic, Chetan Bhatt authored an appealing article, delving into the Salafi-Jihadi "virtuous" violence and political universe. He recognizes that Salafi-Jihadism adopts an "extra-territorial cosmic vision,"[366] meaning that

> the conclusive distinction is between the imagined cosmic war and a variety of actual regional and subnational "jihads". It is the latter, collectively, that many western commentators usually refer to as "global jihad", whereas for Salafi-Jihadis these typically represent the temporary materialization of a vaster, more important cosmic conflict (which Salafi-Jihadis indeed refer to as "global jihad") that has nothing to do with regional conflicts in principle.[367]

In this comprehensive view, all local conflicts are hijacked by Salafi-Jihadi actors in order to establish "the sovereignty of primordial, transcendental law over the planet,"[368] that is to say, the immanent *eschaton*, the transfigured humanity, the golden age – echoing Ayman al-Ẓawāhirī's words: "The struggle for the establishment of the Muslim state

---

364 Ibid., p. 158. Italics in the text.

365 Anwar al-'Awlaqī, *Constants in the Path of Jihad by Shaykh Yusuf al-'Uyayree* (n.p.: at-Tibyān Publications, n.d.), p. 19.

366 Chetan Bhatt, 'The Virtues of Violence: The Salafi-Jihadi Political Universe', *Theory, Culture & Society*, vol. 31, no. 1 (2014): p. 35.

367 Ibid.

368 Ibid., p. 36.

cannot be considered a regional struggle."[369] All means are valid as long as they are used in the name of jihad. Whatever action the *mujāhid* must do, "*he will go to heaven anyway*,"[370] he is saved by the simple fact that he joined the ranks of the *mujāhidūn* army. The mere belonging to the "saved sect" guarantees salvation for the militants. In the second number of *Inspire*, AQAP's propaganda magazine, Anwar al-ʿAwlaqī writes that "the prize awaiting the *shahīd* ["martyr"] is Paradise,"[371] regardless of what he/she has really achieved. "Waging jihad against the infidels is the basis of glory,"[372] said Ayman al-Ẓawāhirī. "Neglecting jihad [...] is a grievous sin,"[373] adds bin Laden.

Abū Ḥamza al-Maqdisī (d. 2018), one of the leaders of the self-proclaimed Islamic State in the Sinai Peninsula, describes the Salafi-Jihadi task as following: "Our aim is clear. It is to spread Islamic *sharīʿa* among the sons of our people through the ways for which Islam calls, to repel evil, and to perform jihad."[374] Combating evil becomes a self-assigned task, taken over by a group of fighters and torn from the hands of God. Jihad takes on metaphysical connotations.

A curious personality in the Salafi-Jihadi galaxy is Yūsuf al-ʿUyayrī, first leader of AQAP, for whom, as we have said above, the *mujāhid* has a superior knowledge and a stronger insight into reality (*wāqiʿ*). After a deep analysis of al-ʿUyayrī's work, Roel Maijer acknowledges that, for al-ʿUyayrī, "transforming reality (*taghyīr al-wāqiʿ*) is the real goal of jihad."[375] In his intellectual work, it is possible to clearly discern gnostic tones. First of all, the "victorious group" (*al-ṭāʾifa al-manṣūra*), which possesses superior knowledge thanks to its involvement in the jihad, "have the task to 'enlighten' the people"[376] and to lead the *umma* in the struggle against Evil (with the capital letter). The following quotation is crucial for the general discourse: according to Yūsuf al-ʿUyayrī,

369 Al-Ẓawāhirī, 'Knights under the Prophet's Banner', p. 201.
370 Meijer, 'Re-Reading al-Qaeda', p. 17.
371 *Inspire*, n. 2 (October 2010): p. 64.
372 Al-Ẓawāhirī, 'Jihad, Martyrdom, and the Killing of Innocents', p. 161.
373 Osama bin Laden, 'Bin Laden's Truce Offer to the Americans', in *The Al Qaeda Reader. The Essential Texts of Osama Bin Laden's Terrorist Organization*, ed. by Raymond Ibrahim (New York: Broadway Books, 2007), p. 225.
374 Abū Hamza al-Maqdisī, 'Gaza Salafist Leader Abu Hamza Al-Maqdisi, Interview On Salafi Jihadi Groups in Gaza, Ramallah, 20 August 2009', *Journal of Palestine Studies*, vol. 39, no. 4 (Summer 2010): p. 163.
375 Roel Meijer, 'Yūsuf al-'Uyairī and the Making of a Revolutionary Salafi Praxis', *Die Welt Des Islams*, vol. 47, issue 3-4 (November 2007): p. 424.
376 Ibid., pp. 442-443.

> Jihadism has the additional advantage of ending alienation. By being both an individual achievement in resisting all forms of temptation and overcoming personal trials, Jihadism leads to a personal achievement of salvation and redemption, while at the same time submitting the individual to the superior forces, the collectivity following the will of God, or embodied in laws of history – in the Marxist case – or the general good *(al-maṣlaḥa al-ʿāmma)*, *tawḥīd* or *ʿaqīda* in the Salafist case. In this sense, like Marxism, the Salafist causes constitute a form of sublimation, liberation, or even in a more mystical sense, self-abnegation, self-transcendence and redemption.[377]

I would add: self-redemption.

This activist dimension of salvation is strongly stressed by al-ʿUyayrī. Meijer continues by saying that "in general political terms, jihad is the ultimate creative modernist project of total destruction in order to build a new world of total submission to an ideal, a concept of absolute purity. In its violence it creates a *tabula rasa* for a new beginning."[378]

Basically, Yūsuf al-ʿUyayrī depicts a jihad that is eternal, since it will not have an end before God's laws are inherited throughout the whole earth; that is unlimited and boundless, applicable in every time and space; that is not defensive nor offensive but a combination of the two; that could employ any means of offense and resistance; and that is, in brief, "more than a physical struggle."[379] This worldview promises individual and collective redemption as well as a new reality as a result of the destructive action of the *mujāhidūn*. Prometheusly transforming reality and actively achieving redemption are the two fundamental operations that lie at the basis of revolutionary Gnosticism.

God is banished: it is no longer Him to provide salvation to humankind nor to create and recreate the world to His liking. Even though Salafi-Jihadis speak of God, it seems that the army of the *mujāhidūn* has taken His place. After all, the salvific knowledge (diagnosis-therapy of human alienation) is already in their hands and the future is unveiled to their eyes. Salafi-Jihadism "reduces the moral visions and civilizing experience of Islam to only a dynamic of power,"[380] flattening the spiritual depth of Islam on a merely secular and earthly level.

From what has been said, it is evident in Salafi-Jihadi thought the presence of "the need for a 'shared *eschaton*', a salvation to be achieved thanks to

---

377 Ibid., p. 444.
378 Ibid., p. 447.
379 Ibid., p. 449.
380 David A. Charters, 'Something Old, Something New…? Al Qaeda, Jihadism, and Fascism', *Terrorism and Political Violence*, vol. 19, no. 1 (2007): p. 74.

the action of the *umma*, brought by the hand of some believers elected by God:"[381] the divine election is the psychological mechanism through which a religious group masks its Promethean and voluntary action – the same as the Anabaptists and the Puritans, and which is common to the Bolsheviks as well, who were persuaded to embody and personify the laws of history. For these and other experiences, "the omnipotence of God can be transferred entirely to the faithful,"[382] and humankind "replaces God, to dispose, at least for a moment, of His annihilating power." [383] Indeed, "by viewing their actions as divinely mandated, jihadis can carry out inhumanities on a massive scale, secure in the belief that they are not personally culpable for them."[384] Fethi Benslama coined the notion of "super-Muslim" to describe this very attitude; he explains it as the posture of those who "conceive themselves as voices of God, […] who submit themselves to God by subjecting Him to themselves,"[385] and who carry out the so-called "'incest man-God', since a human being claims to be confused with his alleged creator to the point of acting in His name."[386]

The Salafi-Jihadi individuals legitimate themselves to purify the world. They see themselves as political and religious saviors and, as Barry Cooper reminds us, "for spiritually disordered individuals violence is not, as Arendt argued, a pragmatic mode of human activity. It is a magic instrument capable of transfiguring reality."[387] Their violent actions (murdering, killing, kidnapping, raping…) are intended to be both altruistic and sacrificial[388] – "jihad is a collective act of worship,"[389] said ʿAbdallāh ʿAzzām – in line with their pneumpathological personality. In a gnostic perspective, altruistic killing converts into altruistic genocide, which in

381 Francesco Furlan, *La figura del Mahdī. All'incrocio dei tre monoteismi* (Rome: Aracne, 2015), p. 313.
382 Martelli, *Teologia del terrore*, p. 55.
383 Di Cesare, *Terrore e modernità*, p. 70.
384 Simon Cottee, 'Mind Slaughter: The Neutralizations of Jihadi Salafism', *Studies in Conflict & Terrorism*, vol. 33, issue 4 (2010): p. 341. Cottee quotes the following passage of al-Qāʿida's declaration of war against Americans to prove his point: "By Allah's leave we call upon every Muslim who believes in Allah and wishes to be rewarded *to comply with Allah's order* to kill the Americans and seize their money wherever and whenever they find them" ('Al-Qaeda's Declaration of War Against Americans', p. 13. Emphasis added).
385 Benslama, *Un furioso desiderio di sacrificio*, pp. 74-75.
386 Ibid., p. 75.
387 Cooper, *New Political Religions*, p. 25.
388 See, for example, *Rumiyah*, n. 1 (September 2016): p. 34: "The kafir's blood is halal to you, so shed it."
389 ʿAzzām, *Join the Caravan*, p. 28.

turn is "a prelude to altruistic omnicide."[390] Salafi-Jihadi violence "serves a purifying aim, bent ultimately on participating a cosmic struggle and the end of times."[391]

Graem Wood explains that "the Islamic State [and other Salafi-Jihadi actors] preyed on a constant feeling of self-incrimination, a reminder that no life is sinless. […] They then weaponized that fanatical sense of shame by declaring their jihad the only absolution."[392] Absolution through jihad, then.

Salafi-Jihadis, in their effort to speed up the end of time, assume a gnostic attitude, in the sense that they are forcing and antedating the end of times by the fulfillment of the prophecies. It is a real *acceleration of the divine plan*, virtually legislating over God's laws, in the certainty of being already saved due to the total adhesion to the salvific plan of jihad. Salafi-Jihadism gives *propulsive* force to a "*retrospective* utopia"[393] since, on the one hand, it aspires to go back to the golden era of the *al-rāshidūn* Caliphs ("Let's have a look at the terminology used by Islamic integralism: the word 'rebirth' often recurs"),[394] and, on the other, the objective is to bring about the future of the end of the world. In this way, the full revolutionary potential of this ideology is triggered, and revolutionary Gnosticism emerges as the engine of such a political and meta-political project.

It is in the light of these considerations that it becomes possible to realize the co-presence of two apparently conflicting attitudes: "The themes of indiscriminate, cleansing, cosmic violence co-exist with ones obsessed with authoritarian order."[395] The tension between apocalypse and order, between anarchism and fascism (broadly understood), acquires meaning only against the background provided by revolutionary Gnosticism, for which before the final collapse, the perfect society and political construction must arise. Rational state-building logic is consistent with a true apocalyptic thinking: the Caliphate, that is to say, the perfect and ultimate Islamic society, is a temporary structure that has the function of accelerating the Final Judgement, leading to an – eschatological but immanent – situation

390 Cooper, *New Political Religions*, p. 68.

391 Audrey Borowski, 'Al Qaeda and ISIS: From Revolution to Apocalypse', *Philosophy Now*, issue 111 (December 2015), https://philosophynow.org/issues/111/Al_Qaeda_and_ISIS_From_Revolution_to_Apocalypse (accessed December 8, 2016).

392 Wood, *The Way of the Strangers*, chap. 2, Kindle.

393 Massimo Campanini, *Il pensiero islamico contemporaneo* (Bologna: Il Mulino, 2009), p. 163.

394 Luigi Zoja, *Nella mente di un terrorista* (Turin: Einaudi, 2017), p. 59.

395 Bhatt, 'The Virtues of Violence', p. 44.

of liberation from all the oppressive structures. Salafi-Jihadis "perceive themselves belonging to an apocalyptic movement as a way to reverse their situation, a sort of revival of the class struggle."[396] And in fact,

> as an ideology, the Salafi-jihad has much in common with radical leftist ideologies of 20th century Europe. Like the radical left, the Salafi-jihad describes its action in part as a revolt against injustice, and it rejects bourgeois values, imperialism and materialism. The goal of both the leftist movements and Salafi-jihadists is essentially an elusive quest to help bring about a more just society – violence is seen as a justified means to an end. Both Salafi-jihadists and radical leftist revolutionaries believe that the scope of their activities and the importance of their actions are global in nature, as are their goals. As Stephen Holmes observed, for Salafi-jihadists the caliphate "is the religious equivalent of Marx's Communist utopia."[397]

The only remark I would like to make about the quote is that Salafi-Jihadism is not a quest for a *more just* society but for the *best* society ever.

To conclude, it is evident that individual and collective redemption is achieved through the participation in a global jihad with metaphysical connotations – hence, it is no longer a redemption given by God to pious faithful, but it is a true self-redemption accomplished following a political-revolutionary action aimed at creating a *tabula rasa* of current *jāhiliyya* to make room for the restored golden age of the *al-Salaf al-Ṣāliḥ*, creating a paradise on earth. The *mujāhid* is immediately saved, meaning that he/she does not need the mediation of any particular prayer or pious act to get to heaven. It is true that all these traditional operations are asked to be performed within Salafi-Jihadi circles; nevertheless, absolution passes through jihad only due to the fact that all those Muslims across the globe who do not adhere to the cause of Salafi-Jihadism are deemed as *murtad*s if not *kuffār*, and consequently damned. In the concise words of bin Laden: "The peak of this religion is jihad."[398]

4.3.7 *The world like a chessboard: sociological dualism*

The corollary of the previous five points is that if one group, the chosen one, possesses the salvific knowledge and is willing to implement it in order to save humankind in its entirety, all the other people, consequently,

---

396 Ignacio Rojas Gálvez, *I simboli dell'apocalisse* (Bologna: EDB, 2016), p. 212.

397 Assaf Moghadam, 'The Salafi-Jihad as a Religious Ideology', *CTC Sentinel*, vol. 1, issue 2 (February 2008): p. 15.

398 Bin Laden, 'From Somalia to Afghanistan', p. 49.

are considered to be ignorant and evil as long as they slow down and even prevent the application of the gnostic plan over earth. Therefore, there are only two camps, the good and the bad, according to a black/white mentality that leaves outside of its purview all the existing shades of grey. And if light is embodied by the revolutionary gnostics, darkness is the environment of all those who live in the ignorance of the "truth". Hence, those who do not possess the Gnosis are not only simple political adversaries but rather cosmic enemies that should not only be defeated but totally annihilated – which configuration follows a Schmittean approach according to which the enemy is now an "absolute" enemy. The enemy is stripped of his/her humanity and may be killed in a multitude of ways, in that to eradicate the enemy of the "truth" is assimilated to the action of a medical doctor who fights a disease. "The more intense the violence is, the more it seems benevolent, since it saves time of pain."[399]

It is no secret that a Manichaean worldview is present in Salafi-Jihadism. "The jihadist education denies the existence of a third category alongside that of Good and Evil."[400] The Salafi-Jihadi legion follows the right path, whereas all others are driving humanity to the brink of perdition. The best description of this sharp division is found in the first issue of *Dābiq* magazine:

> The world today has been divided into two camps and two trenches, with no third camp present: the camp of Islam and faith, and the camp of *kufr* (disbelief) and hypocrisy – the camp of the Muslims and the *mujāhidūn* everywhere, and the camp of the Jews, the crusaders, their allies, and with them the rest of the nations and religions of *kufr*, all being led by America and Russia, and being mobilized by the Jews.[401]

Similarly, Osama bin Laden said: "I say that there are two sides in the struggle: one side is the global Crusader alliance with the Zionist Jews, led by America, Britain, and Israel, and the other side is the Islamic world."[402]

The first thing that stands out from these quotations is the clear-cut division between two camps. In a certain sense, this partition of the world is traditional: the division among *dār al-islām* (house of Islam) and *dār al-ḥarb* (house of war) "start occurring frequently with Ṭabarī's *Tafsīr*

---

399 Jean Guitton, *Il puro e l'impuro* (Casale Monferrato: Piemme, 1993), p. 31.

400 Orsini, *ISIS*, p. 130.

401 *Dābiq*, n. 1 (July 2014): p. 10.

402 Osama bin Laden, 'A Muslim Bob', in *Messages to the World. The Statements of Osama bin Laden*, ed. by Bruce Lawrence (London and New York: Verso, 2005), p. 73.

(fourth/tenth century)"[403] and it refers to the legal distinction between two areas, the one governed by *sharīʿa* and the other under the domination of *kufr*. Then it entered the mainstream of Islamic vocabulary, even though "not even the jurists who coined these terms and used them widely in their writings gave a definition or dealt with them in a separate section."[404] This fact gave a wide margin of interpretation, and these concepts became easy prey to the ideological reinterpretation made by Salafism-Jihadism.

According to Osama bin Laden, "the crusaders and the Jews have joined together to invade the heart of *dār al-Islām*,"[405] leaving the boundaries assigned to them by historical contingencies and teaming up against Islam. Interestingly, bin Laden "has repeatedly cited President George W. Bush's 20 September 2001 proclamation, 'Either you are with us, or you are with the terrorists' as 'proof' of the existence of the two worlds."[406] The two narratives – the one pertaining to the so-called War on Terror and the other referring to global jihad – reciprocally intermingle and support each other.

A similar radical and uncompromising dichotomous worldview makes Salafi-Jihadis believe that a cosmic coalition exists and that is ready to eradicate Islam from the earth. In particular, the Western involvements in Palestine, Iraq, Afghanistan, Chechnya, Bosnia, Somalia, Pakistan, Libya and other places are seen to be part of a long-lasting crusade: "These battles cannot be viewed in any case whatsoever as isolated battles, but rather, as part of a chain of the long, fierce, and ugly crusader war,"[407] bin Laden denounces. In line with this reasoning, bin Laden talks of a *Jewish-*

---

403 Giovanna Calasso, 'Introduction: Concepts, Words, Historical Realities of a "Classical" Dichotomy', in *Dār al-islām/dār al-ḥarb. Territories, People, Identities*, eds. by Giovanna Calasso and Giuliano Lancioni (Leiden and Boston: Brill, 2017), p. 4.

404 Ibid., p. 2.

405 Osama bin Laden, 'Al-Qa'ida Recruitment Video (2000)', in *Anti-American Terrorism and the Middle East*, eds. Barry Rubin and Judith Colp Rubin (New York: Oxford University Press, 2002), p. 174.

406 Joseph J. Hobbs, 'The Geographical Dimensions of al-Qa'ida Rhetoric', *The Geographical Review*, vol. 95, no. 3 (July 2005): p. 308. In a 2002 interview to Al-Jazeera, bin Laden declared that "Bush stated that the world has to be divided in two: Bush and his supporters, and any country that doesn't get into the global crusade is with the terrorists. What terrorism is clearer than this?" ('Transcript of Bin Laden's October Interview', *CNN*, February 5, 2002, http://edition.cnn.com/2002/WORLD/asiapcf/south/02/05/binladen.transcript/).

407 Osama bin Laden, 'Bin Laden Rails Against Crusaders and UN', *BBC*, November 3, 2001, http://news.bbc.co.uk/2/hi/world/monitoring/media_reports/1636782.stm.

Crusader alliance, the "international alliance of evil,"[408] a sort of cosmic army that is destined to clash with the *mujāhidūn*, "waiting for excuses to launch its wars of extermination against Muslims"[409] ("this battle is not between al-Qaeda and the U.S. This is a battle of Muslims against the global Crusaders")[410]. This Christian-Jewish conspiracy[411] against Islam is called "the greater external enemy"[412] and it is at the basis of "a recurring war,"[413] namely, the "struggle between Truth and Falsehood, until Allah Almighty inherits the earth and those who live on it."[414]

Salafi-Jihadis "present jihad and self-sacrifice as the antithesis to everything the West stands for."[415] Abū Ayman al-Hilālī, a Saudi al-Qāʿida-affiliate writer, once said that "the vital contradiction to the Zionist and American enemy is the doctrine of jihad and martyrdom."[416] The divergence and contradiction between the two blocks is total, and Yūsuf

---

408 Bin Laden, 'To the Muslims of Iraq', p. 246. Ayman al-Ẓawāhirī even lists the tools the alleged crusaders adopt to fight Islam: "The United Nations; the friendly rulers of the Muslim peoples; the multinational corporations; the international communications and data exchange systems; the international news agencies and satellite media channels; the international relief agencies, which are being used as a cover for espionage, proselytizing, coup planning, and the transfer of weapons" (Ayman al-Ẓawāhirī, 'Why Attack America (January 2002)', in *Anti-American Terrorism and the Middle East*, eds. Barry Rubin and Judith Colp Rubin [New York: Oxford University Press, 2002], p. 132).

409 Al-Qāʿida, 'A Statement From Qaidat al-Jihad Regarding the Mandates of the Heroes and the Legality of the Operations in New York and Washington', *DSpace -Digital Repository Unimib*, April 24, 2002, https://scholarship.tricolib.brynmawr.edu/handle/10066/4796 (accessed 21 March, 2017).

410 Osama bin Laden, 'The Afghan Soviet Paradigm', in *The Al Qaeda Reader. The Essential Texts of Osama Bin Laden's Terrorist Organization*, ed. by Raymond Ibrahim (New York: Broadway Books, 2007), p. 262.

411 More than once bin Laden declared that "the Jewish lobby has taken America and the West hostage" ('The Zionist Lobby', in *The Al Qaeda Reader. The Essential Texts of Osama Bin Laden's Terrorist Organization*, ed. by Raymond Ibrahim [New York: Broadway Books, 2007], p. 276).

412 Osama bin Laden, 'Interview With Usama bin Laden (December 1998)', in *Anti-American Terrorism and the Middle East*, eds. by Barry Rubin and Judith Colp Rubin (New York: Oxford University Press, 2002), p. 155.

413 Osama bin Laden, 'Transcript of Bin Laden's October Interview'.

414 Al-Ẓawāhirī, 'Ayman al-Zawahiri Interview Four Years After 9/11', p. 182.

415 Assaf Moghadam, 'Motives for Martyrdom. Al-Qaida, Salafi Jihad, and the Spread of Suicide Attacks', *International Security*, vol. 33, no 3 (Winter 2008/09): p. 62.

416 Cited in Reuven Paz, *Qa'idat Al-Jihad. A New Name on the Road to Palestine* (Herzliya: International Policy Institute for Counter-Terrorism, 2002), http://publikationen.ub.uni-frankfurt.de/oai/container/index/docId/12025 (accessed July 6, 2019).

al-ʿUyayrī frames this struggle in terms of a conflict "between the program of truth (*manhaj al-ḥaqq*) and the program of falsehood (*manhaj al-bāṭil*) or Western program (*manhaj al-gharb*)."[417]

Among the five essential characteristics of Salafi-Jihadism that Shiraz Maher lists in his book (*tawḥīd*, *ḥākimiyya*, *al-walāʾ wa-l-barāʾ*, jihad, and *takfīr*), those that meet sociological dualism are two, and namely, *al-walāʾ wa-l-barāʾ* and *takfīr*: the former sets the boundaries and the right distance between the two blocks, whereas the latter monitors who is or is not Muslim, policing the correct collocation of each individual on the correct side and, if need be, disqualifying some alleged Muslim to place him/her among the ranks of the enemy.

The "nefarious Zionist-Crusader plot to annihilate Muslims"[418] must be dismantled and eradicated once and for all. Today, al-Ẓawāhirī maintains, "a clash between it [the Salafi-Jihadi movement] and the Jewish-US alliance is inevitable."[419] There is no third party but Muslims and their enemies. The opponent is dehumanized and Satanized, irrevocably transformed into a diabolical force. The enemy is an "ethic and ontological threat"[420] for the Muslim community because in the Salafi-Jihadi vision "the distinction between adversary (*inimicus*) and enemy (*hostis*) has no value in itself."[421]

Neither peace treaties nor temporary alliances are possible between the two groups, in that any hesitation would slow down and retard the regeneration of humankind. The revolutionary gnostic is uncompromising and categorical and against any possibility of peaceful coexistence: the only viable way is revolution, while all the reformist approaches (such as the Muslim Brotherhood's) are considered ineffective, useless, harmful and, above all, to be solutions that betray Islam. There is no space for opportunist positions. Yet, in the Islamic theological elaboration "from very early on, another juridical category was established, called *dār ul-ʿahd* (the domain of treaties), that allowed for peaceful trade and social intercourse

417 Meijer, 'Yūsuf al-'Uyairī', p. 436.

418 Quintan Wiktorowicz and John Kaltner, 'Killing in the Name of Islam: Al-Qaeda's Justification for September 11', *Middle East Policy*, vol. 10, no. 2 (Summer 2003): p. 85.

419 Al-Ẓawāhirī, 'Knights under the Prophet's Banner', p.135.

420 Paolo Maggiolini and Andrea Plebani, 'La centralità del nemico nel califfato di al-Baghdadi', in *Il marketing del terrore. Twitter e jihad: la comunicazione dell'ISIS*, eds. by Monica Maggioni and Paolo Magri (Milan: Mondadori, 2016), p. 78.

421 Ibid., p. 49.

between Muslim and non-Muslim territories."[422] Well, this notion is totally wiped out, removed, and cancelled from the language of Salafi-Jihadism.

Even regular Western citizens should be killed because they participate in the democratic life of their own countries, backing the decisions the government takes including those regarding the policy in the Middle East. More than once, several Salafi-Jihadi personalities have denounced this situation in order to justify violent attacks against civilians. For instance, in November 2001, just after 9/11, bin Laden said that

> the American people should remember that they pay taxes to their government, they elect their president, their government manufactures arms and gives them to Israel and Israel uses them to massacre Palestinians. The American Congress endorses all government measures, and this proves that all of America is responsible for the atrocities perpetrated against Muslims. All of America, because they elect the Congress.[423]

Hence, civilians are guilty of having chosen tyrannical leaders, although not themselves directly responsible for the aggression against Muslims.

Salafi-Jihadism dehumanizes the enemies and considers them inferior in all respects; "they are defined not as individuals, but solely in terms of a derogatory collective master status: they are, variously, 'infidels', 'unbelievers', 'kufir', 'apostates', 'pagans', 'Satan-worshipers', 'godless', and 'slags'."[424] Curiously, "to see the world in Islamic terms, as [radically] divided between *dar al-Islam* and *dar al-harb*, is not so different from seeing it in Marxist terms, as divided between a socialist world and a capitalist imperialist world."[425] This, in fact, is a common feature among all the gnostic phenomena I have listed above, namely, radical Anabaptism, Puritanism, Jacobinism, Nazism and Bolshevism. The world is a chessboard with black and white boxes and only two armies facing each other. The annihilation of the enemy through the magic and transformative revolutionary jihad would result in a palingenesis for the whole universe and in the restoration of the golden age, the last step in human history before the End of Time. At that moment, Islam will thrive and the *umma* will dominate the earth.

---

422 Talal Asad, *On Suicide Bombing* (New York: Columbia University Press, 2007), p. 12.

423 Osama bin Laden, 'The Price of American Democracy', in *The Al Qaeda Reader. The Essential Texts of Osama Bin Laden's Terrorist Organization*, ed. by Raymond Ibrahim (New York: Broadway Books, 2007), p. 282.

424 Cottee, 'Mind Slaughter', p. 341.

425 Thomas Hodgkin, 'The Revolutionary Tradition in Islam', *History Workshop*, no. 10 [Autumn 1980]: p. 149.

CONCLUSION

Salafi-Jihadism is a "conservative, millenarian, Wahhabi, pan-Islamic, apocalyptic, conspiratorial, neo-fundamentalist, and counter-hegemonic"[1] ideology, a revolutionary theory and practice based on a world-shaping project which promises the regeneration of humanity and, by assuming a backward-looking posture, seeks both to recreate the model Islamic community of the golden era (the first three generations after the Prophet) and to hasten the advent of the Mahdī (the Muslim eschatological savior) in view of the End of Time. In other words, it aspires at restoring the golden era of Islam by means of violence – jihad as a revolution.

From this brief and concise description, the fact that Salafi-Jihadism is a revolutionary gnostic construction comes to the fore. Salvation is reached through human action, and the jihadi army – the army of *those who know* – has the task of taking humanity to the apocalypse.

The first conclusion is that "religion plays a key role in Islamist movements, but not due to doctrinal specifies or the religiosity of Islamists."[2] As a matter of fact, even other gnostic revolutionaries such as the radical Anabaptists and the Puritans were nominally Christians, but they also shared a gnostic worldview. The same could be said of Salafi-Jihadis, whose background is certainly Islamic but whose mentality and approach are gnostic.

Hence, Islam is the environment where revolutionary Gnosticism accidentally found the possibility of growing and emerging, exploiting the spaces of freedom of interpretation left open by the process of secularization. As Paolo Branca says, "Many of the current Islamist movements share with the modernizing reformers the criticism of *taqlīd* (spirit of imitation) and base their strength precisely on direct access to

1 John Turner, 'From Cottage Industry to International Organisation: The Evolution of Salafi-Jihadism and the Emergence of the Al Qaeda Ideology', *Terrorism and Political Violence*, vol. 22, no. 4 (September 2010): p. 553.

2 Anne Marie Baylouny, 'Emotions, Poverty, or Politics? Misconceptions About Islamist Movements', *Connections. The Quarterly Journal*, vol. 3, no. 1 (March 2004): p. 46.

the scriptures, without relying on the mediation previously assured by the class of the *'ulamā'* and on the canonical forms of their teachings."[3] This means that Islam is the actual background where revolutionary Gnosticism found the perfect conditions for emerging once again into the appearance of a new revolutionary force.

The definition of a gnostic pattern consisting of six features has proved to be a useful tool for framing revolutionary phenomena in gnostic terms, making it possible to exclude some political experiences from the "gnostic family" (for instance, Italian Fascism is left out because it "did not aim to remodel humanity"[4] nor did it mean to bring about the *eschaton* and free humankind from all evils.)

Once the presence of all six points of the gnostic pattern was found within the ideological narrative of Salafi-Jihadism, it was rather intuitive to equate this extreme Islamist ideology to revolutionary Gnosticism. The conclusion is that Salafi-Jihadism adopts a gnostic mindset and a non-Islamic framework, even though it is articulated in Islamic terms.

In fact, there are many postulates of the activist understanding of redemption given by the gnostic *Weltanshauung* that conflict with Islam, e.g., the fact that humankind saves itself, that the perfect era will be established by global and cosmic violence, that a so sharp and insurmountable distinction between people exists, that there is a salvific knowledge that allows people to know what is wrong with the world and how to remedy that. From these remarks, the inconsistency of Salafi-Jihadism with the very religion of Islam is apparent, despite the heavy application of traditional Islamic ideas by its ideologues and militants.

In the revolutionary gnostic understanding, Gnosis is the "science of self-redemption of humanity,"[5] being both a diagnosis and a therapy. But this kind of definition discloses the atheist character of all gnostic activists even when they claim to act in the name of religious purposes; indeed, self-salvation is incompatible with a divine redeemer – and the claim of fulfilling God's plan is equally atheist, since it tends to hasten the times fixed by God.

Talking of fundamentalist movements, Shmuel Eisenstadt says that "although apparently traditional, these movements are, in a somewhat paradoxical way, anti-traditional. This is because they deny the existing

3 Paolo Branca, *Moschee inquiete. Tradizionalisti, innovatori, fondamentalisti nella cultura islamica* (Bologna: Il Mulino, 2003), p. 24.

4 John Gray, *Black Mass. Apocalyptic Religion and the Death of Utopia* (London: Penguin Books, 2008), p. 55.

5 Luciano Pellicani, *La società dei giusti. Parabola storica dello Gnosticismo rivoluzionario* (Soveria Mannelli: Rubbettino, 2012), p. 281.

tradition, with its complexity and heterogeneity, while supporting a strongly ideological conception of tradition as a principle above the social and cognitive organization."[6] The same is true for Salafi-Jihadism.

To sum up, on the one side, the gnostic anthropological type is defined by the six characteristics included in the gnostic pattern, i.e., anti-cosmism, tripartition of history, immanentizing of the *eschaton*, Gnosis, political-revolutionary self-redemption, and sociological dualism; on the other side, Salafi-Jihadism is identified by the presence of five concepts, *tawḥīd*, *ḥākimiyya, al-walāʾ wa-l-barāʾ*, jihad, and *takfīr*. The narrative of the Salafi-Jihadi activist, who is also a gnostic revolutionary, is the following: the world is corrupted and degraded (anti-cosmism), but in the past there was a golden era that a group of enlightened who possess the knowledge of the mystery of evil and the mystery of history (Gnosis) can restore (tripartition of history) through a violent and total revolution (political-revolutionary self-redemption, jihad) waged against the infidels and those who do not possess true knowledge (sociological dualism, *al-walāʾ wa-l-barāʾ, takfīr)* in order to reduce to an artificial unity the whole of humanity *(tawḥīd*); the restauration of the golden era will transfigure humankind (immanentizing of the *eschaton*) and will make Islam thrive (*ḥākimiyya)* in the wait for the End of Time (tripartition of history in its apocalyptic consequence).

The Salafi-Jihadi ideology so exposed reveals its very nature, that is to say, a Promethean, activist and atheist conception of the world that stands in the forgetfulness of a pure transcendent dimension, notwithstanding the constant references to God and to Paradise. In the appendix of the present book, Luciano Pellicani even argues that revolutionary Gnosticism is a form of Satanism for the simple reason that it proposes the exact reversal of the model of spiritual salvation that monotheistic religions provide – the savior is no longer God, the Creator, but humankind, the created.[7]

---

6 Shmuel N. Eisenstadt, *Fondamentalismo e modernità. Eterodossie, utopismo, giacobinismo nella costruzione dei movimenti fondamentalisti* (Rome-Bari: Laterza, 1994), pp. 58-59.

7 We must be careful in using all these labels. In commenting the first draft of this book, Giacomo Samek Lodovici pointed out that atheism and Satanism are two opposing conceptions, since Satanism is a form of theism (traditionally, Satan rebels against God), while atheism is the negation of God. In light of this useful clarification, the claim that revolutionary Gnosticism is a form of Satanism should be intended in the minimal meaning expressed above, that is to say, as the reversal of the model of spiritual salvation of all monotheistic religions – in other and more simplistic words, man that saves himself. In the same vein, saying that revolutionary Gnosticism is a form of atheism should be understood in the minimal sense that once that man saves himself, then God is no more, He becomes

In a very interesting study, Hendrik Hansen and Peter Kainz compare the thought of Sayyid Quṭb to Marxism and Nazism. They find the same structure underlying the three thoughts in question: a declining history, a particular group of people that will save the world, and the final restauration of the utopia "of the classless society, the natural race struggle, or the purified society of followers of the true faith."[8] But the most remarkable point of the research is the identification of Islamism as a materialist ideology:

> Reducing Islam to a struggle of believers' self-assertion against external evil is basically reducing the spiritual struggle of man with his faith in God (and therefore with his own evil) to an earthly struggle between good and evil men (believers and unbelievers). The focus on this earthly struggle implies a rejection of transcendence. […] Quṭb falls back on the position which he was so desperately fighting against: materialism.[9]

In a thought-provoking book published in 2009 by Ernst Nolte, *Die Dritte Radikale Widerstands-Bewegung: Der Islamismus* (*The Third Radical Resistance Movement: Islamism*), Islamism is compared to Nazism and Communism for having a common inner logic: "A small group that, based on theological or historical-philosophical principles, aspires to bring a lasting salvation to the ruined world […] so as to put an end to the corrupt and conflicting servitude of some men by other men and thus carry humanity to the supreme peace."[10] In this view, radical Islamism is a real revolutionary ideology:

> There is no greater error than to consider Islamism as a new form of that "reaction" condemned by history to failure. What could sound more revolutionary and progressive than this phrase by Maududi?: "Islam is a revolutionary and ideological project that wants to change the social order of the whole world and rebuild it according to its principles and ideals."[11]

---

actually ineffective in the everyday life of the gnostic, who will thus act like there was no God. The immanentization of the *eschaton* is total: although radical Islamists talk also of a further and divine reality, their project concerns this-world only, and religion becomes an ideology.

8 Hendrik Hanse and Peter Kainz, 'Radical Islamism and Totalitarian Ideology: A Comparison of Sayyid Qutb's Islamism with Marxism and National Socialism', *Totalitarian Movements and Political Religions*, vol. 8, no. 1 (March 2007): p. 68.

9 Ibid., p. 69.

10 Ernst Nolte, *Il terzo radicalismo. Islam e Occidente nel XXI secolo* (2009; repr., Rome: Liberal Edizioni, 2012), p. 199.

11 Ibid., p. 204.

These two studies reveal that Salafi-Jihadism and the materialistic ideologies of the 20th-century share the same intellectual framework, though on different doctrinal basis.

The rejection of transcendence is the main finding of similar comparisons, and it is precisely what allows us to frame Salafi-Jihadism as an atheist ideology. The gnostic mentality, common to all these phenomena, is pervasive in every discourse and treatise of ideologues and militants of al-Qāʿida and the Islamic State.

In conclusion, Salafi-Jihadism "is the ideology of a transnational contemporary movement which has assumed the form of a new totalitarianism,"[12] and "what is clear is that [...] it remains an extremely resilient soteriology. Despite domestic repression, civil war, and an international 'War on Terror', it has endured and survived more than three decades of forceful repression."[13] Salafi-Jihadism is the last and desperate attempt to find an all-encompassing meaning for individual and social life by building it with arms and with violence on earth. It is extremely difficult to confront it in that it necessitates first of all a *struggle of ideas*, as it was the challenge with Communism. It is not possible to overcome Salafi-Jihadism by relying only on a military war; first and foremost, what is needed is an intellectual struggle, for Salafi-Jihadism "is primarily a cultural phenomenon, and cultural phenomena are not destroyed by bombs."[14] For this specific reason, the present research fits also the counter-narrative strategy for countering violent extremism: by exposing the gnostic character of Salafi-Jihadism, its grip on people could be less strong, especially because of the activist nature of individual and collective salvation – God is left behind and humankind takes His place. Hence, the present research provides an innovative framework to unmask the ideology of Salafi-Jihadism by showing that its true nature is a distortion of Islamic values inspired by a gnostic mindset that undermines the salvific power of religious precepts, resulting in the "modernization of the concept of jihad in an activist sense."[15]

---

12 Bassam Tibi, 'The Totalitarianism of Jihadist Islamism and its Challenge to Europe and to Islam', *Totalitarian Movements and Political Religions*, vol. 8, no. 1 (March 2007): p. 45.

13 Shiraz Maher, *Salafi-Jihadism: The History of an Idea* (London: Hurst & Company, 2016), p. 211.

14 Alessandro Orsini, *ISIS. I terroristi più fortunati del mondo e tutto ciò che è stato fatto per favorirli* (Milan: Rizzoli, 2016), p. 241.

15 Enzo Pace and Renzo Guolo, *I fondamentalismi* (Rome-Bari: Laterza, 2002), p. 35.

Although this new framing improves our understanding of the phenomenon, it does not exhaust the topic, leaving outside of its scope many other issues to be addressed. For example, it would be interesting to undertake a serious sociological analysis to compare the social and economic context where Salafi-Jihadism flourished with all other gnostic experiences mentioned above. A similar study would integrate the present research and give strength to the claim that Salafi-Jihadism is a gnostic phenomenon born as a reaction to the processes of modernization and secularization – which is a statement that has been made throughout these pages but that nonetheless would need a specific study.

Also, it would be significant to investigate the relevance of Islamic theological and doctrinal concepts belonging to the tradition of the four Sunni schools of law (Ḥanafī, Mālikī, Shāfiʿī, Ḥanbali) and of the mystical practices of Sufism in relation to revolutionary Gnosticism. By defining Salafi-Jihadism in revolutionary gnostic terms, and by saying that its intimate goal is comprised exclusively in the realm of immanence, the orthodox account on matters such as jihad and *ḥākimiyya* needs to be addressed by the same Muslim leaders so as to draw a clear distinction between a gnostic use and a canonical use of this theoretical arsenal. A similar task would likely be assigned to trained imāms and recognized religious leaders; in fact, the exposure of Salafi-Jihadism will always be mainly a duty for Muslim religious leaders since they have the moral authority among the community of believers.

Salafi-Jihadism stands as one of today's most terrifying threats. The end of IS's territorial control in the land of Syria and Iraq and the death of its leader Abū Bakr al-Baghdādī in 2019 are not indications of a certain and clear victory of the Western coalition. History teaches us that after every great victory over Salafi-Jihadism, a greater threat always is born – the most emblematic case is the death of Osama bin Laden which was followed by the rise of the self-proclaimed Islamic State just as the whole West was rejoicing at its victory over the "Terror".

The future is unpredictable, but what we can learn from recent events is that this so-called "War on Terror" is not a conventional war: it is primarily an intellectual struggle, because today ideas spread at the speed of light and arrive everywhere. Jihadists are no longer confined only to Syria, Afghanistan, Libya or somewhere other than Europe and America; as Olivier Roy has many times shown,[16] the identity-reconstruction in the

16 See, for example, Olivier Roy, *Globalized Islam. The Search for a New Ummah* (New York: Columbia University Press, 2004).

age of globalization causes religions and ideologies to be reformulated in various and capricious ways, resulting in an unexpected deterritorialization of ideas and beliefs.

The framing of Salafi-Jihadism as a revolutionary gnostic experience stands as an attempt to weaken the appeal of this ideology and as a warning about its destructive power, since the goal of redeeming humankind through a global revolution is the most dangerous menace a totalitarian group can ever make. The present book is fully within the scope of this great intellectual struggle. Many other studies have to be done to that end, but the road has already been marked.

APPENDIX
A CONVERSATION WITH LUCIANO PELLICANI*

Today's world finds itself in a paradoxical situation: on the one hand, the liberal-democratic model seems to be gaining ground also in lands and cultures that are far-off from the Western world; on the other hand, we are witnessing the emergence of so-called "antagonist" groups, also known as anarchist, and jihadist militias that propagate messages of total liberation from the capitalist Moloch and from the unfaithful Satan. Such liberation often turns into a real *redemption* of humanity, and the political-revolutionary message assumes messianic and eschatological characteristics: the end of the world is near, and a handful of men – those who denounce such a situation – will lead the entire human race to the Promised Land.

I went in Rome to meet Luciano Pellicani in order to study in more depth the process of sacralization of armed struggles, of which he is one of the greatest scholars. The concept of revolutionary Gnosticism has been greatly adopted in his studies, as I have shown in Section 1.6.

Pellicani welcomes me to his house, makes me sit at a table and offers me a citron-juice drink. "There is a mental block with regard to revolutionary Gnosticism," he begins to explain. "The fact is, Eric Voegelin has always been considered a right-wing intellectual," he says. And he continues: "I also, in fact, have known this category from Augusto Del Noce, with whom I have had the pleasure of speaking personally several times. Let's be clear, my cultural orientation is completely different from that of Del Noce", and in fact Pellicani is a reformist socialist, whereas Del Noce was a Catholic of the Christian Democracy party, "but the truth lies where it is, it is neither right- nor left-wing", he continues. "In this regard, as Albert Einstein said, 'I am an incurable opportunist.' In any case, it was Del Noce who had Eric Voegelin's book *The New Science of Politics* published in Italy. And so I started collecting information about Gnosticism."

---

* I had the opportunity to have this conversation with Luciano Pellicani on July 2019. Less than a year later, on April 11, 2020, Pellicani passed away due to Covid-19 at the age of 81. I will forever preserve his memory, his enthusiasm for research and his exuberant personality.

Luciano Pellicani then tells me about his enormous curiosity towards this phenomenon. It seems like Gnosticism has re-emerged several times in different guises, or at least this is what a careful reading of Voegelin and other authors suggests. "The central problem of Gnosticism is evil," Pellicani continues. "Rigorous Gnosticism is nihilism to the very end. In practice, according to the gnostics, being born is a disgrace. The problem of evil is also present in Hegel: Benedetto Croce writes in a passage – that unfortunately he has not developed any further – that Hegelian philosophy is a Gnosis for the simple reason that it tries to make the problem of evil disappear. If every passage of history is a step towards the final goal, which is freedom, then the series of negative phenomena have a meaning precisely because they are propaedeutic to reaching the final goal, and in the end, the evil disappears. Gnosticism, therefore, has a liberating attitude towards evil. After all, from Hegel's Gnosis derives Marx's Gnosis." Pellicani raises his eyes to look at the ceiling. He collects ideas. "It is not possible to avoid confronting Hegel because he is the one who has held the wolf by the ears. It is not by chance that he claims that our time is characterized by the fact that God is dead, actually anticipating Nietzsche. György Lukács, the famous Marxist intellectual, wrote in his diary: 'I should commit suicide because life has lost all meaning.' Think a little, he even began to study the lives of the saints, despite the fact that in the end he reached a conclusion diametrically opposed to Christianity. In any case, Lukács said that this world must be destroyed in order to reach the true goal."

Pellicani stops to reflect. I then ask him a question: "Is it possible to speak of a genetic continuity between the Gnosticism of the 2nd and 3rd centuries and the secularized, modern Gnosticism, that is present in Hegel and eventually merged into Marx and other more or less revolutionary thinkers?" – a question which I tried to answer in Section 1.1. Pellicani's answer intrigues me: "The continuity is undoubtedly genetic," he maintains, "because Hegel clearly says that he refers to Valentinus, the gnostic of the 2nd century, proposing again the triadic scheme of original unity, splitting, and reconstitution of unity. Hegel speaks of this in his *Lessons in the Philosophy of Religion*, if I'm not mistaken."

I reply: "Giovanni Filoramo, however, tends to prefer the possibility of a phenomenological recurrence, a constant attitude that emerges in different historical periods but under similar circumstances. So, let me reformulate the question: is there a phenomenological recurrence between ancient and modern Gnosticism, or is it rather a true and proper doctrinal continuity?"

"The two things are not in conflict," Pellicani emphatically replies. "Hegel's explicit reference to Valentinus is an element to be seriously taken into account: this fact establishes a direct, genetic link between the classical Gnosticism of Valentinus and the neo-Gnosticism of Hegel, Marx and other authors."

I take another sip of citron-juice drink and lean forward. The debate on revolutionary Gnosticism is not easy, I think. At a recent conference in Prague, I was told that perhaps it would be better to avoid using this very name to avoid confusion with the doctrinal peculiarity of a Late-Antique religious phenomenon. I therefore say to Luciano Pellicani: "There are some scholars who prefer to speak of apocalypticism, thus tending to eclipse the name of Gnosticism, considered equivocal by them."

"Gnosticism and apocalypticism are connected," Pelicani replies immediately. "The obsession of both phenomena is the same, that is, evil. How do we eradicate evil? Where does it come from? I would say that this is *the* theme. For example, Léon Poljakov, a French historian of Russian origin known for his studies on the genocide of the Jews, speaks of 'Hitler's theodicy.' It is certainly a curious expression, isn't it? It means that Hitler's theory is about the origin of evil. And it is also a therapy for eradicating evil: that's why we can speak of a Nazi Gnosticism." He takes a break. "From time to time, a gnostic Paraclete arrives and says, 'Behold, I have found the solution for evil in the world.' And down with the list: "It is the Jew,' or 'It is the bourgeoisie' and so on. To eradicate evil in order to purify the world! The concept of purity is essential."

The obsession with purity is often accompanied by bitter criticism to the capitalist market. I make this point to Pellicani, who seizes the moment to say: "Capitalism plays an important role. Most of the doctrines defined as gnostic have a polemical idol in capitalism. For example, the Puritans wanted to destroy capitalism, as Michael Walzer demonstrates in the text *The Revolution of the Saints* – a book that, go figure!, no one mentions anymore. Puritanism was a revolutionary ideology that wanted to break down capitalism and individualism: the opposite of the Weberian vulgate!"

I bring the discussion back to our time, focusing on our era shaken by great changes. I ask: "Is there a risk that revolutionary gnostic phenomena will return today? Has the temptation to redeem the world disappeared, or will it still emerge?"

Luciano Pellicani sighs and thinks about it. "I actually don't have the answer to this question," he says, "but I do know one thing: in the face of an enormous crisis, the ideal audience for gnostic preaching is created. I have insisted a lot during my career on the role played by the First World War, or rather 'the psychology of the trench.' The objective of the soldiers during the Great War was the annihilation of the enemy. The narrative of

Hitler and Lenin corresponded to the new anthropological type that came out of the trenches. Julij Martov, intellectual and political leader of the Menshevik wing of the Russian Social Democratic Party, understood this and wrote a very valuable book entitled *World Bolshevism*. His central thesis is based on the psychology of the trench that produces a mass ready to explode. And when eloquent and skillful demagogues come to speak, well, the audience is already there."

The point that Pelicani touches on is central: the crisis – any crisis, economic, military, political – has always preceded the great revolutionary gnostic explosions. How, then, can we foil any possible upheaval that may take place in the name of a redemptive ideology? The identification of the enemy to be eradicated, the presumed possession of a salvific knowledge, the Promethean will to redo everything again: these elements would be enough to light the fire of a revolution that would be, by its very nature, projected on the international scene. I therefore ask Pellicani whether or not there is a remedy for the emergence of these revolutionary gnostic tendencies.

"It does exist. I am referring to *permanent reformism*. The social strata affected by the crises, be they economic or otherwise, moan, suffer, and await hope, a saving message. In order to avoid popular uprisings, it is necessary to adapt institutions and policies to the constantly changing reality. In England, thanks to the experience of the Glorious Revolution of 1688, such a program was implemented." He reflects a little and adds: "Certainly, the precondition is economic growth. 'If wealth doesn't grow, all the old shit comes back:' that's how Marx literally expresses himself." And he states: "The influence of the October Revolution has altered the expectations of the lower strata of the population. 'Doing what Russia did' was the motto: if it was possible in Russia, it could also be possible elsewhere. In 1917 the world trembled. I repeat that when a mass of disgruntled and exasperated people is created, the demagogue who delivers the right speech promptly arrives, and it is no longer possible to go back. The First World War created this public, which was strengthened by 1917, and the whole of Europe went mad – but not Britain. The Glorious Revolution was moderate and liberal. From that moment on, England's history became a real counter-revolution manual. In other words, the British people have become able to avoid a revolution."

I get up from the chair, move around the room and look at the books that cover the walls of the living room. Many volumes are stacked one on top of the other certainly according to a rational order but still unintelligible at first glance. I am fascinated by all these books. Yet gnostic revolutions have appeared almost everywhere, I suddenly think. Italy, Germany,

Russia, Great Britain before the Glorious Revolution, France: all these are countries that have been involved in disturbances based on the self-redemptive formula of charismatic gnostic Paracletes. I then ask a question: "Can the gnostic anthropological type be exported? Is there a contagion between cultures in this regard?"

"Definitely!" Pellicani asserts. "The whole Leninist tradition is not understandable if we do not keep in mind that Russian populism is essentially Jacobinism adapted to the Russian reality. Lenin clearly says that the Bolsheviks are basically modern Jacobins. And he adds, with an obvious gnostic spirit, that the Bolshevik is a revolutionary in the service of the proletariat, the one who brings revolutionary consciousness to the proletariat. Jacobinism, then, evolved until it reached Pol Pot. The success of Jacobinism on a world scale is impressive."

Jacobinism is one of the most successful gnostic *avatāra* (see Section 2.2.3). Its influence on the rest of the world is truly disconcerting, indeed.

"Hannah Arendt defines Jacobinism as 'the hunt for hidden vice'," Pellicani resumes. "A sweetened version of the Jacobin mentality is offered by Concetto Marchesi, a great scholar of Latin literature. Marchesi proposed the figure of the 'masked fascist,' according to which everyone can be a fascist, even if masked. After all, the fundamental dichotomy of Manichaeism, the eternal struggle between Good and Evil, translated into political terms assumes the (immanent) connotations of the opposition between the revolutionary party that wants to eradicate evil and all those who resist it. In the eyes of the revolutionaries, this last group is deemed a solid monolithic block without internal distinctions, and according to the gnostic doctrine all those who are part of it are practically equivalent and interchangeable."

At this point, Pellicani recalls his personal history and confides to me that during his long academic career he himself was placed several times on the side of those who resist the revolution, a "masked fascist" according to the lexical proposal of Concetto Marchesi. "Many years ago, the Vallecchi publishing house was about to publish my book *I rivoluzionari di professione*, until a message arrived from a parliamentarian who intimidated the publishers with a letter. The letter said: 'Are you really publishing a book by that fascist of Pellicani?' The book was printed anyway, though out of the series. I seriously considered the idea of leaving the country. The scientific journals started not to publish my articles because – this was the reason – 'they were too right-wing.' I was expelled from the scientific committee of the *Italian Review of Sociology* because I had the courage to write a critical note about the Frankfurt School. *Avanti!*, a historical socialist newspaper, was no longer publishing my articles. I repeat: I was thinking of leaving Italy. Then, in 1976, Bettino Craxi was elected Secretary of the Italian Socialist Party. In one of his first interviews, perhaps the first, given to the weekly publication *L'Europeo*, he stated that the Italian Socialist Party had to return to its original values and that, literally, 'it must not forget the lesson of Eduard Bernstein, as Luciano Pellicani has shown.' I immediately called him on the telephone, then we met and the common battle began: to *debolshevize* the Italian left." Pellicani shakes his head. "The people around me were saying they were socialists but actually they were more Bolshevik than the communists themselves. The October Revolution could not have been called into question, otherwise they would have snapped into the air and put themselves on the defensive." The Manichean mentality had breached the Italian left in the 70's and 80's.

I sit down and grab my pen. I try to resume the original thread, leading the discussion back to the theme of revolutionary Gnosticism. One doubt, however, has motivated my years of doctoral research: why using this category? It is a provocative question that, in any case, has stimulated me to specify more and more the reasons for such a particular study and to explain its adoption for the case of Salafism-Jihadism. I ask Pellicani with a touch of provocation: "Is revolutionary Gnosticism a useful category?"

"To understand reality, yes, it is decidedly useful," he replies.

"But what does it reveal about these groups?" I press the point. "What does it say about the various movements defined as gnostic, such as Bolshevism, Jacobinism and Nazism?"

Luciano Pellicani pauses. Suddenly he gets up from his chair and disappears behind a door. He comes back after a few moments with a book in his hands. "I would answer this question with the last pages of my book *La società dei giusti* that refer to Anatole France," he says, waving the book in the air as if it were a flag. "France, a French writer and Nobel Prize winner of literature in 1921, spent his entire life warning his readers of the Jacobin temptation, that is, to create an angelic man, as he himself said. The creation of the angelic man from the Jacobin perspective required Terror, the guillotine – let us remember that the Jacobins wanted to create a purified world, and thought they could achieve that with such a terrorist system. It was certainly madness, and the results could only be disastrous. Yet Anatole France died under the red flag: that is, he himself had become a Bolshevik. What does this mean?" Pellicani almost whispers now. "It means that we are all tempted to finally eradicate evil without come to terms with it – and so Anatole France. That's what the concept of revolutionary Gnosticism tells us."

I think about it for a second. I add: "So nominally Christian phenomena such as certain fringes of Puritans and the radical Anabaptists of Münster can't really be called Christians. They reveal something alien to the Christian doctrinal complex."

Pellicani replies: "Well, after all they are Christian heresies. A heresy is a phenomenon certainly linked to a particular orthodoxy, it arises from it, but then reaches its autonomy, annexing something new that was not included by the original orthodoxy."

"And revolutionary Gnosticism introduces the notion of self-redemption, that is, man that redeems man," I say.

Pellicani's face lights up: "That's right. That's the point. This is precisely the gnostic claim, which is a Satanic revolt. In this regard, Joseph de Maistre imagines a dialogue between a Jacobin and God. The Jacobin turns to God and says to him 'I don't like anything that exists because it is your work, and consequently I want to do it again.' This is, in technical terms, *Satanism*."

I thank Luciano Pellicani for the time he devoted to me. I get up from the chair and shake his hand. But right at the doorstep, Pellicani starts talking again, visibly disturbed by something: "In fifty years or a hundred years they can pop up again, re-explode. I am referring to revolutionary gnostic phenomena. There is a very acute observation in the essay *La speranza nella rivoluzione* by Vittorio Mathieu. The author rightly writes: 'The next challenge we can expect is ecologism.' And in fact, if ecological rhetoric states that capitalism threatens life itself and leads to self-destruction, it becomes a consequence, and indeed a duty, to destroy capitalism. Ecologism is a technique for purifying the world. Already today, several gnostic ecologist Paracletes are appearing. We will see with what follow-up. Although there have been improvements in the ecological field in recent decades, the perception of the problem has worsened considerably." He continues after a break: "The other problem that I cannot see how it can be solved is the one inherent to migrants. How do we stop them? And in the future it will be even worse! I am pessimistic about this. In the end, we will be forced to use the gunboats, a friend of mine told me one day. When Lenin took power, he said that as long as there was the exchange, it would be ridiculous to speak of socialism – pure madness. But the exchange cannot be eliminated. And in fact the black market was enormous in Russia. The people were ready to challenge the authority to the point of death. This black market grew immeasurably during the Stalinist era, it soon became a second economy. The analogy with migrants is clear: if merchants were willing to die – if found with a lot of goods, they were shot on the spot – migrants, too, are now willing to die. If out of desperation, because of hunger, the people run the risk of being shot because of that bag, even the migrants will not halt. How do you stop migration flows? The demographic boom in those countries is immeasurable. Today we are seven billion and two hundred million on the planet; in 2050 we will be nine billion. This growth will come almost entirely from underdeveloped countries, from hungry peoples. And how are we going to stop them? With gunboats? My God... We would become butchers. I just don't understand. It's a cascade that grows and grows."

With these bitter reflections I leave Luciano Pellicani's house. I think back about his words as I descend the stairs. I reach the street. An African walks beside me and passes by. He is perhaps one of the several migrants who arrive periodically with boats on the Italian coast. I can't – but, above all, I don't want to – imagine the consequences of a possible gnostic revolution linked to the migratory theme. I turn around and leave.

Rome, July 12, 2019

BIBLIOGRAPHY

Abdin, Ahmad Zein al-, 'The Political Thought of Ḥasan al-Bannā', *Islamic Studies* 28, no. 3 (Autumn 1989), 219-234.

Abdul-Raheem, Bashir, 'The Concept of Jihad in Islamic Philosophy', *American International Journal of Social Science* 4, no. 1 (February 2015), 141-148.

Addi, Lahouari, 'Islam Re-Observed: Sanctity, Salafism, and Islamism', *The Journal of North African Studies* 14, no. 3/4 (September/December 2009), 331-345.

Ahmad, Jalāl Al-I, *Occidentosis: A Plague From the West.* (1962; repr. Berkeley: Mizan Press, 1984).

Albrile, Ezio, 'La tentazione gnostica', *I Quaderni di Avallon*, no. 30 (1992), 31-46.

Ali, Mohamed, '*Al-Wala' Wal Bara'* (Loyalty and Disavowal) in Modern Salafism: Analysing the Positions of Purist, Politico and Jihadi Salafis', in *Terrorist Rehabilitation. A New Frontier in Counter-Terrorism*, ed. by Rohan Gunaratna, and Mohamed Bin Ali (New Jersey: Imperial College Press, 2015), pp. 153-191.

Allegra, Antonio, 'Trasformazione & perfezione. Temi gnostici nel postumanesimo', in *L'origine & la meta. Studi in memoria di Emanuele Samek Lodovici*, ed. by Gabriele De Anna (Milan: Edizioni Ares, 2015), pp. 151-168.

Alshech, Eli, *The Emergence of the 'Infallible Jihad Fighters' – The Salafi Jihadists' Quest for Religious Legitimacy* (Washington: MEMRI, 2008).

–, 'The Doctrinal Crisis within the Salafi-Jihadi Ranks and the Emergence of Neo-Takfirism. A Historical and Doctrinal Analysis', *Islamic Law and Society* 21, no. 4 (September 2014), 419-452.

Ambrosio, Alberto Fabio, *Danza coi sufi. Incontro con l'Islam mistico* (Cinisello Balsamo: San Paolo, 2013).

Anjum, Ovamir, *Politics, Law, and Community in Islamic Thought: The Taymiyyan Moment* (New York: Cambridge University Press, 2014).

–, 'Salafis and Democracy: Doctrine and Context', *The Muslim World* 106, no. 3 (July 2016), 448-473.

Arendt, Hannah, 'The Origin of Totalitarianism. A Reply', *The Review of Politics* 15, no. 1 (January 1953), 68-76.
–, *The Origins of Totalitarianism* (1951; repr. San Diego: Harcourt Brace & Company, 1976).
–, *On Revolution* (1963; repr. London: Penguin Books, 1990).
Arkoun, Mohammed, *La filosofia araba* (Milan: Xenia Edizioni, 1995).
Armour, Leslie, 'Gnosticism, the Dream Economy and the Prospects for Communism', *International Journal of Social Economics* 21, no. 2/3/4 (1994), 31-53.
Asad, Talal, *On Suicide Bombing* (New York: Columbia University Press, 2007).
Ashmawy, Muhammad Sa'id al-, *Against Islamic Extremism* (Gainesville: University Press of Florida, 2001).
Atta, Muḥammad, 'Suicide Note', in *Anti-American Terrorism and the Middle East*, ed. by Barry Rubin, and Judith Colp Rubin (New York: Oxford University Press, 2002), pp. 233-236.
Avramenko, Richard, 'The Gnostic and the *Spoudaios*', *The Political Science Reviewer* 41, no. 1 (June 2017), 75-99.
'Awlaqī, Anwar al-, 'Tawfique Chowdhury's Alliance with the West', *Anwar al-Awlaki blog*. February 12, 2009. https://archive.org/stream/Anwar.Awlaki.Audio.Archive/Tawfique.Chowdhury.Alliance.with.the_djvu.txt.
–, *Constants in the Path of Jihad by Shaykh Yusuf al-'Uyayree* (n.p.: at-Tibyān Publications, n.d.)
Ayubi, Nazih N.M., 'The Political Revival of Islam: The Case of Egypt', *International Journal of Middle East Studies* 12, no. 4 (December 1980), 481-499.
Azm, Sadik J. al-, *L'Illuminismo islamico. Il disagio della civiltà* (Rome: Di Renzo Editore, 2000).
Azmeh, Aziz al-, 'Islamist Revivalism and Western ideologies', *History Workshop*, no. 32 (Autumn 1991), 44-53.
'Azzām, 'Abdullah, *Join the Caravan.* (1987; repr. London: Azzam Publications, 2001).
–, *The Tawḥīd of Action* (n.p.: at-Tibyān Publications, n.d.)
Baaren, Th. P. Van, 'Towards a Definition of Gnosticism', in *The Origins of Gnosticism. Colloquium of Messina*, ed. by Ugo Bianchi (Leiden: Brill, 1967), pp. 174-180.
Badar, Mohamed, Masaki Nagata, and Tiphanie Tueni, 'The Radical Application of the Islamist Concept of Takfir', *Arab Law Quarterly* 31, no. 2 (June 2017), 134-162.

Bannā, Ḥasan al-, *Majmū'at rasā'il al-imām al-shahīd Ḥasan al-Bannā* (Kuwait: International Islamic Federation of Student Organizations, 1996).

–, 'Our Message In A New Phase', *The Qur'an Blog* (blog), https://thequranblog.files.wordpress.com/2008/06/_5_-our-message-in-a-new-phase.pdf.

–, 'Oh Youth!', *The Qur'an Blog* (blog), https://thequranblog.files.wordpress.com/2008/06/_9_-oh-youth.pdf

Barkun, Michael, 'Millenarianism in the Modern World', *Theory and Society* 1, no. 2 (Summer 1974), 117-146.

Bāz, 'Abd al-'Azīz bin, *Explanation of Important Lessons For Every Muslims* (Riyadh: Darussalam Publishers, 2002).

Becker, Carmen, 'Muslims on the Path of the Salaf Al-Salih', *Information, Communication & Society* 14, no. 8 (2011), 1181-1203.

Benslama, Fethi, *Un furieux désir de sacrifice. Le surmusulman*, (Paris: Le Seuil, 2016).

Bergen, Peter L., *Holy War, Inc. Inside the Secret World of Osama bin Laden* (New York: The Free Press, 2001).

Berger, Peter L., and Thomas Luckmann, *Modernity, Pluralism and the Crisis of Meaning. The Orientation of Modern Man* (Gütersloh: Bertelsmann Foundation Publishers, 1995).

Bernet, Claus, 'The Concept of the New Jerusalem among Early Anabaptists in Münster 1534/35. An Interpretation of Political, Social and Religious Rule', *Archiv für Reformationsgeschichte* 102, no. 1 (2011), 175-194.

Bettetini, Maria, *Distruggere il passato. L'iconoclastia dall'Islam all'Isis* (Milan: Raffaello Cortina Editore, 2016).

Bhatt, Chetan, 'The Virtues of Violence: The Salafi-Jihadi Political Universe', *Theory, Culture & Society* 31, no. 1 (2014), 25-48.

Bonanate, Ugo, ed., *I puritani. I soldati della Bibbia* (Turin: Einaudi, 1975).

Bonvecchio, Claudio, 'Potere della gnosi e gnosi del potere: un percorso sapienziale', in *Gli arconti di questo mondo. Gnosi: politica e diritto*, ed. by Claudio Bonvecchio, and Teresa Tonchia (Trieste: EUT, 2000), pp. 309-369.

Borghesi, Massimo, 'L'Islam tra fondamentalismo e modernità. Il problema teologico politico', in *Critica della teologia politica. Da Agostino a Peterson: la fine dell'era costantiniana* (Genova-Milan: Marietti, 2013), pp. 331-338.

Borowski, Audrey, 'Al Qaeda and ISIS: From Revolution to Apocalypse', *Philosophy Now*, no. 111 (December 2015), https://philosophynow.org/issues/111/Al_Qaeda_and_ISIS_From_Revolution_to_Apocalypse.

Black, Antony, *The History of Islamic Political Thought. From the Prophet to the Present* (Edinburgh: Edinburgh University Press, 2011).

Branca, Paolo, *Introduzione all'Islam* (Cinisello Balsamo: Edizioni San Paolo, 1995).

–, *Voci dell'Islam moderno. Il pensiero arabo-musulmano fra rinnovamento e tradizione* (Genova: Marietti, 1997).

–, *Moschee inquiete. Tradizionalisti, innovatori, fondamentalisti nella cultura islamica* (Bologna: Il Mulino, 2003).

–, 'Il califfato fra storia e mito', in *Il marketing del terrore. Twitter e jihad: la comunicazione dell'ISIS*, ed. by Monica Maggioni, and Paolo Magri (Milan: Oscar Mondadori), pp. 2016 29-47.

–, *Islamismo* (Milan: Editrice Bibliografica, 2017).

–, 'From Nahda To Nowhere?', in *The Struggle to Define a Nation. Rethinking Religious Nationalism in the Contemporary Islamic World*, ed. by Marco Demichelis, and Paolo Maggiolini (Piscataway, NJ: Gorgias Press, 2017), pp. 469-496.

Brown, Jonathan A.C., 'Is Islam Easy to Understand or Not?: Salafis, the Democratization of Interpretation and the Need for the Ulema', *Journal of Islamic Studies* 26, no. 2 (May 2015), 117-144.

Bulliet, Richard W., *La civiltà islamico-cristiana. Una proposta* (Rome-Bari: Laterza, 2005).

Bunzel, Cole, *From Paper State to Caliphate: The Ideology of the Islamic State* (Washington DC: Brookings Institution, 2015).

–, *The Kingdom and the Caliphate. Duel of the Islamic States* (Washington DC: Carnegie Endowment For International Peace, 2016).

Buruma, Ian, and Avishai Margalit, *Occidentalism: The West in the Eyes of Its Enemies* (New York: The Penguin Press, 2004).

Buttafuoco, Pietrangelo, *Il feroce saracino. La Guerra dell'Islam, il califfo alle porte di Roma* (Milan: Bompiani, 2015).

Byman, Daniel, 'Fighting Salafi-Jihadi Insurgencies: How Much Does Religion Really Matters?', *Studies in Conflict & Terrorism* 36, no. 5 (2013), 353-371.

Cahana, Jonathan, 'None of Them Knew Me or My Brothers: Gnostic Antitraditionalism and Gnosticism as a Cultural Phenomenon', *The Journal of Religion* 94, no. 1 (January 2014), 49-73.

Campanini, Massimo, *Introduzione alla filosofia islamica* (Rome-Bari: Laterza, 2004).

–, *Il Corano e la sua interpretazione* (Rome-Bari: Laterza, 2004).

–, 'L'utopia nel pensiero politico dell'Islam. A proposito del *Medieval islamic Political Thought* di Patricia Crone', *Oriente Moderno* 84, no. 3 (2004), 671-683.

–, *An Introduction to Islamic Philosophy* (Edinburgh: Edinburgh University Press, 2008).

–, *Il pensiero islamico contemporaneo* (Bologna: Il Mulino, 2009).

–, 'Il salafismo e le sue fenomenologie', in *Quale Islam? Jihadismo, radicalismo, riformismo*, ed. by Massimo Campanini (Brescia: La Scuola, 2015), pp. 61-100.

Campodonico, Angelo, 'Rifiuto del finito, dell'articolazione dei saperi e della diversità', in *L'origine & la meta. Studi in memoria di Emanuele Samek Lodovici*, ed. by Gabriele De Anna, (Milan: Edizioni Ares, 2015), pp. 139-150.

Castellano, Danilo, 'La gnosi come "anima" dell'utopia rivoluzionaria contemporanea', in *L'origine & la meta. Studi in memoria di Emanuele Samek Lodovici*, ed. by Gabriele De Anna (Milan: Edizioni Ares, 2015), pp. 257-274.

Chakrabarty, Dipesh, *Provincializing Europe. Postcolonial Thought and Historical Difference* (Princeton: Princeton University Press, 2000).

Charters, David A., 'Something Old, Something New…? Al Qaeda, Jihadism, and Fascism', *Terrorism and Political Violence* 19, no. 1 (2007), 65-93.

Chiapparini, Giuliano, 'Gnosticismo: fine di una categoria storico-religiosa?', *Annali di Scienze Religiose*, no. 11 (2006), 181-217.

Chignola, Sandro, ed., *La politica: dai simboli alle esperienze* (Milan: Giuffré Editore, 1993).

Cohn, Norman, *The Pursuit of the Millennium: Revolutionary Millenarians and Mystical Anarchists of the Middle Ages* (New York: Oxford University Press, 1970; trad. it, *I fanatici dell'Apocalisse*, Turin: Edizioni di Comunità, 2000).

Cook, David, 'Muslim Apocalyptic and Jihad', *Jerusalem Studies in Arabic and Islam* 20 (1966), 66-104.

–, *Understanding Jihad* (Berkeley: University of California Press, 2005).

–, *Contemporary Muslim Apocalyptic Literature* (Syracuse: Syracuse University Press, 2005).

–, *Islam and Apocalyptic*. (Boston: Center for Millennial Studies, 2005).

–, 'Islamism and Jihadism: The Transformation of Classical Notions of Jihad into an Ideology of Terrorism', *Totalitarian Movements and Political Religions* 10, no. 2 (June 2009), 177-187.

–, 'Armageddon nell'Islam: le bandiere nere di Isis', *Oasis*, no. 21 (June 2015), 83-89.

Cook, Michael, *Il Corano* (Turin: Einaudi, 2001).

–, *Ancient Religions, Modern Politics. The Islamic Case in Comparative Perspective* (Princeton: Princeton University Press, 2014).

Cooper, Barry, *New Political Religions, or An Analysis of Modern Terrorism* (Columbia: University of Missouri Press, 2004).

Corbin, Henry, *Storia della filosofia islamica* (1964; trad. it. Milan: Adelphi, 1991).
Cottee, Simon. 'Mind Slaughter: The Neutralizations of Jihadi Salafism', *Studies in Conflict & Terrorism* 33, no. 4 (2010), 330-352.
Couliano, Ioan Petru, *I miti dei dualismi occidentali. Dai sistemi gnostici al mondo moderno* (Milan: Jaca Book, 1989).
Crone, Patricia, *Medieval Islamic Political Thought* (Edinburgh: Edinburgh University Press, 2004).
Cross, George, 'Millenarianism in Christian History', *The Biblical World* 46, no. 1 (July 1915), 33-8.
Cui, Shoujun, and Joshua Glinert, 'Jihadi-Salafi Ideology: The Suspension of Dialectic and Radicalization of Thought', *Journal of Middle Eastern and Islamic Studies (in Asia)* 10, no. 4 (2016), 101-120.
Dābiq, 15 vols.
Damir-Geilsdorf, Sabine, and Mira Menzfeld, 'Who are "the" Salafis? Insights Into Lifeworlds of Persons Connected to Salafis(m) in North Rhine-Westphalia, Germany', *Journal of Muslims in Europe* 6, no. 1 (March 2017), 22-51.
Dawson, Lorne L., *The Failure of Prophecy and the Future of IS* (The Hague: International Centre for Counter-Terrorism, 2017).
De Benoist, Alain, *Terrorismo e "guerre giuste". Sull'attualità di Carl Schmitt* (Naples: Alfredo Guida Editore, 2007).
De Graaff, Bob, 'IS and its Predecessors: Violent Extremism in Historical Perspective', *Perspectives on Terrorism* 10, no. 5 (October 2016), 96-103.
Dei, Fabio, *Terrore suicida. Religione, politica e violenza nelle culture del martirio* (Rome: Donzelli, 2016).
Del Noce, Augusto, 'Pensiero cristiano e comunismo: "inveramento" o "risposta a sfida"?', in *Opere 1945-1964*, by Felice Balbo (Turin: Boringhieri, 1966).
–, 'Tradizione e rivoluzione', in *Tradizione e rivoluzione. Proceedings of the 27th Conference at Centro di Studi Filosofici, Gallarate, 1972* (Brescia: Morcelliana, 1973), pp. 23-53.
–, 'Il problema filosofico della violenza', in *Violenza. Una ricerca per comprendere. Proceedings of the 34th Conference at Centro di Studi Filosofici, Gallarate, 1979* (Brescia: Morcelliana, 1980), pp. 9-12.
–, 'Violenza e secolarizzazione della gnosi', in *Violenza. Una ricerca per comprendere. Proceedings of the 34th Conference at Centro di Studi Filosofici, Gallarate, 1979* (Brescia: Morcelliana, 1980), pp. 195-216.
–, 'Eric Voegelin e la critica dell'idea di modernità', in *La nuova scienza politica*, by Eric Voegelin (Rome: Edizioni Borla, 1999), pp. 5-28.
–, *Il suicido della rivoluzione* (Turin: Nino Aragno Editore, 2004).

Di Cesare, Donatella, *Terrore e modernità* (Turin: Einaudi, 2017).
Di Donato, Marco, *Salafiti e salafismo* (Brescia: La Scuola, 2018).
Dolcetta, Marco, *Nazionalsocialismo esoterico. Studi iniziatici e misticismo messianico nel regime hitleriano* (Rome: Cooper & Castelvecchi, 2003).
Doresse, Jean, 'La gnosi', in *Gnosticismo e manicheismo*, ed. by Henri-Charles Puech (Rome-Bari: Laterza, 1988), pp. 3-65.
Douglass, Bruce, 'The Break in Voegelin's Program', *The Political Science Reviewer* 7, no. 1 (Fall 1977), 1-21.
Duderija, Adis, 'Islamic Groups and Their World-Views and Identities: Neo-Traditional Salafis and Progressive Muslims', *Arab Law Quarterly* 21, no. 4 (2007), 341-363.
Ebner, Julia, *The Rage: The Vicious Circle of Islamist and Far-Right Extremism* (London: I.B. Tauris, 2017).
Eco, Umberto, 'Ur-Fascism', *The New York Review of Books* 42, no. 11 (June 1995).
Eickelman, Dale F., 'Islam and the Languages of Modernity' *Daedalus* 129, no. 1 (Winter 2000), 119-135.
Eisenstadt, Shmuel N., *Fundamentalism, Sectarianism, and Revolution. The Jacobin Dimension of Modernity* (Cambridge: Cambridge University Press, 1999).
–, 'Multiple Modernities', *Daedalus* 129, no. 1 (Winter 2000), 1-29.
Emberley, Peter, and Barry Cooper, ed., *Faith and Political Philosophy. The Correspondence Between Leo Strauss and Eric Voegelin*, 1934 – 1964 (Columbia: University of Missouri Press, 2004).
Étienne, Bruno, *L'islamismo radicale* (Milan: Rizzoli, 1988).
Faraj, Muḥammad 'Abd al-Salām, *Jihad. The Absent Obligation* (1981; repr. Birmingham: Maktabah Al Ansaar Publications, 2000).
Filiu, Jean-Pierrem, *L'apocalisse nell'Islam* (Milan: ObarraO Edizioni, 2011).
Filoramo, Giovanni, *Il risveglio della gnosi, ovvero diventare dio* (Rome-Bari: Laterza, 1990).
–, 'Riflessioni in margine alla teologia politica degli gnostici', in *Gli arconti di questo mondo. Gnosi: politica e diritto*, ed. by Claudio Bonvecchio, and Teresa Tonchia (Trieste: EUT, 2000), pp. 37-49.
'Final document', in *The Origins of Gnosticism. Colloquium of Messina*, ed. by Ugo Bianchi (Leiden: Brill, 1967), pp. xx-xxix.
Fiorini, Fabrizio, *I figli della conoscenza. Storia critica dello Gnosticismo e del neo-Gnosticismo* (Milan-Udine: Mimesis, 2018).
Flood, Finbarr Barry, 'Idol-Breaking as Image-Making in the "Islamic State"', *Religion and Society: Advances in Research*, no. 7 (September 2016), 116-138.

Fouad Allam, Khaled, *L'Islam globale* (Milan: Rizzoli, 2002).

–, 'L'Islām contemporaneo', in *Islām*, ed. by Giovanni Filoramo (Rome-Bari: Laterza, 2007), pp. 219-308.

Franz, Michael, *Eric Voegelin and the Politics of Spiritual Revolt* (Baton Rouge: Louisiana State University Press, 1992).

–, 'Gnosticism and Spiritual Disorder in *The Ecumenic Age*', *Political Science Reviewer* 27, no. 1 (Fall 1998), 17-43.

–, "Voegelin's Analysis on Marx." *Occasional Papers* 18 (August 2000): 5-56.

–, 'Commentaries on the Work of Eric Voegelin', *Political Science Reviewer* 30, no. 1 (Fall 2001), 202-296.

–, 'The Concept of Gnosticism and the Analysis of Spiritual Disorder', *Political Science Reviewer* 34, no. 1 (Fall 2005), 28-47.

–, 'Caution and Clarity in Thinking About ISIS and Apocalyptic Activism', *VoegelinView*, January 21, 2018, https://voegelinview.com/caution-clarity-thinking-isis-apocalyptic-activism/.

Fumagalli, Sergio, 'Gnosi moderna e secolarizzazione nell'analisi di Emanuele Samek Lodovici e Augusto Del Noce', PhD diss., Pontifical University of the Holy Cross, Rome, 2005.

Furlan, Francesco, *La figura del Mahdī. All'incrocio dei tre monoteismi* (Ariccia: Aracne, 2015).

Gambetta, Diego, and Steffen Hertog, *Engineers of Jihad. The Curious Connection between Violent Extremism and Education* (Princeton: Princeton University Press, 2016).

García-Arenal, Mercedes, 'Il messianismo nell'Islam moderno', in *Le religioni e il mondo moderno*, vol. 4, *Nuove tematiche e prospettive*, ed. by Giovanni Filoramo (Turin: Einaudi, 2009), pp. 142-159.

Gaudino, Ugo, 'Leggere Schmitt a Raqqa. Teoria del partigiano e terrorismo islamico', *Sistema Informativo a Schede*, no. 5 (2016), 5-25.

Gatti, Roberto, '"*Nul N'Est Parfait Ici-Bas*": Rousseau gnostico post-cristiano?', in *Gli arconti di questo mondo. Gnosi: politica e diritto*, ed. by Claudio Bonvecchio, and Teresa Tonchia (Trieste: EUT, 2000), pp. 185-224.

Gerges, Fawaz A., *The Far Enemy. Why Jihad Went Global* (Cambridge: Cambridge University Press, 2005).

Germino, Dante, 'Eric Voegelin on the Gnostic Roots of Violence', *Occasional Papers* 7 (February 1998), 5-60.

Giunchi, Elisa, *Nel nome di Allah. L'autorità religiosa nell'Islam* (Milan: Jouvence, 2017).

Gray, John, *Al Qaeda and What It Means to be Modern* (London: Faber and Faber, 2007).

–, *Black Mass. Apocalyptic Religion and the Death of Utopia* (London: Penguin Books, 2008).

Griffel, Frank, 'What Do We Mean By "Salafi"? Connecting Muḥammad 'Abduh with Egypt's Nūr Party in Islam's Contemporary Intellectual History', *Die Welt Des Islams* 55, no. 2 (September 2015), 186-220.

–, 'What is the Task of the Intellectual (Contemporary) Historian? – A Response to Henri Lauzière's "Reply"', *Die Welt Des Islams* 56, no. 2 (August 2016), 249-255.

Guitton, Jean, *Il puro e l'impuro* (Casale Monferrato: Piemme, 1994).

Gunther, Karl, 'The Origins of English Puritanism', *History Compass* 4, no. 2 (March 2006), 235-240.

Guolo, Renzo, *Avanguardie della fede. L'islamismo tra ideologia e politica* (Milan: Guerini e Associati, 1999).

–, *Il fondamentalismo islamico* (Rome-Bari: Laterza, 2002).

–, *L'ultima utopia. Gli jihadisti europei* (Milan: Guerini e Associati, 2015).

Hafez, Mohammed M., 'The Alchemy of Martyrdom: Jihadi Salafism and Debates over Suicide Bombings in the Muslim World', *Asian Journal of Social Science* 38, no. 3 (January 2010), 364-378.

Haniff Hassan, Mohammad, 'The Danger of Takfir (Excommunication): Exposing IS' Takfiri Ideology', *Counter Terrorist Trends and Analyses* 9, no. 4 (April 2017), 3-12.

Hanratty, Gerald, 'Gnosticism and Modern Thought, I', *Irish Theological Quarterly* 47, no. 1 (1980), 3-23.

–, 'Gnosticism and Modern Thought, II', *Irish Theological Quarterly* 47, no. 2 (1980), 119-132.

–, 'Gnosticism and Modern Thought, III', *Irish Theological Quarterly* 48, no. 1/2 (1981), 80-92.

Hansen, Hendrik, 'Islamism and Western Political Religions', *Religion Compass* 3, no. 6 (2009), 1026-1041.

Hansen, Hendrik, and Peter Kainz, 'Radical Islamism and Totalitarian Ideology: A Comparison of Sayyid Qutb's Islamism with Marxism and National Socialism', *Totalitarian Movements and Political Religions* 8, no. 1 (March 2007), 55-76.

Hashemi, Nader A., 'Islamic Fundamentalism and the Trauma of Modernization: Reflections on Religion and Radical Politics', in *An Islamic Reformation?*, ed. by Michaelle Browers (Lanhan, Maryland: Lexington Books, 2004), pp. 159-177.

Hatina, Mair, 'Redeeming Sunni Islam: Al-Qa'ida's Polemic Against the Muslim Brethren', *British Journal of Middle Eastern Studies* 39, no. 1 (April 2012), 101-113.

Haykel, Bernard, 'On the Nature of Salafi Thought and Action', in *Global Salafism. Islam's New Religious Movement*, ed. by Roel Meijer (Oxford: Oxford University Press, 2013), pp. 33-57.

Hegghammer, Thomas, "ʿAbdallah ʿAzzām, l'imam del jihad", in *Al-Qaeda. I testi*, ed. by Gilles Kepel (Rome-Bari: Laterza, 2006), pp. 87-108.

–, 'Global Jihadism after the Iraq War', *Middle East Journal* 60, no. 1 (Winter 2006), 11-32.

–, 'Jihadi-Salafis or Revolutionaries? On Religion and Politics in the Study of Militant Islamism', in *Global Salafism. Islam's New Religious Movement*, ed. by Roel Meijer (Oxford: Oxford University Press, 2013), pp. 244-266.

Hegghammer, Thomas, and Stéphane Lacroix, 'Rejectionist Islamism in Saudi Arabia. The Story of Juhayman al-'Utaybi Revisited', *International Journal of Middle East Studies* 39, no. 1 (February 2007), 103-122.

Heine, Peter, 'I Am Not the Mahdi, But…', in *Apocalyptic Time*, ed. by Albert I. Baumgarten (Leiden: Brill, 2000), pp. 69-78.

Henry, Michael, 'Civil Theology in the Gnostic Age: Progress and Regress', *Modern Age* 47, no. 1 (Winter 2005), 37-47.

Hodgkin, Thomas, 'The Revolutionary Tradition in Islam', *History Workshop*, no. 10 (Autumn 1980), 138-150.

Hutin, Serge, *Lo Gnosticismo. Culti, riti, misteri* (Rome: Edizioni Mediterranee, 2007).

Ibrahim, Raymond, ed., *The Al Qaeda Reader. The Essential Texts of Osama Bin Laden's Terrorist Organization* (New York: Broadway Books, 2007).

Introvigne, Massimo, *Il ritorno dello Gnosticismo* (Carnago, VA: Sugarco, 1993).

Jabri, Mohammed Abed al-, *Democracy, Human Rights and Law in Islamic Thought* (London: I.B. Tauris, 2009).

Jackson, Sherman A., 'Jihad and the Modern World', *Journal of Islamic Law and Culture* 7, no. 1 (Spring/Summer 2002), 1-26.

Jaspers, Karl, *The Origin and Goal of History* (New Haven: Yale University Press, 1953).

Jonas, Hans, 'Gnosticism, Existentialism and Nihilism', in *Gnostic Religion: The Message of the Alien God and the Beginnings of Christianity*, by Hans Jonas (Boston: Beacon, 1963), pp. 320-340.

–, 'Delimitation of the Gnostic Phenomenon – Typological and Historical', in *The Origins of Gnosticism. Colloquium of Messina*, ed. by Ugo Bianchi (Leiden: Brill, 1967), pp. 90-108.

–, *Gnosi e spirito tardoantico* (Milan: Bompiani, 2010).

Juergensmeyer, Mark, *Terror in the Mind of God. The Global Rise of Religious Violence* (Berkeley: University of California Press, 2000).

Kassim, Abdulbasit, 'Defining and Understanding the Religious Philosophy of jihādī-Salafism and the Ideology of Boko Haram', *Politics, Religion & Ideology* 16, nos. 2-3 (2015), 173-200.

Kepel, Gilles, *Jihad: The Trail of Political Islam* (Cambridge: Harvard University Press, 2002).

–, 'The Origins and Development of the Jihadist Movement: From Anti-Communism to Terrorism', *Asian Affairs* 34, no. 2 (July 2003), 91-108.

–, ed., *Al-Qaeda. I testi* (Rome-Bari: Laterza, 2006).

–, *Jihad. Ascesa e declino* (Rome: Carocci Editore, 2015).

Khatab, Sayed, 'Hakimiyyah and Jahiliyyah in the Thought of Sayyid Qutb', *Middle Eastern Studies* 38, no. 3 (July 2002), 145-170.

Kolakowski, Leszek, *Lo spirito rivoluzionario. La radice apocalittico-religiosa del pensiero politico moderno* (Milan: PGreco Edizioni, 2013).

Lacroix, Stéphane, *Awakening Islam. The Politics of Religious Dissent in Contemporary Saudi Arabia* (Cambridge: Harvard University Press, 2011).

Lahoud, Nelly, 'In Search of Philosopher-Jihadis: Abu Muhammad al-Maqdisi's Jihadi Philosophy', *Totalitarian Movements and Political Religions*, vol. 10, no. 2 (June 2009), 205-220.

Lamb, David, 'Hegelian-Marxist Millenarianism', *History of European Ideas* 8, no. 3 (1987), 271-281.

Lami, Gian Franco, *Introduzione a Eric Voegelin. Dal mito teo-cosmogonico al sensorio della trascendenza: la ragione degli antichi e la ragione dei moderni* (Milan: Giuffrè Editore, 1993).

Lasch, Christopher, 'Gnosticism, Ancient and Modern: The Religion of the Future?', *Salmagundi*, no. 96 (Fall 1992), 27-42.

Lauzière, Henri, 'The Construction of *Salafiyya*: Reconsidering Salafism From the Perspective of Conceptual History', *International Journal of Middle East Studies* 42, no. 3 (August 2010), 369-389.

–, *The Making of Salafism. Islamic Reform in the Twentieth Century* (New York: Columbia University Press, 2016).

–, 'What We Mean Versus What They Meant by "Salafi": A Reply To Frank Griffel', *Die Welt Des Islams* 56, no. 1 (April 2016), 89-96.

Lav, Daniel, 'Salafī Jihādīs and the Theology of Faith', in *Radical Islam and the Revival of Medieval Theology* (New York: Cambridge University Press, 2012), pp. 120-166.

–, *Radical Islam and the Revival of Medieval Theology* (New York: Cambridge University Press, 2012).

Lawrence Bruce, ed., *Messages to the World. The Statements of Osama bin Laden* (London: Verso, 2005).
Lazier, Benjamin, 'Overcoming Gnosticism: Hans Jonas, Hans Blumenberg, and the Legitimacy of the Natural World', *Journal of the History of Ideas* 64, no. 4 (October 2003), 619-637.
Lévinas, Emmanuel, 'Reflections on the Philosophy of Hitlerism', *Critical Inquiry* 17, no. 1 (Autumn 1990), 62-71.
Levy, Ran A., 'The Idea of *Jihād* and Its Evolution: Ḥasan al-Bannā and the Society of the Muslim Brothers', *Die Welt Des Islams* 54, issue 2 (2014), 139-158.
Lewis, Bernard, *The Political Language of Islam*. (Chicago: The University of Chicago Press, 1988).
Lia, Brynjar, *Architect of Global Jihad. The Life of Al-Qaida Strategist Abu Mus'ab al-Suri* (New York: Oxford University Press, 2014).
Lingua, Graziano, *Esiti della secolarizzazione. Figure della religione nella società contemporanea* (Pisa: Edizioni ETS, 2013).
Lister, Tim, 'What does Isis really want?' *Cnn*, December 11, 2015, http://edition.cnn.com/2015/12/11/middleeast/isis-syria-iraq-caliphate/.
Logan, Alastair, 'Truth in a Heresy? Gnosticism', *The Expository Times* 112, no. 6 (March 2001), 187-191.
Löwenthal, Leo, 'Caliban's Legacy', *Cultural Critique*, no. 8 (Winter 1987-1988), 5-17.
Löwith, Karl, *Meaning in History* (Chicago: University of Chicago Press, 1949).
Maggiolini, Paolo, and Andrea Plebani, 'La centralità del nemico nel califfato di al-Baghdadi', in *Il marketing del terrore. Twitter e jihad: la comunicazione dell'ISIS*, ed. by Monica Maggioni, and Paolo Magri (Milan: Oscar Mondadori, 2016), pp. 49-80.
Maggiolini, Paolo, 'Dal jihad al jihadismo: militanza e lotta armata tra XX and XXI secolo', in *Jihad e terrorismo. Da al-Qa'ida all'Isis: storia di un nemico che cambia*, ed. by Andrea Plebani (Milan: Oscar Mondadori, 2016), pp. 3-44.
Magris, Aldo, *La logica del pensiero gnostico* (Brescia: Morcelliana, 2011).
Maher, Shiraz, *Salafi-Jihadism: The History of an Idea* (London: Hurst & Company, 2016).
Malka, Haim, 'Jihadi-Salafi Rebellion and the Crisis of Authority', in *Religious Radicalism after the Arab Uprisings*, ed. by Jon B. Alterman (Lanham: Rowman & Littlefield Publishing Group, 2015), pp. 9-35.
Mannheim, Karl, *Ideology and Utopia* (1929; repr. London: Routledge & Kegan Paul, 1979).

Mansfield, Laura, ed., *His Own Words. A Translation of the Writings of Dr. Ayman al Zawahiri* (Old Tappan: TLG Publications, 2006).

Maqdisī, Abū Muḥammad al-, *Millat Ibrāhīm* (n.p.: at-Tibyān Publications, n.d.)

–, 'Monotheism and Jihad – The Distinguished Title', *Pulpit of Monotheism and Jihad* (blog), July 24, 2009, https://muwahhidmedia.files.wordpress.com/2013/06/abu-muhammad-asim-maqdisi-montheism-and-jihad-the-distinguished-title.pdf.

–, *Democracy: A Religion* (Sprinvale South: Al Furqan Islamic Information Centre, 2012).

Marega, Stella, 'L'attesa dell'Apocalisse: dall'antico Gnosticismo alla moderna rivoluzione', *Metábasis*, no. 1 (March 2006), 1-22.

–, 'Il regno della fine dei tempi: una premessa mitico-simbolica all'analisi delle politiche apocalittiche', *Heliopolis*, no. 2 (2016), 147-161.

Martelli, Michele, *Teologia del terrore. Filosofia, religione e politica dopo l'11 settembre* (Rome: Manifestolibri, 2005).

Mathieu, Vittorio, *Cancro in Occidente. Le rovine del giacobinismo* (Milan: Editoriale Nuova, 1980).

–, *La speranza nella rivoluzione* (Rome: Armando Editore, 1992).

Mawdūdī, Abū l-Aʿlā al-, *The Islamic Law and Constitution* (Lahore: Islamic Publications, 1960).

–, *Conoscere l'Islam* (Rome: Edizioni Mediterranee, 1977).

–, 'The Meaning of the Qur'ān', *Quran411.com* (blog), https://www.quran411.com/quran/quran-tafseer-maududi.pdf.

–, *Islam: An Historical Perspective* (Birmingham: U.K.I.M. Dawah Centre, 1996).

McCants, William, *The ISIS Apocalypse. The History, Strategy, and Doomsday Vision of the Islamic State* (New York: St. Martin's Press, 2015).

–, 'Apocalypse Delayed', *Jihadica* (blog), October 16, 2016, http://www.jihadica.com/apocalypse-delayed/.

McKnight, Stephen A., 'Understanding Modernity: A Reappraisal of the Gnostic Element', *Intercollegiate Review*, no. 14 (1979), 265-271.

–, 'Il contributo di Eric Voegelin alla filosofia della storia', in *La scienza dell'ordine. Saggi su Eric Voegelin*, ed. by Gian Franco Lami, and Giovanni Franchi (Rome: Antonio Pellicani Editore, 1997), pp. 95-106.

–, 'Gnosticism and Modernity: Voegelin's Reconsiderations Twenty Years After *The New Science of Politics*', *Political Science Reviewer*, no. 34 (2005), 122-142.

Meijer, Roel, 'Re-Reading al-Qaeda Writings of Yusuf al-Ayiri', *International Institute for the Study of Islam in the Modern World (ISIM) Review*, no. 18 (Autumn 2006), 16-17.
–, 'Yūsuf al-'Uyairī and the Making of a Revolutionary Salafi Praxis', *Die Welt Des Islams* 47, no. 3-4 (November 2007), 422-459.
–, Introduction to *Global Salafism. Islam's New Religious Movement*, ed. by Roel Meijer (Oxford: Oxford University Press, 2013), pp. 1-32.
Miliopoulos, Lazaros, 'The Revolutionary Global Islamism – Politicized or Political Religion? Applying Eric Voegelin's Theory to the Dynamics of Political Islam', *Religion Compass* 7, no. 4 (2013), 126-136.
Mitrofanova, Anastasia V., 'Religious Aspects of International Terrorism', *Age of Globalization*, no. 3 (2013), 99-107.
Moghadam, Assaf, 'The Salafi-Jihad as a Religious Ideology', *CTC Sentinel* 1, no. 2 (February 2008), 14-16.
Moraldi, Luigi, 'La nascita dello Gnosticismo', in *Gli arconti di questo mondo. Gnosi: politica e diritto*, ed. by Claudio Bonvecchio, and Teresa Tonchia (Trieste: EUT, 2000), pp. 25-35.
Morganti, Aldo, 'L'immagine e il nulla. Alcune metamorfosi contemporanee dello Gnosticismo di massa', *I Quaderni di Avallon*, no. 30 (1992), 79-104.
Mura, Andrea, 'A Genealogical Inquiry Into Early Islamism: The Discourse of Hasan al-Banna', *Journal of Political Ideologies* 17, no. 1 (February 2012), 61-85.
–, "Teologia politica e islamismo. Tra universalismo e caduta apocalittica nel pensiero di Sayyid Qutb', in *Teologie e politica. Genealogie e attualità*, ed. by Elettra Stimilli (Macerata: Quodlibet, 2019), pp. 279-300.
Murawiec, Laurent, *The Mind of Jihad* (Cambridge: Cambridge University Press, 2008).
Naef, Silvia, *La questione dell'immagine nell'Islam* (Milan: ObarraO Edizioni, 2011).
Naji, Abu Bakr, *The Management of Savagery* (2004; repr. Harvard: Institute for Strategic Studies, 2006).
Nannipieri, Luca, *Arte e terrorismo. Sulla distruzione islamica del patrimonio storico artistico* (Soveria Mannelli: Rubbettino, 2015).
Nawas, John, 'A Reexamination of Three Current Explanations for al-Mamun's Introduction of the Mihna' *International Journal of Middle East Studies* 26, no. 4 (November 1994), 615-629.
–, 'The Appellation *Ṣāḥib Sunna* in Classical Islam: How Sunnism Came To Be', *Islamic Law and Society* 23, no. 1-2 (2016), 1-22.

Neumann, Peter R., 'Fundamentalism and Modernity', in *Fundamentalisms. Threats and Ideologies in the Modern World*, ed. by James D. G. Dunn (London: I.B. Tauris, 2016), pp. 119-136.

Niemeyer, Gerhart, 'Eric Voegelin's Philosophy and the Drama of Mankind', *Modern Ages*, no. 20 (Winter 1976), 28-39.

Nisan, Mordechai, 'PLO Messianism: Diagnosis of a Modern Gnostic Sect', *Terrorism: An International Journal* 7, no. 3 (1984), 299-312.

Nolte, Ernst, *I tre volti del fascismo* (Milan: Mondadori, 1971).

–, 'I nuovi giacobinismi: da Robespierre a Bin Laden', 2002, available at: http://www.liberalfondazione.it/archivio/numeri-speciali/748-i-nuovi-giacobinismi-da-robespierre-a-bin-laden.

–, *Il terzo radicalismo. Islam e Occidente nel XXI secolo* (Rome: Liberal Edizioni, 2012).

Ohtsuka, Kazuo, 'Salafi-Orientation in Sudanese Mahdism', *The Muslim World* 87, no. 1 (January 1997), 17-33.

Orbach, Danny, 'Tyrannicide in Radical Islam: The Case of Sayyid Qutb and Abd al-Salam Faraj', *Middle Eastern Studies* 48, no. 6 (November 2012), 961-972.

Orsini, Alessandro, *Anatomy of the Red Brigades. The Religious Mindset of Modern Terrorists* (Ithaca: Cornell University Press, 2011).

Osborn, Ronald, 'On the Path of Perpetual Revolution: From Marx's Millenarianism to Sendero Luminoso', *Totalitarian Movements and Political Religions* 8, no. 1 (March 2007), 115-135.

Pace, Enzo, and Renzo Guolo, *I fondamentalismi* (Rome-Bari: Laterza, 2002).

Paz, Reuven, 'Debates within the Family: Jihadi-Salafi Debates on Strategy, Takfir, Extremism, Suicide Bombings and the Sense of Apocalypse', in *Global Salafism. Islam's New Religious Movement*, ed. by Roel Meijer (Oxford: Oxford University Press, 2013), pp. 267-280.

Pellicani, Luciano, 'Capitalismo, modernizzazione, rivoluzione', in *Sociologia delle rivoluzioni*, ed. by Luciano Pellicani (Naples: Guida Editori, 1976), pp. 11-43.

–, *Revolutionary Apocalypse. Ideological Roots of Terrorism* (Westport: Praeger, 2003).

–, *Jihad: le radici* (Rome: Luiss University Press, 2004).

–, 'La città sacra e la città secolare', *Filosofia e Questioni Pubbliche* 14 (2010), 179-209.

–, *La società dei giusti. Parabola storica dello Gnosticismo rivoluzionario* (Soveria Mannelli: Rubbettino, 2012).

–, *L'Occidente e i suoi nemici* (Soveria Mannelli: Rubbettino, 2015).

–, 'Produzione simbolica e potere: gli intellettuali come classe', *Orbis Idearum* 3, no. 2 (2015), 53-62.
Pizzimento, Paolo, *L'apocrifo di Giovanni. Lo Gnosticismo, il Mito e la Metafisica* (Catania: Tipheret, 2018).
Plebani, Andrea, *Jihadismo globale. Strategie del terrore tra Oriente e Occidente* (Florence: Giunti, 2016).
–, 'From Terrorist Group to Self-Proclaimed State: The Origins and Evolution of IS', in *Daesh and the Terrorist Threat: From the Middle East to Europe*, ed. by Hedwig Giusto (Brussels: Foundation for European Progressive Studies, 2016), pp. 34-41.
Polia, Mario, and Gianluca Marletta, *Apocalissi. La fine dei tempi nelle religioni* (Milan: Sugarco Edizioni, 2008).
Poljarevic, Emin, 'In Pursuit of Authenticity: Becoming a Salafi', *Comparative Islamic Studies* 8, no. 1-2 (2012), 139-164.
Porter, Clifford F., 'Eric Voegelin on Nazi Political Extremism', *Journal of the History of Ideas* 63, no. 1 (January 2002), 151-171.
Qā'ida, al-, 'A Statement From *qaidat al-jihad* Regarding the Mandates of the Heroes and the Legality of the Operations in New York and Washington', DSpace – Digital Repository Unimib, April 24, 2002, https://scholarship.tricolib.brynmawr.edu/handle/10066/4796
Queiroz, Maria Isaura Pereira De, *Riforma e rivoluzione nelle società tradizionali* (Milan: Jaca Book, 1970).
Quṭb, Sayyid, 'The American I Have Seen: In the Scale of Human Values', in *America in an Arab Mirror. Images of America in Arabic Travel Literature. An Anthology 1895-1995*, ed. by Kamal Abdel-Malek (New York: St. Martin's Press, 2000), pp. 9-28.
–, *Milestones* (New Delhi: Islamic Book Service, 2002).
–, *La battaglia tra Islam e capitalismo*. (Venice: Marcianum Press, 2016).
Rahman, Fazlur, *La religione del Corano. Le radici spirituali di una grande civiltà* (Milan: Net, 2003).
Rainini, Marco, 'Maria nelle opere di Gioacchino da Fiore', in *Storia della mariologia. Dal modello biblico al modello letterario*, ed. by Enrico Dal Covolo, and Aristide Serra (Rome: Città Nuova Editrice, 2009), pp. 700-725.
–, 'Apocalittica e/o progresso. Le molte reputazioni di Gioacchino da Fiore', in *Filosofia ed escatologia*, ed. by Claudio Ciancio, Maurizio Pagano, and Ezio Gamba (Milan: Mimesis, 2017), pp. 155-178.
Ramadan, Tariq, *Wester Muslims and the Future of Islam* (New York: Oxford University Press, 2004).
Ramsay, Gilbert, and Sarah Victoria Marsden, 'Radical Distinctions: A Comparative Study of Two Jihadist Speeches', *Critical Studies on Terrorism* 6, no. 3 (2013), 392-409.

Rapoport, Yossef, and Shahab Ahmed, eds., *Ibn Taymiyya and His Times* (Oxford: Oxford University Press, 2010).
Reck-Malleczewen, Friedrich, *A History of the Münster Anabaptists* (New York: Palgrave Macmillan, 2008).
Redaelli, Riccardo, *Fondamentalismo islamico* (Florence: Giunti, 2007).
Redissi, Hamadi, *Islam e modernità. L'incontro dell'Islam con l'Occidente* (Verona: Ombre Corte, 2014).
Rhodes, James M., 'The Young Voegelin on Religion', *The Review on Politics* 50, no. 4 (1988), 747-749.
Rich, Paul B., 'How Revolutionary Are Jihadist Insurgencies? The Case of ISIL', *Small Wars & Insurgencies* 27, no. 5 (2016), 777-799.
Rojas Gálvez, Ignacio, *I simboli dell'Apocalisse* (Bologna: EDB, 2016).
Rossbach, Stefan, 'Understanding in Quest of Faith. The Central Problem in Eric Voegelin's Philosophy', in *Politics & Apocalypse*, ed. by Robert Hamerton-Kelly (East Lansing: Michigan State University Press, 2007), pp. 219-261.
Roy, Olivier, *Globalized Islam. The Search for a New Ummah* (New York: Columbia University Press, 2004).
–, *Holy Ignorance. When Religion and Culture Part Ways* (Oxford: Oxford University Press, 2013).
–, *Jihad and Death. The Global Appeal of Islamic State* (New York: Oxford University Press, 2017).
Rumiyah, 13 vols.
Rusconi, Carlo, 'Gnosi e salvezza', *I Quaderni di Avallon*, no. 30 (1992), 23-30.
Russo, Francesco, 'Alle radici della società neognostica. Emanuele Samek Lodovici & Augusto Del Noce', in *L'origine & la meta. Studi in memoria di Emanuele Samek Lodovici*, ed. by Gabriele De Anna (Milan: Edizioni Ares, 2015), pp. 181-198.
Said, Edward, *Orientalism* (London: Routledge and Kegan Paul, 1978).
Samek Lodovici, Emanuele, *Metamorfosi della gnosi. Quadri della dissoluzione contemporanea* (Milan: Ares Edizioni, 1979).
–, 'Dominio dell'istante, dominio della morte', *Archivio di Filosofia* (1981), 469-480.
–, 'La gnosi e la genesi delle forme', *Rivista di Biologia* 74, nos. 1-2 (1981), http://emanuelesameklodovici.it/Scritti/La%20gnosi%20e%20la%20genesi%20delle%20forme.pdf
Samek Lodovici, Giacomo, 'Transumanesimo, immortalità, felicità', *Etica & Politica/Ethics & Politics* 20, no. 3 (2018), 517-538.
Samir, Khalil Samir, 'Origini e natura dell'Islam', in *Islam: una realtà da conoscere*, ed. by Elisa Buzzi, (Genova: Marietti, 2001), pp. 15-35.

Sandal, Nukhet, 'Apocalypse Soon. Revolutionary Revanchism of ISIS', in *The Future of ISIS. Regional and International Implications*, ed. by Feisal al-Istrabadi, and Sumit Ganguly (Washington, DC.: Brookings Institution Press, 2018), pp. 17-38.

Scaraffia, Lucetta, 'Gnosticismo & femminismo', in *L'origine & la meta. Studi in memoria di Emanuele Samek Lodovici*, ed. by Gabriele De Anna (Milan: Edizioni Ares, 2015), pp. 169-181.

Schmitt, Carl, *The Theory of the Partisan* (1963; repr. Michigan: Michigan State University, 2004).

Sedgwick, Mark, 'Al-Qaeda and the Nature of Religious Terrorism', *Terrorism and Political Violence* 16, no. 4 (2004), 795-814.

Shāyegān, Dāryush, *Lo sguardo mutilato. Schizofrenia culturale: paesi tradizionali di fronte alla modernità*. (Milan: Edizioni Ariele, 2015).

Shepard, William, 'Islam and Ideology: Towards a Typology', *International Journal of Middle East Studies* 19, no. 3 (August 1987), 307-335.

–, 'Islam as a "System" in the Later Writings of Sayyid Qutb', *Middle Eastern Studies* 25, no. 1 (January 1989), 31-50.

Sivan, Emmanuel, *Radical Islam. Medieval Theology and Modern Politics* (New Haven: Yale University Press, 1990).

Smith, Richard, 'The Modern Relevance of Gnosticism', in *The Nag Hammadi Library*, ed, by James M. Robinson (Leiden: Brill, 2002), pp. 532-549.

Soage, Ana Belén, 'Ḥasan al-Bannā and Sayyid Quṭb: Continuity or Rupture?', *The Muslim World* 99 (April 2009), 294-311.

Steinberg, Guido, 'Jihadi-Salafism and the Shi'is: Remarks about the Intellectual Roots of anti-Shi'ism', in *Global Salafism. Islam's New Religious Movement*, ed. by Roel Meijer (Oxford: Oxford University Press, 2013), pp. 107-125.

Stern, Jessica, and J.M. Berger, *ISIS: The State of Terror* (Manhattan: Ecco Publisher, 2015).

Stout, Mark, 'In Search of Salafi Jihadist Strategic Thought: Mining the Words of the Terrorists', *Studies in Conflict & Terrorism* 32, no. 10 (October 2009), 876-892.

Tacchini, Davide, *Radicalismo islamico* (Milan: ObarraO Edizioni, 2015).

Taylor, Charles, *The Malaise of Modernity* (Toronto: House of Anansi Press, 1991).

Tibi, Bassam, *Il fondamentalismo religioso alle soglie del Duemila* (Turin: Bollati Boringhieri, 2001).

Tomasello, Dario, *Luci sull'Islām. 66 voci per un lessico* (Milan: Jouvence, 2018).

Toynbee, Arnold J., 'Islam, the West, and the Future', in *Civilization on Trial* (London: Oxford University Press, 1946), pp. 184-212.

Tucker, Ernest, 'Primitivism as a Radical Response to Religious Crisis: The Anabaptists of Münster in the 1530s and the Taliban of Afghanistan in the 1990s', in *An Islamic Reformation?*, ed. by Michaelle Browers (Lanhan, Maryland: Lexington Books, 2004), pp. 147-158.

Turner, John, 'From Cottage Industry to International Organisation: The Evolution of Salafi-Jihadism and the Emergence of the Al Qaeda Ideology', *Terrorism and Political Violence* 22, no. 4 (September 2010), 541-558.

Varshizky, Amit, 'Alfred Rosenberg: The Nazi Weltanschauung as Modern Gnosis', *Politics, Religion & Ideology* 13, no. 3 (September 2012), 311-331.

Ventura, Alberto, 'Alle radici del fondamentalismo islamico', in *Il fondamentalismo islamico*, ed. by Angelo Iacovella, and Alberto Ventura (Rome: ISIAO, 2006), pp. 17-35.

–, 'L'Islām sunnita nel periodo classico (VII-XVI secolo)', in *Islām*, ed. by Giovanni Filoramo (Rome-Bari: Laterza, 2007), pp. 77-202.

–, 'L'Islām della trandizione (XVII-XVIII secolo)' in *Islām*, ed. by Giovanni Filoramo (Rome-Bari: Laterza, 2007), pp. 203-218.

–, 'Confessioni scismatiche, eterodossie e nuove religioni sorte nell'Islām', in *Islām*, ed. by Giovanni Filoramo (Rome-Bari: Laterza, 2007), pp. 309-406.

–, *Sapienza sufi. Dottrine e simboli dell'esoterismo islamico* (Rome: Edizioni Mediterranee, 2016).

Voegelin, Eric, 'The Formation of the Marxian Revolutionary Idea', *The Review of Politics* 12, no. 3 (July 1950), 275-302.

–, Review of *The Origins of Totalitarianism* by Hannah Arendt, *The Review of Politics* 15, no. 1 (January 1953), 68-76.

–, 'Apocalisse e rivoluzione', in *1867/1967. Un secolo di marxismo*, ed. by Vittorio Frosini et al. (Florence: Vallecchi Editore, 1967), pp. 113-135.

–, 'The Eclipse of Reality', in *Phenomenology and Social Reality*, ed. by Maurice Natanson (The Hague: Martinus Nijhoff, 1970), pp. 185-194.

–, 'Response to Professor Altizer's "A New History and a New but Ancient God?"', *Journal of the American Academy of Religion* 43, no. 4 (December 1975), 765-772.

–, *Autobiographical Reflections* (1989; repr. Columbia: University of Missouri Press, 2011).

–, 'Joachim of Fiore (Flora)', in *The Collected Works of Eric Voegelin.* Vol. 20, *History of Political Ideas, vol. II*, ed. by Peter Von Sivers (Columbia: University of Missouri Press, 1997), pp. 126-134.

–, 'The People of God', in *The Collected Works of Eric Voegelin,* vol. 22, *Renaissance and Reformation*, ed. by David L. Morse, and William M. Thompson (Columbia: University of Missouri Press, 1998), pp. 131-214.

–, 'The English Revolution', in *The Collected Works of Eric Voegelin,* vol. 25, *History of Political Ideas, vol. VII*, ed. by Jürgen Gebhardt, and Thomas A. Hollweck (Columbia: University of Missouri Press, 1999), pp. 73-114.

–, 'The Political Religion', in *The Collected Works of Eric Voegelin.* Vol. 5, *Modernity Without Restraint*, ed. by Manfred Henningsen (Columbia: University of Missouri Press, 1999), pp. 19-74.

–, 'The New Science of Politics', in *The Collected Works of Eric Voegelin.* Vol. 5, *Modernity Without Restraint*, ed. by Manfred Henningsen (Columbia: University of Missouri Press, 1999), pp. 75-242.

–, 'Science, Politics, and Gnosticism', in *The Collected Works of Eric Voegelin.* Vol. 5, *Modernity Without Restraint*, ed. by Manfred Henningsen (Columbia: University of Missouri Press, 1999), pp. 243-314.

–, 'Hitler and the Germans', in *The Collected Works of Eric Voegelin.* Vol. 31, *Hitler and the Germans,* ed. by Detlev Clemens, and Brendan Purcell (Columbia: University of Missouri Press, 1999), pp. 51-257.

–, 'Gnostic Politics', in *The Collected Works of Eric Voegelin.* Vol. 10, *Published Essays 1940-1952*, ed. by Ellis Sandoz (Columbia: University of Missouri Press, 2000), pp. 23-240.

–, 'Wisdom and the Magic of the Extreme: A Meditation', in *The Collected Works of Eric Voegelin.* Vol. 12, *Published Essays 1966-1985*, ed. by Ellis Sandoz (Columbia: University of Missouri Press, 2000), pp. 315-275.

–, 'Order and History, vol. IV, The Ecumenic Age', in *The Collected Works of Eric Voegelin.* Vol. 17, *The Ecumenic Age*, ed. by Michael Franz (Columbia: University of Missouri Press, 2000), pp. 45-410.

–, *Anni di guerra. Per una comprensione dei conflitti nel sec. XX* (Soveria Mannelli: Rubbettino, 2001).

–, 'Recovering Reality: An Interview with Eric Voegelin', interview by Peter Cangelosi, and John William Corrington, *New Orleans Review*, 1973. Available at *Voegelinview.com*, https://www.voegelinview.com/recovering-reality-pt-1/.

Voll, John O., 'Wahhabism and Mahdism: Alternative Styles of Islamic Renewals', *Arab Studies Quarterly* 4, no. 1/2 (Spring 1982), 110-126.

Wagemakers, Joas, 'A Purist Jihadi-Salafi: The Ideology of Aby Muhammad al-Maqdisi', *British Journal of Middle Eastern Studies* 36, no. 2 (2009), 281-297.

–, 'Invoking Zarqawi: Abu Muhammad al-Maqdisi's Jihad Deficit', *CTC Sentinel* 2, no. 6 (June 2009), 16-18.
–, *A Quietisti Jihadi. The Ideology and Influence of Abu Muhammad al-Maqdisi* (Cambridge: Cambridge University Pres, 2012).
–, 'The Transformation of a Radical Concept: *al-wala' wa-l-bara'* in the Ideology of Abu Muhammad al-Maqdisi', in *Global Salafism. Islam's New Religious Movement*, ed. by Roel Meijer (Oxford: Oxford University Press, 2013), pp. 81-106.
–, 'What Should an Islamic State Look Like? Jihadi-Salafi Debates on the War in Syria', *The Muslim World* 106, no. 3 (July 2016), 501-522.
–, 'Jihadi-Salafism in Jordan and the Syrian Conflict: Divisions Overcome Unity', *Studies in Conflict & Terrorism* 41, no. 3 (2018), 191-212.
Wainwright, E.H., 'Eric Voegelin: An Inquiry into the Philosophy of Order', *Politikon: South African Journal of Political Studies* 5, no. 1 (June 1978), 67-93.
–, 'Political Gnosticism and the Search for Order in Existence', *Politikon: South African Journal of Political Studies* 6, no. 1 (June 1979), 51-62.
Waldstein, Michael, 'Hans Jonas' Construct "Gnosticism": Analysis and Critique', *Journal of Early Christian Studies* 8, no. 3 (Fall 2000), 341-372.
Walsh, David, 'Voegelin's Response to the Disorder of the Age', *The Review of Politics* 46, no. 2 (1984), 266-287.
Walzer, Michael, 'War and Revolution in Puritan Thought', *Political Studies* 12, no. 2 (1964), 220-229.
–, *The Revolution of the Saints. A Study in the Origins of Radical Politics* (Cambridge: Harvard University Press, 1965).
Watt, William Montgomery, *Islamic Fundamentalism and Modernity* (London: Routledge, 1988).
Webb, Eugene, 'Le differenziazioni della coscienza', in *La scienza dell'ordine. Saggi su Eric Voegelin*, ed. by Gian Franco Lami, and Giovanni Franchi (Rome: Antonio Pellicani Editore, 1997), pp. 203-215.
–, 'Voegelin's "Gnosticism" Reconsidered', *Political Science Reviewer* 34, no. 1 (Fall 2005), 48-76.
Weismann, Itzchak, 'New and Old Perspectives in the Study of Salafism', *The Middle East Book Review* 8, no. 1 (2017), 22-37.
–, 'A Perverted Balance: Modern Salafism between Reform and Jihād', *Die Welt Des Islams* 57, no. 1 (2017), 33-66.
Wiktorowicz, Quintan, 'The New Global Threat: Transnational Salafis and Jihad', *Middle East Policy* 8, no. 4 (December 2001), 18-38.

–, 'The Salafi Movement. Violence and the Fragmentation of Community', in *Muslim Networks from Hajj to Hip Hop*, ed. by Miriam Cooke, and Bruce B. Lawrence (Chapel Hill: University of North Carolina Press, 2005), pp. 208-234.

–, 'A Genealogy of Radical Islam', *Studies in Conflict & Terrorism* 28, no. 2, 75-97.

–, 'Anatomy of the Salafi Movement', *Studies in Conflict & Terrorism* 29, no. 3 (August 2006), 207-239.

Wilson, Bryan R., 'An Analysis of Sect Development', *American Sociological Review* 24, no. 1 (February 1959), 3-15.

Wiser, James L., 'From Cultural Analysis to Philosophical Anthropology: An Examination of Voegelin's Concept of Gnosticism', *The Review of Politics* 42, no. 1 (January 1980), 92-104.

Wood, Graeme, 'What ISIS Really Want', *Atlantic*, March 2015.

–, *The Way of the Strangers* (New York: Random House, 2017).

Zarqāwī, Abū Muṣ'ab al-, *Letter to bin Lāden*, 2004. https://2001-2009.state.gov/p/nea/rls/31694.htm.

–, 'Our Creed and Methodology', DSpace – Digital Repository Unimib, April 13, 2005, https://scholarship.tricolib.brynmawr.edu/bitstream/handle/10066/5026/AQI20050321.pdf?sequence=3&isAllowed=y.

Ẓawāhirī, Ayman al-, 'Knights Under the Prophet's Banner', in *His Own Words. A Translation of the Writings of Dr. Ayman al Zawahiri*, ed. by Laura Mansfield (Old Tappan: TLG Publications, 2006).

–, 'Realities of the Conflict Between Islam and Unbelief', *As-Sahab Media*, December 2006, https://www.cia.gov/library/abbottabad-compound/67/67BD026383A5C82BEBB2AD11BB31A1E9_Dr_Aiman_Reality_of_the_Conflict_En.pdf.

Žižek, Slavoj, 'Robespierre, or the "Divine Violence" of Terror', in *Virtue and Terror*, by Maximilien Robespierre (London: Verso, 2007), pp. VII-XXXIX.